The New York Times

TRULY TOUGH CROSSWORD PUZZLES

First published in the United States by St. Martin's Griffin, an imprint of
St. Martin's Publishing Group

THE NEW YORK TIMES TRULY TOUGH CROSSWORD PUZZLES.
Copyright © 2020 by The New York Times Company. All rights reserved.
Printed in the United States of America. For information, address
St. Martin's Press, 120 Broadway, New York, NY 10271.

www.stmartins.com

All of the puzzles that appear in this work were originally published
in *The New York Times* from January 6, 2012, to June 23, 2012;
from July 12, 2013, to December 28, 2013; from April 21, 2017,
to August 5, 2017; or from August 3, 2018, to August 3, 2019.
Copyright © 2012, 2013, 2017, 2018, 2019 by The New York Times Company.
All rights reserved. Reprinted by permission.

ISBN 978-1-250-25311-8

Our books may be purchased in bulk for promotional, educational,
or business use. Please contact your local bookseller or the Macmillan Corporate
and Premium Sales Department at 1-800-221-7945, extension 5442, or by email
at MacmillanSpecialMarkets@macmillan.com.

First Edition: January 2020

10   9   8   7   6   5   4

The New York Times

TRULY TOUGH CROSSWORD PUZZLES
200 Challenging Puzzles

Edited by Will Shortz

ST. MARTIN'S GRIFFIN ✠ NEW YORK

Looking for more Hard Crosswords?

The New York Times

The #1 Name in Crosswords

ACROSS

1 Factor in calculating an object's momentum
5 Commercial lines?
15 Get in the game
16 Complete, as a skeleton
17 Record label for Otis Redding
18 Complains vocally
19 Four-finger gestures
21 Somewhat
22 Henry Higgins, to Eliza Doolittle
23 "Another thing I forgot to mention . . .": Abbr.
25 Diagonal sail support
27 Breakfast cookware item
33 Rock band with four(!) self-titled albums
35 OS X runner
36 Feeling after a guilt trip
37 "Don't ___"
38 Monet that isn't worth much money, say
40 Keogh plan alternative
41 Channel that used to show a clip of the 1969 moon landing every hour
42 Nothing, in Nantes
43 Says goodbye to a lover
45 Scathing
48 Four-legged friend
49 Extras on TV's "Doctor Who"
50 Digitally endorse
52 What Adderall treats, for short
55 Singer whose "Thinking Out Loud" won the 2015 Grammy for Song of the Year
59 Cancel on someone

62 Plagues
63 Cab charge?
64 Urban garden locale
65 Bronze producer
66 Burgoo or callaloo

DOWN

1 Corn flour in Latin American cuisine
2 Prefix with thesis
3 1991 sci-fi film sequel
4 Cosmopolitan feature
5 "Li'l Abner" creature
6 Italy's ___ alla Scala
7 Croupier's implement
8 When "et tu" was spoken
9 A trilogy has three: Abbr.
10 "___ Dieu!"
11 Words said with one's glass raised
12 French vanilla ice cream ingredient
13 Cartoon character who plays a saxophone
14 Skeleton vehicle, in the Olympics
20 Claptrap
23 Take second
24 Popular holiday dessert
25 Washington establishment, so it's said
26 Sauce with the same consonants as what it's used on
28 Children's author who wrote "Did you ever stop to think, and forget to start again?"
29 Bygone record giant
30 Stir crazy?
31 Containing gold
32 Poetic preposition
34 Symbols of control
39 Animation
44 Turns a corner?
46 Singer/songwriter who composed the Captain & Tennille's #1 hit "Love Will Keep Us Together"
47 Fuze competitor
51 Bright look
52 Start of learning
53 Stop bringing up
54 Hamburger, maybe
55 Dreamland
56 Touched
57 Skin softener
58 You might be careful opening something with this label
60 Sir ___ of the Round Table
61 Back

by David Steinberg

2

ACROSS

1 Buzz source
5 Right
11 Leader in a chorus line?
14 Conversation stopper
15 Love of Cyrano de Bergerac
16 One not abstaining
17 Husband of Octavia
18 With 10-Down, literally, now and then
20 Feature of a moat
21 Things a smartphone has lots of
22 Cash payment?
23 With 7-Down, literally, neither wins nor loses
25 Pick up
26 Some spicy brews
29 Like ranches, typically
30 European river that originates from a glacier
31 Ones not abstaining
33 Some Tesla employees, in brief
34 Only French-produced film to win an Oscar for Best Picture (2011)
37 Chest-thumping, for short?
40 Abide
41 Old Gremlins and Hornets
45 Eye
47 Makings of a population
49 Ran in place
50 With 8-Down, literally, one just taking up space
51 Preps, as cappuccino milk
53 Lamebrain
55 Pen lead-in
56 With 1-Down, literally, downright dastardly
58 Place for a post
59 Put something past?
60 Electrically insulating material around nerve fibers
61 Wild country
62 Ancient title
63 Divorcé, e.g.
64 Tech review site

DOWN

1 Makeshift technique for female modesty
2 "Yep, perfectly clear"
3 "The Astronomer" painter
4 ___ pop
5 Groundhog Day celebration, typically
6 Knock about
7 Buffoons
8 Course number
9 "May It Be" singer, 2001
10 Never putting down roots for long
11 Coin-flipping "Batman" villain
12 Ringmaster?
13 Sees (to)
19 Calpurnia's dream of Caesar's death, e.g.
21 Alternative to a mandolin, informally
24 Provide job support
27 Take it for a ride
28 Member of the "magnificent" 1996 U.S. women's gymnastics team
29 Unwanted state for a would-be lover
32 ___ humain (person: Fr.)
35 Commute in the afternoon, say
36 Appetizer that may accompany sangria
37 Popular snack for bikers and hikers
38 "Star Wars" sporting event
39 Quaint item on an office desk
42 Exercise in student diplomacy, for short
43 It's performed on hands and knees in yoga
44 Dexterity
46 Etta of old comics
48 Job ad abbr.
52 It goes to hell
53 ___ Fleck and the Flecktones
54 End note?
57 Bottom line?
58 Airer of the children's news program "Newsround" since 1972

by Sam Trabucco

ACROSS

1. Insolent talk
5. Wagner's oeuvre
11. "Well, looky here!"
14. Pacific capital
15. Least believable
16. $100 bill, in slang
17. Where a rocky relationship may end
19. "Automatic for the People" band, 1992
20. It's no six-pack, ironically
21. One way to stand
23. Where the brachialis muscle is found
24. ___-Caps (candy)
25. Like the Oscars and the Emmys
26. ___ Rock, N.J.
28. Wayfarers
31. Kind of pressure
33. Slip
34. Begin writing
39. Contribute
40. Something New York and Los Angeles each have
42. Black-and-white
46. Prefix with -metry
47. Big name in movie rentals
48. "Alea iacta ___": Julius Caesar
51. Time in Italy
52. Inept sort
53. All-time record setter on 4/8/1974
56. Herbert of the "Pink Panther" films
57. Angry shout to an umpire
59. "Do Ya" grp.
60. "Seven Words You Can Never Say on Television" comedian
61. Believes
62. Ranch sobriquet
63. Board
64. Info to use against somebody, metaphorically

DOWN

1. Wind sources
2. Something that may be stiff
3. It might include "New Folder" and "Close Window"
4. "You make a point"
5. Multi-time Pro Bowl tight end Greg
6. Big name in conditioning
7. Oscar winner Jannings
8. Bank
9. System of unspoken words, for short
10. Setting for the first Mickey Mouse cartoon
11. Main antagonist in George Orwell's "1984"
12. Followed
13. Sedated, say
18. TV channel with the slogan "Very funny"
22. One who arrives around Halloween
25. Frontier figure
27. Southwestern tree with needles
29. Big name in coverage
30. Miracle-___
32. It was launched with Sputnik
35. Regards
36. Actor Cage, informally
37. Superstore
38. "Rotary phone," for one
41. S.O.B.
42. Farm young 'un
43. Peter of "My Favorite Year"
44. Stumblebum
45. "La Loge" artist
49. Shut out
50. Move to the right incrementally
53. Chervil or chives
54. Jean Auel heroine
55. Jessica of "Sin City"
58. Weapon in medieval warfare

by Damon Gulczynski

4

ACROSS

1 Alternatives to strollers
11 Stumpers?
15 Repetitive farewell from "The Sound of Music"
16 Place
17 Show around the area?
18 Word from the Latin for "seaweed"
19 Swam with the fishes, say
20 Prominent instrument in raga music
21 Put on __
22 Creek relative
24 It was launched on the same day as Windows 95
25 Proud, passionate type, supposedly
28 Downturn
29 Rapper __ Khalifa
30 Blarney stone?
33 Problems resulting from a poor paternal relationship
34 Simple business, frankly speaking?
35 Trick
36 It comes before long
37 Main antagonist in "Toy Story"
38 Bit
41 Causing change
44 Former Spice Girl Halliwell
45 __ Falls, N.Y.
46 Auction figures
50 Emmy-winning newsman Roger
51 Seller of shooting equipment
52 Saucony competitor
53 Spitball, e.g.
54 Tammany Hall cartoonist
55 Elite operative, for short

DOWN

1 Aromatic resin
2 Studmuffin
3 Two-pointed hat worn by Napoleon
4 All these __ . . .
5 Show signs of a sore loser
6 Spike
7 Subject of devotion
8 Frasier's brother on "Frasier"
9 Scientists who measure the exact shape and size of Earth
10 Big __
11 Everyday
12 Houston and Dallas, historically
13 Passport or driver's license
14 International soccer star Luis __
20 First name in psychoanalysis
23 People of southern Kenya
25 Equipment found in warehouse stores
26 Author Welty
27 Places to go out and have a gas?
30 Excess
31 Trash-talk
32 Massive resource: Abbr.
33 What Hawaii has that Alaska lacks?
34 Extremely, informally
35 Comedian
38 Expert on bugs
39 Shaded ring
40 Drive away
42 Stop by
43 Titular misanthrope in a Shakespeare play
44 Hearts
47 Already: Fr.
48 "Go back" button abbr. on some remotes
49 Off-color
51 Computer hardware inits.

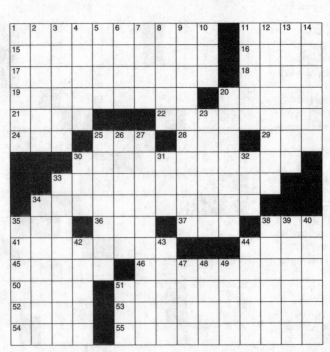

by Ryan McCarty

ACROSS

1 Lake of rock's Emerson, Lake & Palmer
5 One who crosses the line
9 Dunderheads
14 Bare
16 He said "If you wish to make an apple pie from scratch, you must first invent the universe"
17 Fifth wheel
18 Small protuberance
19 "Ingredient" of success
21 Sound at a spa
22 Still
23 Amish, e.g.
24 Verbal shrug
26 Hallucinogenic edibles, in slang
28 They're often blitzed
29 Lieutenant Minderbinder of "Catch-22"
31 Wore an outfit with panache, informally
33 Constellation between Cygnus and Aquila
36 See 44-Across
37 Real identity
39 Pro ___
40 City north of Des Moines
41 Try to get something from a bag
44 Court figure whose job is to detect 36-Across
46 "___ said . . ."
47 Oaf
50 Lines around Chicago
51 Primer finish

54 "Pretty, pretty please?"
56 Grueling grillings
57 Trim
58 Process by which neutrinos are produced
59 Fix, as a bow
60 Attended (to)
61 Merrill in movies

DOWN

1 Full of hot air
2 Money in Nepal
3 Formally establish
4 "Young Frankenstein" co-star
5 Mill owner in the California gold rush
6 Big name in oil
7 Tap attachment

8 Une couleur primaire
9 Showed one's disapproval, in a way
10 Ashy
11 30-foot-long dinosaur able to walk on either two legs or four
12 Samuel L. Jackson has been in six of his movies
13 Some sketch show V.I.P.s
15 Drives
20 ___ Systems, computer networking giant
25 Applies to
26 Most cunning
27 Disorderly do
29 Preserves variety

30 "So much for my theory"
32 Offered unwanted advice
33 Big cheese wheels?
34 Country singer Clark
35 Oktoberfest offering
38 Diet-friendly, say
42 New England prep school attended by J.F.K.
43 Former Supreme Court justice Stone
45 Online periodical
47 You can count on them
48 Spinner?
49 Cushy course
52 Doesn't just tear up
53 Struck out
55 Prefix with cycle

by Jeff Chen

ACROSS

1 Certain fish . . . or sailboats
10 Jon of 2010's "The Town"
14 Cover for a cowboy
15 Here, in Honduras
16 Beset, as a castle
17 Garb
18 Ones frequently called on to give, for short
19 Makeshift fly swatter
21 Toward the poop deck
22 ___ the King Prawn (Muppet in "Muppets Tonight")
23 Urban open space
26 Hit with a charge
27 Charm
29 Tea party member
34 Ones in charge, for short
35 Primitive wind instrument
36 Turned
38 Story of past glories, maybe?
39 Private leaders
41 City along the old Oregon Trail
43 IV, to III
44 Hint of things to come
46 Up to snuff
50 Priest in the Books of Samuel
51 "___ problem"
52 Suffer in the sun
53 Picked rock against paper, say
55 Open investigation?
58 State as a matter of fact
59 Computer statisticians
60 TV host who won a Mark Twain Prize for American Humor
61 Ink holders

DOWN

1 Like twice-told tales
2 Make psyched
3 "You know who I am"
4 Symbols of wave functions
5 Regular guy
6 Lee with three Oscar-garnering films
7 President between James and Grover
8 Lead female role in "Singin' in the Rain"
9 Gets down, in a way
10 Made a meal of
11 In-pool fitness program
12 Rejuvenating treatment at a spa
13 Vegetable aisle freshener
14 Give an unexpected hand
20 Rigby of songdom
23 "My Kind of Town" lyricist
24 Almost-sacrificed son in the Bible
25 Summer
26 Add cornstarch to
28 ___ of the earth
29 Defensive ring
30 Selfless gesture
31 One use for arsenic
32 Former news agent
33 Gulf Coast flier
37 Concern for TV's Aunt Bee
40 Mariah Carey holiday song that was a #1 Adult Contemporary hit
42 Out of sync
45 Irked constantly
46 Curling venue
47 Exchanged some crosses
48 Figures in a classic logic problem
49 National Mall liners
50 Airline in the early 1950s' Operation Ali Baba
52 Minor deviation
54 Derek Jeter's retired number
56 Top of Scotland
57 Bit of dance club equipment

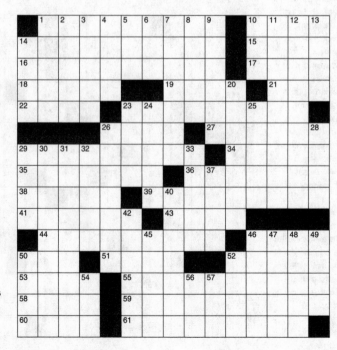

by Mark Diehl

ACROSS

1 Coolest thing about a train?
16 Secret advantage
17 Caribbean home of Blackbeard's Castle
18 Divided land: Abbr.
19 Amenable sorts
20 Bucko
21 Modifier of a low price
22 Most of an S O S
24 Crude shelter
27 Quidditch position in the Harry Potter books
31 Correo ___
32 Accolade for "Mad Men" in four consecutive years
35 Agouti relative
36 "That ___!"
37 WordPress creation
38 Like most theater popcorn containers
40 St. Peter's Basilica attraction
41 Sale indicator
42 Sweeps the board?
43 Ian of "Alien"
45 College town east of Greensboro
46 "___ Walks in Beauty" (Byron poem)
49 Part of a racing bike
51 Swimming center?
54 Real-life villain who was an antagonist in Robert Ludlum's "The Bourne Identity"
57 Neil Armstrong or Jesse Owens, say
58 Flirt with disaster

DOWN

1 One of four in a Scrabble set
2 Repercussion
3 "The foundation of most governments," per John Adams
4 Futuristic play of 1921
5 "That's my intention"
6 ___ eyes
7 Log unit
8 Bundle of nerves
9 Plant ___
10 Foes of the Bolsheviks
11 Frederick Law ___, designer of New York's Central Park
12 1978 Grammy nominee Chris
13 Honeycomb component
14 Big name in athletic footwear
15 Accordion part
21 Here
23 Like Novak Djokovic, by birth
24 Palate stimulus
25 Cast with difficulty
26 Went like a birdie
28 Vegetables high in beta carotene
29 Act unprofessionally?
30 Eastern melodies
32 Trade, in brief
33 Printemps follower
34 Latin conjunction
36 Zero
39 Island just north of the Equator
40 C_3H_8, familiarly
42 Biblical prophet who was fed by ravens
44 One way to the Smithsonian
45 Governor or senator follower
46 "Out!"
47 In good shape
48 Director ___ C. Kenton
50 Hitchcock double feature?
51 Scratched (out)
52 Helgenberger of "CSI"
53 Liqueur flavor
55 You'd expect to see it before long
56 "Evita" narrator

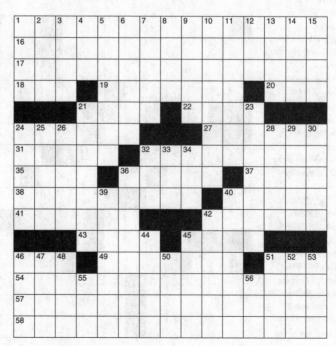

by Roland Huget

8

ACROSS

1 Tex-Mex morsel
10 "Ooh-la-la!"
15 Pop group with the 1993 #2 hit "All That She Wants"
16 Polite rejection
17 Tough crowd?
18 Artifacts, to archaeologists
19 Program-closing command on a PC
20 Gripes
22 Mountain home
24 Equatorial Guinea joined it in 2017
25 Lay the groundwork?
27 This blows!
28 Common classroom adornment
32 Acts all-powerful
35 Detective in "The French Connection"
36 Lamb, by another name
37 Scissors
40 Big name in cookware
41 ___ business
43 Maritime graphic
45 Ration
48 Material in translation
49 Some chats, briefly
50 Behind
51 First chairman of the E.E.O.C., familiarly
53 Wager
56 Heat
59 Group in feminist writing
60 Air traveler?
62 Whence the line "Beauty, terrible beauty! A deathless goddess—so she strikes our eyes!"
63 "Told you!"
64 ___-Poo, son of the Mikado
65 "Abso-freakin'-lutely!"

DOWN

1 One running for the Senate?
2 Supercelebrity
3 Yoko Ono, artistically, in the 1960s
4 Equivalent of a megagram
5 In a way
6 Sweet-and-spicy sports bar snack
7 Theme of Cirque du Soleil's "O," appropriately
8 "Hurry!"
9 Renowned pirate captain during the Golden Age of Piracy
10 First, second and third place
11 Primitive attire
12 "Who ___?"
13 Department store section
14 Where victims of arrests are taken, for short
21 Mental health org.
23 Historic town in Berkshire
25 Certain bank deposit
26 Basic skateboarding trick
29 Classic musical with the song "A Hymn to Him"
30 Freak out
31 Hides
33 Talk, talk, talk
34 "Yo mama" joke, e.g.
38 Ideal, in teenspeak
39 Contents of a playground box
42 We
44 Coiner of the words "chortle" and "frabjous"
46 Modern connection inits.
47 Home of Vegas's World Series of Poker
52 Turquoise or aquamarine
53 Bugs Bunny's girlfriend
54 Exiled ruler of 1979
55 Auto dial
57 Good name for a landscaper?
58 ___-Willets Point (subway station in Queens, N.Y.)
59 The "1" in 1-9
61 –

by Sam Ezersky

ACROSS

1 Garage installation
7 Bud
12 He works with kids
14 Go all out, whatever the cost
15 Florid drapery fabrics
16 Early stage of development
17 Can opener?
18 Burden
20 Downtown Julie Brown's former employer
22 Dolly, e.g.
23 Subject of Marie Curie's isolation
26 ___ d'amore
27 Not yet apparent
28 "Family Feud" host Harvey
29 Epitomizes
32 Makes new connections to, perhaps
34 Stem (from)
35 Pop singer's second album before "Jagged Little Pill"
37 Currency replaced by the euro
38 They might be drawn at night
39 Org. with a top 10 list
42 Old-fashioned cooler?
43 Scandal suffix
44 Self-satisfied smile
46 Naïve sorts
48 Source of many box office bombs?
51 MacArthur Fellowship-winning author of "Between the World and Me"
53 Pandora's domain
54 Cornish meat pie
55 1994 Denis Leary comedy

DOWN

1 Remain valid
2 "White Buildings" was his first collection of poetry
3 Court order?
4 Support staff
5 Country singer who uses her first two initials
6 Tongue twister pronoun
7 Jazzed
8 Satisfy
9 Security figure, in brief
10 Many a range
11 Lionizing lines
12 Architectural high point
13 British-based relief organization

14 Playwright who wrote "Walk! Not bloody likely. I am going in a taxi"
15 Revolutionary figure
19 Surpassed
21 Some hand signals
24 Took in
25 Make potable, in a way
26 Manufacturer of indoor cars
27 Toon named after one of Matt Groening's sisters
28 Watch words?
29 Subject of a museum in St. Petersburg, Fla.
30 Portrayer of Hulk in 2003
31 Colonial stingers
33 Downfall

36 Sleep next to
38 Washtub
39 Fuzz
40 Eighth-day rite
41 Half of a candy duo
43 Frank who designed Walt Disney Concert Hall
45 Recurring symbol
47 ___ salad
49 Plot element?
50 Bellow
51 Bit of advice
52 Predetermined

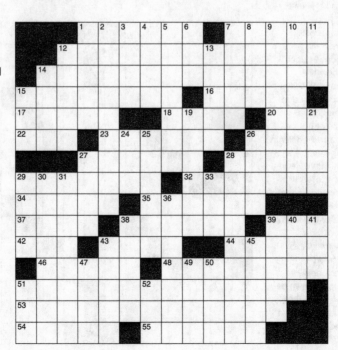

by Peter Wentz

ACROSS

1 Lively dances in 2/4 time
7 Smallest country in mainland Africa
13 Had a fit?
15 Indian or Mexican
16 Frazzled commuter's comment
17 One getting on
18 How someone may be interrupted
20 Country club figure
21 Language with a trilled "r"
22 Verb in the first telegraph message
23 They're encouraged on a ketogenic diet
24 Encouraging words
25 Japanese stock holder
26 Lead-in to comic
27 "Super" thing in games, once
28 Force of nature?
30 Bit of belt-tightening
31 Longtime talk show host with a degree from Harvard
34 Ethnic group that makes up about 18% of the world's population
37 Silly tricks
38 Ones on Telemundo
39 Athlete known as "The Black Pearl"
40 "What, will these hands __ be clean?": Lady Macbeth
41 Wee warbler
42 Luxurious Italian house
43 Abbr. for those who don't like parties
44 Bisector of the Fertile Crescent
46 Road Runners' race classification
48 Neighbor of an Austrian
49 Part of an oven
50 Money in the Bible
51 What's left
52 Prepare to go

DOWN

1 Secretary of war to Taft, Roosevelt and Truman
2 First word of the Constitution after the preamble
3 Messes up
4 Wild things
5 Shop shapers
6 Any minute
7 Mean Miss of "The Wizard of Oz"
8 Second
9 Ed.'s inbox filler
10 Cameo
11 Resistance to change
12 Kind of can
14 Overhyped event, in slang
15 One who gets bent out of shape
19 Connecticut Yankee, e.g.
23 Pedal pushers
25 "Love ___"
26 Emulated Rumpelstiltskin
28 Hunter College is part of it, in brief
29 Summer coolers
30 Attorney general before Reno
31 Disbeliever's question
32 Prelims
33 Is unobliged to
34 "My word!"
35 Chewy, in a way
36 Proximate
39 Dividing shrub
41 Toon with a middle initial
42 Drudge
44 List
45 Smeltery refuse
47 Nowhere to be found, for short

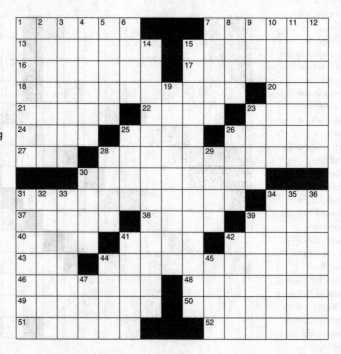

by Randolph Ross

ACROSS

1 LP, e.g.
5 Stories with many chapters
10 Instagram and others
14 Getting paid, say
16 Trouble with a tap
17 Part of a Central American grove
18 Field mouse
19 Beam shooter
20 Mel in Cooperstown
21 ___ dixit (unproven assertion)
22 Jerks
23 It takes time to sink in
25 ___ Decor (magazine)
26 Demand from a school bully
27 Hi or lo follower
28 Spit out
29 More minimalist, say
30 Series of rounds
31 Place to fish from
32 "___ the Sheep" ("Wallace and Gromit" spinoff)
34 Potential drain obstruction
35 Fate worse than a ticket
38 What goes after the wrong type?
40 Fall Out Boy's "Sugar, ___ Goin Down"
41 Pipe sellers
42 Brad's gal in "The Rocky Horror Picture Show"
43 Tombstone figure
44 Cheap beer option, for short
45 Country
46 Hotel/casino on the Vegas Strip
47 Foul

49 Go on a tweetstorm, say
50 Aquanaut's chamber
51 Leg up
52 Word with skirt or strip
53 Pastoral verse

DOWN

1 Eponymous Austrian physicist who studied waves
2 Owing money
3 London burial place of John Donne and Horatio Nelson
4 "As ___ as unsunn'd snow": Shak.
5 Mark of a villain, maybe
6 Not mainstream, informally

7 One of a series of attempts
8 Vinegary
9 Resource for an artist to draw on?
10 Like some boards
11 Balloonist's tankful
12 Tall, slender, footed glass
13 No-wait
15 What a colon might denote
23 Drop
24 Store name with a big red initial
26 What shuttles leave from
28 What the Egyptian deity Ammit devoured
30 Chrome dome, so to speak
31 Google ___

32 Like some fish and olives
33 Court procedure
34 Dress down
35 Comfy safari digs
36 Stewart's onetime TV sparring partner
37 Battery type
38 Bundle up
39 Fictional figure whose name means "hole dweller"
40 Hot green stuff
42 Psychologist who coined the word "synchronicity"
45 Venue for broomball
48 AWOL, so to speak

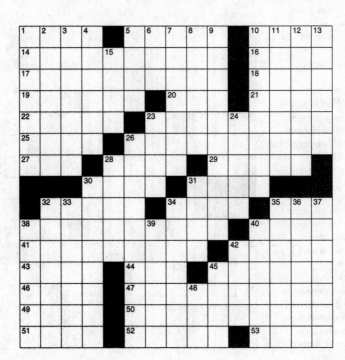

by Josh Knapp

12

ACROSS

1. Principal
6. High note?
11. Balkan land, on Olympic scoreboards
14. Island that's the first word of the Beach Boys' "Kokomo"
15. Central principle of the Baha'i faith
16. Work containing more than 3.5 million citations, for short
17. Balm of Gilead, e.g.
18. Practice roster for an N.F.L. team
20. Half of a 1980s sitcom duo
21. Scratch on the table?
22. Horse's mouth, so to speak
23. Follower of Kennedy or Clinton
24. Baker's unit
26. Fits snugly
27. Florentine, for example
29. Cons
31. One-up
32. Only facility in the world to have hosted the Olympics, Super Bowl and Final Four
35. V8 ingredient
37. People at a theater who didn't pay for their tickets
39. Bananas
42. Crack, say
43. Name for a big wheel
45. Dark
47. Kind of pressure
49. Small square
50. Superhuman, in a way
52. Smoked delicacy
53. Whole grain component
54. Periodical whose founder has appeared on every cover since its 2000 launch
56. Speaks with a pleasing rhythm
57. ___ score
58. Lab dept.
59. Esteem highly
60. 1994 U.S. Open champ
61. Like many student films
62. Excalibur's place

DOWN

1. Sell
2. It provides only partial coverage
3. "Hold your horses!"
4. Stage award
5. Went quickly
6. Do the job
7. Ones sharing some shots
8. Movies, informally
9. Moving walkway maker
10. Boxer with a cameo in "The Hangover"
11. Links
12. Changes color, say
13. Farthest out there
19. Celine Dion, by birth
21. Seven-piece puzzle
24. Dancer's support
25. Certain pilgrim
28. Resting on one's laurels
30. Deeply felt
33. Ill, in Ithaca
34. Quite a ways
36. Useful list when troubleshooting a computer
38. Member of the Hoboken Four
39. "Porgy" novelist ___ Heyward
40. Many an Aesop character
41. Jerks' creations
44. Wits
46. Accessory for a bride, maybe
48. Indigent
51. Industry authority
53. Remain
55. 1099-___ (bank-issued tax form)
56. Head, for short

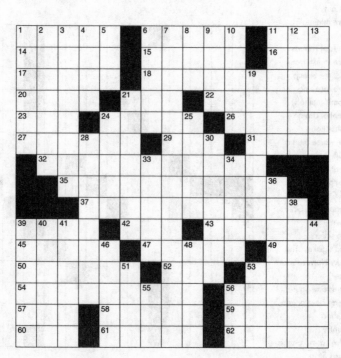

by Andrew J. Ries

ACROSS

1 Differences between colors
12 Duchamp contemporary
15 "Well, what do you know?!"
16 Accessory for Miss Piggy
17 Six-time Grammy winner who is half of the group Gnarls Barkley
18 Some buzzer followers, for short
19 End of a count?
20 Toil and trouble
21 MTV toon teen
23 Reebok rival
24 Most clipped
25 "Fiddler on the Roof" setting
28 Embarrassed
29 Net ___
30 Establish
31 Shorts go-with
32 Still vying
33 Bits of sweat
34 Offensive line
35 Natl. Library Card Sign-Up Month
36 Desktop accessories
37 Novelist Ephron
38 Course outline
40 Helen who helped establish the 46-Down
41 School copier, maybe
42 Minute Rice instruction
43 Like Mercury vis-à-vis Mars
44 Future reporter
45 Shepard of "Parenthood"
48 Darth Vader's boyhood nickname
49 Type unprofessionally
52 Sleep study acronym
53 "Hallelujah!"
54 Change the locks?
55 "Brilliant!"

DOWN

1 Extensive
2 Reddit Q&A sessions, briefly
3 Circlers at airports
4 Oocyte, e.g.
5 Rest on, as chances
6 Register
7 Where Hercules slew the lion
8 Some Pontiacs
9 Night that "Friends" aired: Abbr.
10 Distant stars?
11 Led
12 Supercilious
13 Spit spot
14 Become legally certified
22 "My baby at my breast," to Shakespeare's Cleopatra
23 Boba ___, "Star Wars" bounty hunter
24 Sounds of failure
25 Leafy vegetable related to a beet
26 1974 Abba hit
27 Mazurka meter
28 Individually wrapped hotel amenities
30 Pelvis-patella connector
33 Member of the 1920s Murderers' Row
34 Bout ender
36 Grounds for a 15-yard penalty
37 Tragic heroine of Irish legend
39 Muscle used in pull-ups, briefly
40 Sarah who hosted the podcast "Serial"
42 Support pieces
44 Saves or assists
45 Liter lead-in
46 See 40-Across
47 Classic Jaguars
50 D.O.D. division
51 It might receive zero stars

by John Guzzetta

ACROSS

1 Admissions might give one away
10 Order at an osteria
15 Winner of the inaugural College Football Playoff
16 x+0 = x, e.g.
17 Equal rights subject
19 Homer's father
20 3-Down inventor's inits.
21 Best Picture after "The Last Emperor"
22 Fear-inducing phrase
25 Word with reel or rule
26 Scamps
28 Actress Michelle of "Crazy Rich Asians"
30 One showing firm leadership?
33 Early major-league game setting
34 Destination of Muhammad in his Night Journey
36 Persian for "place of"
37 Skedaddle
38 "Dr. T and the Women" star, 2000
39 Squirt
41 Over
42 Conference member: Abbr.
43 Fixes
44 Wool sources
45 Late major-league game setting: Abbr.
46 Those needing onboarding
48 "D'oh!"
52 British grandma
53 EWR alternative
56 Auto-mated things?
59 "M" or "Z"
60 Print source
61 Thwacks
62 Progress

DOWN

1 Thing: Sp.
2 Literary character likened to a "mute, maned sea-lion"
3 Reproductive system?
4 "Star Wars: The Last Jedi" pilot
5 Company whose headquarters were built from its own product
6 Unbelievable bargains
7 Ceilings
8 Site of some credit card skimming, for short
9 Flavor of some eau de vie
10 Lepers
11 Canceling
12 Neighbor of India and China on a Risk board
13 Senate coverage?
14 "Yes, exactly!"
18 Fricassee relative
23 Pompeii, e.g.
24 Narrow margin
26 Says harsh words?
27 The "o" of Verizon's Fios
29 N.B.A. coach Spoelstra
30 New year, metaphorically
31 Like a howl at night
32 Howls at night, maybe
34 Relative of a .png file
35 College Station player
37 One looking for a hand
40 Scanned smartphone graphics
41 Requites
44 Like most of the Home Depot logo
45 "Come ___!"
47 Permanently
48 Ideologies
49 "Got milk?"
50 Part of 20-Across
51 Ride
54 Purchase
55 Cousins of garters
57 Through
58 L.C.D. forerunner

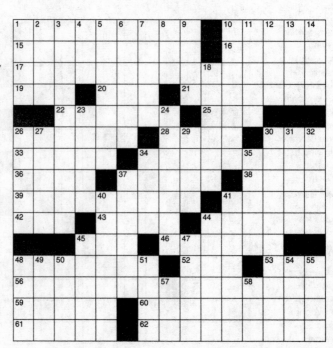

by David Liben-Nowell

ACROSS

1 Dress down
6 El Chapo, notably
15 Caravan destinations
16 Western vacation spot
17 Split tickets?
18 1924 to 1953
19 Instagram filter shade
20 Trailer, e.g.
21 Gas
26 Roadside danger, for short
27 ___ Ski Valley, one of the highest municipalities in the U.S. (9,207 feet)
28 Effect of surplus oil
29 They're indispensable
31 Household nickname
32 Fruits that ripen after being picked
34 Raise
36 Follower of "sweet" or "in your"
39 Polenta base
41 Clear
43 The mathematician Fibonacci, for one
46 Pen noise
47 F.S.U. player, to fans
48 "So that's ___?"
49 Many commercial slogans
51 Alternative to stone
54 Console pioneer
55 Sight in many a Japanese restaurant
59 Downton Abbey, e.g.
60 Skating site
61 Growth on buoys
62 Took courses under pressure
63 Core group?

DOWN

1 Mollycoddles
2 Unwanted messages
3 "Yeah, maybe"
4 Entries in red
5 Think piece
6 Streaming alternatives
7 Groove
8 Tarbell who took on Standard Oil
9 Goes soft
10 Eastern city whose name sounds weird?
11 Actor Eric
12 Tot's attire
13 Unabomber's writing, e.g.
14 Glass pieces
22 Not be steadfast
23 Retired justice who wrote "Out of Order: Stories From the History of the Supreme Court"
24 G.O.P. org. . . . or letters after Senator Richard Burr's name
25 It's not going anywhere
29 "Do You Hear What I Hear?," e.g.
30 That: Sp.
32 Door-to-door giant
33 Rapper with the double-platinum album "If You're Reading This It's Too Late"
35 Pres. Obama's signature achievement
37 Tim Roth's character in "Reservoir Dogs"
38 Marco Polo was on it for 24 years
40 Brand of facial brush
42 Fancies
43 French aperitif
44 Whole
45 Colleague of 23-Down for 15 years
47 Christmas, in Italy
49 Plugs away
50 Baby carriers
52 Rhinestone-covered appurtenance for Elvis
53 Nashville-based awards show, familiarly
56 Goat's cry
57 Make believe
58 One of 18 on a golf course

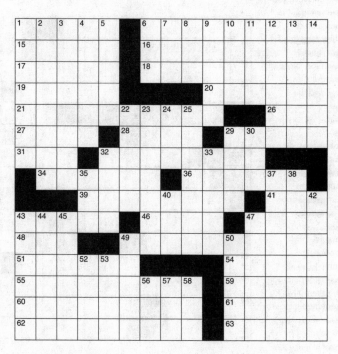

by Zhouqin Burnikel

ACROSS

1 Eats before dinner?
10 Gamble
14 Dangerous toy
16 Dramatic opening
17 No light amount of work
19 Photo ___
20 Gets hitched
21 Overseas dissent
22 Exploit
24 Go down or come up
26 Shot contents
28 Garment originally fashionable in the late 1950s
32 Childhood home of Grant Wood and Elijah Wood
34 Talk show host named in the #MeToo movement
35 Dance in which "you bring your knees in tight"
36 Way to get around writer's block?
37 Makes tingly, in a way
41 Dinner from the oven
42 Home of the 11,000-foot-deep Cotahuasi Canyon
43 External: Prefix
44 Fully accept
51 Wine aperitif
52 TV series whose first episode was titled "Where Is Everybody?"
55 Polo on the small screen
56 They typically revolve around steps
57 Polite reply to Aunt Polly
58 Subject of many emo songs

DOWN

1 Orchard pests
2 River from the Appalachians
3 Program that analyzes the structure of input
4 Emergency key
5 So
6 City SW of Kansas City
7 "___ 101" (former Nickelodeon sitcom)
8 Connection concerns, in brief
9 Renaissance painter Guido
10 Org. in 2017's "Dunkirk"
11 What laying a king on its side in chess means
12 "Elektra" composer
13 Their checks don't check out
15 Like half a deck
18 Pictures that might make you hungry
23 Owner of the Cheshire Cat, with "the"
25 Harden the outside of through cooking
27 Hearty entree
28 Actress Hayek
29 Spring arrival
30 Certain racing teams
31 ___ Zor-El, Supergirl's birth name
33 Problem for a plumber
34 Crib users
35 Counterpart of an iamb
36 Fairly
38 River to the South China Sea
39 Comes with
40 Least in question
45 Unaccounted for, briefly
46 Unappealing trumpet sound
47 Frosty film
48 Jon who wrote and illustrated "Smart Feller, Fart Smeller and Other Spoonerisms"
49 Julie ___, host of TV's "Big Brother"
50 Italian diminutive suffix
53 ___ O'Hara, Martian's host on old TV's "My Favorite Martian"
54 Wine shop offering, informally

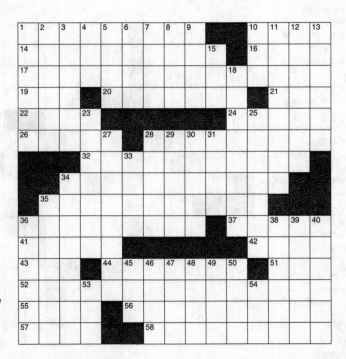

by Sam Trabucco

ACROSS

1 Suzanne Somers's role on "Three's Company"
8 Wind River tribe
15 Cornmeal treat
16 Crescent-shaped
17 Called things off
18 Star-studded event held annually at the Anna Wintour Costume Center in New York
19 Highway divider
20 Marriott competitor
21 "You ain't ___!"
22 Six-time All-Star Ron
23 Where college students might take a stand?
24 Inclined
25 Some acts
27 Mercedes line
30 2001 Destiny's Child #1 hit with the lyric "I don't think you ready for this jelly"
33 Notoriously spoiled sort
36 Figures in the Edda
38 Peak that marks the eastern boundary of Yosemite Natl. Park
41 LP, e.g.
42 Dennings of "2 Broke Girls"
43 Apple picker
44 Writer whose room at the University of Virginia is now a mini-museum
45 Big name in house paint
46 Gizmodo or Engadget
50 Autobiographer who wrote that tennis is "the loneliest sport"
52 Preferred seating, for some
53 Wreck
54 Colorful beach sighting
55 Started fuming
56 King's staff
57 Marched

DOWN

1 Place to get solutions, in brief
2 Spy who trades sex for secrets, informally
3 User of a popular social news site
4 Strand during the winter, say
5 Actress Thompson of "Family"
6 Hide
7 Besides
8 Revlon cosmetics brand
9 Wanted to take back, say
10 Not having
11 Boxers
12 Setting for the 1996 best seller "Into the Wild"
13 Symbols of innocence
14 Jungle swingers, for short
20 Certain adopted pet
22 Salon jobs
25 Vacuum brand
26 Super-super
27 Does some computer work
28 Like the equation $ax^3 + bx^2 + cx + d = 0$
29 What the Clintons each took before they met, in brief
31 ___ steak
32 Nonmainstream
34 Store that really should have a spokesperson
35 "Why not!"
37 Zebralike
38 Olympic marks
39 Network V.I.P.
40 Call
44 Remote button
45 The assassin Sparafucile, in "Rigoletto"
47 Online lead-in
48 One who's "knackered" when exhausted, informally
49 Big vein
50 Spanish sweetheart
51 Cancún kitty
53 Drill master: Abbr.

by Kameron Austin Collins

18

ACROSS

1 Balaclava, for one
8 Approximately five milliliters: Abbr.
11 Invasive plant?
14 "Don't mean any disrespect," in modern lingo
15 Powerful tablet
17 Add to a database
18 Walgreens competitor
19 Level
20 Bolster
21 Algae touted as a superfood
22 Equipment used with goggles
23 Bánh ___ (Vietnamese cake)
24 Dope
25 Like idol worshipers
31 Commercial name that becomes a Native American tribe if you move its first letter to the end
35 Counterpart of 6-Down
36 Daring way to go
37 Not go in a straight line
38 Give a whoop
39 Part of some love triangles
41 Word before or after "one"
43 Ahead of, old-style
44 Infrequent losers
48 Natural fuel source
52 Decides to abstain
53 Juice brand owned by Coca-Cola
54 Nutty confection
55 Indian restaurant fixture
56 It may be broken in a library
57 Major Tuscan export
58 Gang members
59 ___ Prize (onetime annual $1 million award)
60 Person who's spectacularly awful

DOWN

1 Places for braces
2 Specific occasion
3 Sassy response to a scolding
4 Green land
5 Where models are assembled?
6 "See ya!"
7 ___ Landing (part of Philadelphia)
8 Runs out of gas
9 Three-cornered sail
10 Rhetoric class concept
11 Back slap?
12 Sales figure
13 Go through a voice change?
16 Formal opening
25 Not forward
26 Little wiggler
27 Gold standard
28 Turn
29 "I'm gonna be sick!"
30 Stick in a ball-and-stick game
32 Classic film with a screaming boy on its poster
33 Monthly travelers?
34 Sty, e.g.
40 2013 hit for 2 Chainz and Wiz Khalifa
42 Formally choose
44 Thicket
45 When the Boston Marathon is held
46 Most of a sugar cane
47 Charger
48 Screw up
49 Locale of America's deepest gorge
50 Lineup in 44-Across
51 Colorful wraps

by David Steinberg

ACROSS

1 Exclamation appropriate for 1-Across
11 It's where it's at
15 Purple-blue shade or the flower it's named after
16 Series finale
17 You might use it in dressing
18 Props for a Broadway play?
19 Salinger title teen
20 Heels
21 Bucks, e.g.
22 Not quite keep up
23 Salon supply
25 Cargo area
29 Time, proverbially
30 U.S.'s first so-called "Public Enemy No. 1"
31 Krugerrand, e.g.
34 "Fore!," for one
35 Dance move of the 2010s
36 Looney Tunes's Speedy Gonzales, e.g.
37 Fiddled (with)
39 V.I.P. section?
40 King maker
41 Brewski
42 Held in contempt
44 Young 'un
45 Dark suit
46 Of the flock
48 Actress Jessica
52 "Take this . . ."
53 Crux of "The Crucible"
55 Medieval weapon
56 Waiting to come out
57 Get a lode of these!
58 Military leader known for being chicken?

DOWN

1 Place for a shrine
2 Court equipment
3 Perfumery measure
4 Craftiness
5 Pecorino Romano source
6 Protector of the heart
7 Bring to the boiling point
8 Ratified
9 Seemingly spontaneous gathering
10 Supplied
11 More than just won
12 "See!"
13 Roger ___, fifth chief justice of the Supreme Court
14 "Family Ties" mother
21 Vulcan telepathy technique
22 Some camping gear
24 Verizon acquisition of 2015
25 Jazzy style
26 Anklebones
27 Like a code anyone can use
28 Honey bunch?
31 Travel (about)
32 Will go ahead as planned
33 State bird whose name sounds like its call
35 Newsroom concern
38 LAX to ORD or JFK: Abbr.
39 One who's got game . . . but shouldn't
41 Like a kid in a candy store, e.g.
42 Sap
43 Intelligible
47 Start of a subj. line
48 Seed case
49 Kind of trap
50 Captures
51 It may precede second thoughts
53 Lose it, with "out"
54 Eastern rival

by Robyn Weintraub

20

ACROSS

1 Took out
6 First-ever comedian to appear on the cover of Time (1960)
10 Singer with the 2017 #1 R&B album "Ctrl"
13 Data storage sites
15 Cookie for the calorie-conscious
17 ___ number
18 Like some pans
19 Me-first attitude
21 Surprised salutation
22 Org. in 2007's "Charlie Wilson's War"
23 Make rent
24 "Time for me to shine"
25 Hungarian-born mathematician Paul
27 Does some yard work
28 Embedded
30 Verb repeated throughout Exodus 20
32 Largest sesamoid bone in the body
34 Moving
38 What finger wags indicate
40 University near Penn
41 Grinding away
44 R.E.M. show?
46 Slew
47 Word on a red stamp, perhaps
49 Muscle used in dip exercises, informally
50 Standards
51 Requiring a lot of work
54 Prone to sarcasm

55 Mahi-mahi, by another name
57 Alternative to online dating
58 Regurgitate, as a baby would
59 Penn, e.g.: Abbr.
60 Troubles
61 1), 2), 3), etc.

DOWN

1 Some tragic ends, for short
2 First-termers
3 It may be under pressure during an emergency
4 Bad designs
5 Unmindful
6 Brillo alternatives
7 Counterpart of pizzicato, in music

8 Oscar-winning 1974 documentary about the Vietnam War
9 Buncha
10 Eastern religion
11 Galvanized, chemically
12 Brings to a boil
14 Broke down for careful analysis
16 "Now you're talking!"
20 It made a big splash in 2001
21 [Snort]
26 "Well, whaddya know!"
29 Lead-in to tourism or terrorism
31 What isn't legal for copying: Abbr.
33 "___ qué?"

35 Remove from the ground
36 Equipped
37 Assembly line pioneer
39 Goes with Mr. All Right?
41 They're not in the script
42 Claw
43 Congenital
45 Lionel Richie's "You ___"
48 Woman's name that rhymes with a part of the world
52 Inverse of giga-
53 Minor concessions
56 Special ___

by Lewis Dean Hyatt

ACROSS

1 Bitter end?
5 Many a line from Benjamin Franklin
10 Fool, in British slang
14 Numerical prefix
15 First name in rap history
16 Look (for), as a compliment
17 Question after "Hey!"
20 Bathroom or beach supply
21 Eye intently
22 "Awake in the Dark" author
23 Mic holders
26 Soccer superstar Lionel
27 Gutenberg's Bible, e.g.
28 Workers, dismissively
30 Jean who wrote "Wide Sargasso Sea"
31 [Don't you think you're milking it a bit too much?]
32 Enid who wrote "National Velvet"
34 ___ milk
35 Checker of someone's vitals
36 2008 presidential campaign topic
37 Name associated with chicken
38 Unwavering
39 Takes off
40 Focus of Boyle's law
41 Relative of philia and agape, to the Greeks
43 Fortune 500 company whose products have a trademarked green-and-yellow color scheme
44 Capital of South Sudan
45 Hertfordshire neighbor

47 Provider of a traveler's check, for short
48 Like
49 Item suggested visually by the black squares in this puzzle's grid
52 Like many an ESPN Deportes watcher
55 Full-bodied
59 Redress
60 Reduplicative dance name
61 Impressively tough, slangily
62 Marched

DOWN

1 "Hmm . . ."
2 Millennials, in relation to their parents
3 "Hope" and "Friendship," for two
4 HBO's "Veep," e.g.

5 Envelope abbr.
6 "OB-viously!"
7 Parrot
8 Go on and on
9 Vaper's device
10 Big name in pharmaceuticals
11 Not be in the driver's seat
12 Simple
13 "In other words . . ."
18 Juicer
19 Group of whales
23 Heavy metal band with the double-platinum album "Countdown to Extinction"
24 Victory
25 Seafood known for its sweet taste and delicate texture
28 Peeled

29 Group running together
32 Tender
33 Many profs
42 ___ Kyle, Catwoman's alter ego
44 Go on and on
46 Places for pedestrians to be alert, informally
48 Drink with a straw
50 Sez
51 Some wares in a china shop
52 The International Space Station, e.g.
53 DuVernay who directed "A Wrinkle in Time"
54 ___ Baker (British clothing retailer)
56 Italian cardinal
57 Bummed
58 ___ time

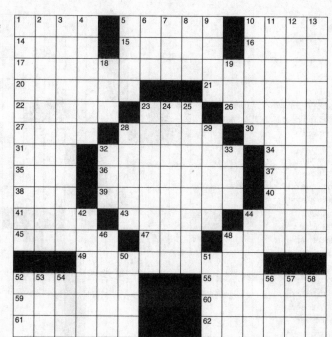

by Erik Agard and Bruce Haight

ACROSS

1 Rhimes who created "Grey's Anatomy"
7 Dieter's time of indulgence
15 Reach the limit
16 2016 film whose climax is on the planet Scarif
17 They might be made to reconcile
18 2006 Emmy winner for "The West Wing"
19 Give extra medication
20 Got cracking
21 Problems with a collection
22 Org. that might take the government to court
24 Symbol of militarism
25 Women's soccer star Krieger
26 Means of drawing up solutions
29 Lead actress in 2017's "The Big Sick"
33 Fair
37 Wraps up
38 Composer Arcangelo who inspired a set of Rachmaninoff variations
39 Not quite blow
40 Small falcons
41 Collaborative principle in improv comedy
43 Nursery cry
44 Take the edge off?
47 Like discussions of metaphysics
49 Theme in some time travel fiction
50 Green refreshers
53 Pill bug, for one
55 Isn't discrete
56 Nissan crossover named for an Italian city
57 "The Son of Man" artist
58 Illuminating comment
59 Try out, as a game
60 Volleyball team, e.g.

DOWN

1 Gets a twinkle in one's eyes?
2 Hit movie with the tagline "A family comedy without the family"
3 Leaning column?
4 Texting while driving, and others
5 Hardly smashes
6 Flummoxed
7 Come home after a night of heavy drinking, say
8 Go into seclusion
9 Jennifer who wrote the Pulitzer-winning "A Visit From the Goon Squad"
10 Title for Princess Anne beginning in 1982
11 Leaves work?
12 Sadness
13 Actress MacDowell
14 First Nobel laureate from Ireland
23 Big Four workers, for short
27 Ancestor of Methuselah
28 One might result from negligence
30 World's most-followed Twitter user, as of 2018
31 Trailblazing athlete of the 1970s
32 Cartoonist's indicator of nodding
34 Exploded
35 In the blink of an eye
36 Served
38 Let go of
40 Diet in the Mideast
42 Virtuosi
44 Fail to tread lightly
45 #2, to #1
46 Lowercase letter resembling a "w"
48 Members of an Arizona tribe
49 Global currency market with a portmanteau name
51 Came to roost
52 Good Tinder outcome
54 Dweller in Apt. 1-A, say

by Kevin G. Der

ACROSS

1 Objective worked toward during crunch time?
8 "Get off the stage!"
15 43-Across that shares its name with part of a flower
16 Catching rays for days, say
17 Need for a certain outlet
18 Outlet's opposite
19 Singer with the 2012 hit "Let Me Love You"
20 "Later, alligator!"
22 Successful hacker's declaration
23 Tubes
24 Agrees to compromise
25 Chihuahua, for one
26 Seriously muscular
28 Hagatna is its capital
30 Big Apple team, on scoreboards
31 Deep blue
32 Word on some Emmy awards
34 Cutting-edge, as an electronic product
36 Alpha male, perhaps?
40 Some Girl Scout cookies
42 Any of three sisters of old Hollywood
43 See 15-Across
46 The worst of times
47 ___ wrench
48 Taps, as a keg
50 Cliff notes?
52 4x platinum album of 2001
53 Eric of "Munich"
54 Hitherto
55 Pound, e.g.
56 Suffered humiliation
58 Early tool
60 Participate in quid pro quo
61 Region of Ghana known for gold and cocoa
62 Plucks
63 Roll of 4 and 6, in craps

DOWN

1 Teacher's timesaver for grading tests
2 PC modem or drive
3 Novelty item in vintage comic book ads
4 Law enforcers, in slang
5 Start of some rock genre names
6 One side of a store sign
7 Real first name of writer Isak Dinesen
8 Rides the waves without a board
9 Prime draft pick
10 Tiny tube travelers
11 Lost all patience
12 Profession in a Eugene O'Neill title
13 "___ and happiness are an impossible combination": Mark Twain
14 Where Nemo was found in "Finding Nemo"
21 Nip in the end
24 A.F.C. North team
25 Notable ring bearer
27 A.F.C. East team, informally
29 Intangible quality
32 Official birds of Quebec
33 Center of a Scrabble board
35 Kind of phase for some teens
37 Place to get ribs or pulled pork
38 Literally, "little wheel"
39 Low-cal version of a classic cookie
41 From
43 Deep blue
44 Director of "The 40-Year-Old Virgin" and "This Is 40"
45 Fail to follow suit
47 Missionaries of Charity founder
49 Button material
51 Mother of Perseus
54 Only
55 Recorder button
57 "Frasier" role
59 Post's Honey ___!

by Trenton Charlson

ACROSS

1 Gang member associated with the color blue
5 Powerful ray
10 Sorority letters
14 Advanced
15 Spinning
16 "I'm so sorry"
17 Marie who married at 14
19 Bean town?
20 Painting of a bouquet, e.g.
21 Israeli P.M. between Netanyahu and Sharon
22 With assurance
23 Make deep cuts in
25 Caesarean section?
26 Easy-to-eat, in a way
27 Wyoming town that's home to the Buffalo Bill Museum
28 Relatives of tails
29 Steamy place
30 Rapping
31 Switzerland's ___ de Neuchâtel
34 Something a lawyer might make
35 Something that's "free" (although that's debatable)
36 They're hard to beat
39 Can't not
40 Head case, so to speak
41 Rich cakes
42 Man with ___
43 Ship-to-ship communication
45 Courts
46 Dead ringers?
47 Best Picture before "12 Years a Slave"
48 Contradict
49 Olympic racer
50 Texter's valediction
51 Does nothing
52 Spy

DOWN

1 Makeup of a high school reading list
2 Mall authority figure
3 Palestinian uprising
4 Astronomer with a geocentric model of the universe
5 Macho
6 "Whose woods these ___ . . .": Frost
7 Modern invitation to hook up
8 Chats
9 A bitter pull to swallow?
10 Guiding light
11 Full-bodied red
12 Joint tenant?
13 Gouged
18 Latin pronoun
21 Stupefy
24 Moth repellent
26 Ended a phone call?
28 King of Cups, e.g.
30 Sing about?
31 "Hey!"
32 Hannah Montana, for one
33 Narrowly spaced
34 Protection from harmful rays
35 "Eight Elvises" and "Sixteen Jackies"
36 Really annoy
37 Bit of news
38 Panegyric
39 Ice planet in "The Empire Strikes Back"
41 Pecks, in a way
44 Role for a young Ron Howard
46 Spy grp.

by Ben Gross and James Somers

ACROSS

1 It might go to the dogs
11 Unaltered
15 Tahoe, for one
16 Costa ___
17 Trendy salad type
18 Plot in Genesis
19 Prey for a dingo
20 "Rush!"
21 Assessment of acidity
23 Platform that many things run on
24 Part of the Trinity
25 Maniacal laugh
26 Traditional retirement present
27 Ambiguity
28 Selection ___
30 Breezes (along)
31 Knights, bishops, rooks, etc.
32 Fluff pieces
33 See 47-Down
34 Not final
35 Word before "I hate that!"
36 "I'm ___!"
37 An almanac and Google, for a crossword solver
38 Extra keys, e.g.
40 Excel-using exec, maybe
41 What officials need to get cleared before speaking?
42 Bladder, e.g.
43 Subway operator, for short
46 Stuffed appetizer
47 Relative of sepia
48 Cable inits. popular with female viewers
49 Starting
50 "That's not me anymore"
53 Hilton alternative
54 "Take your time"
55 Funny Martha
56 Wheedles

DOWN

1 Part of the original "Star Trek" cast
2 National alternative
3 88 or 89
4 That can't be right
5 Boxes
6 September and October, for pumpkins
7 Expletive-free
8 Farrier's tool
9 Going by
10 Postarrest ritual
11 "___ Arrives" (1967 soul album)
12 Pitched horizontally
13 Polar features
14 Seat of Orange County, Calif.
22 Kansas' Fort ___
25 Escort
26 Rehearsed
27 Too lean
28 Major lobbying group, colloquially
29 United
30 "Blue ___" (Irving Berlin tune)
32 Lasciviously desires
33 Keeps up
34 Part of one's Twitter page, informally
36 High ___
37 Bills are found in it
39 College assignment, informally?
40 Prestige
42 South American capital
43 High muck-a-muck
44 Move behind?
45 Very long chain
47 First name of a cartoon 33-Across
51 "I shall return," e.g.
52 It checks for leaks, for short

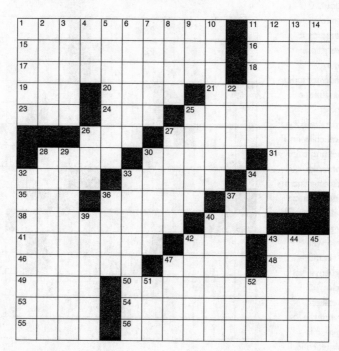

by Evan Kalish

ACROSS

1 Overweight and untidy
9 Fertilizer ingredient
15 Sybaritic pursuit
16 City on the Douro River
17 Bro-ey shout-out
18 1973 Best Actor winner for "Save the Tiger"
19 Knotty tree growth
20 Took sick leave, say
22 Slobbery toon
23 Subject of the documentary "Top Secret Rosies: The Female Computers of W.W. II"
24 Torah vessels
25 "Happy Days" hangout, informally
26 Waiting for a delivery
28 Miss, e.g.
30 23andMe services
33 Ones going on runs
35 Got on the board
37 Like oil spills and clearing of rain forests
41 Jack's other name
42 Certain Febreze targets
44 Paragon
45 Played with the bow, in music
48 "Say Anything . . ." director
49 Embroil
50 Ads that get lots of traffic?
52 Confident self-assessment
53 Tarzan's realm
54 What a hack has
56 Do a double take?
57 Progressive competitor
58 Being
59 Hinged

DOWN

1 Some disguised fishing trawlers
2 Nebulous
3 Method of solving
4 Transferrer of stock?
5 Today preceder
6 "That's lousy"
7 Clocked
8 "Y" with a bar
9 Skunks
10 Take in the paper
11 Winner of five British Opens between 1975 and 1983
12 Hardwear?
13 One with a frog in its throat?
14 Signs of rush hour
21 Capital across the Red Sea from Asmara
26 Idaho's Nez ___ County
27 Makes out
29 Belgium's longest-reigning monarch (44 years)
31 Macbeth met one at Dunsinane Hill
32 Cabbage for canning?
34 Formulaically humorous
36 Mad
38 Woman's name meaning "gift"
39 Decked out
40 Like some aspirin regimens
43 Prepare for a long day ahead
45 At ___ minimum
46 Turn yellow or red, say
47 Fissure
49 Where "The Last Supper" is located
51 Fabric purchase
55 Add up to

by Byron Walden

ACROSS

1 It might give you a headache
4 Tank top
10 "Westworld" network
13 Restaurant chain with a "never-ending pasta bowl"
16 Slip
17 "You wanna fight?!"
18 Remote inserts
19 Doughnut-loving toon
20 ___ Air
21 Kind of ball that's edible
23 Did a pantomime of
24 Ukulele accessory
25 Like many textbook publishers
26 Show letters
28 Game in which I is 1
31 Belt under the waist?
35 Some Tornado Alley residents
36 Explosion cause
37 Country music's ___ Young Band
38 Figures in some "Twilight Zone" episodes, for short
39 9-to-5, maybe
40 [Knock, knock]
42 Has as a tenant
44 Composer of symphonic "verse"
46 "Heck, yeah!"
47 Didn't keep quiet
48 Level
50 Talk smack to
54 Stopped debating
55 Bear in a hit 2012 film
56 Invite, as to one's penthouse
57 ___ package
58 Wasted vacation days?
61 Show with a musical guest, for short
62 Genre for Anthrax and Megadeth
63 An end to jargon?
64 Classic gag gift
65 See 56-Down

DOWN

1 Hot chocolaty drink
2 Simple craft
3 Confidence booster on a test
4 Its teeth are pointy
5 Hollywood title: Abbr.
6 Latin rhythm
7 Unsavory fellows
8 Spot remover?
9 Bits ___ second
10 Hershey toffee treats
11 Its shell has three sides
12 Guesstimate words
14 German wheels
15 Emphatic rejection
22 Fathers' clothes
24 "Sweet"
27 What insomnia causes to build up over time
29 Like Call of Duty: Black Ops
30 This, to Tomás
31 Breezy air
32 Spinoff Nabisco cookies
33 Wimp
34 Establishment to which customers have come for years?
41 Classic TV diner
43 Tears don't rip it
45 Stubborn Dr. Seuss pair
49 Clarifier in texts
51 Very furry, muscular dog
52 Elder of the sisters who visited Narnia in "The Chronicles of Narnia"
53 Said "O-D-O-U-R," e.g.
54 Ukulele accessory
56 With 65-Across, fierce marcher
59 Post cereal made with honey
60 ___ Chang (ex-girlfriend of Harry Potter)

by David Steinberg

ACROSS

1 "I Am ___" (2013 best-selling autobiography)
7 Deals
12 1998 Paul Simon/Derek Walcott musical, with "The"
13 Party leader
14 Jaguar's coat, e.g.
15 Apple ___
16 Classified
17 Little put-down
19 Exorcism, e.g.
20 [Yawn]
22 Addictive pain reliever
24 Baby during its first four weeks
25 "Do something funny!"
26 Nick name
28 Rapper with the 5x platinum album ". . . And Then There Was X"
29 "Crime and Punishment" setting
41 Low
42 U.S. women's soccer star Megan ___
43 Sporty Pontiac of old
44 Dark and forbidding
45 MacFarlane of "American Dad!"
46 Capital of the U.S. from 1785 to 1790, in brief
48 Thick, as toilet tissue
49 Members of familles
51 Tried to follow
53 Company that once had tremendous "quarterly" profits?
54 Light crimson
55 "Fiddler on the Roof" Oscar nominee
56 Showed signs of congestion, maybe

DOWN

1 First name of two Wimbledon winners in the 1980s and '90s
2 Political organization
3 Shepherds, in the Bible
4 Le Pen pal?
5 International treaty subject
6 Ones not calling the shots?
7 Chest part, informally
8 Lovingly, in scores
9 Classic blues song with the line "I'd rather be dead than to stay here and be your dog"
10 When to start on a course
11 Less stressed
12 Singer in Jewish services
14 Small part
16 Tucker out, in a way
18 Hobble
21 Press secretary who inspired C. J. Cregg of "The West Wing"
23 ___-de-sac
27 Graduate of a Red Cross training course, for short
29 Resists change
30 Go along with
31 Stuck
32 Ordinary joe
33 "Full Frontal With Samantha Bee" network
34 Word with game or building
35 One letting you know before going for a bite?
36 Some malicious programs
37 Intolerant
38 One-footed creature
39 South Pole discoverer Amundsen
40 Millennials, by another name
47 "Seriously?!"
50 Part of R.S.V.P.
52 Morale-boosting grp.

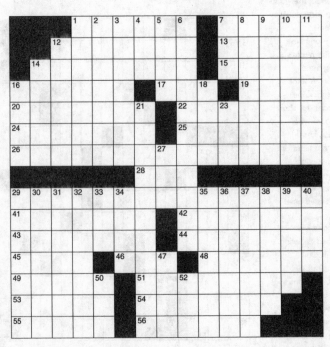

by Ryan McCarty

ACROSS

1 High-occupancy vehicles?
10 Madres' kin
14 Some high-rise constructions
15 "This one's ___"
16 Backward
17 Soup noodle
18 Drapers' units: Abbr.
19 Wig out
20 Friendly greetings
21 "Fish are friends, not ___" (line from "Finding Nemo")
22 Leaves
24 Made a case
27 Touchy sort?
28 ___ Bar, Ireland's oldest pub, dating to A.D. 900
29 Pioneer mover
33 Call mean names, say
34 Old Speckled Hen, for one
35 Dispenser item
36 "The Devil's playthings"
38 Crinkly fabric
39 Provides, as aid
40 Calls funny names, say
41 "Vamoose!"
44 Liner, e.g.
45 Butterfly chrysalises, e.g.
46 Fishing basket
48 Eponymous Belgian resort town
51 Like some early learning, for short
52 Like some college applicants
54 Something found near the tongue?
55 Ones who find it difficult to go out?

56 Group whose past members have included six U.S. presidents
57 Much of Generation Z, today

DOWN

1 Rep
2 Agreeable answer to an invitation
3 "Jingle Bells" contraction
4 Sentry's query
5 Reprobate
6 First-aid brand
7 Urgent letters
8 Adjusts the parameters of
9 General direction of I-77: Abbr.
10 Times Square, you might say
11 Setting for "Siddhartha"
12 ___ friends
13 Impression
14 Take a sip of
20 Breaking it might be cause for celebration
21 Fair fare
23 Complimentary composition
24 Wine town in Piedmont
25 Follow the script
26 Caesar's conquest of 58-50 B.C.
27 Gets into shape?
29 Common Christmas decoration
30 Raw materials
31 Look of astonishment
32 Astonishes
37 Largest carrier in Japan
40 J. J.'s sister on "Good Times"
41 First U.S. company to be valued at $1 trillion
42 Certain street art
43 Dot
44 Determined about
47 Stop lying
48 Competitor of Us Weekly
49 Bodybuilder's pride
50 Trailers, e.g.
52 Romeo's was "a most sharp sauce," per Shakespeare
53 You: Ger.

by Robyn Weintraub

ACROSS

1 Pole stars?
10 Shop contents
15 Smetana composition inspired by a river
16 Too good for
17 Flexible attire
18 Chicken
19 ___ Lovegood, friend of Harry Potter
20 Chemistry test?
22 One-eighth of a data set
25 777, e.g.
26 Target of some shots
28 Creature that can walk on lava
29 Shoots
30 Opposite of pobre
32 Sierra and others
35 Leslie's friend on "Parks and Recreation"
36 Mutant villain of Marvel Comics
39 Gambler's spot
40 Bottom of the barrel
42 Former Senate majority leader who was once an amateur boxer
43 Single cut
45 Wheels
47 Group with a satellite truck
49 10–12 on a Little League team, maybe
52 Romeos
53 Activity at a comic con
54 Reminder of a hit
55 Fancy restaurant topping?
56 "The Mikado" and "The Merry Widow"
61 What sharks take interest in
62 Rebel fighter during the Mexican Revolution
63 Pressure group?
64 Edgy newspaper type, informally

DOWN

1 Dump
2 E'en if
3 Neither long nor short: Abbr.
4 Survivor's cry
5 Mass appeal
6 Thickness-adjusting tool
7 Woman's name meaning "pleasure"
8 One might be paid to talk
9 Certain bar order
10 Dangling part of a turkey
11 Persistent
12 Subject of a classic six-volume work by Edward Gibbon
13 One might have clickable "Yes" and "No" buttons
14 Event in which the Four Questions are read
21 ". . . never mind, then"
22 Butcher's scraps
23 "I Fall to Pieces" singer
24 Like landscape paintings that focus more on color and lighting than fine detail
25 Harebrained
27 It's a feeling
31 Turn over
33 Hard ___
34 Shoots out
37 Place for matches
38 Abandoned
41 Carolina Panthers mascot with a rhyming name
44 Dog depicted by Monopoly's dog token
46 Chicago political dynasty
48 TV show created by Vince McMahon
49 Go haywire
50 28-Across, e.g.
51 Dumplings at a Japanese restaurant
54 Was lachrymose
57 Bucko
58 [Oh, no you didn't!]
59 Loser to New England in Super Bowl LI: Abbr.
60 "Come to think of it . . ."

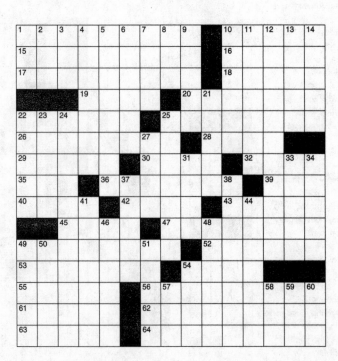

by Will Nediger

ACROSS

1 What all capital letters may indicate
9 Octet in "The Twelve Days of Christmas"
14 Online magazines, blogs, etc.
15 Speaks highly of
17 Canvas application
18 Bring under control
19 One might be written to an idol
20 Von Trapp father in "The Sound of Music"
22 Sport whose participants are called rikishi
23 Scoopers for baba ghanouj
26 Supreme Court clerk's reading
28 Solver with a set of clues, for short
29 ___ testing
31 Pre-euro money
33 A chorus line?
36 Pride : lions :: ___ : monkeys
37 Leukocytes
40 Who said "There's only one Elizabeth like me, and that's the queen"
41 Massaged
42 More run-down
45 Jacques of film
46 French plural of "son"
47 Challenge for a mover
49 Arcade game button
53 Name on the ESPY Courage Award
55 Inspiration for some fake social media accounts, informally
57 What "torah" means
58 Neighbor of Suisse
60 Capital of South Australia
63 2015 Best Actress winner Brie
64 "It's fine, don't worry"
65 Older brother of Malcolm on "Malcolm in the Middle"
66 "Faster, faster!"

DOWN

1 Pry
2 Heitkamp of North Dakota politics
3 Young prey for a bobcat
4 Make the calls, informally
5 Break during a cricket match
6 "Understood, man"
7 Pool game
8 Bulldog's N.C.A.A. rival
9 Combination
10 Big name in men's deodorant
11 Suffix with sinus
12 Bite-size breakfast treat
13 Jellylike organism once classified as a fungus
16 Popular movie theater candy
21 Cleanse
24 Quieted down
25 Pertaining to the moon
27 Billionaire types
30 Key in?
32 Byline, e.g.
33 Like the highest-rated restaurants in Michelin Guides
34 Car-pooling arrangement
35 Copacetic
37 Spiced holiday drink
38 Precisely
39 Raiders' org.
43 Period of great climate change
44 Paris's ___ de Rivoli
48 Tribes
50 What a politician's promises and actions should do
51 Windmill blades, essentially
52 One may be quoted in the news
54 "What ___?"
56 ___ Rexha, pop singer with the 2017 #2 hit "Meant to Be"
59 Neighbor of the island Santorini
61 Edge
62 Give it ___

by Kyle Dolan

ACROSS

1 Going in
8 Inferior-quality item, informally
15 Player of the mother on "Black-ish"
17 Pitch for a whole season?
18 Couple on the road?
19 "Yum!"
20 ___ king
21 High-ranking suits
22 Susquehannock Indian relatives
23 Part of Q.E.F.
24 Basic cable inits.
25 Mantle's cover
26 Dashed off, say
27 Name on 2016 campaign buttons
28 Vessels with sharp bows
29 Features of jack-in-the-boxes
31 *scratches head*
32 Animal cry in a nursery rhyme
33 Dolly user
34 Singer of the 1989 #1 hit "Opposites Attract"
35 Plied, in a way
36 It's measured in degs.
39 Dirty
40 Is up on
41 Georgia ___
42 "Baudolino" novelist
43 Foal : horse :: cria : ___
44 Word from the Italian for "crush"
45 2011 musical with the highest-charting Broadway cast album since "Hair" in 1969
48 Band since 1922
49 Doing super-well
50 Removes roots and all

DOWN

1 Staple, e.g.
2 Apex predators of the past
3 Big name in late-night
4 Some causes of brain freeze
5 Guns
6 Die on one side of Italy?
7 Trials
8 Hang in there!
9 "It has one syllable" and "Its fourth letter is T"
10 Play honor
11 Cards on a scoreboard
12 Retro picture
13 Set apart
14 End of some affluent community names
16 Work together (with)
22 Actress Alexander of "Get Out"
23 Missed out, e.g.
25 Amsterdam feature
26 Blown away
27 World capital that's an anagram of Azerbaijan's capital + L
28 Pacific types
29 Gem that's been polished but not faceted
30 Heyday of many serials
31 Kia Rio competitor
32 System used for computer code
33 Spanish term of endearment
35 More watery
36 Tony-winning musical with three B'way runs
37 Play starter
38 Summer slip-ons
40 Novelist Mario Vargas ___
41 Homme land?
43 Rich store
44 Ask
46 Melt alternative, for short
47 Catlike Pokémon with an onomatopoeic name

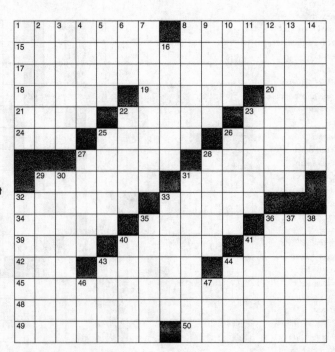

by Doug Peterson and Erik Agard

ACROSS

1 Airer of "Orphan Black" and "Almost Royal"
11 Foreign dishes?
15 Dislikes intensely
16 Stop
17 Ginormous quantities
18 ___ Reville, Alfred Hitchcock's wife and collaborator
19 Jocular response to "How did you know?!"
20 Baby rabbit
21 Presented in rows and columns
23 Home of Colbert and Corden
25 Cobbler's job
26 Craft for J.F.K. in W.W. II
29 Li'l
31 Org. behind the magazine America's 1st Freedom
32 Fuel holder
33 Science class for ambitious H.S. students
34 Lead role on TV's "30 Rock"
35 "Get your act together!"
36 It covers the floor
37 One to swear by?
38 ___ Gardens
39 Patch growth
40 Tennis's only two-time Grand Slam winner
41 Sightings in 11-Across
42 Some flashlight needs
43 Things drawn during the Napoleonic Era
44 Classless
46 Urges
48 Site on the National Mall
50 1970 title lyric after "Simple as do re mi"
51 State without words?
54 Like some tracks

55 Number 2, for one
58 Old World blackbird
59 Warner Bros. cartoon series presented by Steven Spielberg
60 Short orders to a short-order cook?
61 Raise

DOWN

1 Core political support
2 Some cookouts, informally
3 Major success
4 Lead-in to right or wrong
5 Relative of a malt shop
6 Win the help of
7 Bonnie with five 1990s Top 40 hits
8 Four-time Japanese premier
9 Word before sign or after red
10 One making a killing
11 Many a trailer
12 Get hit by one of Cupid's arrows
13 Musical standard from "Show Boat"
14 Daydreamers
22 Laddie
23 Family name of Hollywood brothers
24 One might say "All access"
26 Important item for a '50s greaser
27 Not live in the present?
28 Explodes
30 Way up a ski mountain
33 Where the Olympics were held for the first time in 1964

36 Box of 64, maybe
37 Quick strikes
39 Thai currency
40 Something "grand" that's not really so grand
43 Poor
45 Places for small herb gardens
47 Lakshmi of "Top Chef"
49 Largest river to the Laptev Sea
51 ___ bowl (dish for the health-conscious)
52 Absorb, as body moisture
53 If-then-___ (computer coding statement)
56 Feel ill
57 Medical research org.

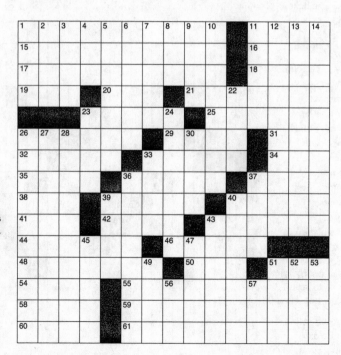

by Temple Brown

ACROSS

1 "Dora the Explorer" catchphrase
16 Demanding
17 It's not backed up
18 Cry for attention, maybe
19 Mephitis
20 K'ung Fu-___ (Confucius)
21 Sign of a sensation
22 Radio freq. unit
23 Japanese room divider
25 What's done up in an updo
27 Unsavory
30 Capitol vehicle
33 First name in fragrance
34 Angel's antithesis
35 Number below #
37 He hit his 600th home run in 2007
38 How some bonds are sold
40 Suffers humiliation
42 Four-time Emmy-winning drama
44 Specialized
45 Quinn of CBS's "Elementary"
47 Stanford rival, informally
48 Cool ___
51 Home of the largest grain elevator in the world: Abbr.
53 Ancestor of a cell
55 U.S. financial giant, for short
56 One way to lose your balance?
59 "Things get ugly"
60 Classic Dr. Seuss title

DOWN

1 Levels
2 Like EE vis-à-vis E
3 Digs in the snow?
4 "I'm exhausted!"
5 Trio of mummies
6 Bad record
7 Philosopher who said "What does not kill me makes me stronger"
8 Part of YOLO
9 Blows away
10 Big name in jam
11 Not just down
12 One way to stand
13 Spark provider
14 E-4 and E-5, but not E-3

15 Good name for someone tracing family history?
22 Actor who said "It takes a smart guy to play dumb"
24 ___ J, singer with the 2014 hit "Bang Bang"
25 Straw mat
26 It's a wrap
28 Drink flavorer
29 ___ big
30 Dora the Explorer, e.g.: Abbr.
31 Fred Astaire, at times
32 Taciturnity
34 Sound of a sock
36 Starter at un restaurant

39 Drink that competes with Monster
41 Big name in shipping
43 2010s dance craze
46 Abbr. on a food wrapper
48 "Ville-d'Avray" painter
49 On the wrong side (of)
50 ___ Tatin (upside-down pastry)
51 Singer Perry
52 Pine
54 "That's ridiculous!"
55 Title for a fox
57 10/
58 Member of a crossword aviary?

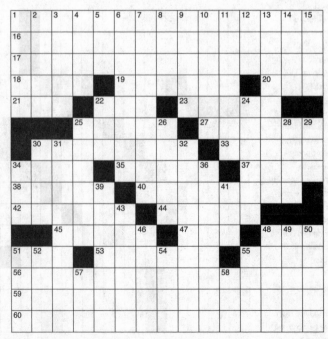

by David Steinberg

ACROSS

1 "You Don't Mess Around With Jim" singer, 1972
6 Resort in Salt Lake County
10 Hill worker
13 Modern phrase said before doing something foolish
15 Coping mechanisms?
17 Homer's specialty
18 Website for tech whizzes
19 Eastern state
20 One might tell you to do the math
21 Kind of dog found in New York City
22 Warm and toasty, e.g.: Abbr.
23 Follower
25 Render harmless, in a way
28 Little suckers
29 In play
30 Put off
33 Lets go
34 "___ anniversaire!"
35 County in a Pulitzer-winning play title
36 Holders of solutions
38 Mountaineer's tool
39 Often-misspelled contraction
40 Court suspension
41 Neat
43 Ran fast
44 Runs
45 ___ Smetanina, first woman to win 10 Winter Olympic medals
47 'Vette alternative
50 Flier from Asia
51 "Take a chill pill!"
53 Shakers, e.g.
54 Employer of some shepherds
55 Call, in poker
56 Japanese bowlful
57 Title character of a "Dora the Explorer" spinoff

DOWN

1 Fancy restaurant name starter
2 Skip it!
3 "This Is Us" producer Ken
4 Org. behind the surveillance report FluView
5 They may have rooms to spare
6 Acts as a decoy for, possibly
7 Mother of Artemis
8 University of Maryland athletes
9 Secret ending?
10 Not just chilly
11 Overprotective government, so to speak
12 Message that might be sent in a storm?
14 Fawns, e.g.
16 Possible reason to forgo mascara
21 Like many laundromat appliances
22 Advance notice for an event
24 Jost's "Weekend Update" co-anchor
25 Bonkers
26 Fashion designer ___ Saab
27 Activity for newlyweds at a wedding reception
28 Some succulents
30 "Something" can be heard on it
31 Bigwigs may have big ones
32 Cubs' places
37 Address that's not often written down
40 Fiddler's aid
41 Units equivalent to volts per ampere
42 California's Point ___ Peninsula
43 Synergistic promo
46 "Felice ___ nuovo!"
47 Plastered
48 Bit of kindling
49 Not falling for
51 Big 12 sch.
52 Determination from a Breathalyzer test, for short

by Robyn Weintraub

ACROSS

1. Counts
10. Los ___, West Coast home of Netflix
15. Carnival transport
17. "Drive happy" sloganeer
18. Bed in many a Thai dish
19. High as a kite
20. One may make Us money
21. Fabergé egg collector
23. Genesis name
24. Org. with the "Give Kids a Smile" initiative
25. Like many matches
28. "___ Sylphides" (ballet)
30. Super ___
31. Roman who wrote "Whatever advice you give, be brief"
34. Ibizan inn
36. Head shot
38. Activity involving a leader and a follower
39. Elliptical settings
40. Get tangled up
41. They're used at the border
42. Derby head
43. Add
45. Some E.R. cases
46. Not lie, say
49. Frappe Chiller offerer
51. Brand name that spells something not nice backward
54. Sentiment on 14 de febrero
56. Started back
58. Fratty Silicon Valley techie, stereotypically
61. Quiet
62. Fitting place to order craft beer?
63. Name on a planter
64. Doesn't do anything rash

DOWN

1. "E lucevan le stelle" source
2. Quit stalling
3. Girl saved by Don Juan
4. Get ready to play, with "up"
5. Reason to ask "What do you see?"
6. England's Isle of ___
7. Its East African equivalent is "bwana"
8. Building block
9. Muscle shirt wearer's pride
10. Gift that's not always welcome
11. Lead-in to unfortunate news
12. Go out of one's way
13. Lowest pack member
14. Tab holder, e.g.
16. Very, informally
22. Was in a sorry state?
26. Golfer's approach, often
27. Annual spring chore, for many
29. People with great head shots?
31. Subject of the 2009 biography "Stormy Weather"
32. Sorceress exiled on Aeaea
33. Cut out
35. Budges
36. Vehicle with wing-shaped tail fins
37. ___ Fett, "Star Wars" bounty hunter
38. Game with royal marriages
39. Was blue
44. "Oom" producer
46. Option for 38-Across
47. Words after a verbal slip
48. Yankees manager after Showalter
50. Auto specification
52. Parts of some neuro exams
53. Class
55. Crew at a big accident
57. Make blue, say
59. Mean in school, for short
60. Rob ___

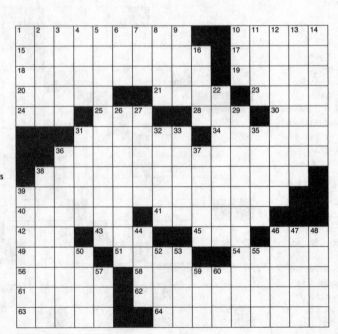

by Ryan McCarty

ACROSS

1 "Are we clear?"
12 E.R. figures
15 Eager to a fault
16 Sound of alarm
17 Joseph, to the Catholic Church
18 "Transformers" technology, for short
19 Roth of cinematic gore
20 Father of the Amazons, in myth
21 Total taken in?
23 Peaceful scene
24 Mindless followers, in slang
25 Event for an enumerator
28 Hand-held game devices
29 Trinity test subject, informally
30 Lessen
31 Family of computer games
32 Quipster's delivery
33 [Mwah!]
36 Major suit
37 They, in Portugal
39 Tax __
40 N.C.A.A. hoops powerhouse
42 Running numbers?
44 Lowly workers
45 Southern corn bread
46 Like Easter eggs
47 Castigate
48 Partner for life
49 Religious trip

52 Solo flying?
53 Military assistants
56 Dungeons & Dragons baddie
57 Help for ordering some affordable furnishings
58 With 54-Down, river of the Carolinas
59 Base of some aquaculture farms

DOWN

1 Really cool
2 You might make one in your lap
3 Fabulous creature
4 "Catch-22" pilot
5 Emmy-winning "Orange Is the New Black" actress
6 Eight English kings
7 Prop at a sales meeting
8 "Ah well, we tried"
9 Père d'une princesse
10 Urge to raid the fridge, with "the"
11 Think a lot of
12 "Transformers" antagonist
13 Wining and dining
14 Higher education?
22 Some antique buses
23 Real close?
24 Protest action
25 Seller of lenses

26 Viral fear of the 2010s
27 "Dream on!"
28 Paths left by storms
30 Grease
34 Catchy 1952 slogan
35 They never fail
38 Mennonites, e.g.
41 Chew on this
43 Believers in world spiritual unity
44 Time to work out
46 Ball club?
48 Clue for a detective
49 Robust
50 Mythical shooter
51 Some PC image files
54 See 58-Across
55 Hipster

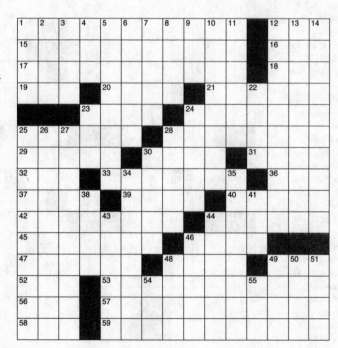

by Sam Trabucco

ACROSS

1 Informal font
10 Rock climber's challenge
14 Out and about?
15 Break
16 Symbol created in 1958 as the logo for the Campaign for Nuclear Disarmament
17 Ermine predator
18 It follows directions
19 Talisa Maegyr's portrayer on "Game of Thrones"
21 It's a long story
23 Like "Wonder Woman"
24 They're no good
26 Doctors Without Borders, e.g., briefly
27 Open courts
29 Really clicks with a partner, say?
35 Film villain with one eye
36 Access to the slopes
38 Plot device?
39 Deep-fried ball of cornmeal
41 Goody two-shoes
43 John, overseas
44 Honey
45 "You decide"
51 High in the Andes?
54 Sarcastic political meme that started in 2009
56 Vietnam's Dien Bien ___
57 Some "Lord of the Rings" characters
58 Cleansing ritual
60 Female name that's the name of a female assistant backward
61 Forger's mark?
62 Trashes
63 Color achieved during tempering

DOWN

1 Gets along
2 Word with light or rock
3 2004 movie featuring a clique called the Plastics
4 Business end?
5 Last Ptolemaic ruler, informally
6 Post masters?
7 Subject of gerontology
8 Plague
9 Match (up)
10 Only three-time inductee into the Rock and Roll Hall of Fame
11 Second-oldest national currency
12 Half of a 1980s sitcom duo
13 John in space
17 Sea with no land boundaries
20 Female deer
22 "Moonlight" actor
25 2016 WNBA champs, informally
27 "That hits the spot!"
28 Greek letter that once symbolized life and resurrection
29 Pro ___
30 Skype or FaceTime, e.g.
31 Info in many a help wanted ad
32 Metaphorical prescription
33 Long division?
34 Go down
37 Mila of "Forgetting Sarah Marshall"
40 Cool air?
42 ___ plancha (pan-fried)
44 Out of fashion
45 High-traffic commercial area
46 Bridge officer on the original Enterprise
47 Arrested
48 Pops
49 He said "I learned to be a movie critic by reading Mad magazine"
50 Dull and flat
52 2012 Nobel Peace Prize recipient, informally
53 Weird
55 "Double" or "triple" move
59 Touch

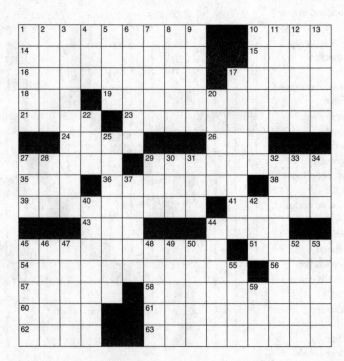

by Trenton Charlson and David Steinberg

ACROSS

1 Commercial line
7 Hit 1980 musical with the song "Join the Circus"
13 Accessory for Minnie Mouse
15 Handle a chopper, say
16 Many a Falcons or Hawks fan
18 "Huddled" group in an inscription on the Statue of Liberty
19 "O.K., I get it!"
21 Jags
22 Org. with many operations
25 Part of a cable network?
27 "The Great Ziegfeld" co-star, 1936
28 Santa ___ Derby
30 Struggles
32 Sail extender
33 Thick cut
34 Station predictions, for short
37 Gathering where burping is encouraged
40 "You're killing me!"
41 Countless centuries
42 Like cinnamon trees
43 Family name of classic TV
45 Dupe
46 Bar fixture
48 Slower than vivace
50 Caesar born in 1922
51 Resident of a halfway house
53 "Star Wars" figures
55 Ones with big shoes to fill
57 Measure of people skills
61 Straightened (up)
62 Napoleon, for one
63 Exceeds the limit
64 Outback offerings

DOWN

1 Nonsense song syllable
2 GPS fig.
3 Word with baron or basin
4 Neutral hue
5 Renounce
6 "Au contraire!"
7 Comic book sound effect
8 Gamer's likeness
9 Uptick
10 Things used on bridges to ease congestion
11 In ___ (gestating)
12 Difficult to sort out
14 1992 comedy based on a long-running "S.N.L." sketch
17 "Hi-diddly-ho!" speaker on TV
20 "No issues yet"
22 Play groups
23 Two cents' worth
24 JFK, for one
26 Place for a stud
29 Hedren of Hitchcock's "The Birds"
31 Ride
35 Creator of the game Centipede
36 Church conclave
38 Veritable
39 Writer of satirical works
44 Let go
46 Certain branches
47 Wildflower of the primrose family
49 Reduces to small bits
52 Scrape, to a tot
54 Ed.'s convenience
56 Campus activist org. revived in 2006
58 Verdant setting
59 Nettle
60 Parts of pecks: Abbr.

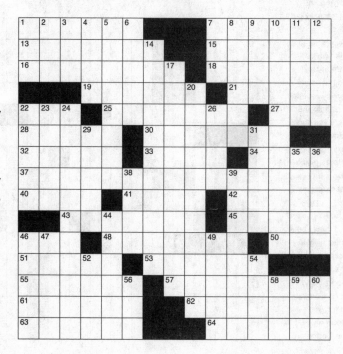

by Andrew J. Ries

ACROSS

1 Athlete with the 1999 guide "Go for the Goal"
5 Folklore monster whose name means "goat-sucker"
15 Cream alternative
16 What might precede a parachute jump
17 Captain Morgan and Admiral Nelson's
18 "I got you"
19 Dog jog
20 Attempts to remove some barriers
21 River with Victoria Falls
23 Wave function symbol in quantum mechanics
24 Having someone's thoughts in mind?
25 Revolving toy
30 1988 security guard comedy
33 Stimulate
34 Prefix with god
35 Jazzman Earl
37 Cardinal point?
38 Put away for later
40 Like agliata sauce
42 Where you might go downstairs for drinks
44 Dir. that's also a suffix
45 [That makes me mad!]
46 Program opening?
50 Didn't think about
55 Product with six fruity flavors
56 #1 hit for the Jackson 5 and Mariah Carey
57 Role for Hugh O'Brian on TV and Kevin Costner in film
58 Tailgaters' tote

59 Shade akin to cerulean
60 Enthusiast's purchase
61 Wet cloud

DOWN

1 Bandwidth unit
2 Maker of the MDX and RDX
3 1983 comedy/drama about a stay-at-home dad
4 Remark of envy
5 Arguing with God, for example
6 One of several French kings
7 ____-approved
8 Sort who entices others to follow
9 Still
10 Assigning stars to?

11 Congratulatory start
12 Science subj.
13 Swindle
14 Connectors
22 Attendance abbr.
25 One method of locating schools
26 United, e.g.
27 Apt surname for an acupuncturist?
28 "By Jove!"
29 "What's ____?"
30 Setting of a 2000s Comedy Central police show
31 Let off
32 Locale for Cubans
34 "Silly me!"
36 Some Winter Olympians
39 Nickname of Doménikos Theotokópoulos

41 Political designation: Abbr.
43 Nova Scotia's Cape ____ Island
46 Crop deity
47 Operation Red Dawn defender
48 Mono, e.g.
49 Overseas worker, perhaps
50 Some family folks, informally
51 Nickname for Ulysses
52 Entered response
53 Some 58-Across contents, in brief
54 Ward with many awards

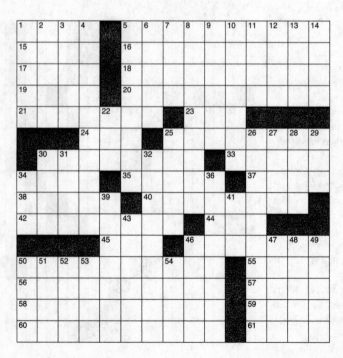

by Erik Agard

ACROSS

1 Striped sea predators
12 Whirlpool site
15 Shot
16 Not you specifically
17 Entertainment for a long ride, perhaps
18 Honoree on the third Friday of Sept.
19 Business ___
20 Fountain fare
21 Expressionist painter James
23 Sends anew
25 Arugula and escarole
26 When the French Open starts
27 One way to ride
29 Use, as a mattress
32 Having zero interest, say
33 Steve of rock guitar fame
34 "Look at me, ___ helpless . . ." (opening to "Misty")
35 Flock
36 Alpine capital
37 Exclamations of exasperation
38 Premonishes
39 "Where ___ fail, music speaks": Hans Christian Andersen
40 Making a mark of a sort
42 Album fill, informally
43 Relief
44 "CSI" prop
48 "Yuck!"
49 Greeting in Britain
51 Ahead of, poetically
52 Org. with a serpent in its logo
53 1987 children's best seller
56 Some grad students, for short
57 Person depicted on the Alabama state quarter
58 Denizen of Fangorn Forest
59 Repeated phrase in the chorus of a classic folk ballad

DOWN

1 River near the Pantheon
2 See 55-Down
3 Stock
4 Johann ___, 16th-century defender of Catholicism
5 Dressing choice
6 Title girl in a 1965 #1 hit
7 They operate around the clock
8 Encouraging start?
9 Shore indentations
10 Keystone enforcer
11 Displayed derision
12 Hall-of-Fame pitcher who once struck out 10 consecutive batters
13 Labor party member's holding?
14 Hides in a cabin, perhaps
22 Mo. neighbor
24 Coverage options, briefly
25 Overcast, in Britain
27 Comics sound
28 They may be dark or fine
29 Film distribution company for "The Hunger Games"
30 Declaration from a volunteer
31 Locale of many a red-eye destination
32 Traditionally red structure
35 Retreat
36 Squarish
38 Elite group
39 Mr. Rochester in "Jane Eyre," e.g.
41 Mails a dupe
42 Warszawa's land
44 Harmonize
45 Casus ___ (action justifying a war)
46 "As You Like It" forest
47 Captain von Trapp's given name
49 Bridge position
50 Manhattan Project scientist Harold ___
54 Bit of derisive laughter
55 With 2-Down, multipurpose

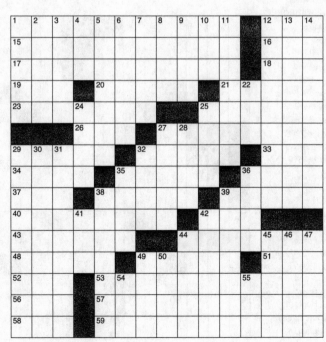

by Peter A. Collins

42

ACROSS

1 Recorded, somewhat quaintly
7 Got wise to?
13 Bond order
15 Court great Goolagong
16 Taking care of responsibilities like an actual grown-up
18 Check in the mail, perhaps
19 Long in films
20 New York's ___ State Parkway
22 Baby food
23 Traveler's boarding areas?
25 Leading
26 Growth medium
27 Frame
29 Director Lee
30 Put on
31 Drinking glasses?
34 Ahura Mazda worshiper
35 Slip covers?
36 Swift quality
37 Big export of Sri Lanka
38 Country that eliminated the U.S.A. in both the 2006 and 2010 FIFA World Cups
42 "Dang!"
43 Substantive
45 Flemish river
46 A.F.L.'s merger partner
47 Gets one under
49 José de ___ Martín, national hero of Argentina
50 Act of noticing
52 Half Dome's home
54 Pragmatist philosopher Charles Sanders ___
55 You can't beat them
56 Lowbrow
57 Protests, but not uprisings?

DOWN

1 Some sultan subjects
2 Literature Nobelist Gordimer
3 Not the classy sort?
4 Hartsfield-Jackson code
5 Surname of father-and-son British P.M.s
6 "Giant Brain" of 1940s headlines
7 Small flourish
8 "___ les compliments de l'auteur" (inscription in a French book)
9 So-and-so
10 What some coin purses do
11 Involves
12 On a fundamental level
14 How Pee-wee Herman often appears to fans
17 Not seeing anyone else, say
21 Talks about one's job, perhaps
24 Induces to commit a crime
26 Ostentatious
28 First female artist with five Billboard #1's from the same album
30 It's what everyone's doing
32 Want ad abbr.
33 Miracle-___
34 Title city of film whose mayor is Leodore Lionheart
35 Squad car
36 Receive as a member
39 Birthplace of St. Clare, the founder of the Poor Sisters
40 Unclutter
41 James of TV's "How the West Was Won"
43 2000s female teen idol, to fans
44 They're positive
47 "Coffee Cantata" composer
48 What Brits call an "articulated lorry"
51 Return destination, for short
53 Crossed

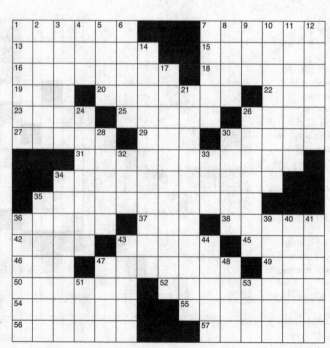

by Joon Pahk

ACROSS

1 Dominant figure
16 High-end Italian sports car
17 1997 Notorious B.I.G. hit whose title lyric precedes "strictly for the weather"
18 Queen who styled herself as Isis, familiarly
19 ___ Lopez opening (chess tactic)
20 Some superhero attire
21 Yankees All-Star pitcher Severino
22 Chris of "The Good Wife"
24 Four-thirds of a dram: Abbr.
25 "___ time!"
26 Brother-to-be
29 Cosmetics company whose letters appear in left-to-right order in "cosmetics company"
30 Electron particle emission
32 Relative of cashmere
34 Money replaced by euros
35 Thrash
36 Prepare for a bomb, say
38 Euphoria
42 Court plea, briefly
43 County east of Devon
45 "If u ask me . . ."
46 America's busiest airport after ATL and LAX
47 ___ América (soccer tournament)
48 Rose
49 Screw up
51 New toy?
53 Legislative body of Russia
54 "Gil Blas" author
58 Everywhere
59 Things that contain 59-Across that contain 59-Across that . . .

DOWN

1 Online gamer's problem
2 Orate
3 "100 Years . . . 100 Movies," e.g.
4 Many employees of the Lego company
5 So
6 Seriously shortchange
7 ___ Little, "The Wire" character
8 Prolific
9 Event of 1964 and 2020
10 It's two hours behind Pacific: Abbr.
11 Memorable time
12 12 points, typographically
13 Many a battery charger
14 Instrument whose name comes from the Latin for "heavenly"
15 Hard to eat quietly, in adspeak
21 ___ Dems (U.K. political party, informally)
23 Highish bridge holding
26 "Je vous en ___" (French for "You're welcome")
27 City on the Mexican border
28 Things that amaze
29 Noted arms manufacturer
31 Designer Gucci
33 Indicator of a coming storm
36 Friend of Tarzan
37 Tar
39 Communication means since 1911
40 Hobbit corrupted by the Ring
41 "That HURTS!"
42 Refusal with a contraction
44 Lewdness
47 Host Bert of old game shows
48 Vim
50 Gucci competitor
52 Corner office, maybe
53 Out of juice
55 Car that went defunct in 1936
56 Place to count sheep
57 Pair of nines?

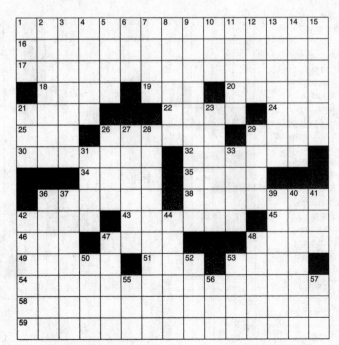

by David Steinberg

44

ACROSS

1 First digit
6 Beam at?
10 4.93 milliliters: Abbr.
13 Purchase that usually ends up in the trash
15 Two stars, maybe
17 "The job's not great, but I can pay my bills"
18 Ordering aid
19 Mortgage agcy.
20 Proclaimed
21 Flinch, e.g.
22 Rejection of a monotheist
23 Take a dive
25 With all one's might
28 African tree with hanging fruit
29 Full of twists
30 "Balderdash!"
33 Credits
34 Palindromic file extension
35 Oil source
36 College division
38 Showed elation
39 Like ogres
40 Not flush, say
41 One with his or her head in the clouds
43 Ranch alternative
45 Highland bodies
46 Fine dining no-no
48 Cry over spilled milk, perhaps
51 "Essays of ___"
52 Mobile home designation
54 John, abroad
55 Function not intended for seniors
56 Up there, so to speak
57 Saves, e.g.
58 Snack usually eaten outdoors

DOWN

1 Exclamation from a weary employee
2 "Poison, I see, ___ been his timeless end": Shak.
3 Celestial animal
4 Deg. from Kellogg
5 They're tops in the theater
6 Some kick-around wear
7 Man's nickname that sounds like two letters of the alphabet
8 Smoother
9 Starting point
10 Fantastic means of travel
11 Natchez and Delta Queen, for two
12 Subject of the 2018 biography "The Shadow President"
14 Brace
16 Mix
21 Pair that clicked in film
22 "I could use some help"
24 ___-eared
25 Statement no.
26 California's ___ Woods National Monument
27 Fake
28 Constrained, with "in"
30 Dwindles
31 This, for one
32 Held
37 Spec for some bargain tix
41 Direction of a ship
42 Ford acquisition of 1999 and sale of 2010
43 Ark unit
44 Main dinosaur in Pixar's "The Good Dinosaur"
47 Counterpart of the Roman god Sol
48 "Triptych Bleu I, II, III," e.g.
49 Bad thing to find in your refrigerator
50 One gets shared a lot
52 Plays at work?
53 Meas. for a steno

by Robyn Weintraub

ACROSS

1 Goddess played by Rene Russo in "Thor"
7 Single-minded pursuits
15 Quit
16 Swimmer off the coast of Greenland
17 Bringing up the rear
18 Having hooves
19 E-4 or E-6, in the Army: Abbr.
20 Stayed close to
22 Kool Moe ___ (first rapper to perform at the Grammys)
23 Shrewdness
26 Brother of the Wild West
27 Laugh hysterically
28 One of the Brady kids
30 Summer broadcast for ESPN
37 What many doctors and lawyers work in
38 It's sanctioned by a "G"
39 Skipper's opposite
40 Risks
41 Gobs
43 Things felt at a casino?
48 Start of a cycle?
49 Nascent stage
51 Riled (up)
52 Lavatory
54 On edge
57 Daughter (and granddaughter) of Jocasta
58 Police
59 Good as new
60 Bundle

DOWN

1 Brief affair
2 Mr. Microphone manufacturer
3 Cool digs?
4 Indian state on the Arabian Sea
5 The Theatre Cat in Broadway's "Cats"
6 Bad way to be left
7 Slowly moves (along)
8 Shooting location
9 Hankering
10 Bubble and squeak ingredient, slangily
11 Communication that's seen but not heard, for short
12 1991 Kenneth Branagh film about reincarnation
13 Diner
14 Computer mode
21 Pull off a spool
24 Didn't pull over
25 Jimmy Dorsey standard with the line "You're like the fragrance of blossoms fair"
26 Common diagnostic for epileptics
28 Caribbean land named by Columbus
29 Rattle off
30 Efficiency stat
31 Word whose first letter is dropped in contractions
32 Country superfans
33 Therapists' org.
34 Squalid
35 Three CDs?
36 Wide shoe spec
41 Having it out
42 Bygone saxophone great, familiarly
43 Collide with in an intersection, perhaps
44 Packing
45 John who wrote "Appointment in Samarra"
46 Money at una casa de cambio
47 Panache
49 So
50 Tie up
53 #1, e.g.
55 Photographer Goldin
56 And all that: Abbr.

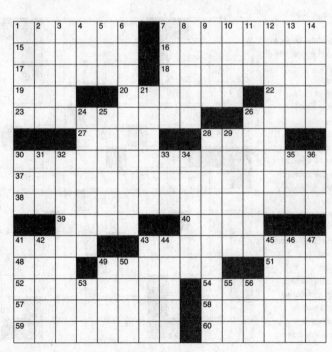

by Adam Fromm

ACROSS

1 Jets are found in it, for short
4 Rep
9 Photo framer's offering
12 Tough person to get information from
14 Like southern Israel vis-à-vis northern Israel
15 Porter of note
16 Acclaimed 1942 film banned in Germany until after W.W. II
18 Alma mater of N.B.A. M.V.P. Russell Westbrook
19 It's found just south of the White House's South Lawn
20 Stadium divertissement
22 Often-braised cut of beef
24 Language of South Asia
25 Home of the Unesco World Heritage Site of Palmyra
26 "It's futile"
28 Ending of eight U.S. presidents' names
29 Quad bike, e.g.
31 Drawing
33 Measures taken to make golf courses tougher in the early 2000s
36 "Let me demonstrate"
37 Hard core
38 Sports star who once declared "I am America"
39 Like some barbecue
41 Guitar accessories
45 Arizona rival
47 Empathize with
49 Some guitar basics
51 Salt
52 Bryophytic growth

53 "What a jerk!"
55 NASA's ___ Research Center
56 Walt Disney's middle name
57 Singer of the song "Shadowland" in "The Lion King"
58 Subj. of the 2017 memoir "Working on the Dark Side of the Moon"
59 British weight
60 Something to build on

DOWN

1 Reach
2 Ostentatious
3 ___ oil
4 Richard who composed the music for "Damn Yankees" and "The Pajama Game"
5 Cheesy crust
6 "___ feste Burg ist unser Gott" (Bach cantata)
7 Narrow part
8 Station
9 Venomous snake
10 The whole time
11 Joining, with "up"
13 Subject of the Supreme Court cases Loving v. Virginia and Obergefell v. Hodges
15 Edge
17 One looking for bugs
21 "Go right ahead!"
23 Conflict that saw the sieges of Ladysmith and Kimberley
27 One overseas
30 Modern game equipment

32 That's the ticket!
33 Sprint and such
34 Home of the Isle of Man
35 Cow or chicken follower
36 Bad choices in it might cost you an arm and a leg
40 Like the lion slain in Hercules' first labor
42 Foreign correspondent, maybe
43 Classic opera set in Cyprus
44 Cross with
46 Have trouble sleeping, say
48 Run out
50 Daring way to fly
54 Calculus calculation, for short

by Andy Kravis and Erik Agard

ACROSS

1 Too fast to be careful
9 Stockpile
14 Gaze at, as someone's eyes
15 Tool used while on foot
16 Be heedful
17 "___ LANDS!" (headline of 1927)
18 Shoe brand that's also a man's name
19 Exact match
20 Euphemism for Satan, with "the"
21 Unctuous utterances
23 Prey for a heron
25 Short
26 TV series inspired by Sherlock Holmes
29 Someone glimpsed in a concert film, maybe
31 Rum cocktail
34 Need settling
35 So-called "Grandmother of Europe," born 5/24/1819
39 Boot
40 Reached out with one's hands?
41 Inventor of a 17th-century calculator
43 One use for a tablet
48 La saison de juillet
49 Backpack and its contents, e.g.
52 What a football penalty may be seen in
53 Time being
55 Odds and evens, say
58 Do so hope
59 Pioneering rocket scientist Wernher von ___
60 Fictional land named in some real-life international law cases
62 Worshiper of the war god Huitzilopochtli

63 Opening of an account
64 Like the sound of an oboe
65 Some descendants of 62-Acrosses

DOWN

1 Patron of sailors
2 Horse-drawn four-wheeled carriage
3 Passions
4 Shade of green
5 By ___ of
6 Over
7 Bring discredit upon
8 Star of Broadway's "The Lady and Her Music," 1981
9 Didn't stray from
10 Cartoon character often shown with his tongue out

11 Mass movement
12 Cold War opponent, informally
13 Not moved at all
14 URL element
22 Rickrolling or the Dancing Baby, e.g.
24 London or Manchester
27 Priciest 1952 Topps baseball card
28 Shabby club
30 National Garden Mo.
32 Passes, informally
33 Part of un opéra
35 Louis ___ (French king)
36 Grp. that no one under 30 can join
37 One way to reduce a sentence
38 Portion of Alexander Pope's work

39 Amenity at many a wedding reception
42 F.B.I., e.g.
44 Source for fine sweaters
45 Jamie ___, co-star in the "Fifty Shades of Grey" movies
46 Modern cause of flooding
47 Kind of jelly
50 Presidential middle name
51 Get more mileage from
54 Signaled to start
56 Colorful breakfast bowlful
57 Who often says "I found this on the web"
61 Sam Spade, e.g., informally

by Stanley Newman

48

ACROSS

1 Speaker's accessory
9 "Phooey!"
15 Not running loose, say
16 ___ Collezioni (fashion brand)
17 One with drawing power in Hollywood?
18 Claptrap
19 With 53-Across, jalopy
20 Establishments whose products might be described by this answer + H
22 Scripture
23 Follow
25 "Poor venomous fool," in Shakespeare
26 Brings in
27 It appears over a tilde
30 Drop ___
32 Emmy/Tony winner Arthur
33 Top of a Pacific island chain
36 Only person to win an Oscar for playing an Oscar-winning actress
37 Book of stars?
38 Tats
39 A's, e.g. . . . or a word following "A"
40 Harrisburg-to-Allentown dir.
41 Handles, with "with"
43 Not the sharpest crayon in the box
45 Cold-weather coat
49 Pro ___
50 The half-blood prince in "Harry Potter and the Half-Blood Prince"
53 See 19-Across
54 "The Little Mermaid" lyricist Howard
57 Insincere welcome
59 Congested, in a way
60 Push-ups, e.g.

61 Creator of Kermit the Frog and Rowlf the Dog
62 Book that doesn't take long to get through

DOWN

1 Uneager
2 Musical with the song "You're Never Fully Dressed Without a Smile"
3 Patriot who said "Moderation in temper, is always a virtue; but moderation in principle, is a species of vice"
4 ___ City (sobriquet for New Haven)
5 Play auditioner's hope
6 #, in chess notation
7 Sardinia, e.g., to locals
8 Website relative of JDate
9 ___ joke (total groaner)
10 Pirate's exclamation
11 Off in biblical lands?
12 Nosh
13 Amateurish
14 Attacks, as in a joust
21 Busted out of jail
24 Tarot card that bears the numeral XIII
26 Enter quickly
28 Willy Wonka's factory output
29 Bygone communication
31 As prompted
33 Event for computer whizzes
34 Epic narratives
35 Jon of "Napoleon Dynamite"

36 Film buff
37 Hebrew scripture commentary
42 Tiffany products
44 One of the Obamas
46 Support group reassurance
47 Fever
48 Wound (up)
51 Creperie equipment
52 Out there
55 Long ___
56 Prefix with binary
58 "I'm With ___"

by Paolo Pasco

ACROSS

1 Stick to one's guns
9 Mission for a Mafia member
15 "You sure about that?"
16 Something a tuning fork has
17 Sort of pricing model with multiple tiers
18 Singer Sharp with the 1962 hit "Mashed Potato Time"
19 ___ bar
20 An "A" in physics?
22 One traditionally dressed in red or green
23 Mounts
25 What "mía" means across the Pyrenees
26 Question from an anxious person
28 Group of close friends, in modern slang
31 Shell game?
33 Light and graceful
34 River that meets the Colorado at Yuma
35 Sports news pro
37 Thomas Dewey or Hubert Humphrey, notably
39 Aquatic source of iodine
40 Uncle ___, main role on "The Fresh Prince of Bel-Air"
42 Verse
43 Creature that might live in a 39-Across forest
44 Verbal attack
46 Glassless glasses
47 –
50 Not twiddle one's thumbs
53 "Bear with me"
55 Man's name that's a number in Italian
56 Longtime head of Duke basketball, to fans
58 Proudly tech-savvy sort
60 Verbal attack
61 Conferral after some two-year programs
62 Not-too-bright subordinate
63 Invasive plant?

DOWN

1 Feature of Algeria and Egypt
2 +1
3 "Everybody has their issues, right?"
4 Can't do it alone
5 Put a stop to?
6 Flexible
7 '18 honoree, today
8 Part of a percussion ensemble
9 Chemical group with the formula -OH
10 "Gotcha"
11 Not just any
12 Green hue
13 Sister company of Peugeot
14 Argument
21 Green hue
24 Like some breakfast bars
27 Didn't go out
28 Performers who take a lot of heat?
29 "I wish it weren't so!"
30 A bajillion
31 ___ bomb (cocktail)
32 Something to take in protest
34 Praise that might be dispensed with a treat
36 Light shower
38 English
41 ". . . per my reasoning"
44 Greeting that might follow a fist bump
45 Leave the country
48 Likely to take a bite out of one's wallet
49 Cornball
50 Opposite of bombs
51 Application of paint
52 Its leaves are used for the Hawaiian dish laulau
54 Abba of Israel
57 Head of lettuce?
59 "Stand" band, 1989

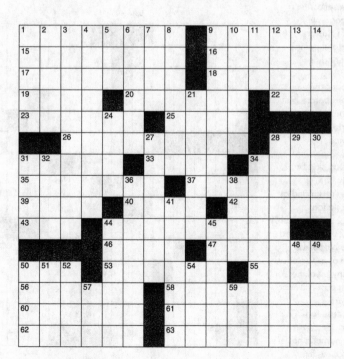

by Sam Ezersky

ACROSS

1 Baseball great who was the subject of the 2006 best seller "Game of Shadows"
6 Authorize, as a digital contract
11 Takes heat from
13 Political figure who became a CNN commentator in 2015
15 Won back
16 Advance showing of a film
18 Annoying bedmate
20 "___ doomed!"
21 Subject of an overnight lab study
23 D.O.T. branch
24 Right now
26 Winner of the lowest-scoring Super Bowl in N.F.L. history (16 total points)
30 Overindulge
31 :(
32 Pool party?
34 Word before bait or buzz
35 Certain grain source
36 Hot wheels?
39 Boston skyscraper, with "the"
40 They're spotted at fire stations
45 "___ so" ("Nuh-uh")
47 Classic baby food
49 Like Napoleon's defeat at Waterloo
51 Many a yak herder
52 Gymnast Biles and others
53 "License to Kill" star
54 Big name in hosiery
55 Longtime film/theater critic Jeffrey

DOWN

1 Start of many a morning commute, informally
2 Some first-years after undergrad
3 ___ astrology, study with horoscopes
4 Means of surveillance
5 Go to pot?
6 Potential recidivists
7 Classic blazer fabrics
8 Ending with quart- or quint-
9 Developed
10 "I'm fine, but thanks"
12 Nonbeliever
13 Part of a fireplace
14 Disturbed
17 Literary anthology
19 Squaw Valley backdrop
22 Backing
25 Wasted word to a housecat
26 Turnovers, e.g.
27 Group working on P.S.A. campaigns
28 Big name in cookware
29 Stood on the hind legs, with "up"
31 Product made with steel wool
32 Dark-skinned grape used in winemaking
33 Locale of London's Leicester Square
35 Abu Simbel statue honoree
37 Activity for new parents
38 Percussionist's wooden sticks
41 As good as it gets
42 Try to get in, say
43 "Suh-weet!," quaintly
44 Do business?
46 Proctor's declaration
48 Septet in Dante's "Purgatorio"
50 Lose crispness, in dialect

by Ari Richter

ACROSS

1 Ibsen heroine
5 Nickname in early jazz piano
10 Mining target
14 "Is there anything else I can help with?"
16 Rocker, perhaps
17 "I'd really appreciate this favor"
18 Of no value
19 "___ mess"
20 They fall apart when the stakes are raised
21 Flat screen?
22 John ___, secret identity of the Lone Ranger
24 Assembly
25 Outline in the Arby's logo
26 What "Mac" means
28 United Christendom movement
32 More than nods
34 Western sidekick
35 To a tee
38 Overlooks
39 Warrant
41 Wife of Albert Einstein
42 They discuss texts
44 Western city that shares its name with a tree
48 Kind of replication
49 One of the friends on "Friends"
51 Kotb on morning TV
52 Key presenter
54 Baseball's Buck
56 Track advantage
57 Dr. Seuss's "And to Think That ___ It on Mulberry Street"

58 All-comers' discussion
60 Popular assistant
61 One who's seen but not heard? Just the opposite!
62 Delicacy
63 Sleep ___
64 "Boy Meets World" boy

DOWN

1 Depths
2 Famous play call?
3 One side in the Brexit vote
4 Answer to one's mate
5 Became one
6 Great pains
7 Early Nahuatl speaker

8 Elevate, redundantly
9 Mention as an afterthought
10 Stiff a restaurant
11 Doing grown-up things, in modern lingo
12 Ring
13 Entente member
15 Lead-in to a meal?
21 May in England
23 "No kidding!"
27 Speedster
29 ___ of America
30 Take in
31 Questionnaire check box option
33 Exit ___
35 Bush in Florida
36 Game with a discard pile

37 Something that might build character over time?
40 Ace of Base genre
41 Heart
43 Steak option
45 Eye site
46 One going over the line
47 Table linens
50 The Beatles' "Hey Jude" vis-à-vis "Revolution"
52 Navigation hazard
53 Land east of the Suez Canal
55 Verdant expanse
58 Results of oogenesis
59 Include surreptitiously, in a way

by Michael Hawkins

52

ACROSS

1 Tech's character set
6 City on a gulf of the same name
10 Blow
14 Tip, say
15 ___ war (conflict unlikely to hurt anyone)
16 Letters on a crucifix
17 Oxymoronic break
20 Love lines?
21 Passes (out)
22 It's a gas
23 Had more than one could handle
25 Sleepy still?
26 Brief flashes
27 Slacker's opposite
29 Stick in the dugout
31 Abbr. after U.S.M.C., maybe
32 Was patronizing, in a way
36 Room backstage at a playhouse
37 Step-by-step instructions?
38 Bit of fudge?
39 Pleasant forecast
40 Palynologists study them
44 Bit of fishing equipment
47 Part of Michelangelo's "David" once maliciously broken with a hammer
49 Send a revealing image, say
50 Stock holding
51 Green film character
53 Chance to take stock, for short
54 Coinage of 2000
57 Risk territory bordering Ukraine and Afghanistan
58 Quash
59 Star of "North Dallas Forty," 1979

60 Public firing?
61 Having the resources
62 Wide gap

DOWN

1 "The Handmaid's Tale" novelist
2 Poorly crafted
3 Proceed wildly
4 Newspaper coverage
5 "Just playing"
6 Cinematographer's consideration
7 Long gestation for a film, informally
8 They often start with elections
9 Rams home, for short
10 Actress/singer Gaynor
11 Local leader
12 Led

13 Descriptor for a police force
18 Plea bargain component
19 Sister company of Yahoo
24 One of the Wayans brothers
26 Nursery bagful
28 Foreign language dictionary abbr.
30 Porters may be found near them
33 ___ Sea, body of water between Borneo and the Philippines
34 Rabbit's favorite chain restaurant?
35 List from an etiquette expert
36 Symbol of San Francisco
37 Like some laws

38 Finally admit, say
41 Ignatius J. ___, protagonist in "A Confederacy of Dunces"
42 Many Lost Generation poets, briefly
43 Puts away
45 Norman Vincent ___, best-selling motivational writer
46 Web address ender
48 Keynote
51 Tar
52 High-quality coffee variety
55 ___ moment
56 Easy pitch

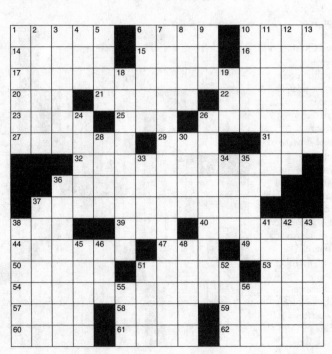

by Andrew J. Ries

ACROSS

1. Cry on the battlefield
7. "Mine!"
15. Reading Fightin Phils, e.g.
16. "Just curious"
17. Expecting, slangily
18. "Cue the violins!" elicitor
19. Loafs
20. Children's Dr.?
21. One on foot, informally
22. Made a web site?
23. 1/746 horsepower
24. Pouty face
25. "It's no use"
27. Celebrity mug shot, typically
28. The key to making a quick exit?
29. Veteran
33. Actors' unions?
37. Famous sights at San Francisco's Pier 39
38. Chap
40. Einstein
43. Simply taboo
45. Only N.F.L. franchise to win championships representing three different cities
46. Villain in "Wonder Woman"
48. Diminishes
49. Occasion for a party
50. Schooled on the field
52. Sweeping
53. [If you catch my drift . . .]
55. Like Antarctica
56. One on a registrar's list
57. Pro QB Manning, by birth
58. Really hot
59. Get down

DOWN

1. "Savvy?"
2. Definite no, informally
3. Put away a sandwich, perhaps
4. Royal stand-in
5. Has a hard time swallowing
6. Alternative genre
7. Implant
8. Die, as a light
9. Round figures
10. Julia Roberts's role in the "Ocean's" series
11. Informal object
12. Pill bug or wood louse
13. Buoyed
14. Action film director Zack
20. Toga go-with
23. Mrs. Flintstone
24. Tequila cocktail, in slang
26. Group who Mao Zedong famously said "hold up half the sky"
27. World's longest wooden roller coaster, with "The"
30. Prefix with -logy
31. Worked (out)
32. Mythological judge of the dead in the underworld
34. Clearance caveat
35. "I" lift?
36. Catch some rays
39. Reply often made with a sigh
40. Steeped
41. Gorge
42. Supreme god of the universe, in ancient Egypt
44. It's only skin-deep
46. Add-on
47. Change, as a lock
50. Hooters
51. Craftiness
52. Banjoist Fleck
54. Clobbered, in brief
55. ___ sleep

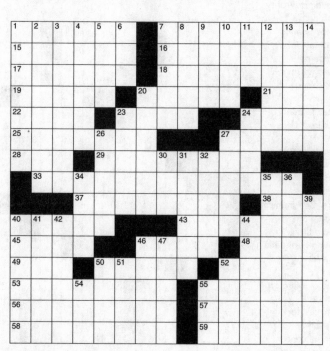

by Caitlin Reid

ACROSS

1 "A pity"
5 Holier-than-thou
9 Possible poker payments
14 Lead role in "Rent"
15 Boxed up, say
16 California's Santa ___ Range
17 "Rocky IV" rival who makes a reappearance in "Creed II"
19 Crack
20 Like the love story in 2013's "Blue Is the Warmest Color"
21 What might precede a bite
23 School 43-Across
24 Home of the Basilica di San Francesco
25 Astronomical rarity
27 Digital native, often
28 Time-consuming environmental procedures
30 Something rain might change, in brief
31 Squeezes (into)
32 Sweet treat since 1924
33 Called to see, in a way
34 Set (on)
37 Whittlers' tools
38 One of 309 in the National Mall
39 Tissue affliction common during the Civil War
40 Reflect
42 World of Warcraft creature
43 23-Across, for one: Abbr.
44 Mood influencer
45 Program on a Billy Blanks DVD

47 Protest item that leaves a powdery mess
49 In a pickle or in a jam
50 Brewery fixture
51 Substance made from seaweed
52 Is disposed (to)
53 Rocker David Lee ___
54 City near Tesla Gigafactory 1

DOWN

1 Question following a holdup
2 What a band plays at a concert
3 Stocked up
4 Penalty box, in hockey lingo
5 Hair care item
6 Say "Not this again!," say
7 Boot brand since the 1970s
8 Voice-activated smart speaker introduced in 2016
9 Wine-colored
10 Agcy. that oversees Ginnie Mae
11 Fruity summer treats
12 Creep, perhaps
13 Great red dragon, in Revelation
18 Burn, in slang
22 Go on disparagingly
25 Home sweet home?
26 Word in the translation of "e pluribus unum"
29 Backing
31 Quarantine locales
32 [Just like that!]
33 Corral
34 Skinflint
35 Grueling kind of race
36 Brain-wave-amplifying device in "X-Men"
37 It's one thing after another
38 Martial arts hold that forces submission
39 "Understood"
41 Like some verbs: Abbr.
44 Website need
46 Figure, briefly
48 Mostly monosyllabic language

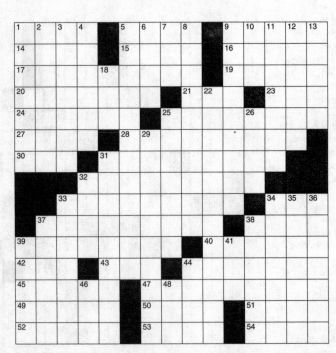

by Ryan McCarty

ACROSS

1 Wanderer's refuge
6 1/8 of a standard stick of butter: Abbr.
10 Part of the eye
14 Big shot?
16 Some deer
17 Words in hide-and-seek
18 Fleece
19 Rafael Nadal's country, in the Olympics
20 What vines do
21 Owner of Bloomingdale's
22 British philanthropist Henry
23 How John Glenn orbited the earth in 1962
25 Insurance department
28 Expert sleuth
31 Wanders
32 Turn a blind eye
33 "Gracious!"
34 Their pockets aren't deep
35 "Dominant" thing
36 "It wasn't my fault"
38 What "de rien" might be a response to
39 Precisely
40 Ted with a cameo in the movie "Ted"
41 Instruction given through a rolled-down window
42 Cross
43 Singer Khan
45 Creaky part of a house
47 Where to stick a toothpick
50 Front part of a saddle
51 Something relatively complicated?
53 Off-the-shoulders hairstyle
54 At all
55 Certain competition
56 "If someone ___ careful . . ."
57 Seriously bother

DOWN

1 "Tom Thumb" antagonist
2 Father of Deimos and Phobos
3 Product sold in bars
4 OB/GYN offering
5 Aids for snoops
6 A crowd, so to speak
7 Shade of white
8 Sign indicating a sign
9 Bettor's winnings
10 Often-repeated bit of modern folklore
11 Some commercial work
12 Hard to grasp, say
13 Sets, as a price
15 Things on the back of a computer
21 ___ reflex, infant's instinctual spreading of the arms
22 Wed
24 Part of the eye
25 Believe it!
26 Enter one's password, maybe
27 Ultramodern
28 Went after
29 Festive mayo day
30 Political commentator Ezra
32 Game with lots of instructions
34 Nail job, for short
37 With 49-Down, early tryout
38 John Updike novel subtitled "A Romance"
40 Dining adornment
42 Light
43 Bud
44 Word before and after against
46 Government sleuth, quaintly
47 Cookout item, for short
48 Entertainer and civil rights activist Horne
49 See 37-Down
51 Org. in "The X-Files"
52 It's in the bag

by Robyn Weintraub

56

ACROSS

1. Impromptu places to conk out for the night
10. Prime spot for a tat
13. Archenemy of the Fantastic Four
15. Home to Matisse, Mondrian and Monet, informally
16. Addendum to a common pentad
17. Sierra Nevadas, e.g.
18. Finally chooses
19. Media big Zuckerman
20. Either constituent of table salt
21. One of the Three Musketeers
23. Ceases production
26. Enjoys oneself immensely
28. Spike Lee's "___ Gotta Have It"
29. With 53-Across, one whom you might blame for something bad that you did
31. Brand owned by Kraft Foods
32. What 100-proof alcohol has
33. Island in NW Greece
35. Touched the ground
36. Paris is found in it
38. Race
39. Fires (up)
40. Handles with care?
42. Perform a Thanksgiving cooking task
44. "Thumbs down from me"
45. Grp. that Ronald Reagan once supported
46. Grp. that Ronald Reagan once supported
47. Congressman who served the most consecutive years as speaker of the House (1977–87)
53. See 29-Across
54. Radio sign-off
56. Go on and on about something
57. Seatbelts, e.g.
58. "Listen!": Sp.
59. Sabermetrics whiz, e.g.

DOWN

1. Stack at a music store
2. They're all over Down Under, informally
3. Top
4. Leave in
5. Tout's offering
6. Brand that treats acid reflux
7. They might work on something for 60 seconds
8. Pulls off
9. Meh
10. Object seen in the Ralph Lauren logo
11. Old Food Network show with the catchword "Bam!"
12. Practices cleromancy
14. Natural mimics
15. Cubs' supporters
22. Rule that Gandhi opposed
23. Passes idly
24. Operatic song-speech
25. "Come on! It's common knowledge!"
26. Crystal clear, as an image
27. Letter before Lima and after Foxtrot when spelling 27-Down
28. Clickable message at the start of an online TV show
30. Democracy in action
34. Graffiti and such
37. Sci-fi author Simmons with the 1989 Hugo-winning novel "Hyperion"
41. ___ skill
43. Old boosted rocket stages
45. "Ish"
48. "Central Park in the Dark" composer
49. Little noodge
50. "Gotcha"
51. Unaccompanied
52. Caravaggio's "The ___ Player"
55. Oral admonishment

by Joe Deeney

ACROSS

1 The "one" in "the old one-two," maybe
8 Chivalrous offer
15 "You bet!"
16 Eyes, slangily
17 Become independent . . . as suggested visually by some of this grid's black squares
19 It's a wrap
20 Cereal with a Berry Berry variety
21 Being, to Sartre
22 Taking action
23 Gulf currency
25 Joint
26 Comical Howard
27 Tourist center handout
29 Fun and games, informally
30 Lord of Rivendell in "The Lord of the Rings"
32 Summer cooler
34 Salon offering
36 Any of 13 popes
37 Suits, briefs, etc.
41 Home of Theseus
45 Q&A on Reddit
46 Body parts that become other body parts if you change the second letter to an A
48 ___ Juan
49 Way off, say
51 Summer cooler
52 Wheels of fortune?
53 Slammin' Sammy
55 Series of ages
56 Like much data
57 Mental eccentricity . . . as suggested visually by some of this grid's black squares
60 Briskly, to equestrians
61 Something a short driver might need?
62 Meet at the river, perhaps
63 Unfavorable

DOWN

1 Like a ballet dancer
2 Language akin to portugués
3 Hide seeker
4 Doctor
5 ___ jacket
6 Opposite of drop
7 Line setter
8 Things you can get credit for
9 French article
10 Wallace who wrote "Ben-Hur"
11 Relative of Aunt Bee
12 Started making money as an athlete
13 Suspect in Clue
14 Soul
18 Actress Dobrev of "The Vampire Diaries"
23 Physician on TV's "Celebrity Rehab"
24 Didn't end as scheduled
27 Over
28 ___ Corner, section of Westminster Abbey
31 Black ___
33 Place for a retired soldier?
35 Ohio town that was the first permanent settlement in the state (1788)
37 Chocolaty nougat-and-caramel product
38 Give off
39 Face-saving aid at a reunion
40 Canon competitor
42 Will have to face
43 Features of smartphones
44 Blandly agreeable
47 ___ Falls Convention (early women's rights gathering)
50 Some bow ties
52 French city near the Belgian border
54 Skinny
56 First name in game shows
58 With 59-Down so-so
59 See 58-Down

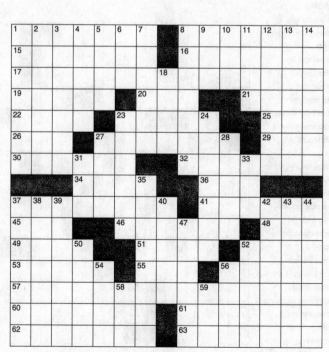

by Bruce Haight and David Steinberg

ACROSS

1 Woman who spends money on a younger lover, in modern lingo
10 Total, in a way
14 Bush-league
16 Book that's the source of the phrase "Physician, heal thyself"
17 End of a bill
18 Land of leprechauns
19 It's just a feeling
20 Effloresces
22 Lambaste
23 Lets out
26 Go (along)
27 Pained expressions
29 Start of a reminiscence
31 Title genie played by Shaquille O'Neal in a 1996 film
34 Big mouth
35 Racer Luyendyk
36 Hoards
38 Freezing
40 Easy stride
41 Country singer McDaniel
43 Liqueur flavorers
44 Like chalk on a chalkboard
46 Something to build on
47 Common tutoring subject
48 Crème de ___ (strawberry liqueur)
50 Farm sound
53 ___ Vikander, Best Supporting Actress for 2015's "The Danish Girl"
55 One may read "Reverse"
58 1983 Apple computer with a girl's name
59 Neighboring
62 Lead-in to boy or girl

63 Fast-food order not for the diet-conscious
64 Actress Cannon
65 Geographical eponym of a 1970s–'80s fad diet

DOWN

1 Dueling weapon
2 Savory sensation
3 Lively dance in double time
4 Juggernaut fighting vehicle in "Star Wars" movies
5 Italian artist Guido
6 Liner of the nose, e.g.
7 "___ we all?"
8 Central
9 Pac-12 sch.
10 Role for Liz Taylor

11 Ancient symbol depicting a serpent eating its own tail
12 Winter transport
13 Certain bikes
15 What ends with Adar
21 Inspiration for Jefferson Airplane's "White Rabbit"
24 Belly, in totspeak
25 Morales of "NYPD Blue"
27 Refuges
28 "Till There ___ You," song from "The Music Man"
30 Understood
31 Crunchy dish with green leaves
32 Principle associated with Machiavellianism
33 Mexican revolutionary
37 Emmy-winning Ward

39 Icon of ambient music
42 Pacific ring?
45 "100 Years . . . 100 Movies" listmaker, for short
49 Hindu precept
50 Santa ___ (historic ship)
51 Soviet workers' group
52 Give ___ of reality
54 James of "The Godfather"
56 Punch lines?
57 Clothesline, e.g.
60 "All My ___ Live in Texas"
61 Club drug, informally

by Kameron Austin Collins

ACROSS

1 Gum-producing plant
5 Addition to a compost pile
9 Rush home?
13 Store discount come-on
15 ___-Turkish War (post-W.W. I conflict)
16 "Doesn't concern me"
17 Take two
18 "Not true!"
19 Former Houston hockey team
20 Illustration, for example: Abbr.
21 Ad time filler, for short
22 Half of an interrogation team
24 Neighbors of Estonians
26 First American film in which a toilet is heard being flushed (1960)
28 Equally distant
31 Cry at a surprise birthday party
33 Shut (up)
34 Pull a fast one on
35 Chill
36 Where a stud might go
37 Big name in Deco design
38 Hipsteresque, in a way
39 Struck out
40 Like bonds designated AAA
42 A-listers
44 Little mischief-makers
46 Fernando or Felipe, once
47 Word with nursing or training
50 Touch of color
51 One making a living by pushing drugs, informally

54 Contend
55 Sound evidence?
56 Good earth
57 Stay with a friend, say
58 Concerning
59 What areology is the study of
60 Synthetic fiber, for short

DOWN

1 Sources of cashmere
2 Openly confident
3 ___ fusion (cuisine)
4 Large quantity
5 Like the role of Albus Dumbledore after the second Harry Potter movie
6 All huffy
7 "Me neither"
8 Poindexter

9 Gives away to a better home, in a modern coinage
10 Back in again
11 One who hates heights
12 Messes around (with)
14 Daffy Duck, notably
15 Addressees of valedictories
23 High point
24 "Nobody ever told me," e.g.
25 Deposits in some banks
27 Bit of punditry
28 "___ Death," movement from "Peer Gynt"
29 Metal in a junk heap
30 Cause of typos, humorously

32 One who gives a lot of orders
35 Be highly regarded
39 Clean lightly, as a floor
41 Listings in a travel guide
43 Metaphor for penthouse suites
45 Back problem
47 "Project Runway" cable channel
48 Turn back
49 Mimic's skill
50 Anklebones
52 Activity for which you need a fair amount of wiggle room
53 On

by Freddie Cheng

ACROSS

1 "No, thanks"
6 Rapper's release
10 Activity that might elicit stares, for short
13 Singer/actress Janelle
14 Theater option
15 Couleur du chocolat
16 "___ Ever" (Elvis song from "G.I. Blues")
17 Yamaha purchase
19 Hazmat regulator
20 USA competitor
21 Construction piece that describes what happens when you compliment me?
22 Kashyyyk denizen, in sci-fi
24 Contents of some sleeves
26 Olympic runner?
27 Up and a little to the left, for short
28 One who might be diagnosed with a polysomnogram
31 Cellist with a Presidential Medal of Freedom
32 Like some legal judgments
33 Singer seen annually on David Letterman's Christmas show
34 "Say no more - I'm on it"
35 "___ Mañanitas" (traditional Mexican birthday song)
38 GPS suggestion: Abbr.
39 Walletful
40 Aid in breaking down doors
42 Go down, so to speak
44 ___ South, div. of the 55-Acrosses
45 Pixy ___
46 #2 image among smartphone users?
49 Not straight up
50 "That's my cue!"
51 Taqueria order, informally
52 ___ Park, Calif.
53 "C'mon, man," in a syllable
54 Wetlands feature
55 See 44-Across

DOWN

1 "Count me in"
2 One of the nine weapons in 2008's expanded version of Clue
3 "That, in spades!"
4 See 8-Down
5 Lead-in to cow, horse or dog
6 Footwear with a tree logo
7 Who said "The Lord will roar from Zion, and utter his voice from Jerusalem"
8 With 4-Down, someone who might repossess your car when you go bankrupt?
9 Prefix with thermic
10 Like some vestments
11 1980s presidential candidate
12 Weak
15 So-so bond rating
18 Conquers
20 English breakfast, for example
23 "Ninotchka" actress, 1939
24 Mayoralty, e.g.
25 Close . . . but not THAT close
29 Unseeded?
30 Trim
31 French homophone of 30-Down
32 Stand-up comedian with the 2005 double-platinum album "Retaliation"
33 Companies known for their net profit
34 "Enough already!"
35 Many a Univision viewer, in modern usage
36 Armpit
37 Poet with the 1967 Pulitzer-winning volume "Live or Die"
41 Big name in parfum
43 Original airer of "Everybody Hates Chris"
44 Cracked
47 ___ Resorts International
48 "Je pense que ___" ("I think so": Fr.)
49 Tsp. or tbsp.

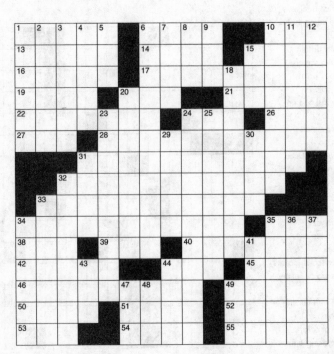

by Erik Agard

ACROSS

1 Means of interstellar travel
10 Supreme Court colleague of Ruth and Neil
15 Oklahoma tribe originally from the Southeast
16 Parts of nerve cells
17 An anchor is at its end
18 Five-time winner of FIFA's player of the year award
19 Sport ___
20 Loser
22 Garners
23 What might hurt a celebrity's Q Score
26 Top of Scotland
28 Main
29 Word with Pacific or basketball
31 Sheep's milk product
32 Arm muscle, informally
33 "This isn't over"
36 Advice column query
37 Some facial treatments
38 Ad ___
39 Forty-niners' equipment
40 First show to win 50 Emmys, in brief
41 Sister company of Century 21
42 Delta Air Lines hub in the Mountain time zone, for short
43 State capital known as the Cherry City
47 Great-great-great-great-great-great-grandfather of Noah
49 This clue's number divided by this clue's answer
53 Cells joined by other cells
54 Alternative to tea leaves
56 Modern information analyst
59 Who sings "Some Enchanted Evening" in "South Pacific"
60 Shortly
61 Kind of cup
62 Travels like the fly in sci-fi's "The Fly"

DOWN

1 Cancel
2 Letter found between two vowels in the alphabet
3 Felt off
4 ___ Dome (former Indianapolis venue)
5 Something on the horizon
6 Like a rock and many a roll
7 Part of Caesar's boast
8 Something to set or pick up
9 Make nice to in a manipulative way
10 "The Lord of the Rings" role
11 Farm team
12 Certain facial piercings
13 Like the sound of surround sound, typically
14 "Again . . ."
21 Much of military history
24 Competition at Pebble Beach
25 Meat cuts that are often barbecued
27 Valkyries, e.g.
30 Drinks made from agave
31 Tricks
33 Hit 1999 film that popularized a slo-mo effect known as "bullet time"
34 Took a gamble
35 Nabisco brand
36 Question asked after opening one's eyes and blinking repeatedly
37 Like cockatoos and iguanas
44 Unlikely partygoer
45 Party, e.g.
46 Selling points
48 Colorful Hindu festival
50 One providing directions
51 Abbr. after a series of 52-Downs
52 See 51-Down
55 Driving aid
57 Its head is usually at the bottom
58 "If u ask me . . ."

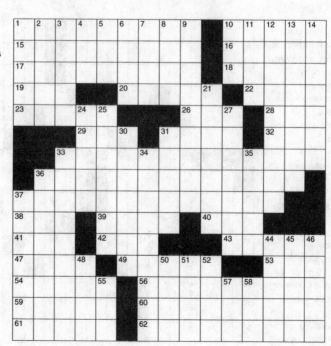

by Evan Kalish

ACROSS

1 "Right?": Fr.
10 Org. whose founders include Cecil B. DeMille
15 Leading man?
16 Sturdy floor wood
17 Potent Hawaiian weed
18 Unsettled feeling
19 High-society people may put them on when in public
20 Alternative to a Lambo
21 A man or a mouse
22 Demolition letters
23 Not so far away
25 It multiplies by dividing
26 "Narcissus and Goldmund" novelist
28 ___ truck
30 Part of a guess in Battleship
31 Only place in the U.S. to host both the Summer and Winter Olympics, informally
34 Vacation souvenir, perhaps
36 Parent company of Pine-Sol
38 Blanket
39 Home of Millennium Park, informally
40 Sharing many of the characteristics of
41 Background noise
42 ___ boy
44 Goods, slangily
48 2019 #1 album by Tyler, the Creator
50 Medicine cabinet glass
53 "Brilliant!"
54 200-milligram units
56 Snow of "Game of Thrones"

57 Bibliographer's abbr.
58 Still around
59 1963 Four Seasons hit
61 Paintings of Adam and Eve, typically
62 Alternative to Kickstarter
63 Bond, e.g.
64 Fully fixed

DOWN

1 Jet popular in the 1960s and '70s
2 Flight attendant in "Airplane!"
3 Periods of growth
4 "Who is ___?"
5 Harsh cry
6 Expressive characters
7 Rough up, in a way

8 Come down (on)
9 Match
10 Boy's name that becomes a girl's name if you move the first letter to the end
11 Tricks
12 Steakhouse selection
13 Not have an accomplice
14 "You want to?"
21 Occult
23 Learn indirectly
24 Taken in
27 Orkneyan or Shetlander
29 Part of a cloverleaf
32 Pixelated, perhaps
33 "Nope"
35 Family hand-me-down?

36 Quickly drink
37 Long car trip?
39 Woman who has traveled to el Norte, maybe
43 Music style that might feature an accordion and a bajo sexto
45 G.I. meal
46 Put some juice into
47 Bless
49 Shade of black
51 Zillow listing
52 Ruined
55 Challenge
57 Fragile projectiles
59 Short smoke
60 House support

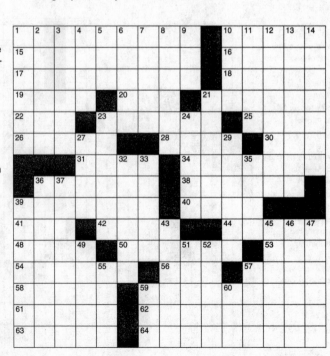

by David Steinberg

ACROSS

1 Like sauvignon blanc and pinot grigio, typically
4 Scrubber
9 Warrior pose in yoga, e.g.
14 Kiss cam displayer
16 Meg who wrote "The Princess Diaries"
17 What's found above a tilde
18 Orange half of an iconic duo
19 Smart set?
20 Things sandals lack
21 Firing locale
22 Repaid
25 Managed
28 Swindling trick
29 Shake off
30 Sapped of resources
31 % on the back of a baseball card, say
32 Get in the end
33 Disturbed states
36 Comic actor Barinholtz
37 Las Vegas casino with a musical name
39 Bites harmlessly
40 Two-time Grand Slam champion of the 1960s
42 Is sure to succeed
44 Some fishing attire
45 Hearty breakfast dish that includes potatoes
46 Pilot production?
47 ___ Games, company behind Fortnite
48 Battleship row
53 One-named singer with the 1993 platinum album "Debut"
54 "Nothing can stop me now!"
55 Mascot of the Winnipeg Jets
56 Pearl Harbor or Norfolk
57 Pulitzer-winning writer of "The Optimist's Daughter"
58 Leslie ___, main role on "Parks and Recreation"
59 Handful

DOWN

1 Spun wax, say
2 Trick
3 Org. offering athletic memberships
4 Very uneven
5 Title tenor role
6 Big name in pest control
7 The other side
8 "Who wants to step up?"
9 Unbeatable blackjack pair
10 Garments worn at beach parties
11 Type least likely to turn up in a hospital
12 New Year's Eve party freebie
13 "I already ___"
15 Caromed
23 Middle of a Latin trio
24 Puts off
25 Shark, to swimmers
26 Everyman
27 All available options?
28 Use smear tactics on
30 Rosy shade of makeup
34 What team leaders must frequently manage
35 Player of the Skipper on "Gilligan's Island"
38 Quite eager
41 Gather on the surface, chemically
43 Underling
44 BBQ restaurant handout
46 Mormon settlement of 1849
49 Country that has approximately 0% arable land
50 Idle
51 Instead
52 Whole bunch
53 Company that makes the Mini

by Peter Wentz

ACROSS

1 Junk dealers?
9 Ghost buster, of a sort
15 Fix without doctoring
16 Many a magnet has one
17 Thought accompanying a light bulb
18 Like speakeasies and fridges, at times
19 One may be copped
20 "Bandleader" with a 1967 #1 album
22 Dr. ___
24 On the ___
25 Go with the wind?
27 '
28 Big times
30 Man's name that's an alphabet run
31 The Panthers of the A.C.C.
32 Commonplace
33 Passes, slangily
34 Comment of complete contentment
37 ___ A. Bank (men's clothier since 1905)
38 Man's name that means "the king"
39 Last word in many company names
40 Tidbit for an echidna
41 Tone-___
42 Of very poor quality, in modern slang
43 Old Model M's and Model T-6s
45 Blues group?: Abbr.
46 It's truly inspired
47 Offerings from Friskies
50 Gradually cut off (from)
54 1962 John Wayne film
55 Hit list
57 Handle, of a sort

58 Descended upon, as mosquitoes might
59 "Another Bud, bud!"
60 Comic con, e.g.

DOWN

1 Prime directive?
2 Nebula Award winner Frederik
3 Guy's gal
4 Pioneering thrash metal band with its own music festival, Gigantour
5 Dating letters
6 Commencement
7 Class in which kids may learn about sin?
8 Best-selling game with a hexagonal board
9 College area of study with no application required?
10 On the double
11 Contents of a bowl or a pot
12 Complained loudly and publicly
13 Kir and Campari, for two
14 Stark family member on "Game of Thrones"
21 What the U.S. and Canadian dollars had, roughly, in the early 2010s
23 Made looser or tighter, in a way
26 Opulence
27 Is perfect, clothing-wise
29 It's got its ups and downs

31 Mobile home?
32 Capital on the Balkan Peninsula
34 Barely open
35 It's going downhill
36 Not a team player
42 Often-reddish quartz
44 1990s' ___ Report
48 Crop
49 Something brought to a supermarket
51 City on a lake of the same name
52 Off-road rides, for short
53 Vote in the Security Council
54 Nucleus
56 Something everyone's doing

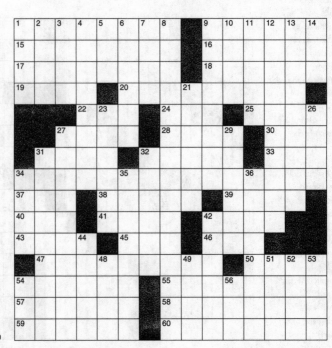

by Sam Trabucco

ACROSS

1 Tarot card, with "the"
5 Bird named for its black-and-white markings
15 Eccentric fashion designer in "The Incredibles"
16 Its deep blue variety is called maxixe
17 Trixie's mom, in the comics
18 Cocktail made from peach schnapps and orange juice
19 Track event
20 Brand once marketed as "The Reincarnation of Tea"
21 Gate announcement, briefly
22 Demand
24 Kind of type
28 Island attire
29 One maturing quickly, informally
30 Skewed
31 Erasable mark
35 Target of some therapy
36 Wrestler Flair
37 It comes from Mars
38 Your heart may go out to it
41 Title for Macbeth
42 Rock and roll, e.g.
43 Their players are often benched
44 Half of an old comedy duo
45 Taboo word
46 Ivy League nickname
48 One of the Everly Brothers
50 Either of the two highest trump cards in euchre
52 Was charming?

56 Queens stadium eponym
57 Body of water between two locks of the Erie Canal
58 The Big Bad Wolf, in old cartoons
59 Reason for going out a lot?
60 Fervor

DOWN

1 Pool surface
2 Sole supporter?
3 Item sold at Burger King but not at most McDonald's
4 Person tasked with locking up
5 Full-figured
6 Peer
7 Hype

8 University of Arkansas mascot
9 One of the March sisters
10 Cooler
11 Portfolio part, for short
12 "Around the World in 80 Days" star, 1956
13 Tech news source
14 Not free to go
23 Pismire
25 Rembrandt or Vermeer
26 "The fierce urgency of now" speaker, familiarly
27 So on and so forth
28 Starch-producing palm tree
29 Oreo ___
31 Small fruit high in pectin
32 "Lemme look!"

33 1939 film banned in the Soviet Union
34 Participants in some awkward meetings
39 Exhibition-funding grp.
40 "Man, it's cold!"
41 Quaint contraction
43 Part of a Rube Goldberg device
44 Dough nut?
45 Uses shamelessly
46 M.B.A. prereq.
47 Singer ___ Del Rey
49 Crate
51 Balance beam?
53 Poker game tell, perhaps
54 Foofaraw
55 ___ soda

by Trenton Charlson

66

ACROSS
1 Spring report
6 Bad fall
12 Performance bonus
14 Print alternative
15 Place for driving lessons
16 Salves
17 Manner of speaking in eastern Virginia
19 Men
20 Hundred Acre Wood youngster
21 45th anniversary gifts
22 Dangerous toy
24 Charged
25 ___ de boeuf en croûte
26 Brings on
27 Roman god invoked by Iago
28 Leveled
29 Canal sight
30 Tragedy that was first performed in 431 B.C.
31 Don
35 Inits. in a bowling alley
36 Bygone magazine spinoff
37 Linguistic borrowing, as "earworm" from "Ohrwurm"
40 One who gets lots of tweets?
41 World capital on the Rideau Canal
42 Moolah
43 Lead-in to weight
44 Simpson who infamously lip-synched a song on "S.N.L."
45 High and thin, as a voice

DOWN
1 Siamese fighting fish
2 Iroquois Confederacy nation
3 Became impassable, in a way
4 Medal with the dates MDCCCXXXIII–MDCCCXCVI
5 What a business might shift resources to
6 Dances taught by a kumu
7 George Orwell's real first name
8 "Just ___"
9 Branches
10 End up as a wash
11 Surmount
13 Checked out
14 Body in our solar system that was considered a planet in the first half of the 19th century
16 Found a new tenant for
18 Gogol's "___ Bulba"
22 Certain obsessive-compulsive
23 Shiny blowfly
25 Maker of rows
26 Trusted
27 Believers who practice ahimsa, strict nonviolence to all living creatures
28 Strips
29 George ___, co-star with Bette Davis in 11 films, including "Dark Victory" and "Jezebel"
30 Unesco's ___ Fund for Girls' Right to Education
31 Cut off
32 Codeine, for one
33 Went from adagio to largo, say
34 In base 6
36 Fleeting moment
38 N.B.A. starter?: Abbr.
39 Reliable

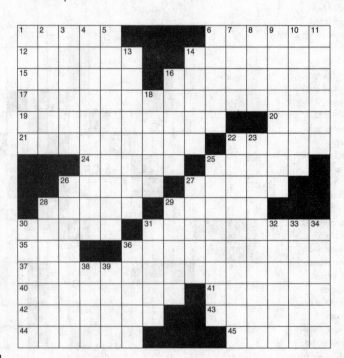

by Byron Walden

ACROSS

1 General plan?
7 Reproductive part
13 Locks that might not be totally secure?
15 Cause of wheezing
16 Put on the line, perhaps
18 Check names
19 It gets cleared for takeoff
21 Bit of gymnastics equipment
22 Important thing to know, if you will
24 Big biceps, in slang
25 Photos from drones, e.g.
26 Trail mix morsel
27 "How ___ it?"
28 Some works by poets laureate
29 Crime for which Al Capone went to prison
33 Yank
34 Put on the line
35 PC "brain"
36 Character raised in "Rosemary's Baby"
38 In the thick of
39 One relatively close either way?
40 Female role in "Pulp Fiction"
41 Silly
42 Pitfall
44 Theater ticket option
46 Debtor's letters
47 Ones flying in circles
48 BBQ offering
50 Settlers of disputes
54 Noted library opened in 2001
55 Traveler who picks up three companions in a classic film
56 Pledge to
57 Ill will

DOWN

1 One-time connection
2 Affected response to an allegation
3 Prickly husk
4 Keeps current
5 First podcast to win a Peabody Award (2015)
6 Job requiring a car, say
7 Fruit in the custard apple family
8 "Here's my two cents . . ."
9 Dump
10 Tony winner set in River City, Iowa
11 "Um . . . er . . ."
12 Doesn't die
14 Singer with the #1 albums "Stars Dance" (2013) and "Revival" (2015)
17 Pie that comes "fully loaded"
20 Green protector
22 Become, finally
23 Colorado's official state dinosaur
24 Wonderful time
25 Tiny bit
27 Roll of bread
29 Road goo
30 Peace sign
31 Pontificate
32 Titian's "Venus Anadyomene," e.g.
34 Lbs. and ozs.
37 Tiny bit
38 "Friends" co-star
41 One of the Gandhis
42 Shankbone
43 Romps
44 Modern handbag portmanteau
45 Shady area
47 Zymurgist's interest
49 Animal that doesn't have a sound coming out of its head?
51 Series end
52 P
53 Aleppo's land: Abbr.

by Andrew J. Ries

ACROSS

1 Calgary nickname, along with "Stampede City"
8 Competitor of Twinings
14 Collapsible chapeau
16 Where Sevastopol is
17 Like Denver
18 Book page size
19 Eat lots of protein and carbs, say
20 Some legal speeders, briefly
22 Cab alternative
23 Pioneering football coach ___ Alonzo Stagg
24 Occupy, as a desk
26 "Let's ___!"
27 "I expected better"
28 They may go on long walks
29 Member of Dubya's cabinet
30 It's filled with energy
32 The Netherlands was the first country to legalize it
35 Celebrated the birth of a child, perhaps
36 Winegrowing region of SW France
37 Them, to us
38 Prefix with tourism or politics
41 "Hmm . . ."
42 Bygone potentates
43 Word with bank or blind
44 Love, by another name
45 Like the ocean
46 Mess up
48 Permanent-press

50 Pogo and others
52 Totally dominating
53 Bad record?
54 Alternatives to S.U.V.s, informally
55 Common "explanation" from a parent

DOWN

1 Private practice?
2 Poppy products
3 "Sure, I guess . . ."
4 Long hauls
5 Island with a state capital
6 Jerked in two directions at once
7 Poke with a lot of needles?
8 Michael ___, "The Office" manager

9 Parentheses, essentially
10 Sloshed
11 Endangered watershed
12 Marine
13 Web-based recovery program, informally
15 Film featuring an assassin from 2029
21 Rubber
25 To a fault
26 Indian flatbreads
28 Trig function
29 Deal in
30 Souchong alternative
31 Boarding points at amusement parks
32 Vessel in a famous 1960s shipwreck

33 Midwest university city
34 Part-time job for many an actor or actress
38 Came after
39 Hannity's former Fox News foil
40 Must pay
42 Sharp tastes
43 Bento box fare
45 Skier Lindsey with three Olympic medals
47 Peak in Thessaly
49 Bravo, e.g.
51 ___ gow (gambling game played with dominoes)

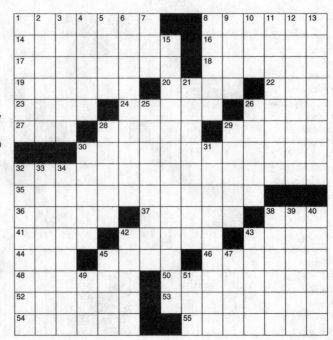

by Ryan McCarty

ACROSS

1 Areas where clerics are seated
6 Play's counterpart
11 Beldam
14 Thin layer of foam at the top of an espresso
15 Selling point
16 The Jazz, on sports tickers
17 Add, British-style
18 Business circles?
20 "Our remedies ___ in ourselves do lie": Shak.
21 Character assassination, for one
23 Collapse
25 Bit of work
26 Brand that's a shortened description of its flavor
27 "Heavens to Murgatroyd!"
31 James, Jimmy or John
32 "Heavens to Murgatroyd!"
33 Omegas represent them
35 Savage of "Savage Love"
36 Cousin of a fjord
37 ___ party
38 Post cereal with an apostrophe in its name
41 Familia members
42 Genre for Miriam Makeba and Ladysmith Black Mambazo
44 Quiet (down)
47 Toon who wears a red hair bow
49 Zhou ___
51 Mac : Scottish :: ___ : Arabic
52 They open in the morning

53 Type for who this clue will be annoying?
57 It's stretched out in yoga class
58 Iconic part of Nancy Sinatra's early attire
59 Kennedy colleague
61 Café freebie
62 Year abroad
63 Unlikely donor
64 Pres. whose given birth name was David
65 Does business
66 Alternative nickname for Liz

DOWN

1 Hurricane or flood
2 Perfunctory
3 Get cozy
4 Producer of a deep drumming call
5 Boobs
6 Law school, so it's said
7 Pungent cheese
8 One who might need an ID
9 Broken-off branch
10 "___ Brand" (Nathaniel Hawthorne tale)
11 Rush
12 Verdi opera based on a historic invader
13 Stranded motorist's boon
19 Eating things
22 Promised one
24 Nobelist Hammarskjöld
28 Rings
29 A batter receives four for a grand slam
30 Shark-jumping sitcom character

34 Beauty ___
38 Bull, essentially
39 Highly anticipated social events
40 Work with intelligence?
41 Latin lover's words
43 One may be essential
44 Classified
45 Foray
46 Hound
48 Doorframe part
50 Repeated boast in a 1987 #1 hit
54 Super
55 Author Jaffe
56 Foot type
60 Get down, in a way

by Damon Gulczynski

ACROSS

1 Skye, the Small Isles, etc.
9 Fiddles (with)
15 Eaglelike
16 Armpit, to a doctor
17 Brown-bag lunch item
18 With wacky irreverence
19 2002 "documentary" with "Don't try this at home" contents
21 Varieties
22 Sounds of pity
23 Fan sound
24 Like an ascot, perhaps
28 Put a dent in, say
29 Jeep model
32 Le Monde material
35 "No, you don't want to do that"
36 First hit for the Police
37 Performed beautifully
38 Managing
39 Psychological mediator
40 "Drop dead, loser"
41 Strike sharply
43 Change one's tone?
44 "Don't ___ thing"
48 Hit 1959 Broadway play starring Sidney Poitier
53 Jam producer
54 Bowed with adversity
55 Book after Proverbs: Abbr.
56 Only woman aboard the Argo, it's said
57 Third-rate
58 "Jezebel" costume

DOWN

1 Faithful pilgrim
2 Congruent
3 Riviera, e.g.
4 Singer with a recurring role on "General Hospital"
5 Guts, in part
6 "Mine!"
7 Slaughter of the Cardinals
8 Record of affairs?
9 Achievements in large-scale topiary
10 Bar ___
11 Historic conflict in and around the Yellow Sea
12 Reducing to splinters
13 ___ Kemper, star of TV's "Unbreakable Kimmy Schmidt"
14 Leo with the 1977 #1 hit "When I Need You"
20 Any I, e.g.: Abbr.
25 What may involve the calf muscles?
26 Managed, with "out"
27 Shade of green
28 Saw
29 Its logo is based on a Pennsylvania Dutch hex sign
30 Derisive reply
31 "The Sopranos" actress
32 Slow sort, informally
33 Patootie
34 ___ Motors, old Lansing manufacturer
36 Tattle
38 Subcompact
40 International treaty subject
41 Coastline features
42 Robert of "Spenser: For Hire"
43 A little tight
45 Simultaneously
46 Round abodes
47 Dancer Pavlova and others
49 Went after, in a way
50 ___ the Great of children's literature
51 Like many folk songs: Abbr.
52 Stood fast

by Adam Fromm

ACROSS

1 Cuckoo
5 Showed
9 Stack (or snack) on a table
14 Literally, "highest city"
16 Mystical characters
17 "This place looks horrible!"
18 Highway through the Yukon
19 Site where top hats and canes might be checked at the door
21 Make
22 Drummer Starkey
23 Sound that might be made while rubbing the arms
25 TV boy with spiked hair
27 In front of, to Shakespeare
29 Org. since 1902 with 50+ million members
30 Throw a long football pass
32 Intermission starter?
33 Part of XXX
34 California's Harvey ___ College
35 Santa player in "Elf"
37 Food sticker
38 "Star Wars" nickname
39 Chucklehead
40 Rebounded
42 Old RR watchdog
43 Like some columns
45 Lacerate
46 Court ruling
47 "Eww, no more!"
48 Memo directive
50 2012 #1 hit by LMFAO

56 Internet hookup
57 Like Sprite
58 Hindu aphorisms
59 Producer of red-and-white blooms
60 Get low
61 Practice
62 No longer a draft, say

DOWN

1 Homey
2 It hurts
3 Ollie's friend on old TV
4 Walked unsteadily
5 Bug exterminator?
6 Mount Holyoke grad, e.g.
7 Act out
8 Sports-themed restaurant
9 Soup go-with
10 Bottom of the sea?
11 Development period
12 Dim
13 Application fig.
15 Oenophile's pride
20 "The Flies" playwright
24 Went pit-a-pat, pit-a-pat
25 Doesn't stay in the hole, as a ball
26 Hooked on
28 Prada competitor
30 Communication service since 2004
31 Pablo Picasso's designer daughter
36 Jared Kushner, as a notable example

37 Where people go to vote
39 Concierge's handout
41 Narrow recess
44 Relative of an alligator
49 Portmanteau garment
51 Prefix with graphic
52 Prefix with graphic
53 Subterfuge
54 Opposite of "Too rich for me"
55 Word with road or blood
56 Pile at a publisher: Abbr.

by David Steinberg

ACROSS

1 Result of a firing
4 English channel
7 It's poorly written
13 Hannibal's men
16 1962 Best Picture setting
17 Fault line?
18 Swimming
19 Shade of green
20 Bind with a belt
22 Certain finish
23 Chanel No. 5 competitor
25 Gridlock consequence
27 Many a Dallas cowboy
28 Comments that lead people to repeat themselves
29 Ones carrying babies on their backs
31 Middle Earth?
32 Dawdles
34 Source of feedback
36 Fictional spy who first appeared in "Call for the Dead"
37 "___ joke"
38 Ranges
39 Go the right way?
42 Mystery in the fossil record
43 Writer with the given names Robert Lawrence
44 Tick off
46 Jointly
48 Whine lover?
50 Undeceived by
51 Capital for King Zog
53 Hooter's location
55 Setting for Sergei Eisenstein's "Battleship Potemkin"
56 Clear brandy
57 Brisk competitor
58 Fist pumper's cry
59 Besides

DOWN

1 PIN money?
2 "Jeez Louise!"
3 Trick-taking card game
4 About 252 cals.
5 Like M. Poirot
6 Competitive, in a way
7 Title of politeness
8 Swimmer's woe
9 Pro ___
10 Slaughterhouse
11 Spent a season in the sun?
12 Rubbery compounds
14 Certain eruption
15 Famed Pop Art subject
21 It's pretty obvious
24 Augmenting, old-style
26 Functional
30 Guinness adjective
31 Modeling medium
32 Long-lasting, in commercial names
33 Good earth
34 Table
35 Some fertilized eggs
36 Unit of explosive capacity
39 Palace of Nations locale
40 Has a home-cooked meal
41 Made a big scene?
43 Import
45 Step on a scale
47 Illustrator Thomas
49 Down
52 Strong, as a bond
54 New Left org.

by Martin Ashwood-Smith

ACROSS

1 Radisson rival
7 Title role for Bryan Cranston in a 2015 biopic
13 Neologism coined by Cole Porter
15 Sea that Homer called "wine-dark"
16 Song whose opening lyric translates to "What a beautiful thing is a sunny day"
17 Missionaries' targets
18 Scratch
19 River bisecting Orsk
21 Squad cmdr.
22 White notes in Monopoly
23 Golf cart foursome
25 1962 Organization of American States expellee
26 Necromancers
27 Crown cover
28 Part of an armada
31 Instructions on where to go?
32 World's oldest currency still in use
33 Total
34 Grate catches?
35 Early automotive pioneer
36 Scoopers for taramasalata
37 Musical group with "energy domes"
41 End of a cause?
42 ___ soup
43 Pole topper
45 LeBron James, by birth
47 Restless sort
49 "She understands her business better than we do," per Montaigne
50 Agricultural outfit
51 Banded metamorphic rock
52 Lively wit

DOWN

1 Substance used in Egyptian mummification
2 Unaided
3 Earthworm trappers
4 Contend
5 Things mailed without a label?
6 Who said "I'm so mean I make medicine sick"
7 Cantina offerings
8 De facto
9 ___ boots
10 Ruler's role
11 Reports of gunfire?
12 Performing for an audience
13 Dummkopf
14 Emancipation proclamation
20 Lay-by : England :: ___ : America
24 "No need to trouble yourself"
25 Firth of "The King's Speech"
26 Make a hash of
27 France's patron saint
28 Conversation piece?
29 Follows the game?
30 They meet at a summit
31 Surname of TV's "Hot Lips"
32 Extend
36 Seven ___ (Civil War battle site)
37 Shut out
38 Things that take guts?
39 Cathedral feature
40 Withdraws, with "out"
42 Opportunity's on it
44 Gefilte fish option
46 Word of agreement that sounds like a pronoun
48 Road map abbr.

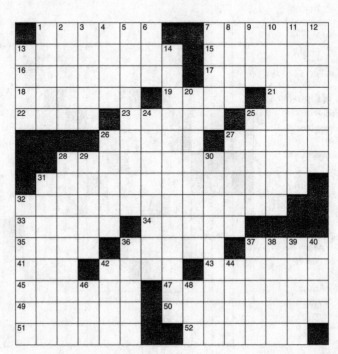

by Patrick Berry

ACROSS

1 Be on K.P., in a way
11 ___ school
15 Sly depiction, often
16 Breakout of a sort
17 Play and movie about a noted 1977 series of interviews
18 Moves unpredictably
19 Partners in many lesbian couples
20 Who said "Politics is war without bloodshed"
21 Lost all patience
22 It disappears after rising
23 Circuit
25 "Doktor Faust" composer
26 Bovarism
27 1983 7x platinum Billy Joel album, with "An"
29 Japanese import that debuted in 1982
31 John in a suit?
32 Hinge (upon)
33 Marine fish related to the cod
35 "Star Trek: T.N.G." counselor
37 They're not complex numbers
40 "___ Sleeps Over" (classic children's book)
42 Some sorority women
46 One asking for Ahmed Adoudi, say
49 Setting for Red Sox games: Abbr.
50 Stick back in the water?
51 See 52-Across
52 With 51-Across, two steps away from AA, informally
53 Torment
54 Acoustics unit
55 Brood

56 It may be just a bit
57 Winner of the 1998 Masters and British Open
60 Prefix with -genous
61 One who won't give kids a shot?
62 It's often picked up in bars
63 One who's gotten good marks?

DOWN

1 Isn't resolute
2 Land
3 Crush
4 Sibilate
5 Feature of only two letters
6 Overnight letter?
7 President Peres
8 Insect, e.g.
9 Old switch extension

10 Start of a sequel, sometimes
11 Intifada locale
12 Former home of the Colts
13 Like some chest pain
14 Lot
21 Vandal
23 Italian bread that's become toast?
24 Currently into something
25 Center of a blowout, maybe
28 Camp sight
30 Balding
34 Long stretch
36 Sticks in the water?
37 Rows
38 Herb of PBS's "Ciao Italia"

39 1981 and 1988 World Series-winning manager
41 1988 Olympics locale
43 Urban lab transporter, maybe
44 Bonds
45 Noah's predecessor
47 Eloise creator Thompson
48 Rapper with the debut album "Hard Core"
54 Jurist's seat
55 Suggestive transmission
57 What's more in Madrid?
58 Beginnings of life
59 Blemish

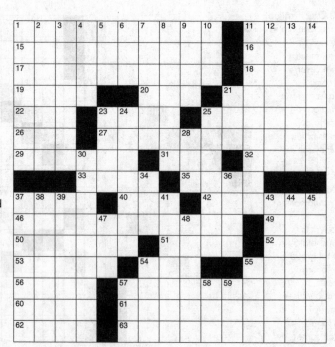

by Joe DiPietro

ACROSS

1 Jumble
9 Heavy metal shortage?
15 Popular song in a children's sing-along
16 Some headgear
17 Continue
18 A real money maker
19 Brief bit of time, in slang
20 Ben-___
21 First lady after Lou
22 Words after shake or break
24 Smallville family
26 Inside look?
27 Not miss
30 I.R.S. Form 1120 filers: Abbr.
31 Proof that a property is yours
32 "Cat ___"
34 Beloved "army" leader
35 Chewing on
38 Long, narrow land
39 Useless
40 Asia's ___ Sea
41 Stone
42 Pulled (in)
46 Fresh
47 Molières : France :: ___ : U.S.
49 Apt. amenity, perhaps
50 Services in the U.K.
52 A good one is important for music
55 Constellation next to Scorpius
56 Where people are often told to look

57 Another day
59 Unconventional sort, en français
60 Fit
61 Laceless, say
62 In the way it used to be

DOWN

1 Nut
2 Philippines' ___ City
3 Shelley's "Ozymandias," e.g.
4 Order repeated before a hike
5 Jibe
6 One of the Near Islands
7 Baby deliverer
8 With it, man
9 They're never minor

10 Things that might sense danger and scams
11 Funny Bombeck
12 First set of choices
13 "Nothing to get upset about"
14 On
21 Not a lot, but ___
23 Assistance for returning W.W. II vets
25 "It's the ___, stupid!"
28 Sweet stalk
29 "Civic" animal
31 "End of discussion!"
33 Ones in the closet?
34 Up to the job
35 Like some heavy-duty trucks

36 Longfellow character
37 What the Irish breathe
38 Residents of Cambridge, England
41 Acquired
43 Close
44 Jazz pianist Garner
45 Bank from which a check is paid
47 Words from a Latin lover
48 Capital on the Han River
51 Record producer Pettibone
53 In
54 Spoils badly
57 Culinary general?
58 Betrayer

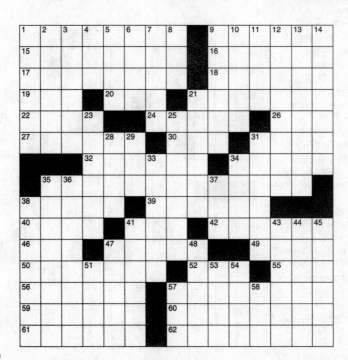

by Bill Clinton and Victor Fleming

ACROSS

1 Tiny cheese sandwiches, of a sort
9 A thread winds around it
14 Nest-raiding insect
16 Surrender
17 Computer icon, e.g.
18 Paid to play
19 Pro's opposite, in slang
20 Places frequented by Dorian Gray
22 Dish made from 7-Down
24 Nonnative plant?
25 Ironman race, briefly
28 Existing
32 Threw
36 One likely to have a large collection of albums
39 Grammy-winning R. Kelly hit of 1996
40 They're often upsetting
41 See 25-Down
42 Flowers named after the Greek word for "star"
43 Went nowhere
44 Abbr. by a blinking light
46 ___ Yantra (sacred Hindu diagram formed by nine interlocking triangles)
48 Stumble out of the gate, say
54 What ":" can mean
57 Teachers of karma
58 High-quality window composition
61 Sphere
62 "Wag the Dog" co-star, 1997
63 Bat around
64 "No need to elaborate"

DOWN

1 Strike
2 Declaration after looking at one's cards
3 ___ stand
4 Band with the gold-certified albums "Tres Hombres" and "El Loco"
5 Ignorant middle class, per H. L. Mencken
6 Fortune Global 500 bank
7 Ingredient in 22-Across
8 Take a shot
9 Inundate
10 Christmas decoration
11 Quinceañera, for 15-year-old girls
12 Neither up nor down
13 Joins
15 "Eww, stop!"
21 They're old and tired
23 Work together.
25 With 41-Across, one bending unexpectedly?
26 1994 Peace Prize sharer
27 Woman's name meaning "peace"
29 Some wasp nest sites
30 Rid of impurities
31 Tree-tapping spigot
33 Some sporty Italian wheels
34 "The Simpsons" aunt
35 Meeting on the DL
37 Powerful tool for Dumbledore
38 Follows a healthful diet
45 Try
47 ___ of Langerhans (part of the pancreas)
48 Cut of meat
49 Boris Pasternak heroine
50 Parting of the clouds, maybe
51 After
52 Baroque artist Guido
53 Strong, sharp smell
55 Instrument with a needle, for short
56 Plant watcher, for short
59 River that forms part of the England/Wales boundary
60 Collected works

by Jeff Chen

ACROSS

1 Walk all over
6 Put back together
10 88 or 98
14 "It's now or never"
16 Converge
17 Nailing a performance
18 Origination point of some drips
19 Sheet music abbr.
20 Having hit successfully, say
21 Weightlifter's concern
22 Obliterates
24 Port whistler
25 Classic arcade game with a glass backboard that shatters
27 86 or 99
29 Still learning the ropes of
31 Large W.W. II area: Abbr.
32 Save
34 Agenda-topping issue
36 Momentarily
38 Started to work
41 Bratty girl on "Little House on the Prairie"
45 Qualifier in 46-Across
46 Messages with emojis
48 Size zero, say
49 Savory Indian appetizer
51 Marking for a very soft passage
53 Show great fondness
54 Abundance
55 Mothered or fathered
58 ___ pros. (lawsuit abbr.)
59 French filmdom

60 Rid of inefficient extras
62 What makes consumers blush?
63 Plays peacemaker
64 Pet sounds
65 They may be soaked up
66 They're favorites

DOWN

1 Moorish castle
2 Heavy rain
3 Wrongly assumed
4 Some patrons: Abbr.
5 Voice-activated Amazon device
6 "The ponytail's hipster cousin," per GQ
7 Its honorees plan to become one

8 Org. for forensic specialist Abby Sciuto
9 Class clown's comeuppance
10 Competitor of Cartier
11 Means of travel for a V.I.P.
12 Get sidetracked
13 Part of a blended family
15 Soupçon
23 Crafty sort
26 Article of attire with strings
28 Convictions
30 W.W. II service member
33 Old-fashioned letter opener
35 Dogged it
37 It shares a key with a caret

38 What motivates people to get to first base during a game?
39 Survivor's cry
40 "Let's get real here . . ."
42 Strong and majestic
43 Half spoken, half sung
44 Naturally blind
47 Flings
50 Eponym of USA Track & Field's highest award
52 It may be poached
56 View from Catania
57 Photo ID issuers
61 Commander during John Brown's capture in 1859

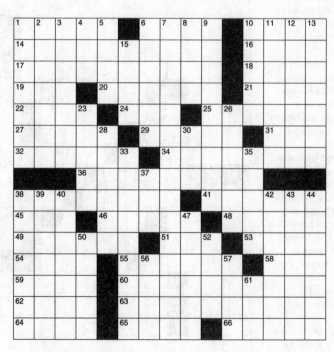

by Matthew Sewell

ACROSS

1 Part of a modern circuit
12 Onetime MTV figures
15 Vegan sushi option
16 Extended stretch
17 Regional coverage plan?
18 Marble ___
19 Bit of work
20 Bit of work
21 Lit
23 Muckraker who pushed for "model tenements"
25 Things with periods in their names
27 Actor Ansari
28 "Look before you leap" source
30 Control+Y on a PC
31 Reading block?
32 Optometrist's favorite musical note?
34 Became clouded over
36 [Just like that!]
38 Hamilton settings
39 Real-life ice age beast seen on "Game of Thrones"
43 Like some light smokes
47 Played for a sap
48 Place to pick up chicks
50 Brazil's fourth-largest state by population
51 The Philippines' ___ Archipelago
52 Egyptian sky god
54 Smart
55 Some chess sacrifices
57 Let
58 Celebratory move popularized by Cam Newton
59 "Mr." who has stitches in his face
60 Sloppy joe ingredient
64 Work that shows love
65 "Meridian" and "The Temple of My Familiar" novelist
66 Edamame discard
67 Metric for gauging female representation in works of fiction

DOWN

1 New Orleans cocktail
2 They can't stay quiet when tickled
3 Like a film that's 2½ hours or so
4 Fish market supply
5 Player, perhaps
6 "None but the Lonely Heart" writer/director, 1944
7 "That's cheating!"
8 Like a blue jay
9 Like bad drivers, often
10 French pronoun
11 "Listen!," e.g.
12 Sprint competitor
13 Driving the wrong way?
14 Welcomed blessing?
22 Snapchat feature that alters one's features
24 Got into a lather
26 Political cartoonist Edward
29 Stem
33 Lab, for one
35 Gearshift part
37 Amplifier for stage actors
39 Bunny picker-upper?
40 "Heck yeah!"
41 Kin
42 Individually
44 Western legend, familiarly
45 Some shooting stars
46 Gullible rodent in a Scott Adams comic
49 Kicked
53 Ski town near Mount Mansfield
56 Run through
61 Stadium cry
62 Spanish seasoning
63 ___-tab

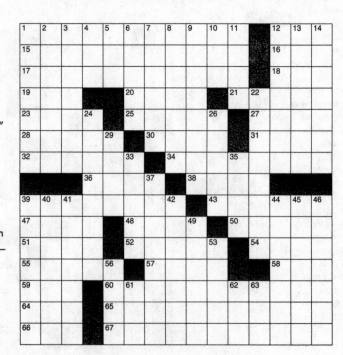

by Paolo Pasco and David Steinberg

ACROSS

1 Living end
12 Writer's deg.
15 What doesn't have a second to lose?
16 Cruet contents
17 "Here's one example . . ."
18 Neighbor of N.Y.
19 Glass with bubbles
20 Coronation, e.g.
21 To God, in a hymn
22 Alternatively
23 Feature of some digital photos
26 Puma parts
27 Quinine, for malaria
29 Met
33 Cricket, to a grasshopper, or vice versa
35 Skirted
36 Highly inflationary
37 Unknowingly reveal
38 Amusing bits of trivia
39 Dora the Explorer, for one: Abbr.
40 Some plum tomatoes
41 Persevere
44 Taking away
48 "Strange Magic" band, for short
49 Smart __
50 Bear in "The Jungle Book"
51 Woven trap
52 A back-seat driver can't do this
55 Org. that promotes Energy Star Day
56 "Tell me more . . ."
57 Part of E.S.T.: Abbr.
58 Miscellany

DOWN

1 __ mocha
2 Something ring-shaped
3 Something ring-shaped
4 Bible belt?
5 Fragrant wood
6 They're often installed in the spring, for short
7 Highway sign abbr.
8 More than concerned
9 They're tender
10 Places to keep 9-Down: Abbr.
11 Sport featuring clay disks
12 Tunes to accompany dimmed lights
13 Content often written by lawyers
14 Choir part
23 Chief justice in the Dred Scott verdict
24 Finished up, as cupcakes
25 Honda's luxury brand
26 Mother of Helen of Troy
28 Some Caltech alums: Abbr.
29 They're hailed on Broadway
30 Stayed out when you shouldn't have?
31 "I'm pleasantly surprised"
32 How some YouTube videos go
33 Talk show hosted by a Harvard grad
34 Lumbering sorts
36 Sport for rikishi
38 Surgical tool
40 Like clarinets
42 Donnie of a 2001 cult film
43 Terse admission of guilt
44 Hanukkah serving
45 The __ Marbles (British Museum holding)
46 Solid
47 Some tracks
48 Feta sources
50 Gutsy
53 Victoria, e.g.: Abbr.
54 River or dynasty name

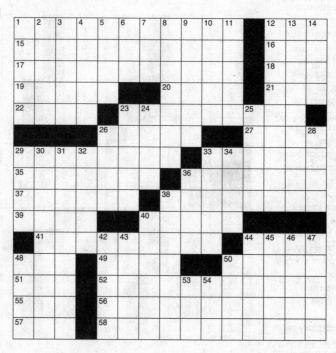

by Robyn Weintraub

ACROSS

1 Honor in a big way
5 "The Aviator" actor, 2004
9 Fictional swordsman
14 Stoked
15 Province of NW Spain
16 Word that's its own synonym when its first two letters are replaced with "w"
17 "At the ___" (subtitle of a 1978 hit)
18 Fellow
19 Relatives of kites
20 N.E.A. member?: Abbr.
21 Language related to Hopi
23 Terse response to an order
24 "Well, yeah!"
25 Md or Rn fig.
26 Notable 1973 defendant
27 Establishes
31 Dickens character "with a dead lull about her"
33 University in Melbourne
35 Occasional meat eater
37 Carl Sagan's sequel to "Cosmos"
39 Gloss
42 Quick to put up, in a way
44 Great Trek figure of the 1830s
45 Spring's cyclic counterpart
47 Company behind Hitchcock's "Notorious"
48 One making bank-to-bank transfers?
49 James and Jones of jazz
51 Battles
52 Dungeons & Dragons race
54 "___ it up and spit it out" ("My Way" lyric)
55 What's more
56 Totally occupy
57 Trailer segment
58 Color close to puce
59 Like many towels
60 One of two areas on a football line
61 Play award?

DOWN

1 Front
2 See how many hits you get, say
3 Five-star
4 Pulitzer-winning novelist Jennifer
5 Fountain growth
6 1994–2000 TV talk show
7 "Who'da thunk it?!"
8 During pregnancy
9 Crush
10 Be subtly and snarkily insulting
11 "Girls" girl played by Lena Dunham
12 Portmanteau in the frozen food aisle
13 Word with sound or storm
22 Part of many a scandal
28 Peddler of religious literature
29 Attempt to cure
30 Like many major highways
32 Less genial
34 Science of nutrition
36 Basic
38 Starts to practice
39 Jim ___, one-handed Yankee who pitched a no-hitter in 1993
40 Knuckle-headed antic?
41 Like Mars vis-à-vis Jupiter
43 Like centerfolds, typically
46 Grill setting
50 9/
51 Use an e-cig
53 Bug catcher, maybe

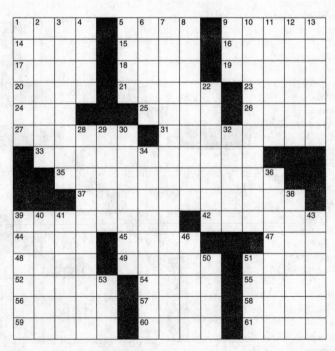

by Damon Gulczynski

81

ACROSS

1 Churchill Downs, to horse racing fans
6 So-called "battery acid"
9 Striking
14 Words after "Stuck" or "High" in hit song titles
15 Control tower projection, for short
16 Susceptible
17 Wendy's burger for "discerning carnivores"
19 It'll give a chip zip
20 "This is gonna be amazing!"
21 Dazzling figure skating feat
22 Abbr. for Lucasfilm
23 Court finales
26 Sandy islet
27 Do some plot work
28 One to one, say
29 Get at
32 Shakespeare's Shylock, for one
35 Eldest of the Pleiades
36 Group of horses?
37 Cher or Adele, e.g.
38 Smallest infinite cardinal number
40 Opposite of narrow
41 Close attention, in brief
42 Uber app abbr.
43 Modicum
44 Simple, simple, simple
48 Stingers from a gun
51 One devoted to Mary?
52 Its logo features a flaming ball
54 He joined the 52-Across in 2004
56 Title role player in 2013's "Mandela: Long Walk to Freedom"

57 Plasma, for one
58 Heartbeat
59 One who might target four minutes
60 What Willy Loman was in
61 "Dream on!"
62 Get rid of

DOWN

1 Company once named Socony-Vacuum
2 Pass
3 Palmlike tropical plant
4 Cousin of a polecat
5 Sally Field's role in "The Amazing Spider-Man"
6 Unleash upon
7 Not the movable type
8 Main villain in "The Phantom Menace"
9 Some execs
10 Many a dweller along the Euphrates
11 Assigned, as to do charity work, in modern lingo
12 Constantly wanting more
13 Unwaveringly committed to
18 Follower of fire or bombs
24 Boston ___
25 Be short
26 Sound in a storm
29 "No clue"
30 Worker always seen with a beard
31 Bit by bit

32 Easily disgusted
33 ___-de-sac
34 Dressage concern
36 "Pain at another's good," per Plutarch
39 Bears
40 Pity party cry
43 Guitarist Hendrix
45 Go down
46 Queen's "We Are the Champions," vis-à-vis "We Will Rock You"
47 Dry out
48 Gorgeous, to Giorgio
49 Ones up in arms?
50 Vacancy sign?
53 Probate figure
55 Relative of "die"

by John Guzzetta and Michael Hawkins

82

ACROSS

1 Horizontal pieces covering joints, in architecture
8 Team that last won the World Series in 1979
15 Ancient Greek land that fought Sparta
16 Weaver of Greek mythology
17 Some farm machinery
18 To the point
19 Personae non gratae
20 Gets in on the game
21 Must pay
22 Often-repeated line
23 Cup holders
25 Things you must choose, it's said
26 Sort
27 Lose-lose
29 Spanish muralist José María __
30 Infrequent ending for URLs
31 Sign of age
35 Part of a watch that holds the face's glass cover
37 __-dieu
41 Like hippies, by nature
43 Thickening agent in cookery
45 Seriously hurt
46 Recipient of a Mailer-Daemon notice
47 Saucy name?
49 Eventually

50 Gives meaning to
51 Slippery
52 Puerto Rican home to the Western Hemisphere's largest radio telescope
53 Open to everyone
54 Sides of blocks
55 Corpus Christi, e.g.

DOWN

1 Shooter's target in soccer
2 Passage between buildings
3 Gather with difficulty
4 "Understand?"
5 Brainstorm
6 Bleachers blaster
7 Unwelcome comeback
8 Amazon rodent
9 Athlete among athletes
10 Harangue
11 Décor features
12 Heraldic emblem of Scotland
13 Guarantor
14 Overlook, as a fault
24 Not wasted
25 "L'Arlésienne" suite composer, 1872
28 1975 Best Musical, with "The"
31 Open-sided shelters
32 Distracted, maybe
33 More severe
34 "Evita" lyricist

35 It may be a write-off
36 Mississippi River explorer
37 Turpentine is distilled from it
38 Philippine strongman __ Duterte
39 Become slippery, in a way
40 Heartfelt
42 Kind of roast
44 Singer Clark
48 Baja bears
49 Places where black-eyed Susans grow

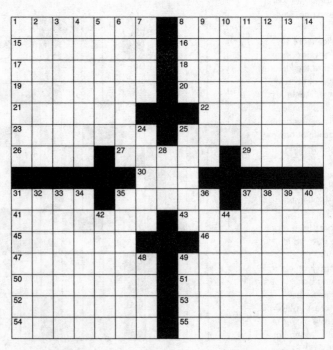

by Roland Huget

ACROSS

1 Road movie producer?
8 Brokerage famous for its "spokesbaby"
14 It'll give you a break
16 Movie villain modeled after Ernst Stavro Blofeld
17 "Nailed it!"
18 Home of the Red Cross
19 Overplay a part
20 Fields of energy
22 −1, for sine: Abbr.
23 Small drinks
24 Unwelcome kind of message
25 Terse refusal
26 "Was ist ___?"
27 Where Manila is
28 Apple apparatus
29 Unit of brilliance?
30 Aussie girl
31 Out for a week or two, say
34 Tie-ups
35 Flight attendants point them out
36 Mañana preceder
37 Hat features
38 Natl. Women's History Month
41 Really long
42 Sweet, in scores
43 Story with many parts
44 Mars, but not Earth
45 Long-distance call?
46 Seltzer, e.g.
47 With 9-Down, Spanish leaders?
49 Like "Roma," to Romans
51 It can dirty your Windows

52 Rears
53 Fulminated
54 "Easy peasy"

DOWN

1 Count (on)
2 Lack of oomph
3 Razor sharpeners
4 Weighs, in a way
5 Manitoba tribe
6 Lab grp.
7 Famous introduction that was never actually used
8 Mystery prize
9 See 47-Across
10 "Star Wars" villain Kylo ___
11 Mass number
12 From on high
13 Korean compact
15 Not right, sarcastically

21 Ginny's brother, in the Harry Potter books
24 They may have images of Mozart and Cervantes
25 Some University of Virginia undergrads in 1969, for the first time
27 1972 top 10 hit that ran for 7+ minutes
28 Markers
29 Garçon's offering
30 Snail trail
31 Rain forest menace
32 Chase with a drink
33 Household brand famous for its infomercials

34 Austin Powers's car with a portmanteau name
37 Dad ___
38 Rep. Waters of California
39 Set of priorities
40 Like AB negative among blood types
42 Treated, in a way
43 Might
45 Time long ago
46 Units of wire thickness
48 "Who ___?"
50 Italian possessive

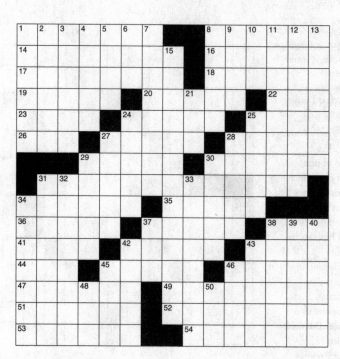

by Steve Overton

ACROSS

1 Begin at the beginning?
9 Fiery
15 Launch of April 1968
16 Set free
17 Staple of a barbershop shave
18 Onerous
19 Seed of a strawberry or sunflower
20 National bird of Trinidad and Tobago
22 Jules or Jim, in "Jules et Jim"
23 "So ___!"
24 Two stars, perhaps
25 Very old school
26 Milky Way maker
27 Mom and pop business?
29 Half of a black and tan
30 Danger for a hiker
31 Fast-food order placed millions of times a day worldwide
32 Separate, as strands of hair
34 It's got teeth
37 Greyhound destinations?
38 Drivel
39 O'Neill contemporary
40 Take some courses
41 Fitting coffee order on a submarine?
42 Ruin
43 Stopwatch ticks: Abbr.
44 Reprimand gruffly

45 Character of book and film who was born John Clayton III
47 Uranus or Neptune
49 Number one advocate?
50 Gothic architecture feature
51 Davy Jones's locker, with "the"
52 Spot almost halfway through a course

DOWN

1 Epithet meaning "great soul"
2 Momentous
3 Absent
4 Fixes
5 It's all the same
6 Victor at Brandywine
7 Forerunner in a race?
8 Income for general expenses?
9 Skydivers' aids
10 Bright camp wear
11 Deli supply
12 Like the Golden Horde
13 Koan contemplator
14 Trim
21 Subservient sort
24 Running around with one's hair on fire
25 Abbr. in a bibliographic citation
27 Kids, typically
28 Runs, for instance
30 Runner's place

31 Relative of a cod
32 Ship's capacity
33 Physics class project testing impact safety
34 Refuse work?
35 One way to look
36 "Are you kidding me?!"
37 Passed the dessert?
38 "___ Carey," 9x platinum 1990 album
41 Bob who narrated "How I Met Your Mother"
43 Scout uniform part
44 Lived
46 Bad spot
48 Staple of modern sci-fi movies, for short

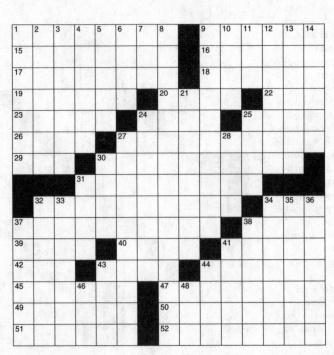

by Mark Diehl

ACROSS

1 Alternatives to olives
7 Went for a run
13 Spanish spread
14 "Told ya!"
15 More affected
16 Drill setting
17 Part of many arena names: Abbr.
18 "Sign me up!"
20 Situation with no up side
21 Evidence of a hard landing
23 Not bogus
24 Michael who directed the 2015 film "Blackhat"
25 "That makes two of us"
27 Spooky grp.?
28 Like some sent documents
29 Moving between male and female
32 Sore helper
33 Old baseball mascot with a "C" on his cap
35 Toaster components
38 Major beef source
41 Blue
42 Big name in 1990s hip-hop
44 Like white panthers
45 Co-Nobelist with Yitzhak and Shimon
47 2002 Grammy nominee John
48 Popular nail polish brand
49 School once headed by Mies van der Rohe
51 21st in a series of 24
52 Neighbor de Ibiza
54 Add subtly
56 Used up
57 "Hel-l-lp!"
58 Makeup problems
59 Past the point of caring

DOWN

1 Swift writings
2 It has four tusks
3 Shows disregard for privacy
4 Discovery magazine subj.
5 Unidentified gossip source, often
6 French philosopher who wrote "Reflections on Violence"
7 Greet with disdain
8 Abbr. before a colon and a name
9 Potent pot component, for short
10 Impetus for a colonial "party"
11 Wolverine's cousin
12 Hinge
14 Instagram and such
16 Major uncertainty
19 Classified key to success
22 Onetime host with 11 Daytime Emmys
24 Fared
26 Just sits
28 Who's there
30 Green on the silver screen
31 Party server
34 "Always one of a kind" sloganeer
36 One of a White House couple until 2017
37 Dish often garnished with white radish
38 Salivation stimuli
39 Flamethrower option
40 Radiator protector
43 Big name in disposable tableware
45 Crocheter's collection
46 Rene of "Nightcrawler"
49 Vulgarian
50 Bulgarian, e.g.
53 Big Apple airport code
55 "___ changed"

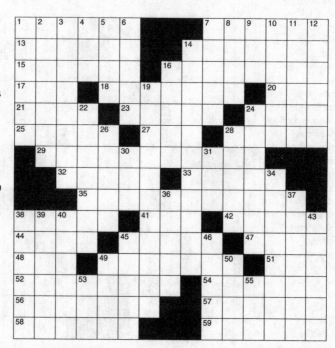

by Zhouqin Burnikel

ACROSS

1 Meal maker?
7 "Vamoose!"
13 Fats Domino's real first name
15 Skin-care brand
16 Austrian treats
18 Put down hard
19 Rows
20 Barbershop staple from "The Music Man"
22 Shiraz setting
23 Ones putting down quadrels
24 Practice composition?: Abbr.
26 Whole note, to a Brit
28 Port on Ishikari Bay
30 Friends
32 SpaceX head Musk
33 Sibling trio in "Hamilton"
37 "Would ___?"
38 One might be a "n00b"
39 Dry runs, e.g.
41 Commonsensical
45 Cartoon word often seen with a lightning bolt
46 Channel swimmer Gertrude
48 ___ floresiensis (extinct "hobbit")
49 Day of doom, in Scandinavian mythology
51 "It's déjà vu all over again" speaker
52 Sea seen from Ithaca
53 Destination proclamation
55 Fifth of eight parrying positions in fencing
56 Wearying work schedule
57 Equilibria
58 Call of Duty tally

DOWN

1 French anise-flavored liqueur
2 Uncut
3 Flow
4 Flow stopper, of a sort
5 Preserves covers?
6 Memphis-to-Nashville dir.
7 Big character in children's literature
8 Very much
9 Lead-in to méxico
10 Poet Sara who wrote "I Shall Not Care"
11 Shaking like a leaf, maybe
12 Runner's ___ (marathoner's woe)
14 Title actress on Netflix's "Unbreakable Kimmy Schmidt"
17 Early Mercedes-Benz racing car
21 Part of Sherlock Holmes's attire
23 Part of a merry refrain
25 Goes for the bronze?
27 Believe
29 Some pyramids, though not the ones at Giza
31 Drawn-out campaign
33 ___ bath
34 Leave en masse
35 Historical name of the Iberian Peninsula
36 Kakuro calculation
40 Group of 100 people
42 Bothered terribly
43 "Jackpot!"
44 Ta-Nehisi who wrote the best seller "Between the World and Me"
47 Builders of the original Legoland
50 Generates, with "up"
51 Reduce in force or intensity
52 They're high at M.I.T. and Stanford
54 About to explode

by Ryan McCarty

ACROSS

1 They may make the rounds
5 Lounging wear
15 Coat color
16 Question often asked after twirling
17 Some O.K.'s
18 Rambo sort
19 Word with hatch or room
21 Coffee shop freebies
22 Many a Wall St. hire
23 Fracking target
24 Circumspect
25 Amazon icon
26 Saint's place
28 Pastel shade
29 Low-___ diet
30 "O" follower
31 Part of Wayne Manor
35 Request to Dad, maybe
36 Like a pact with the Devil
37 Modern-day home of the classical poet Hafez
38 Jobs in tech
39 Subject of a 1984 mockumentary
44 Flag
45 Spill something
46 First name in country
47 Part of an embassy address, for short
48 "Oh, darn!"
49 Edible seed of a pumpkin or squash
50 Some baby talk
53 Rostrum
54 1983 hit with the line "She's been living in her white bread world"
55 Look at on the beach, say
56 College application components
57 Backpacker's pack

DOWN

1 "Gunsmoke" actor James
2 Kind of pork
3 Antic
4 Marked down
5 One going everywhere on foot?
6 Peso : Mexico :: ___ : Korea
7 Baby animal in a parable in II Samuel
8 Esteem
9 Sycophant
10 Figures usually held in one's head
11 Like
12 Movie with the Oscar-winning song "It Goes Like It Goes"
13 Patriot leader
14 Book of celestial maps
20 Bedsheet material
24 Abraded
25 Bop
27 Bandmate of Micky, Peter and Michael of the Monkees
28 Bloodshed
30 Co-star of Ferrell in 2003's "Elf"
31 Laugh heartily
32 Benedict X, but not IX or XI
33 "Tonight Show" house band
34 Arm that's tucked away
35 Copy illegally
37 Thin tablet
39 Nancy's friend in the comics
40 Sycophant
41 Ranking system of a sort
42 Verdi opera set in the fifth century
43 Particle beam weapon
45 Rodeo sight, informally
48 Female whales
49 Buds
51 Caught
52 Kaplan book subj.

by James Mulhern and Ashton Anderson

88

ACROSS
1 Wine barrel sources
5 Enhance
10 Handouts, with "the"
14 Old competitor of Bikini Bare
15 Audible sign of age
16 Flanged support
17 Things analyzed in dendrochronology
19 Bean in a pod?
20 Desperately wish
21 Von Rothbart's daughter, in ballet
22 New Age retreat in Big Sur
23 Paradise is next to it
25 Diamond cutter?
26 Holiday pie ingredient
27 Now-regulated growth regulator
28 Mr. Moneybags types
29 One-named singer with the 2013 top 5 hit "Gentleman"
30 Standing out
31 Dreadful date, maybe
34 Lifeline providers
35 Jazz Fest setting, informally
36 Dollars for quarters?
39 Card count in ombre
40 Annual event covering about 1,000 miles
41 It might contain a discography
42 Rats' hangouts
43 Like some harsh weather
45 People bond with it
46 Was similar to
47 Lack of pressure
48 Many a nature walk
49 Big intro?
50 Producers of highlights
51 "Get Yer ___ Out!" (1970 live album)
52 "Love is not ___" ("Tears on My Pillow" lyric)

DOWN
1 Worthy of notice
2 Some whipped creams
3 Kids' game with a ball
4 A.F.C. North player
5 Follow, as a lead
6 It may put you to sleep
7 Activity requiring a crash course?
8 Company with striking footwear
9 Sanctions
10 Jeweled headwear
11 Do a 28-Down for
12 One of the Teletubbies
13 Cline who wrote the 2011 best seller "Ready Player One"
18 End with speed
21 Running gold medalist Steve
24 Some hospital work
26 The Secret Service dubbed her "Radiance"
28 See 11-Down
30 Cocina and baño, e.g.
31 Combination undergarment
32 Bosom buddy
33 Routine
34 Foyer furniture
35 Brand once advertised with "Take it off. Take it all off"
36 Like tailgates and trapdoors
37 Beck album with the alternative hit "Where It's At"
38 Handle badly
39 Goose, e.g.
41 Botanical trunks
44 Karaoke stand-in?
46 Be worth it

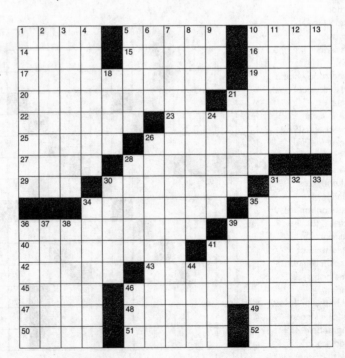

by Stu Ockman

ACROSS

1 Given the short end of the stick
8 Prone
11 What many Brits don't spell "realize" with
14 500, e.g.
15 Natural energy source
17 Designer behind the Dolly Girl perfume
18 Really stress
19 Wind sounds
20 Strong connection?
21 Locale in "Do the Right Thing"
24 Where the Shannon flows
25 One may be straight
26 Put down
29 Disconcert
32 Spirit
34 Excessively sentimental
35 No more
36 Trim, in a way
38 Own (up)
39 Tapes, maybe
41 Impudence, slangily
42 For the taking
43 Bacchanals
45 Flower girl, sometimes
47 Like a control freak
48 Classic sitcom sign-off
52 Big appetite
55 House shower
56 H&M competitor
57 Providers of limited coverage?
59 Noodge
60 1983 song that begins "Hate New York City"
61 Only word spoken in Mel Brooks's "Silent Movie"
62 Back again
63 "That's no challenge"

DOWN

1 Rogue
2 Tower of ___ (classic math puzzle)
3 Desi Jr. of the 1960s group Dino, Desi & Billy
4 His assassination sparked W.W. I
5 Tarboosh feature
6 Coin introduced by Louis IX
7 ___ gratia
8 Famed Indian burial site
9 Took for a fool
10 Food processors, informally
11 One involved in monkey business?
12 Titular Salinger girl
13 Puma prey
16 Campaign of flattery
20 Humorous as opposed to strange
22 Wished could be undone
23 Key
27 Place to pray
28 Where Molson Coors is TAP
29 Feeling that everyone's having fun without you, in modern lingo
30 More than conjecture
31 Place of outdoor meditation
33 Tennis's Petrova
37 ___ Vogue
40 Harbor seal
44 Dieter's piece of cake?
46 Crackpot
49 Trouble in the night
50 Catches in the act
51 Retract
52 Skiing great Lindsey
53 Nondairy spread
54 Newbie
57 Jot
58 1969 Peace Prize agcy.

by Damon Gulczynski

ACROSS

1 Noodle house noodles
5 Checkout counter option
15 The opposing side
16 "Attention!"
17 Mother in "Hairspray"
18 Optimist's mantra
19 Time out?
20 Becomes well known
21 "Take THAT, sucka!"
23 It "will find a way," according to Virgil
24 Fraternité fellows
25 Some hard rock
26 What's the matter?
28 Western tribe
29 "The Simpsons" sycophant
31 "Duuude"
32 "Man will do many things to get himself loved, he will do all things to get himself __": Mark Twain
33 Certain two-wheeler
36 Cable channel that once won a Four Freedoms Award for freedom of speech
37 Early showings
39 __ latte
41 Easternmost of fashion's "Big Four" cities
42 "Kanthapura" novelist Raja __
43 "A __ should not mean / But be": Archibald MacLeish
44 Lean
45 Foo Fighters founder Dave
47 Paragons
50 Disney queen voiced by Idina Menzel
51 Mozart's "Il Re Pastore," e.g.
52 Unit of work
53 Sexennial event
54 Cultural leader?
55 Bad-mouths
56 What seeds often have

DOWN

1 Investments often associated with CDs
2 "Yikes!," quaintly
3 Economist who shared a Daytime Emmy with Jimmy Kimmel in 1999
4 Master of strings
5 Ballet move
6 "Kiss Me Deadly" rocker
7 Guru residences
8 Is closefisted
9 Nail-biting
10 "__ Dinka Doo" (theme song of Jimmy Durante)
11 Place to celebrate the Autumn Moon Festival
12 Turned into
13 Estée Lauder fragrance for men
14 Some inheritances
22 Baba ghanouj ingredient
27 Typical Snapchatter
28 Strong recommendation
30 Soap-making equipment?
31 A new computer program may be in it
33 Source of sodium in the wild
34 Study of the atmosphere
35 "Uh-huh . . . ri-i-i-ght"
37 Kind of deposit
38 Classic Stanislaw Lem sci-fi novel
39 Mini maker, originally
40 Capital that's home to Last Chance Gulch
41 City and county of central California
43 German toast
44 48-Down subgroup
46 Help for users
48 University department, for short
49 Freelancers' enclosures, for short

by David Phillips

ACROSS

1 Filing station?
10 Bookbag part
15 Kept sacred
16 Public speaker's asset
17 2016 film that won Best Picture
18 Photo app, slangily
19 It's a little less than a pound
20 Where to stick a needle
22 NASA project launched in 1973
25 Shifted, in a way, as a skirt
26 CNN host Burnett
28 Fairy tale sister
31 Posts an intentionally mysterious status update on social media
35 Estadio cheer
36 Swelling
37 "In case it's of interest . . ."
38 "Mosses From an Old ___" (Hawthorne short story collection)
40 Grind
41 Kobe Bryant made it 15 times
43 Geek Squad company
46 Court painter of Charles IV of Spain
47 Title Roman tribune of an early Wagner opera
49 Hanna-Barbera feline
53 Elvises in Las Vegas, e.g.
56 Chocolate/caramel candy
57 Show on which Key and Peele got their start
58 "Promises, Promises" writer
61 Member of the working class
62 Putting teeth into
63 More sheltered
64 Furniture and such onstage

DOWN

1 European textile city that gave us the word "denim"
2 Actress Aimée
3 Common wedding dress color
4 Flooring option
5 G, in the key of C
6 Mahershala ___, Best Supporting Actor for 17-Across
7 Internet annoyances
8 Lead-in to -wise
9 Business meeting?
10 Things seen on a bookshelf
11 Mandarin or Mandingo
12 Like someone who invests in volatile stocks
13 Piedmont city famous for its sparkling wine
14 Three follower, in sports
21 A couple words?
23 Bailiwick
24 Lobster catcher?
27 Dimensions without planes
29 Lohengrin's love
30 Regard
31 Win, lose or draw
32 Together, in music
33 Deep-sixes
34 "Thimble Theatre" surname
38 Part of a club
39 Not without consequences
41 Not-so-distant relative
42 What may have a strong net effect?
44 "i" dot
45 Oregon State mascot
48 Woman's name meaning "peace"
50 Funny
51 And no one else
52 Blacksmith's tool
53 Little rascals
54 Actress Kate of "House of Cards"
55 Search
59 Cut (off)
60 ___ Lankan

by Andy Kravis

ACROSS
1 Contemptible sort
4 One may be cast-iron
9 "No ___!"
13 From quite a while back
16 Hard to get hold of
17 What can't hold still during lectures?
18 1960s TV character who says "Aw, shucks"
19 Kind of walk
20 Plant-monitoring org.
21 Bear trap fearer
22 Intriguing meeting
24 Breakdance maneuver
26 Midsize bra parts
28 Bunch of, informally
29 Braggadocio
33 Comparatively bright
35 Vituperate
36 Lace place
37 Free Wi-Fi, e.g.
39 Little beefs?
40 Links words
41 Ancient theater
43 Wickedness
45 Largest Italian seaport
50 Score symbol similar to a tie
51 Miss, for instance
52 Città about 250 miles SE of 45-Across
53 In prime condition
54 Summer cooler
58 Certain Confucian compilation
59 Sci-fi transporter
60 Links

61 Site of Hercules' first labor
62 Square root of nove

DOWN
1 Change into something else
2 Hours-long meal
3 ___ good (amazing)
4 Pitches
5 Gamboling place
6 Connection letters
7 Nursery rhyme girl
8 "Challenge not accepted"
9 Supervised
10 Climactic scene in the Eminem film "8 Mile"
11 Competitor with a map and compass
12 Pub game
14 Concert lineup
15 Out of juice
23 Capital of Georgia
24 What "O" may symbolize
25 Doing away with
27 Site that reviews 44-Down products
29 Outlet for artisans
30 Cousin of tartar sauce
31 Judge's call
32 Juice extraction device
34 Longtime Knicks nickname
38 "Challenge accepted"

39 "Wasn't I right?"
42 Certain PC storage area
44 See 27-Down
46 Conclusion preceder
47 Really lean
48 Astrologer known for annual forecast books
49 "Storage Wars" channel
55 Historic vehicle, briefly
56 Dudgeon
57 Shooting grp.

by David Steinberg

ACROSS

1 Perennial loser
8 Event featured in every Summer Olympics
14 Automatics lack them
16 Captured by cameras, maybe
17 Pasta with ribs
18 "Charmed" actress Milano
19 Touch
20 Washington insider, informally
21 Alongside
22 Singing ability, informally
24 Protective garment
26 S.&P. rating
27 Made objections
30 Pet
31 Pier group?
34 High tops?
35 Traditional holiday meals
36 Extraction targets
37 Nullifies
38 Greek vowel
39 Southwest language
41 Classes
45 Short-legged item of furniture
47 Montreal is part of it: Abbr.
50 Playwright who wrote "Hell is full of musical amateurs"
51 Grammys competitor
52 Fully ready
54 Musical with the song "Beauty School Dropout"

55 Advance copy sent to a critic
56 Mailroom device
57 Brand sold by Sears

DOWN

1 Throw away
2 Whodunit story?
3 Managed to find
4 Chartered financial institutions
5 Do one's part
6 Martial arts film hit
7 Number-picking game
8 Popular backache remedy
9 Blue arm
10 Moon of Pluto discovered in 2012
11 Pair in "Carmen"
12 Flight destination?
13 Beach grass that prevents erosion
15 Optimists' discoveries
23 Fabric with diagonal lines
25 Rostand who wrote about Cyrano
28 Onetime owner of Skype
29 Opposite of spread out, as a paper
30 Alpha Centauri, for one
31 From now on
32 ___ regni
33 Large, shallow pan
34 Fink's portrayer in "Barton Fink"

35 IDs tied to one digit
39 "Siddhartha" novelist
40 Web-footed creature
42 Vinyl enthusiast's need
43 Breathless
44 Delivered an oath?
46 Turin-based automaker
48 Pawn
49 Stories that might not be true
53 Winter home, perhaps

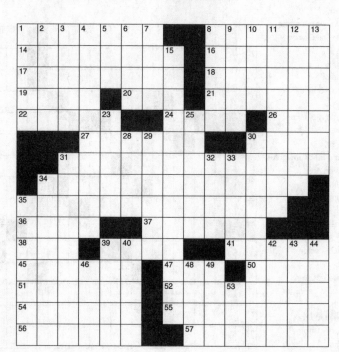

by Patrick Berry

ACROSS

1 Incredible, in modern slang
11 Veep between Al and Joe
15 Diminishing returns?
16 By and by
17 Like Nafta
18 Blazed
19 The Tritons of the N.C.A.A.
20 & 21 U.S. Open champ of 1985-87
22 Seat in Parliament?
24 Least naive
25 Deplorable
28 Deplorable
31 Maker of Friskies
33 The Wasp and Black Widow, for two
36 Boston Tea Party leader
37 Lets go
38 Capital whose name means "city inside rivers"
39 Sweetheart's brothers?
41 It's moved by a keystroke
42 Cantaloupe, by another name
44 Pull (out)
45 Gives a lot of unwanted attention
47 Tree line?
49 Mammals that may weigh up to 12,000 pounds
50 Tea Party, e.g.
52 "PT 109" actor Robert
56 Cheese, for some
57 Excessive desire for wealth
59 Problem to face?
60 Celebrity affair, maybe
61 Crib
62 Digital barrage

DOWN

1 W.W. II's Battle of ___
2 Podcaster Maron
3 Japan was a member of it
4 Video game character rescued by Link
5 Spacewalk, for short
6 Castro overthrew him
7 Alternative to "Sincerely"
8 Turkey bacon?
9 Something to float
10 Show for which Louis C.K. unsuccessfully auditioned in '93
11 Sweetener in a health food store
12 By some measure
13 Hammock holders
14 Prepared to confess sins, say
21 Traditional rite of passage among the Masai
23 Scours
24 2014 U.S. Women's Open champion
25 Beauty spots
26 Lamborghini owner
27 "The Fast and the Furious" activity
29 Oscar nominee for "The Great Dictator"
30 Major employer of pharmacists
32 Offers as a sacrifice
34 One that can only go straight
35 Part of a pedigree
37 Watt per ampere squared
40 A.T.M. deposits: Abbr.
41 Throw together
43 He said "He who knows does not speak; he who speaks does not know"
45 Desperately, informally
46 Lords of film
48 Slight
50 Ruined, in a way
51 Like a five-star hotel
53 Backup software option?
54 Trust buster?
55 Conceal cleverly
57 Rose Bowl setting, for short
58 ___ adelante (later on: Sp.)

by Zachary Spitz

ACROSS

1 Many consultants, for short
5 Flash
9 Wayne's friend in "Wayne's World"
14 Waterway whose construction began in Rome
16 Word repeated before "to you and you and you," in a show tune
17 Emphatic parental turndown
18 "Ciao"
19 Words from one about to break into tears
21 Master of ___
23 Cards
24 "Ain't that the worst!"
25 Add oil to, maybe
26 Sleep phenomena
30 "___-Ami" (Guy de Maupassant novel)
31 Jessica of "The Texas Chainsaw Massacre"
32 Frequent fodder for crossword clues
34 Believer in spirits
36 Trapped
37 Bit of finger food
38 Stirs
39 Lady Gaga's "___ It Happens to You"
40 Place for barnacles
41 Dispense
43 ___ Martin, French firm since 1724
44 Formally approve, as a document, old-style
46 No worries
47 "Mo Money Mo Problems" rapper
51 Early Indus Valley settler
52 Devotee of Mötley Crüe or Megadeth
56 Spike who directed "Being John Malkovich"
57 Player of a drug kingpin on "The Wire"
58 Puts money on the table, say
59 One-named singer with the 2016 #1 hit "Pillowtalk"
60 Plan, for short

DOWN

1 Dudes
2 Dude
3 Quarterback's asset
4 Involved with
5 "___ the Virgin" (CW show)
6 Behind closed doors
7 DraftKings competitor
8 They might be wished for at fountains
9 Polka forerunner
10 1949 Hepburn/Tracy courtroom film
11 Initiation practice
12 This puzzle's constructor, for one
13 What words can do, in an admonishment
15 Christmas decoration
20 Is forbidden to
21 Faddish dance move done to the 2015 hit "Watch Me"
22 Facebook Chat status denoted by a green dot
24 Arizona ballplayer, casually
25 Nationalism, per Einstein
27 Modern requests for participation
28 Dr. Evil's sidekick in Austin Powers movies
29 "Sorry to say . . ."
31 Marcel Marceau persona
33 Dorm V.I.P.'s
35 Topic in feminist film criticism
36 Something prohibited by the Ten Commandments
38 Island in San Francisco Bay
42 "Do You Hear the People Sing?" musical, to fans
43 Outbreaks of eczema, e.g.
45 Great scores in Olympic diving
46 Lawful ends?
47 State bordering California, informally
48 Press
49 Peer ___
50 Reclined
53 They're game
54 Half a Hamilton
55 Pop

by Paolo Pasco

ACROSS

1 Time-tested
8 Being tried
13 Pouring one's heart out at a coffee-house?
15 Lead female role on Netflix's "House of Cards"
16 Sweepstakes exhortation
17 Radiance, in England
18 Exhibit flexibility
19 Biting words?
21 Descend upon en masse
22 "What is ___ ?"
23 Wearer of an "H"-inscribed hat
24 Snapchat's ghost, e.g.
25 Pluto, to Saturn
26 Home to the Museum of El Greco
27 Lieutenant of 1970s TV
28 "___ Fancy has been quelled": Longfellow
29 Awesome successes
31 Attempt to establish an online connection
34 What some caddies carry
35 The ___ Store
36 Smoother, now
37 Much-mimicked entertainer
39 Budgeter's concern
42 Dodgers' pursuers
43 Like H-U-M-O-U-R
44 Monastery head
45 1950s song syllable
46 Major port near the Persian Gulf
47 Sticks in the mud
48 Maker of hospital cuts
50 Airport monitor
52 Hard-wired
53 Words next to an X
54 Heavens
55 Key

DOWN

1 Slip preventers
2 Shore line?
3 Reach
4 Manual sequence
5 Rockefeller Center muralist
6 Actor Hunter or singer Hunter
7 Sports stick
8 Application to a cut
9 U. 2's?
10 Cartoon avatars on Snapchat
11 Confident to a fault
12 Some athletic footwear
14 Certain social media notifications
15 Big role for Liz Taylor
20 Bistro offering
23 Fail to be
24 Big-box store founded in 1946
26 Seminary study
27 Single-serve coffee holders
28 Sportscaster Rich
30 Cry of exasperation
31 Bit of sports fan paraphernalia
32 Show for which Laurie Metcalf won three Emmys
33 Ocean areas
34 Does not disturb
38 Competitor of Mt. Olive
39 Drive like hell
40 Ankh-holding deity
41 Baby blue, e.g.
43 Be adequate for
44 Word before or after green
46 Over and under, e.g.
47 Michael who directed "The Insider"
49 Fire
51 Sensitive conversation topic

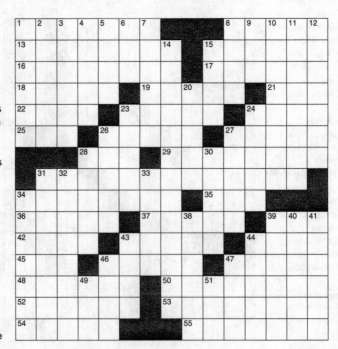

by Zhouqin Burnikel

ACROSS

1 Award for "Hairspray" but not "Hair"
12 Some party hirees
15 Famous 1980s movie quote
16 Breakfast morsel
17 XXX, for example
18 Land in la mer
19 A goner
20 Platform locale: Abbr.
21 Texting app that was so 2012
23 Tequila sunrise direction
24 "Ten ___ Commandments" (song from "Hamilton")
25 Response to an affront
26 Parisian crowd?
27 Burl who sang about Rudolph
29 Evidence of a change of mind
33 Grooms
35 Lug nut hiders
36 Have as emergency backup, say
37 Crosses the threshold
38 Dispute settler, maybe
39 Caution
40 Like some myths
41 Fire's need
43 ___ Decor (Hearst magazine)
44 Alternatives to lumps: Abbr.
48 Like some divorces
49 "O, ___ the day!" (exclamation from Miranda in "The Tempest")
50 Intimate
51 Lead-in to duct
52 Oversee to a fault
55 Home of Paradise: Abbr.
56 Bluntly honest
57 Rock band?
58 Dangerous situation

DOWN

1 The Divine Miss M
2 Guiding beliefs of a people
3 Jack ___
4 "___ Colors Don't Run" (flag maxim)
5 Big name in Champagne
6 College, in British lingo
7 Aesthetically pleasing
8 "Big thumbs-down!"
9 Some lipstick shades
10 Word from a Latin lover
11 Lamb Chop puppeteer
12 Question from the unwilling
13 Sriracha ingredients
14 Reversal of a 29-Across
22 Lawyer's need
24 Roller coaster features
26 Bolshevik's target
28 Figs. in a 3-2-4 format
29 Muse (on)
30 Have a hot body
31 Meddling
32 Dramatic parts
33 Aplomb
34 It may be carved in stone
36 Coppola film family name
38 Fill with crayons
40 Big showcase prize on "The Price Is Right"
42 Body fluid
44 Dovetail component
45 Support for a garden plant
46 House aides
47 Vessel opener
48 Little bit of MSG?
50 Breaches
53 U.N. worker protection grp.
54 Tucson hrs.

by Robyn Weintraub

ACROSS

1 Heating system network
6 "Jeez, why don't you just mind your own business?!"
14 Floored
15 Gain with little effort
16 Its first cover, in 1970, said "Dynamite Afros"
18 "Rests one's eyes"
19 Grammy category
20 Class of fliers?
21 Fragrant biblical gift
23 It passes Luxor Temple
24 1984 Summer Olympics star
26 Setting after resetting
27 Ayn Rand hero
28 Players rush for them: Abbr.
29 Amalgamate
31 In a darling way
33 Fuzzy food
34 First name on "Keeping Up With the Kardashians"
35 Pair on a table at a nice restaurant
37 Orange side
38 Stuff "tested" in the 1960s' Acid Tests
41 "Close one!"
42 When Supreme Court sessions start: Abbr.
44 Overturn
46 European capital
47 "Don't worry about it," slangily
49 Octavia's "others"
50 Trap during a ski trip, say
52 Sunset, e.g.
54 Basketball tactic
56 Rings
57 ___-Carthage International Airport
58 Eschews overnight shipping?
59 How you might feel after finishing this puzzle

DOWN

1 Like some religious laws
2 Not backed up
3 Haunted house sights
4 Most affectedly dainty, to a Brit
5 Political century: Abbr.
6 Firebird alternative
7 Rapper with a role in the 2015 film "Dope"
8 Eli Manning's team, on scoreboards
9 Certain congregation leader
10 Hackers' helpers
11 C. S. Lewis piece?
12 Through bribery
13 Hole near a tongue
15 Recess rhyme starter
17 2015 N.F.L. M.V.P.
22 Measurement in a celestial coordinate system
25 Boo-boo
30 One lighting up the dance floor
32 It can crawl or fly, but not walk
33 Dinar spenders
35 Selena Gomez or Eva Longoria, e.g.
36 Hyatt hotel line
38 Fitness legend Jack
39 Adds to the pot
40 Least happening
41 Ready
43 Crashes into, in a way
45 Parted with
48 Family planning options, briefly
51 Roberts of romance
53 Pond juveniles
55 Verizon purchase of 2006

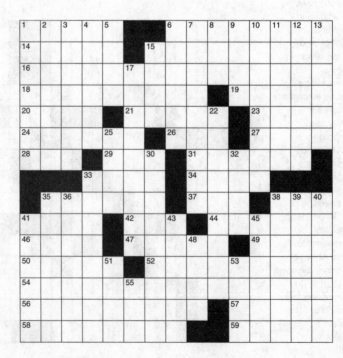

by Erik Agard

ACROSS

1 Some undergrad degs.
4 Plans nefariously
9 Rout
13 "That's a shocker"
16 ___ number
17 Labor market short on long-term work
18 Gunn of "Breaking Bad"
19 3-year-old in 2015 sports news
21 "Sorta"
22 Ahead of, old-style
23 Like pawns and puppets
26 Point guard, e.g.
32 Historic "restructuring"
35 Grp. with the 1976 platinum album "A New World Record"
36 Nova Scotia's Grand ___ National Historic Site
37 Who said "All I need to make a comedy is a park, a policeman and a pretty girl"
38 Bass part
39 Ellipsis alternative, maybe
40 Quaint evening reading material
42 Low-level computer work
44 Like many indie films
45 Chafe
46 It appears at the top of a page
48 Autocrat known as "the Liberator"
57 What fish or chicken can be, but not turkey
58 They're light-years away
59 Nuisance
60 Band featured in the mockumentary "The Great Rock 'n' Roll Swindle"
61 Seizure
62 White Cloud competitor
63 ___-mo

DOWN

1 N.Y.C. racetrack, informally
2 Level
3 Learned
4 Doggy
5 Chinese tennis star who has won both the French and Australian Opens
6 Go crazy with, in a way
7 Many a sub
8 Teammate of Hammerin' Hank in 22 All-Star Games, with "the"
9 The N.I.H. is based in it
10 City near Pyramid Lake
11 Bone involved in pronation
12 Eliciting a "meh"
14 Pooh-pooh
15 Longtime TV procedural
20 Fendi rival
23 Hiked
24 Maker of the iComfort line
25 At attention
26 Brooklyn art institute
27 Horse or gazelle, at times
28 The ___ School (Manhattan dance institution)
29 Sour, fermented milk drink
30 "Burnt Norton" poet
31 "The Daily Show" correspondent Chieng
33 White of the eye
34 Like ingrates
41 Object of a scout's search
43 Modern travelers' marketplace
46 Black
47 Food figs.
48 "Modern Family" rating
49 Brand
50 Cantatrice's delivery
51 C.F.O., e.g.
52 Love letters
53 Datum for a secy.
54 Some old fire trucks
55 "___ do"
56 Playground rejoinder

by Damon Gulczynski

ACROSS

1 Double-digit figure?
10 See 20-Across
15 Spider producer
16 Lacking dexterity
17 Untouched
18 Reform?
19 Colosseum greeting
20 National beverage of 10-Across
21 Scratch
22 Apple field
24 Not thought out
26 Christmastime musical/comedy stage show, in England
27 Input
29 "You don't have to tell me twice!"
31 Bit of Disneyana
33 Floor
34 Cult follower?
35 Mace-wielding DC Comics superhero
39 Joint
41 Actress Ortiz
42 Bullet point
44 Put away
45 Unembellished type
48 Skip the lines, say
52 On-line jerks?
53 Draft picks?
55 0, for 0 degrees
56 Toward el sol naciente
57 Brisk pace
59 Title for Queen Isabella: Abbr.
60 Mushroom added to udon soup
62 Expert on the drums?
64 Third-longest river in Africa
65 Get through lines quickly
66 Rumble in the night
67 1966 album ranked #2 on Rolling Stone's "500 Greatest Albums of All Time"

DOWN

1 It's a matter of taste
2 Number of sides on a loonie
3 Make a difference to
4 Monopoly token since 2013
5 Eight-year presidencies, e.g.
6 Kind of cell
7 "Don't worry about me"
8 Beginnings
9 San Francisco's ___ Valley
10 Good name for a personal trainer?
11 Winter coat
12 Yearly
13 Smartphone home screen option
14 High degree of proof?
23 "Darn it!"
25 Covers for locks
26 Party animal?
28 Not paying attention
30 Dance with strong percussion
32 Behind
35 Old stars
36 Who wrote "We do not see things as they are, we see them as we are"
37 "Interested in one of my tickets?"
38 Enemy captain in 2009's "Star Trek" film
40 Pharma supply
43 Collection of favorites, of a sort
46 Position in Quidditch
47 Relative of a skunk
49 "Now see here . . ."
50 Encroachment
51 Things studied by pogonologists
54 Branching-out points
58 Rumpus
61 Cause of an explosion
62 Picking things up?
63 Word on une bouteille de vin

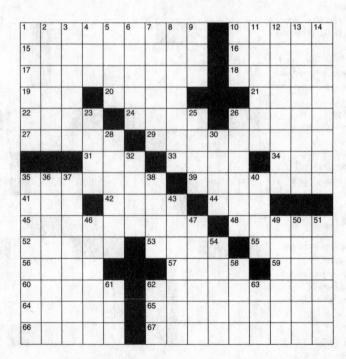

by David Phillips

ACROSS

1. "Not much at all for me, please"
10. Bare
15. Director Michelangelo
16. Big name in movie theaters
17. What gets the shaft?
18. Struck, as by God
19. *Basketball area
20. Unlike Iago
22. *100%
23. Not run, maybe
25. Co. that introduced Dungeons & Dragons
26. Cane material
28. Abhorrent
30. Symbol of modesty
32. *Water cooler
33. British critic Kenneth who created "Oh! Calcutta!"
34. Women, old-fashionedly
36. Bit of flimflam
38. Third-place candidate in the 1920 presidential election who ran his campaign from jail
39. Skiing mecca
43. *Submerged
47. Outwits
48. Alternative indicator
49. Ageless, in an earlier age
50. Portmanteau food brand
52. Microscopic messenger
54. Sets (on)
55. *Had charges
56. Pizarro contemporary
59. Cousin of a cistern
60. Messed (with)
62. Many British mathematicians
64. Came (from)
65. So that one might
66. Wood fasteners
67. Revolutionary invention for restaurants?

DOWN

1. Something good to hit
2. Asleep, say
3. What an agoraphobe does
4. Big load
5. Symbol of life
6. Daisies and the like, botanically
7. Stable colors
8. Even or close to even, in a tennis set
9. Circlegraph shapes
10. '14s in '14, e.g.
11. Lead on
12. Relatives of guinea pigs
13. Grind
14. Product that might be used with a blessing
21. Like "Have a nice day," for example
24. Takes off
27. Nearly
29. Left over
31. ___ of the earth
34. Gets set
35. Feudal thralls
37. Table leaves?
39. Target, in a way
40. Like Europe in 1945
41. Cry in hide-and-seek
42. Image
44. Those who should follow the advice in the sounded-out answers to the five starred clues
45. Wikipedia precursor
46. Uses for support
49. Grill, e.g.
51. Words of explanation
53. Cramming aid
57. ___ Zátopek, four-time Olympic track gold medalist
58. Delta 88, e.g., informally
61. Paris's Avenue ___ Champs-Élysées
63. Money of Romania

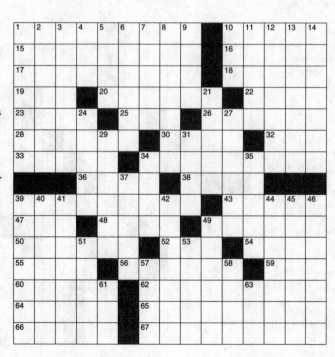

by Matt Ginsberg

ACROSS

1 Back order?
7 Main means of defense?
15 First city bombed in W.W. II's Baedeker Blitz
16 Opted to duck
17 1954 Audie Murphy western
18 Prom amenity
19 It comes with lots of extras
21 "Every hero becomes a ___ at last": Emerson
22 W's is 74
23 Not hunched over
24 Biased writing?: Abbr.
25 Pounded side
26 Scrooge's portrayer in "The Muppet Christmas Carol"
27 Soul
28 Pens
30 Jaguar, for one
31 Classic brand in men's apparel
32 Occur
33 Occur
36 Christ the ___ (Rio de Janeiro landmark)
40 Grace
41 Small, round and shiny
42 Letters on some overseas packages
43 Person taking drugs
44 Dark green?
45 Automotive plural selected in a 2011 promotion
46 Court position
47 They're off on casual Fridays
49 ___ chicken
51 Indignant denial

52 Frozen treat with Alexander the Grape as one of its flavors
53 2010 U.S. Open winner McDowell
54 Setting of the Levant
55 Tito's successor as head of the Non-Aligned Movement

DOWN

1 Superman accessory
2 Apply to
3 Of pions and kaons
4 When clocks are set back for the end of daylight saving time
5 Pi Day celebrant, perhaps

6 Late October to March, in West Africa
7 Malaria enlarges them
8 It might be in a jam
9 Not satisfied
10 Midori on ice
11 "White Christmas" singer, informally
12 Beyond silly
13 Obama descriptor
14 Show reverence to, in a way
20 Called out
26 Deceive
27 "Revelations" choreographer
29 Expert in facial recognition?
30 Recall reason
32 They may be stoked

33 Jazz legend who turned the Benny Goodman Trio into the Benny Goodman Quartet
34 Worship
35 Cornmeal mush
36 It often comes with a "Thank You"
37 Devil dogs
38 Height
39 Whoop it up
41 Unpaid mine workers
44 One of two components of the drug Sinemet
45 Some athletic shoes
48 Manhattan's ___ D. Roosevelt Park
50 A heavy metal band may have it

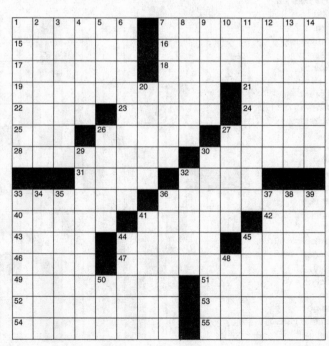

by Byron Walden

ACROSS

1 Winning smile, e.g.
6 International cricket event
15 Too-familiar
16 Road built during the Samnite Wars
17 Press conference segment
18 Game ender, possibly
19 Working for
20 Republican who won Bentsen's vacated Senate seat
21 Band with a person's name
23 1970 Kinks album title starter
24 Afternoon reception
25 Orange growers
26 Joe who was retired in 1997
27 Folk medicine plant
29 Music genre prefix
30 Clears the mind, with "up"
31 Chow
33 Chase off
34 "Things Fall Apart" novelist
37 Escort, as to the door
38 What the name "Rhoda" means
42 Trying minors
43 What repellent might prevent
45 New Deal program, for short
46 Heady feeling
47 She and Clark Gable were known as "the team that generates steam"
49 Surrounded with foliage
51 Impressive, as accommodations
52 Player of Sal in "The Godfather"
53 Call to mind
54 "Don't decide right away"
55 Parties with mai tais, maybe
56 Titan's home
57 Shrill cries

DOWN

1 British P.M. when W.W.I began
2 One who's unseated?
3 Land line?
4 Tribal bigwig
5 Claw
6 Five-time N.C.A.A. basketball champs from the A.C.C.
7 Uniform ornament
8 Thwarts for petty reasons
9 Add color to
10 1968 novel set in Korea
11 Opposed to the union, say
12 Couple
13 Performer on the road?
14 Note books used in church?
22 Stevedore's burden
26 Gentle murmur
28 "Music should strike fire from the heart of man, and bring tears from the eyes of woman" speaker
30 Undercover item?
32 Exercise target
33 Begin planning the nuptials
34 Way to walk while conversing
35 Fall apart
36 Fallen star
37 How Congress might adjourn
39 Major error in soccer
40 "Louder!"
41 Seal classification
43 Magna Carta's drafters
44 Without doubt
47 Largely hollow bricks
48 Flo Ziegfeld offering
50 Erase

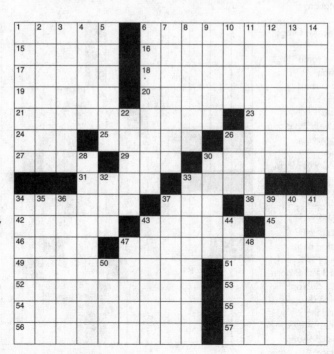

by Patrick Berry

104

ACROSS

1 1993 hit with the lyric "Keep playin' that song all night"
8 Credit
15 Gross, to a toddler
16 Blue dress wearers
17 A guillotine is used to remove them
18 Good with
19 Cause for cardiological concern
20 Something to hop on
22 Not cut, say
23 Took to the ground?
25 Shed material?
27 Friday, e.g.
31 Successor to Gibson on "ABC World News"
34 It's in general circulation
35 Oriente
36 Subject for Gregor Mendel
37 Shows some emotion
40 End up short
41 Ends up short, maybe
43 Grp. with the motto "Deo vindice"
44 Seeking
46 1957 Dell-Vikings hit
49 Paris Hilton, e.g.
50 [Why me?!]
54 Area of need
56 It's feedable
58 Speaker of the house, perhaps
59 Famed kicker born with a clubfoot
61 Fashion designer behind the fragrance Rock Me!
63 Hydrocortisone producer
64 Gets on the line?
65 ABC's first color program, with "The"
66 Big spinning effort

DOWN

1 Tow bar
2 Place for une faculté
3 "See what I'm talkin' about?"
4 What often comes with a twist?
5 Sch. with a Hartford campus
6 Sweets
7 Nez Percé war chief
8 Org. that endorsed Obamacare
9 He hit 106 more home runs than Barry Bonds
10 Like "Zorba the Greek" novelist Nikos Kazantzakis
11 Concern for a lifeguard
12 Concerning
13 Think piece?
14 Abbr. before a year
21 Take in more
24 Take in less
26 What you see here
28 Some-holds-barred sport
29 Audi model retired in 2005
30 "So sweet was ___ so fatal": Othello
31 It may be submitted to an architect
32 México lead-in
33 Meanie's lack
38 ___ speak
39 Cousin of a jaguarundi
42 Gets hot
45 Infusion aid
47 Jordache alternative
48 Literary son of Jenny Fields
51 "Orfeo" composer Luigi
52 Wear during re-entry
53 It's known for its varieties
54 Setting of "Love Me Do": Abbr.
55 Need to tan
57 Standout
60 Real Salt Lake's org.
62 Tortoise's beak

by Tim Croce

ACROSS

1 First rock band whose members received Kennedy Center Honors
7 Jiffy
11 Shade of black
14 Fix, in carpentry
15 Undoubtedly
17 Dropped a line?
18 Olympians' food
19 Figures for investors
20 Animal that catches fish with its forepaws
21 Ward on a set
22 Shade of gray
24 Work __
25 Annual with deep-pink flowers
28 Miles off
30 Tailor
33 Part of the Dept. of Labor
34 All-Star Martinez
35 "Guys and Dolls" composer/lyricist
37 Like dirty clothes, often
39 Secondary: Abbr.
40 The muscle of a muscle car, maybe
42 Soup scoop
43 Fill
44 ABBA's genre
46 "Alice" actress Linda
48 Kyrgyzstan's second-largest city
49 Game discs
53 Uncopiable, say
55 Quick session for a band
57 Springsteen hit with the lyric "Only you can cool my desire"
58 Noted graffiti artist
59 Viking, e.g.
60 Philosophize, say
61 Strike leader?
62 Breather
63 Trained groups

DOWN

1 Sights at the dentist's office
2 Three-time Olympic skating gold medalist
3 Georgia of "The Mary Tyler Moore Show"
4 1955 Pulitzer-winning poet
5 Rushed
6 Maxim
7 Pot and porn magazines, typically
8 Norton Sound city
9 Diplomat who wrote "The Tide of Nationalism"
10 Reform Party founder
11 Legitimate
12 Construction project that began in Rome
13 Rush
16 "Yeah . . . anyway"
23 Ultra sound?
26 Boolean operators
27 Charging things?
29 Ensnare, with "in"
30 "It wasn't meant to be"
31 Literally, "the cottonwoods"
32 Those with will power?
36 Exactly 10 seconds, for the 100-yard dash
38 Spanish greeting
41 Tending to wear away
45 Illogically afraid
47 Draw (from)
50 Actor Werner of "The Spy Who Came in From the Cold"
51 Heroic tale
52 Lid afflictions
53 Cleaner fragrance
54 They're sometimes named after presidents
56 Squat

by Brendan Emmett Quigley

106

ACROSS

1 Fictional amnesiac portrayer
10 Out
15 Mix and match?
16 Total
17 Identifies with
18 Old computing acronym
19 Head Start program service, briefly
20 Some drillers, for short
21 Prefix with gram
22 Stay (with)
23 Turned on a friend, maybe?
24 Painting surface
28 Proscribed
30 Destination in the "Odyssey"
32 "No need to go on"
37 Without embellishment
39 Vitamin in meat, milk and eggs
40 Resolve a bromance spat, say
42 Crime scene sight
43 Muscle Beach sights
45 Backs
46 Garden decorations
50 Evade
52 2007 horror sequel
53 It may be hard to reach
54 Fool
58 1970s subcompact
59 Member of a medical minority
61 British running great Steve
62 Start of a Dickensian request
63 Clipped
64 Emulate Ferris Bueller

DOWN

1 Dealer's amt.
2 Parrot
3 Communications leader?
4 Big Indonesian export
5 "Silent Spring" topic
6 Gland: Prefix
7 Costumed figure
8 Suleiman the Magnificent, for one
9 Modernists
10 Difficult sort
11 Addition
12 Common subject of medieval art
13 Blank ___
14 Title role for Charlton Heston
22 Election-related nonprofit since 1990
23 Cymbal sound
24 "Mystic Pizza" actress Annabeth
25 Dramatic accusation
26 Cut with more than one layer
27 Bit of Bollywood attire
29 Mac
31 Base for some incense
33 Dry
34 Tynan player in "The Seduction of Joe Tynan"
35 "Severn Meadows" poet Gurney
36 Retreats
38 "Delish!"
41 Presentation by Bill Clinton in 2007 or Bill Gates in 2010
44 Cores
46 Sensitive subject?
47 Green
48 Sports league V.I.P.
49 Paws
51 Tawdry
53 They're a handful
54 What might put you through your paces?
55 Minor opening?
56 Wave function symbols
57 Suffixes with mountain and cannon
60 Grp. involved in the Abbottabad raid

by John Lieb and David Quarfoot

ACROSS

1 Food item resembling an organ
11 Not long-departed
15 Question after a public shellacking
16 Plutoid just beyond the Kuiper Belt
17 Many a detective film cover-up
18 Squire
19 Lack of authorisation?
20 "Casablanca" carrier
22 It really stands out
25 Be loud at a funeral, say
26 Many 56-Across users
29 It may have check marks
30 General exercise?
31 Stretches out
35 "We're in trouble now!"
36 Abbr. on a sports ticker
37 Topics at some religious retreats
41 Cousin of a screwdriver
44 Largest city in the South Pacific
45 Go back on
46 Six bells in the morning watch
49 Prefix with geek
50 Hand picks?
52 Monogram of the author of "A Charge to Keep: My Journey to the White House"
55 Kind of block
56 It replaced the Indian rupee in 1932
60 Winnipeg's ___ Franko Museum
61 Ithaca is at its southern end
62 Be inclined
63 His Secret Service code name was Providence

DOWN

1 Classic name in New York delis
2 Subject precursor
3 Like some eggs
4 Intro to Euclidean geometry?
5 Letter abbr.
6 Casual assent
7 As
8 Weena's race, in fiction
9 Generally speaking
10 Big name in video streaming
11 Five and ten, e.g.
12 Ticketmaster info, maybe
13 Coloring
14 Compact first name?
21 Formation on 28-Down
22 About 186,282 miles
23 Marathoner Pippig
24 NASA's Aquarius, e.g.
26 Done some strokes
27 Routine reaction?
28 See 21-Down
32 Home of the Black Mts.
33 Crow relatives
34 Stock mover
38 Shrimp
39 Midas's undoing
40 Katana wielder
41 Curt
42 Beauregard follower
43 GPS abbr.
46 Cheerleader's move
47 Relative d'un étudiant
48 Many an animal rights activist
51 Baseball Hall-of-Famer who played for the Giants
52 Bother, with "at"
53 After-life gathering?
54 Backwoods relative
57 Starting device: Abbr.
58 Code word
59 Publisher of World of Work mag.

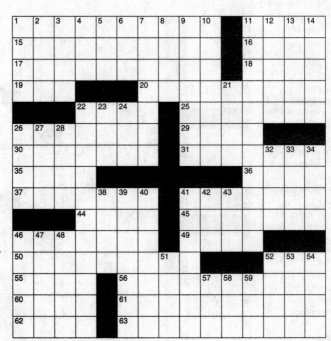

by Barry C. Silk

ACROSS

1 Bar fixture
4 Person who might suit you well?
15 Start of many a "Jeopardy!" response
16 Transported
17 Org. with an Office of Water
18 "Poor Little Fool" hitmaker, 1958
19 Danny who composed the theme music for "The Simpsons"
21 Eponymous Dr. Asperger
22 Onetime Michael Jackson bodyguard
23 Benders
24 Sight on a "Hee Haw" set
25 Hindu god often depicted with a bow and arrow
26 A choli may be worn under this
27 "Star Trek: T.N.G." role
28 Name on the cover of "Yosemite and the High Sierra"
29 Verb suffix?
30 Ancient scribe's work surface
32 Treadmill runners, maybe
34 "Sex is an emotion in motion" speaker
37 Not reliable
39 Empire State tech school
40 "Pride ___ before destruction": Proverbs
42 Be uncooperative
43 Showroom window no.
44 Discipline
45 European hub
46 Show stoppers?
47 Leipzig-to-Zurich dir.
48 Columnist Collins
49 Was triumphant in the end

50 Inventor's undoing?
53 Mineralogical appendage?
54 Avatar setting
55 Base man
56 Image on Utah's state quarter
57 Baker's dozen for the Beatles, for short

DOWN

1 Tree also known as a sugar apple
2 "You've got to be kidding!"
3 Perfectly
4 Wedding rings?
5 Have ___ (be advantageously networked)
6 Secret attachment, for short
7 South Bend neighbor

8 Court group
9 Dominick who wrote "A Season in Purgatory"
10 Some Snapple products
11 Conan O'Brien's employer from '88 to '91
12 1899 painting used to promote gramophones
13 Massive, as a massif
14 National service
20 Internal investigation, for short?
24 Hybrid menswear
25 Grasped
27 Texas Ranger Hall of Fame and Museum site
28 Many are blonde
30 Among
31 Enjoy the moment

33 Copier giant absorbed by the Kyocera Corporation
35 Appear suddenly
36 Track consultants
38 Banana Republic defender, maybe
40 Ersatz blazer
41 Speaker of Shakespeare's "If music be the food of love, play on"
43 Calculus calculation: Abbr.
45 Like some gruel
46 Pioneer in cool jazz
48 Mapped item
49 "Marjorie Morningstar" novelist
51 Got out of the way
52 Head of state?

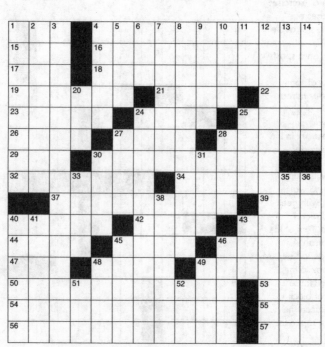

by Brad Wilber and Doug Peterson

ACROSS

1 Where Union Pacific is headquartered
6 Chinese ___ (popular bonsai trees)
10 Medieval drudge
14 Sister of Castor and Pollux
15 Fighter getting a leg up?
17 Site of Tiberius' Villa Jovis
18 Page on the stage
19 Comfortable
21 Taking place (in)
22 One-point throws
24 Appliance sound
25 Checkers, for instance
26 Play critic?
28 Hype
32 Onetime Arapaho foe
33 Grooming tool
36 Vietnamese holiday
37 O-shaped
38 Priest in I Samuel
39 Dread Zeppelin or the Fab Faux
41 Sports div. that awards the George Halas Trophy
42 Gold Cup venue
43 Quote qualification
44 Coin of many countries
45 Pretension
48 Get more inventory
50 Country whose flag is known as the Saltire
54 Bubble handler?
55 Foundation devoted to good works?
57 Uniform
58 Bag lady?
59 Less often seen
60 Deep black
61 Twist
62 America's Cup trophies, e.g.

DOWN

1 Broadway musical with two exclamation points in its name
2 They might have bones to pick
3 Like characters in a script
4 Some wetlands wildlife
5 Miyazaki film genre
6 Hosp. record
7 Creates an account?
8 Fast-food debut of 1981
9 Go along effortlessly
10 Vending machine drink
11 What to do when you have nothing left to say?
12 Peace Nobelist Cassin
13 Dance-pop trio Right Said ___
16 Symbol of happiness
20 Off the mark
23 English Channel feeder
27 Bad line readings
29 Launched the first round
30 Narcissistic one
31 Hand-held "Star Trek" devices
33 Sea creature whose name means "sailor"
34 Huxtable family mom
35 Surgical cutter
40 Gondoliers, e.g.
44 Like a poli sci major, maybe
46 Woodworking tools
47 Underhanded schemer
49 American Airlines hub
50 Drink served in a masu
51 Zodiac symbol
52 Palindromic man
53 "My man!"
56 Plaintive pet sound

by Patrick Berry

110

ACROSS

1 Title trio of a 1980 Pulitzer winner
16 One-on-one with a big shot
17 Gist
18 French preposition
19 "Just what I need"
20 Stamp purchases
23 "Cool dad" on "Modern Family"
24 Hill minority: Abbr.
28 Top honors for atletas olímpicos
29 They're often taken on horses
30 Happening
31 ". . . we'll ___ a cup o' kindness . . .": Burns
32 First name in Harlem Renaissance literature
33 Quail
34 Winged it
37 Napkin material
38 Son of 30-Down
39 "___ wise guy, eh?"
40 Very little (of)
41 A quarter of acht
42 Second-largest city in Nicaragua
43 Tree-hugger?
44 Youthful and fresh
45 Longtime late-night announcer
46 Breakout company of 1976
48 Spearfishing need
49 Moment's notice?
56 Vetoes
57 Some government checks

DOWN

1 It might tell you where to get off
2 Sch. founded by a Pentecostal preacher
3 Turn down
4 Dances around
5 Dangerous things to weave on
6 Ballparks at J.F.K.?
7 Her, to Henriette
8 Grabbed some sack time
9 Self-confidence to a fault
10 Vehicular bomb?
11 Romance novelist's award
12 Looking ecstatic
13 One of the Romneys
14 New Deal inits.
15 Snicker bit
20 Home of Sanssouci Palace
21 Wind River Reservation native
22 Hiawatha's grandmother in "The Song of Hiawatha"
23 Philatelist's concern, briefly
25 Clean type
26 Lab growth need
27 Designer Gabbana of Dolce & Gabbana
29 Stamp purchase
30 Father of 38-Across
32 Limoncello ingredient
33 K. J. ___, 2011 Players Championship champion
35 Univ. in Manhattan
36 Smaller cousin of a four-in-hand?
41 100 bits?
42 San Diego suburb
44 Russian retreat
45 One trying to avoid a banking crisis?
47 Loss from a guillotine
48 They're issued to cruisers, briefly
49 Little chances?
50 Fruitcake
51 It's H-shaped
52 First year of the Liang dynasty
53 "Kung Fu" actor Philip
54 Part of U.S.S.R.: Abbr.
55 Charlotte-to-Raleigh dir.

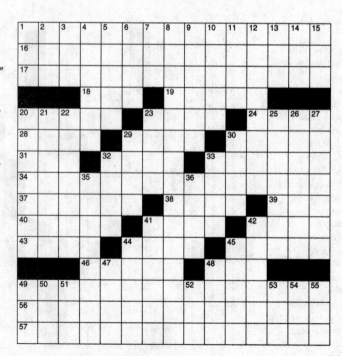

by Chris A. McGlothlin

ACROSS

1 Fighting
6 Amscray
10 They get taken easily
14 ___ Road (W.W. II supply route)
15 Hospital bed feature
16 Nail
17 Circular side?
19 Unisex name meaning "born again"
20 Many a security point
21 Straight
23 Form of "sum"
24 Sound name
25 Tom who won a Tony for "The Seven Year Itch"
26 Ones keeping on their toes?
29 The City of a Hundred Spires
31 Triage determination
32 Home of "NerdTV"
35 Line of rulers
37 Big game plans?
39 Argument-ending letters
40 Short distance
42 Occasions for bulldogging
43 Hot-and-cold menu item
45 Mathematician Cantor who founded set theory
48 Going without saying?
49 Aid in getting back on track
52 Means of reducing worker fatigue
54 Kraft Nabisco Championship org.
55 Color also known as endive blue
56 Classic Hitchcock set
58 Quiet place to fish
59 Suffixes of 61-Across
60 Rich of old films
61 Contents of some ledges
62 "___ Wedding" ("The Mary Tyler Moore Show" episode)
63 Occasioned

DOWN

1 Flat, e.g.
2 Fixes flats?
3 Hospital patient's wear
4 See 5-Down
5 With 4-Down, lost control
6 Feature of some western wear
7 Pathfinder?
8 Reagan was seen a lot in them
9 Word after who, what or where, but rarely when
10 Things driven on construction sites
11 Anti-inflammatory product
12 Authorities might sit on one
13 Wonderful
18 Kind of wheel
22 One putting the pedal to the metal
24 Summer symbol?
27 One of the Eastern elite
28 Aviation safety statistic
29 Straightaway
30 Manhattan choice
32 Broken into on TV?
33 Kind of lab
34 Nemesis of some dodgers: Abbr.
36 Fellow chairperson?
38 Use a 24-Down
41 Like pigtails
43 Talks tediously
44 Hacker's achievement
45 American company whose mascot has a Cockney accent
46 Diamond flaw
47 Diagonal rib of a vault
50 One getting cuts
51 Early: Prefix
53 Exit lines?
54 Ethnologist's interest
57 254,000 angstroms

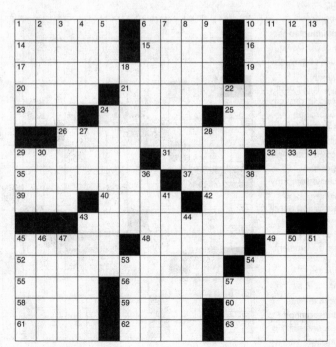

by Dana Motley

112

ACROSS

1 Baker's predecessor
5 "The Daily Rundown" carrier
10 Steinbeck siren
14 Vindaloo accompaniment
15 Admission about a story
16 Skillful, slangily
17 Brother's keeper?
20 In thing
21 In place
22 What one should take in: Abbr.
23 Engagement rings?
25 Muhammad, e.g.
27 Ready for another round
28 Packer in a bookstore
31 Young turkey
32 Strong order?
35 Compliment to the chef
36 Drawers hitting the pavement?
42 County whose seat is La Junta
43 Means of changing one's mind
44 One way to catch the game
45 Quaint letter-opening abbr.
47 Took the wrong way
48 13th Spanish letter
49 Ear plug?
53 Big inits. in power
54 Remark after holding someone up
57 War head?
58 Thrill
59 Strauss's "Tausend und ___ Nacht"
60 Backwoods agreement
61 Many a Madrileño
62 Walked all over

DOWN

1 Where to observe some workers
2 Napa Valley setting
3 Clipboard's relative
4 One way to fly: Abbr.
5 "Carota" and "Blue II," for two
6 Start of many an operation
7 Trivial objections
8 Blast from the passed?
9 Software box item
10 Peck, e.g.: Abbr.
11 Den mother's charge
12 Tony with an Emmy
13 Like many sonatas' second movements
18 Mad person's question
19 Leave to scrap, maybe
24 Indigent individuals
26 Numbered relations
28 "___ wind that bloweth . . ."
29 Bass parts
30 Legendary spring figure
33 Pier grp.
34 Bras ___ Lake (Canadian inland sea)
36 Rumor opener
37 Agenda opener
38 They're thirsty much of the time
39 What gobs take in
40 The Merry Mex of golf
41 Feeling no pain
46 Jewel cases?
47 Bill with barbs
50 Fruit giant
51 Home of the daily Hamshahri
52 Raiders Hall-of-Famer Jim
55 Coin feature
56 Unlike 38-Down

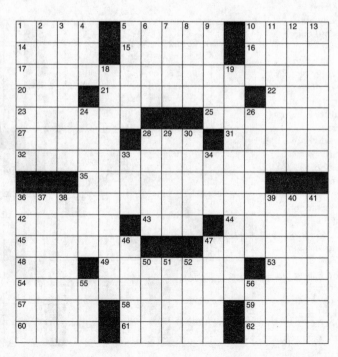

by Ed Sessa

ACROSS

1 Human-powered transport
8 Lingerie enhancements
15 Japanese "thanks"
16 Consumed
17 Like some Mideast ideology
18 Grammy-winning singer from Barbados
19 "___ me later"
20 Barrister's deg.
21 Belief opposed by Communists
22 Hammer and sickle
24 Small arms
25 "Be right there"
29 Labor outfits
30 Bubbly brand, for short
34 Oral reports?
35 Des Moines-to-Cedar Rapids dir.
36 It's known to locals as Cymraeg
37 "Money" novelist, 1984
38 Orange entree, informally
40 Not take a back seat to anyone?
41 Diner freebies
45 Fisherman's Wharf attraction
46 Young colleen, across the North Channel
48 Browns' home, for short
49 Bring to a boil?
52 By the boatload
53 Wastes
55 Cubs' home
56 Improbable victory, in slang
57 Potentially embarrassing video
58 Mezzo-soprano Troyanos

DOWN

1 Quebec preceder, to pilots
2 Meaningful stretches
3 Soft touch?
4 Supermarket inits.
5 Some bank offerings
6 Totally flummoxed
7 Spring figure?
8 Pitcher Blyleven with 3,701 strikeouts
9 Oatmeal topping
10 Close
11 Unit of wisdom?
12 "Little Girls" musical
13 Actress Kirsten
14 Hits with some trash
22 Sporty auto options
23 Torch carriers
25 Capital of South Sudan
26 Old one
27 Her voice was first heard in 2011
28 It's already out of the bag
30 Parts of a school athletic calendar
31 Designer Cassini
32 "Mi casa ___ casa"
33 Segue starter
36 Everything, with "the"
38 Trip
39 Fried tortilla dish
40 Landlocked African land
41 Collectors of DNA samples
42 Hides from Indians, maybe?
43 Chill
44 All-points bulletin, e.g.
47 Final word in a holiday tune
49 Locale for many political debates
50 Perdition
51 Site of the Bocca Nuova crater
54 Poli ___

by Ian Livengood

114

ACROSS

1 Start of a phobia?
5 All the best?
10 Five-time U.S. Open winner
14 Immensely
15 Leisurely
16 Sign of virtue
17 Malted alternatives
20 Be ruthless
21 Run-___
22 Pair of word processors?
23 Instinctive reaction
24 Verbal gem
25 Bygone country name or its currency
28 Safe to push off
34 It springs from Monte Falterona
35 Brush off
36 Place for tiger woods?
37 Get going
39 Not at all sharp, maybe
40 A shot
41 Plant production: Abbr.
42 "Go figure!"
48 One of the muskrats in the 1976 hit "Muskrat Love"
51 Play savior
53 Dual diner dish
54 Stickler's citation
55 "Or else ___ despiser of good manners": Shak.
56 Newton, e.g.
57 Event with body cords
58 Not at all sharp
59 Lands

DOWN

1 Brand of blades
2 Brand of literature
3 Where seekers may find hiders
4 Almost never
5 Go-for-broke
6 Proceeded precipitately
7 IV component
8 Chain of off-price department stores
9 Guzzle
10 Home of the world's largest artificial lake
11 Ground crew gear?
12 Like prairie dogs, notably
13 "Pippin" Tony winner
18 As if scripted
19 "Get the lead out!"
23 Get inside and out
25 Director/ screenwriter Penn
26 "Exodus" character
27 Magazine with an annual "500|5000" conference
28 Likely result of excess 17- and 53-Across
29 Prefix with 36-Across
30 Seemed to be
31 Bit of chiding
32 Not dally
33 "That's fantastic news!"
35 One bound to hold notes?
38 Venom
39 Spot ___
41 Actress Matlin
42 Words of support
43 Do the final details on
44 Not coming up short
45 Frost, to François
46 Human Development Report publisher, in brief
47 About 50% of calls
48 Turnover alternative
49 Tax burden?
50 Measures up to
52 Like many a goody-goody

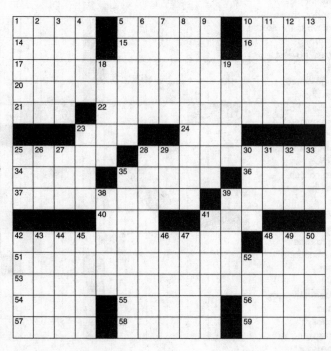

by Frederick J. Healy

ACROSS

1 First female candidate to win the Ames Straw Poll
16 War paths
17 It airs in the morning, ironically
18 Case builders: Abbr.
19 Copy from a CD
20 Understood
21 Show featuring special agents
22 Red Cloud, e.g.
24 Player of the bad teacher in "Bad Teacher"
26 Rear
27 Possible rank indicator
29 Overseas relig. title
30 Big name in car monitors
32 Beat it
34 "Keep dreaming!"
36 Word after a splat
37 Like some lovers' hearts
41 Strikes
45 She may be fawning
46 Colorful cover-ups
48 Brandy letters
49 Grilling test
51 Misses abroad: Abbr.
52 Newborn abroad
53 ___ Hedin, discoverer of the Trans-Himalaya
55 Folman who directed the 2013 film "The Congress"
56 Comcast Center hoopster
57 Alternative to a breakfast burrito
61 Big source for modern slang
62 Some critical comments from co-workers

DOWN

1 Yellowstone setting: Abbr.
2 Odysseus, e.g.
3 Dopes
4 Knocks off
5 Control tower info
6 Re-serve judgment?
7 Female adviser
8 Ill-humored
9 Norwegian Star port of call
10 Old oscilloscope part, briefly
11 Turns over in one's plot?
12 Was reflective
13 Its adherents are in disbelief
14 Formula one?
15 Neighbor of Victoria: Abbr.
21 Top kick, for one: Abbr.
22 Puck and others
23 Some exact likenesses
25 Part of Queen Elizabeth's makeup?
27 Certain league divisions
28 Forerunners of discs
31 Kind of cross
33 They may be returned with regrets: Abbr.
35 458 Spider and F12 Berlinetta
37 Production
38 Definitely
39 Give some space, say
40 Grind
42 Stormed
43 Modern mouse hole?
44 Ring bearer, maybe
47 Emulates Homer
50 Actor Burton
52 Competitor of Lauren and Klein
54 Numerical prefix
56 First name in footwear
57 "Two, three, four" lead-in
58 Org. with a clenched fist logo
59 Org. created right after the cold war
60 MS-DOS component: Abbr.

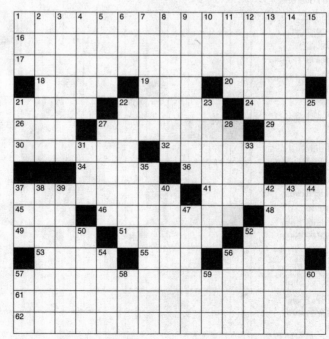

by David Steinberg

ACROSS

1 TV host who won a Best Comedy Album Grammy
12 Vegan lunch option, informally
15 Cry used to pump up a crowd
16 Following
17 Fortune
18 Beast in a Marco Polo tale
19 Old station name
20 Abbr. in a birth announcement
21 Request in pool or beer pong
23 Hudson River school?
25 "Eww!"
27 Soundtrack to many a bomb-defusing scene
28 Prizes given to good docs?
31 "Kazaam" star, informally
32 Crying need?
36 A wedge might come out of it
37 Beast hunted by Hemingway in "Green Hills of Africa"
38 Work set mostly in Cyprus
40 Herbal quaff
42 Wilde wrote "De Profundis" in one
43 Lion runner
45 Unlike a showboat
46 Rash application
47 Reception opening
49 Hull sealer
51 1-Across's home, once: Abbr.
52 Resistance figure
57 Like pickle juice
59 Dated
61 Many a donor, in brief

62 Go around, but not quite go in
63 W.W. II defense
66 Sun ___
67 Fall fallout, some believe
68 Short agreement
69 Scorsese film before "Alice Doesn't Live Here Anymore"

DOWN

1 "The Two ___" ("Chinatown" sequel)
2 Like 1-Across, by descent
3 Quick set
4 "Oh no!"
5 His, modern-style?
6 Roll up and bind
7 Source of the word "alcohol"
8 Glass protector

9 Velázquez's "___ Meninas"
10 Repute
11 Orange and blue wearer, for short
12 It opens during the fall
13 Some trade barriers
14 Nada
22 On the line
24 Dangerous thing to sell
26 Humphries of the N.B.A.
29 Southern site of an 1865 battle
30 Weak spots
32 Wrap session?
33 Slant one's words, in a way
34 Picture with a lot of gunplay
35 Game controller button

39 Cholesterol-lowering food
41 First-choice
44 Hand over (to)
48 Self-titled debut album of 1991
50 Sign at a game
53 "Au Revoir, Les Enfants" writer/director
54 Sporty Lotus model
55 Put one's foot down, in a way?
56 Accord indicators
58 Protection
60 "I ___ tell"
64 1998 Angelina Jolie biopic
65 49-Across source

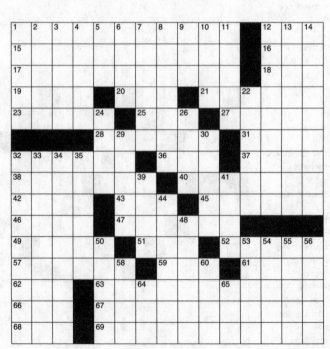

by Josh Knapp

ACROSS

1 Old Hollywood low-budget studios, collectively
11 "Oh, God!" actress
15 Wine bottle contents in Hitchcock's "Notorious"
16 Only event in which Venezuela medaled at the 2012 Olympics
17 Dessert often with cream cheese icing
18 Ironwoman org.?
19 Singer born Eithne Ní Bhraonáin
20 Map inits. created in the wake of the Suez Crisis
21 Now-rare connection method
23 Blather
25 Big name in markers
26 Nitroglycerin, for one
29 Director's alternative to a dolly
32 It was dissolved in 1991
34 Time in TV ads
35 Fused
36 Fortify
38 Domingo, e.g.
39 Onetime TV music vendor
41 Kind of community
43 Avocado relative
45 Ross Sea sights
46 Interrupts
47 Strike out
48 Excoriates
49 "Revolution 9" collaborator
51 It may slip in the back
55 L.B.J. biographer Robert ___
56 One-third of a triangle, maybe
59 Hindi relative
60 The goddess Kali appeared on its first cover
61 Bygone
62 New Jersey childhood home of Whitney Houston and Queen Latifah

DOWN

1 Brownish purple
2 Port where Camus set "The Plague"
3 Fluctuate
4 Brings to a boil
5 Rock in ___ (major music festival)
6 "Coppélia" attire
7 Hit from the 1978 disco album "Cruisin'"
8 More than chuckle
9 Planet first mentioned on "Happy Days"
10 It's used to define a border
11 Colorful dessert
12 Press production
13 Doing a government agency's job
14 Garner
22 Not the party type?: Abbr.
24 Part of 20-Across
25 Substance that citrus peels are rich in
26 Endor natives
27 Site of the last battle of the Cuban Revolution
28 Barriers used in urban renewal projects
29 Ire
30 Get a hint of
31 Party tray array
33 Vexing
37 Country name
40 Releases
42 Baseball's ___ Line (.200 batting average)
44 Prime meridian std.
47 Skip
48 Smallish lingerie spec
49 Electrical units
50 Ordered
52 "You can count on me"
53 Provided backup, in a way
54 Deep or high lead-in
57 Org. with inspectors
58 "A defeat for humanity," per Pope John Paul II

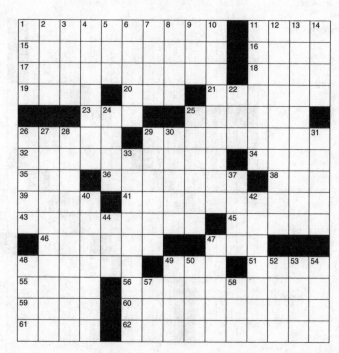

by Brad Wilber and Doug Peterson

118

ACROSS
1 World's tallest building
12 Instagram post
15 One way to cruise along
16 7 a.m. staple, briefly
17 They come out of many mouths
18 Protection from pirates: Abbr.
19 Sets forth thoroughly
20 Trite
22 Guitar maker Fender
23 She's beautiful, per a popular song
24 So-called "weekend pill"
28 Like some liquor stores
29 Like 30-Down
30 Room at the top, maybe
31 Spa treatment, for short
32 Unsurprising outcome
33 Radios, e.g.
34 "Sweet!"
35 Starz alternative
36 Belfast is on its shore
37 Mind
38 Site of the Sibelius Monument
40 Castle's place, initially
41 Took up some of
42 Big time
43 Trepanning targets
44 Some partial appointments
49 Blood
50 Big time
52 It may be cracked or packed
53 "C'est la vie"
54 Co. purchased by Wizards of the Coast
55 Hail Marys, e.g.

DOWN
1 Champion between Holyfield reigns
2 It has "batch" and "patch" commands
3 Not be smooth-talking?
4 Activity with holding and throwing
5 Singer of the 1987 #1 country hit "Do Ya"
6 Buds
7 "I shall not find myself so ___ die": Antony
8 Fictional accounts
9 Text attachment?
10 Bygone yellow-roofed kiosks
11 Forward, back or center
12 Like every Bond film since 1989
13 Virginal

14 Moor
21 Karate trainee in 2010's "The Karate Kid"
23 Agatha Christie's "There Is ___ . . ."
24 Is unable to cut the mustard
25 Form of strength training
26 It'll help you breathe easier
27 Fast flight
28 One in a religious majority
30 Brand on a face
33 Largest river of southern California
34 Norah Jones's "Tell ___ Mama"
36 Not amounting to much

37 "Holy" group in 17th-century literature
39 Something to beg pardon for
40 Ill-paid laborer
42 Something to beg pardon for
44 Not be gratuitous
45 ___ Sant'Gria (wine choice)
46 Servant in the "Discworld" novels
47 Kind of pudding
48 Whole bunch
51 Both Barack and Michelle Obama have them: Abbr.

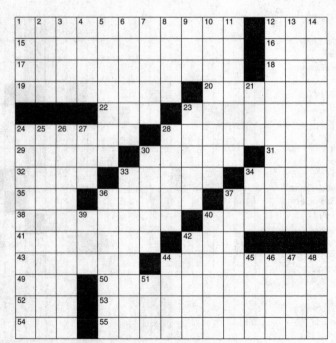

by Julian Lim

ACROSS

1 Holding
9 Way of looking at things
14 Reading light for an audiobook?
16 Detergent component
17 Going nowhere?
18 Pine for
19 Org. always headed by a U.S. general or admiral
20 Baltic native
22 "After ___"
23 Seat cushions?
25 Old airline name
28 Roofing choice
29 "According to reports . . ."
32 Wedded
33 They make a racket
34 Cell alternatives
35 Like each word from this clue
37 Many a time
40 Change places
41 White spread
42 Heavy and clumsy
43 White of the eye
45 The Dom is the third-highest one
46 A whole bunch
49 Blows a fuse
50 Nation with the most Unesco World Heritage Sites
53 Winner over Ohio State in 1935's so-called "Game of the Century"
55 Suez Crisis setting
56 Startling revelation
57 Xerox competitor
58 Buffalo Bill and Calamity Jane wore them

DOWN

1 Hold firmly, as opinions
2 Stuff used to soften baseball mitts
3 Generally
4 Hill house
5 "A whizzing rocket that would emulate a star," per Wordsworth
6 Big name in storage
7 Boortz of talk radio
8 Swinger?
9 Diane Sawyer's employer
10 Land on the Arctic Cir.
11 Most dismal
12 Mouthwash with the patented ingredient Zantrate
13 Shakespearean stage direction
15 Depression creator
21 Crab apple's quality
24 Old-fashioned respirator
26 Not as outgoing
27 Communist bloc news source
30 Experienced
31 Fountain drinks
33 Wrist bones
34 Lamebrain
35 It's not fair
36 Car collectors?
37 Greek salad ingredient
38 They arrive by the truckload
39 Movie trailers, e.g.
40 Carriage with a folding hood
41 Turbine parts
44 Advanced slowly
47 School door sign
48 Amendment to an amendment
51 Southeast Asian language
52 Dark side
54 Ikura or tobiko

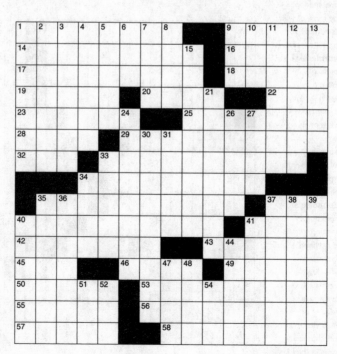

by Patrick Berry

ACROSS

1 Where a lot of dough gets thrown around
11 See 51-Across
15 Fuel for a warp drive engine on "Star Trek"
16 Resignation exclamation
17 Sleep aid, for some
18 BMW of North America and others: Abbr.
19 Zip around a field?
20 Makes happen
21 Assistant played by Bruce Lee
22 Wanting for nothing
24 "Celebrity Jeopardy!" show, briefly
25 Took revenge on
26 Broadview ___, O.
29 Become stiff
33 Get by force of will?
37 Punk's cousin
38 Info about a person's education and work history
39 Smooths
40 Follows a military order
41 Their habits give them away
42 Follows a military order
44 Time of long journées
45 Lets go through
46 Brief albums, in brief
48 Needing hand cream, maybe
51 With 11-Across, biblical woman who met a bad end
53 Board
56 "That gives me an idea . . ."
58 First spaceman's first name

59 Setting for "The Misfits"
61 Polo competitor
62 "My bad"
63 Musical production
64 Symbols of sharpness

DOWN

1 One with promotional potential
2 "___ Steps" (Christian best seller)
3 "10" is inscribed on it
4 Temple imperfection
5 Subject of the 2012 book "Circle of Treason"
6 Porter created by Burroughs
7 Winnebago relatives
8 "Incorrect!"
9 Babes in the woods?

10 Smartphone that preceded the Pre
11 Do the impossible, metaphorically
12 Anxious
13 It's never wrong
14 Standard breakup creation
23 Temptation for Luke Skywalker
25 Follow the sun?
27 Sniffs out
28 First capital of the Last Frontier
30 Like some fogs
31 Ham's handoff
32 Name associated with a mobster or a monster
33 Skyscraper component
34 Brief period of darkness?
35 Eager

36 Event with unmarked choices
43 Trial lawyer who wrote "O.J.: The Last Word"
47 Basidium-borne body
49 Adjective on taco truck menus
50 Crumple
51 "Can't Believe Your ___" (1988 Neil Young song)
52 Drink said to have originated on Lesbos
53 Titles for distinguished Indians
54 Main character in "The Paper Chase," e.g.
55 Cousin of a congo eel
57 Blabbers
60 See, in Santiago

by Jeff Chen

ACROSS

1 Offer to host
8 W.W. II vessels
15 Expressed slight surprise
17 "But really . . ."
18 ___ Empire
19 Deep-seated
20 What you might be overseas?
21 Part of A.M.A.: Abbr.
22 Principal
23 Leave in
24 Rx specification
25 Industry leader
26 Part of a place setting
27 Swelters
28 Absolutely correct
29 Relatives of spoonbills
31 Voyeur
32 Staggered
33 Many chains are found in them
34 Ticked off
35 Works at a museum, say
36 One of the girls
39 Going ___
40 Gnats and mosquitoes
41 Powerful engine
42 Pipe holder?
43 Watch brand once worn by 007
44 One of 24
45 1959 #5 hit with the B-side "I've Cried Before"
48 What a board may be against
49 Euripides tragedy
50 Satyrs, say

DOWN

1 Mountains of ___ (Genesis locale)
2 Strauss opera
3 "Trees" poet
4 Werner of "The Spy Who Came in From the Cold"
5 "In that ___ . . ."
6 Hall-of-Fame outfielder Roush
7 Throws off
8 Flag carried on a knight's lance
9 Blake's "burning bright" cat
10 Pessimist
11 Outmoded: Abbr.
12 Three-time Haitian president
13 Super-wonderful
14 Make more attractive
16 Warriors with supposed powers of invisibility and shapeshifting
22 Ready for an on-air interview
23 "Your mama wears army boots" and such
25 Put a charge into?
26 Leans precariously
27 "L'Arlésienne" composer
28 Workout targets, informally
29 Copycat
30 Long-haired cat breed
31 Simple and serene
32 Fox relative
33 Old arm
35 Pale shades
36 Fought
37 Shot-putter, e.g.
38 Puts in
40 "Positive thinking" pioneer
41 Grounds for a medal
43 Pet
44 Place for a jerk?
46 "Captain Video" figures, for short
47 '50s politico

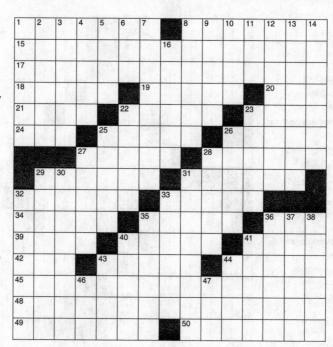

by Mangesh Ghogre and Doug Peterson

ACROSS

1 They aren't straight
6 "Aarrghh!"
13 Shove off
15 Lures
16 "Oo la la!" jeans, informally
18 Preceder of John Sebastian at Woodstock
19 Scott Joplin's "The Entertainer" and others
21 Chain
22 Heralds
24 Produces lush sounds?
25 Heavily populated areas, informally
26 They adhere to brains
28 Temple inits.
29 Lieutenant colonel's charge
30 Students with outstanding character?
31 See 48-Across
32 Its arms are not solid
35 Difficult journey
36 Gifted trio?
37 Follow the party line?
38 Round trip for one?
40 Direction givers, often
42 Superexcited
43 Delicate needlepoint lace
45 Is so inclined
46 Do some work between parties

47 Brings in for more tests, say
48 Fast parts of 31-Across
49 Meteorological probe

DOWN

1 Like wolves vis-à-vis foxes
2 Not at length
3 Takes up onto the surface
4 Susan's family on "Seinfeld"
5 The Father of the Historical Novel
6 Group of football games played at the beginning of Jan.

7 Dog it
8 Pardons
9 Choose in the end
10 Flawlessly
11 Areas next to bull's-eyes
12 Strongmen of old
14 Remedy for a bad leg
17 Fastballs that drop sharply near the plate
20 Durable cover
23 Wise sort
27 2002 Best Original Screenplay Oscar winner for "Talk to Her"
29 Spotted hybrid house pet

30 1980s Olympic star with the autobiography "Breaking the Surface"
31 Grant
32 Geisha's instrument
33 Expelled
34 Pressure gauge connection
35 Mechanic, say
36 Beyond that
37 Shop keeper?
39 "___ Lucy" (old sitcom)
41 Florida's De ___ National Monument
44 Wii ancestor, briefly

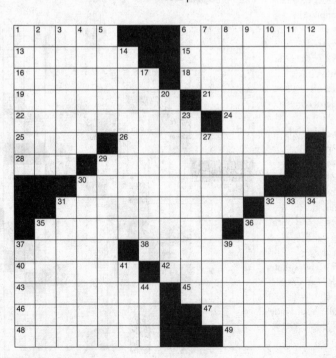

by Tim Croce

ACROSS

1 Begin
10 Donizetti heroine
15 Catches up to
16 Magnetron component
17 Relative of a spouse
19 "Just playin'"
20 Things often dropped in Harvard Yard?
21 Big name in winter vehicles
22 Fixer, perhaps
23 In the way of
24 Phony blazers
25 Birthplace of the Franciscan order
27 "Before My Birth" collagist, 1914
28 ___-yo (cold treat, briefly)
29 With 36- and 39-Across, go from 1- to 61-Across
31 10-year-old Best Supporting Actress
33 Robert W. Service's "The Cremation of Sam ___"
36 See 29-Across
37 Robert W. Service output
38 Soothing flora
39 See 29-Across
41 Bumped into
42 Bumped into
43 Razor target, maybe
47 Pack into a thick mass
50 Ottoman bigwig
51 Tan in a library
52 Anatomical ring
53 Direction de Paris à Nancy
54 Vegan gelatin substitute
55 Stopgap supervisor's duty
58 ___ Montoya, swordsman in "The Princess Bride"
59 Prefixes featured on some maps
60 Baden-Powell of the Girl Guides
61 End

DOWN

1 One known for riding out of gear?
2 Brings out
3 Sends in
4 He'll "talk 'til his voice is hoarse"
5 The Who's "___ Hard"
6 ___ Romanova, alter ego of Marvel's Black Widow
7 Landmark anime film of 1988
8 Many pulp heroes, in slang
9 Picking up skill?
10 Cheerful early risers
11 Preposition on a business-hours sign
12 Unit charge
13 "&" or "@," but not "and" or "at"
14 Restricted flight items
18 By yesterday, so to speak
23 Indication of some oxidation
24 Hug or kiss, maybe
26 Drink brand symbolized by a polar bear
27 39th vice president
30 "The Dark Knight Rises" director, 2012
31 Grammy category
32 What's typical
33 "Lordy!" in Lodi
34 Snow job?
35 Been chosen, as for office
40 One-two in the ring?
42 Pavlova portrayed one over 4,000 times
44 Storied place of worship
45 Eastern lodging
46 "2 Fast 2 Furious" co-star Gibson
48 Grand Caravan maker
49 Jumbles
50 One of Jacob's sons
53 Ser, across the Pyrenees
54 Loads
56 Piece of the street
57 ___-fi

by Peter A. Collins

124

ACROSS

1. Clemson Tigers logo
9. Mistreating
15. Not left hanging, say
16. Draws
17. Mimosas and such
19. Toddler seats?
20. ___ Day (May 1)
21. ___ gratia
22. Become completely absorbed
23. Florida's ___ National Park
25. Rhone feeder
26. It can be found beneath the lower crust
27. "Look ___" (Vince Gill hit)
28. Sauce often served with oysters
32. See 43-Across
33. Beginning of time?
34. Mao's designated successor
35. Snoop Dogg, to Cameron Diaz [fun fact!]
37. Kind of check: Abbr.
38. Coeur ___
39. Capitale européenne
40. Angry Birds or Tetris, e.g.
43. With 32-Across, study of Hesse and Mann, informally
44. W.W. II battle site, for short
45. One might be a couple of years old
46. 2013 women's singles champ at Wimbledon

47. Shows levelheadedness
50. Mobile advertising medium?
51. Hardly like the pick of the litter
52. "Oh man, that's bad"
53. Words after "say" or before "bad"

DOWN

1. Ring accompaniers
2. Like stunt pilots' stunts
3. Headed toward bankruptcy
4. Printer rollers
5. Release a claim to, legally
6. What the French think?

7. Marxist Andrés and writer Anaïs
8. Boom source
9. Centennial, e.g.
10. Good at drawing?
11. Continental abbr.
12. Attention-seeking, say
13. Woodenware
14. Davis of Hollywood
18. Put off
23. Occupy opponent
24. Suffix with hex-
26. Eyeshades?
28. Like a customer who may get special notice
29. Plastic that can be made permanently rigid
30. See red?

31. Corroded
33. Braggadocios
36. Inauguration recitation, maybe
37. Confirmed
39. Ones above military heads
40. Lists
41. "Would that it were!"
42. Former Israeli president Katsav
43. Adorned, per menus
46. Something with round parts?
48. Draw
49. Part of 8-Down

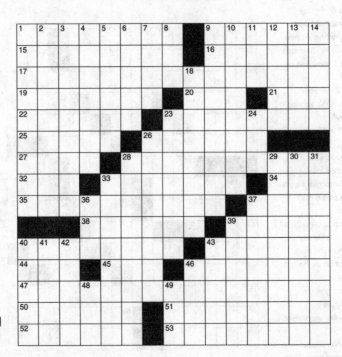

by Joe Krozel

ACROSS

1 Hall-of-Fame rock band or its lead musician
8 It sends out lots of streams
15 Very long European link
16 Rust or combust
17 It flies on demand
18 Skunk, at times
19 Some P.D. personnel
20 One who may be on your case
22 The Spanish I love?
23 What a couple of people can play
25 Stand-out performances
26 Chocolate bar with a long biscuit and caramel
27 Subject of the 2003 book "Power Failure"
29 Without hesitation
30 Subsist on field rations?
31 Its flowers are very short-lived
33 Like a sawhorse's legs
35 Critical
36 Party staple
37 Catered to Windows shoppers?
41 Noodle taxers?
45 Observes
46 Abbr. after 8-Across
48 Last band in the Rock and Roll Hall of Fame, alphabetically
49 "The Hudsucker Proxy" director, 1994
50 Columbia and the like
52 French river or department
53 "___ mentioned . . ."
54 Images on some lab slides

56 Lima-to-Bogotá dir.
57 Frankenstein, e.g.
59 Its passengers were revolting
61 Theodore Roosevelt Island setting
62 Destroyer destroyer
63 Colorful cooler
64 Makeover options

DOWN

1 Like some milk
2 Sashimi staple
3 Changing place
4 Blockbuster?
5 Mediums for dummies, say: Abbr.
6 Where it all comes together?
7 Ex amount?
8 Appointment disappointments
9 Nationals, at one time
10 Flag
11 Tablet banner, say, briefly
12 Reserve
13 Inventory
14 Duped
21 Gradual, in some product names
24 Giant in fantasy
26 Bar that's set very high
28 Physicist Bohr
30 Display on a red carpet
32 Basic solution
34 Without hesitation, in brief
37 Does some outdoor pitching?
38 "Don't joke about that yet"
39 Took away bit by bit

40 Event occasioning 7-Down
41 Cryotherapy choice
42 Artificially small
43 What might take up residence?
44 Truncated trunks?
47 Zero times, in Zwickau
50 Back-pedaler's words
51 About 7% of it is American
54 Vapor: Prefix
55 Apple assistant
58 Lib. arts major
60 Coral ___ (city near Oakland Pk., Fla.)

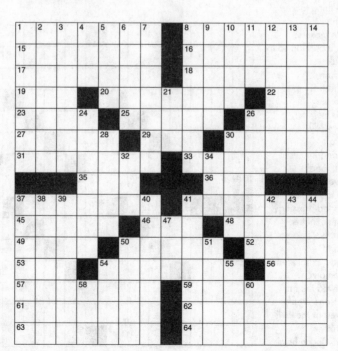

by Bruce R. Sutphin

126

ACROSS

1 It may provide closure in a tragedy
8 Discarded
15 City named for Theodore Roosevelt's vice president
17 Word search technique?
18 Webby Award winner who accepted saying "Please don't recount this vote"
19 With 11-Down, animal called "stubbin" by locals
20 Nascar stat that rises under caution flags
21 Diddly
22 Opening in the computer business?
23 Bad thing to lose
24 Flights
25 Taste makers?
26 Has it bad for, so to speak
27 -i relative
28 Largest city in Moravia
29 Mob member, informally
30 Morale
35 Second in command?
36 Cloverleaf section
37 Flat top
39 Blended dressing?
42 Shutter shutter
43 Literally, "I do not wish to"
44 Sauna exhalations
45 Solomonic
46 Chewed the fat
47 Watson's creator
48 Lowest of the low?
49 Prankery
50 1965 Beach Boys hit
53 Mission

54 Jason Mraz song that spent a record 76 weeks on Billboard's Hot 100
55 Outcries

DOWN

1 Outgoing
2 Lot arrangement
3 Draws
4 Some refrigerants
5 Reinforcement pieces
6 Mantel piece
7 Nissan bumpers?
8 Annual event since 1929, with "the"
9 Hard to pick up
10 Cigarette paper source
11 See 19-Across
12 Author of 1980's "The Annotated Gulliver's Travels"
13 Macedonia's capital
14 "El día que me quieras" and others
16 Large monitors
22 Abandon one's efforts, informally
23 "The Hound of the Baskervilles" backdrop
25 It's around a cup
26 1 Infinite ___ (address of Apple's headquarters)
28 Dover soul
29 Force in red uniforms: Abbr.
31 Course data
32 Palliate
33 Hit hard, as in an accident
34 Tip used for icing
38 They will be missed

39 Lightly hailed?
40 Major report
41 "Yowza!"
42 Hound
43 Dresden decimator of 1945
45 Something beyond the grate divide?
46 Herod's realm
48 1879's Anglo-___ War
49 "Fantastic Mr. Fox" author
51 War on Poverty agcy.
52 Advisory grp. that includes the drug czar

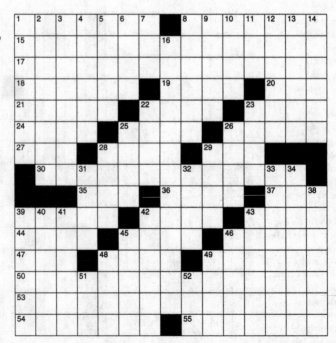

by Byron Walden

ACROSS
1 Forest newcomer
5 Group whose last Top 40 hit was "When All Is Said and Done"
9 To-do list
14 Sound after call waiting?
15 Sense, as a 14-Across
16 Nobel winner Joliot-Curie
17 Turkey sticker
20 "Everybody Is ___" (1970 hit)
21 Response to a threat
22 Old co. with overlapping globes in its logo
23 1960s civil rights leader ___ Brown
25 Katey who portrayed TV's Peg Bundy
27 Benchwarmer's plea
33 Drain
34 Bobby's follower?
35 Fibonacci, notably
36 Hockey Hall of Fame nickname
38 Alternative to ZzzQuil
40 Stat. for Re, La or Ti
41 "___ needed"
43 Papa ___ (Northeast pizza chain)
45 Now in
46 "That subject's off the table!"
49 Luster
50 They have edible shells
51 Whse. sight
53 "Philosophy will clip an angel's wings" writer
56 French class setting
59 Universal query?
62 Uncle Sam, say
63 One featuring a Maltese cross
64 Turkic word for "island"
65 Browser history list
66 Couldn't discard in crazy eights, say
67 Court suspensions

DOWN
1 Relief provider, for short
2 Blasts through
3 "And now?"
4 Sealing worker
5 "Per-r-rfect!"
6 ___-red
7 Alfred H. ___ Jr., founding director of MoMA
8 Like G.I.'s, per recruiting ads
9 Interval
10 Were present?
11 Gets payback
12 Sensed
13 They may be used in veins
18 They may be used around veins
19 All-Star Infante
24 Drone
26 1998 hit from the album "Surfacing"
27 False start?
28 Stockholder?
29 Like some hemoglobin
30 ___-A
31 Plantation habitation
32 Cybermemo
37 Something taken on the stand
39 Ring
42 They're on hunts
44 Revolving feature
47 Revolving features?
48 "Psst . . . buddy"
51 1/20 tons: Abbr.
52 Whence the word "bong"
54 Day of the week of Jul. 4, 1776
55 Wizened up
57 Indiana, e.g., to Lafayette
58 Some use electric organs
60 River Shannon's Lough ___
61 Sudoku segment

by Peter A. Collins

128

ACROSS

1 Angry missive
10 Body parts often targeted by masseurs
15 Trailing
16 Hatch in the upper house
17 Chutes behind boats
18 Treaty of Sycamore Shoals negotiator, 1775
19 Taking forever
20 Antimissile plan, for short
21 Part of Duchamp's parody of the "Mona Lisa"
22 Octane booster brand
24 San ___, Calif. (border town opposite Tijuana)
26 Discount ticket letters
29 In the main
31 Stuffed bear voiced by Seth MacFarlane
34 Not likely to be a "cheese" lover?
36 Pens for tablets
38 Learn to live with
39 Like the sound holes of a cello
41 1986 Indy 500 champion
42 Champion
44 Venetian mapmaker ___ Mauro
45 Driver's license requirement
47 Portugal's Palácio de ___ Bento
48 What a movie villain often comes to
50 Faced
52 Enter as a mediator
54 Tribe whose sun symbol is on the New Mexico flag
56 Grandson of Abraham
60 Roadster from Japan
61 Sites for shark sightings
63 Gut trouble
64 Group in a star's orbit
65 Disney Hall architect
66 Sci-fi battle site

DOWN

1 Beats at the buzzer, say
2 Like a control freak
3 Houston ballplayer, in sports shorthand
4 Spring events
5 Word spoken 90 times in Molly Bloom's soliloquy
6 Desperately tries to get
7 "Criminal Minds" agent with an I.Q. of 187
8 Singer of the #1 single "Try Again," 2000
9 Half a couple
10 Vacancy clause?
11 Like the crowd at a campaign rally
12 Some mock-ups
13 One in a Kindergarten?
14 Three-time All-Pro guard Chris
21 Owen Wilson's "Midnight in Paris" role
23 Glenda Jackson/Ben Kingsley film scripted by Harold Pinter
25 Cunning one
26 Wolf (down)
27 ___ gun
28 Battle site of June 6, 1944
30 Grand Slam event
32 John Paul's successor
33 Inflicted on
35 Green org.
37 Shade that fades
40 Musical with a cow that's catapulted over a castle
43 Area inside the 20, in football
46 Appetite
49 More likely
51 Sadness symbolized
52 Complacent
53 Plaza square, maybe
55 Least bit
57 Blind strip
58 Morsel for a guppy
59 One with a password, say
61 Street crosser, briefly
62 "You wanna run that by me again?"

by John Farmer

ACROSS

1. 1999 rap hit featuring Snoop Dogg
9. "Sin City" actress
13. Classic TV family
15. Represent
16. 45°, for 1
18. Wild things?
19. Puts on eBay again
20. Cuban province where Castro was born
22. Zoological groups
23. Diamond deal
24. Software plug-in
25. Mode of transportation in a 1969 #1 hit
26. Filmdom family name
27. Israel's Sea of ___
28. Silence fillers
29. Informal name of the 45th state
30. Softball question
33. Clean, now
34. Songbird Mitchell
35. Turkey ___, baseball Hall-of-Famer from the Negro leagues
37. Breaks
38. They get tested
39. ___ system, part of the brain that regulates emotion, behavior and long-term memory
40. 2000s CBS sitcom
41. Sextet at Woodstock
42. "El Condor ___" (1970 Simon & Garfunkel hit)
43. Golda Meir and Yitzhak Rabin led it
45. Division d'une carte
46. Place of outdoor meditation
47. Mock words of understanding
48. Price of an opera?

DOWN

1. Gangster nickname
2. "Carmen" figure
3. Covers
4. Share a secret with
5. From the Forbidden City
6. Bad impressions?
7. Poverty, metaphorically
8. Dutch city ESE of Amsterdam
9. Shape shifters?
10. Try to hear better, maybe
11. Knock-down-drag-out
12. First name in shooting
14. Winter set
17. Didn't make it home, say
21. Arm
23. Email ancestors
25. "Wordplay" vocalist, 2005
27. "In your dreams!"
29. Mary ___ (doomed ship)
30. Italian region that's home to Milan
31. Chances that a year ends with any particular digit
32. Florida's Key ___
33. Musician who arranged the theme from "2001"
34. Fruit-filled pastry
35. Where to bury the hatchet?
36. Olympic ice dancing gold medalist Virtue and others
37. ___ Alley
38. Hypercompetitive
39. About 40–60 beats per minute
41. Volume measure
44. Volume measure

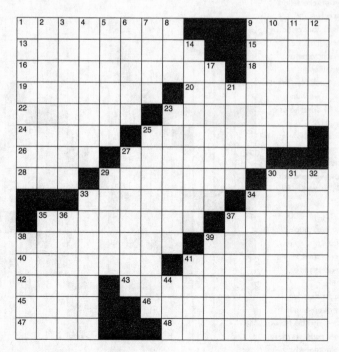

by David Steinberg

130

ACROSS

1 1980 new wave classic
7 1996 hybrid animation/live-action film
15 Cole ___, 2008 World Series M.V.P.
16 "Ahh" sloganeer
17 Juices
18 Hot numbers
19 "Bait Car" channel
20 Some hotels and old cars
21 Lays flat
22 It can precede masochism
23 Kind of mile: Abbr.
24 Location from which the phoenix rose
25 Ulan-___ (city in Siberia)
26 Biographer biographized in "Poison Pen"
29 Wear for Teddy Roosevelt
31 Amt. of copper, say
32 Surmounted
33 Dirty Harry fired them
37 Upstate N.Y. sch.
38 1985 #1 whose video won six MTV Video Music Awards
39 Rhode Island cuisine specialty
43 Rapper with the 2000 single "Party Up (Up in Here)"
44 "___ Story" (2007 Jenna Bush book)
45 Symbols of strength
46 Zales inventory
47 Give some juice
48 Benefits
50 Have thirds, say
51 Jockey competitor
53 Jin dynasty conqueror
54 Female novelist whose given name was Howard
55 Rhyme for "drool" in a Dean Martin classic
56 Something between 49-Downs
57 Out of alignment

DOWN

1 "How's it goin', dawg?"
2 Hobby with Q codes
3 Fresh
4 Gnocchi topper
5 "___ It" (2006 Young Jeezy single)
6 100 metric drops: Abbr.
7 Dirt, in slang
8 Like the Simpson kids' hair
9 Dramatic opening
10 Lewis ___, loser to Zachary Taylor in 1848
11 Prefix with tourism
12 1995–2013 senator from Arizona
13 1985–93 senator from Tennessee
14 Raymond who played Abraham Lincoln
20 Cowboy feature
23 What a leadfoot may do
24 City that's headquarters for Pizza Hut and J. C. Penney
26 Former Australian prime minister Rudd
27 Supposed sighting off the coast of Norway
28 Where faces meet
30 Tight shoe wearer's woe
33 Mercury and Saturn, once
34 Follower of one nation?
35 Soup line
36 Marketing mantra
38 Return service
39 Sci-fi's ___ Binks
40 Many an early tie
41 Safe spots
42 First marketer of Cabbage Patch Kids
46 Outrageously freewheeling
48 ___ concours (unrivaled: Fr.)
49 Way off
50 Bearded mountain dweller
52 Bit of action
53 Deg. from 37-Across

by Peter Wentz

ACROSS
1 Wiped the floor with
16 Use of blockades, say
17 Western daily
18 Lobby
19 Watch things
20 Limited edition?
21 Suffix with electr-
22 Blasting, musically
24 Bay, say . . . or bring to bay
28 Tempest, to Theodor
31 Bellyaches
33 ___ Rose
34 One may be tapped out
37 Brunch orders, briefly
38 McKinley's Ohio birthplace
39 Title priestess of opera
40 Aim
42 Setting of 10, maybe
43 Sony output
44 Bulldogs' sch.
46 Painter ___ della Francesca
48 Certain advertising medium
55 It's not word-for-word
56 Old French epics
57 Idolizes

DOWN
1 1970s–'80s sitcom setting
2 "I'm ___" (Friday declaration)
3 Doctor's orders
4 Passing people
5 What Hamilton called the wealthy
6 "Sure, let's try"
7 ___ Arden Oplev, director of "The Girl With the Dragon Tattoo"
8 Mid third-century year
9 Gershwin biographer David
10 Guarders with droopy ears and pendulous lips
11 Some collectible lithographs
12 It hasn't happened before
13 Sans spice
14 Sought-after rock group?
15 Fun or laugh follower
22 Send quickly, in a way
23 Finders' keepers?
25 What stars may indicate
26 Cause of a class struggle?
27 Allure alternative
28 Sun blocker
29 Pearl Harbor attack initiator
30 Polaris bear
31 Limb-entangling weapon
32 Second-greatest period in the history of something
35 1931 Best Picture
36 Utility bill details
41 Light measures
43 Like much arable land
45 "I ___ Lonely" (1954 hit for the Four Knights)
46 Lead-in to deux or trois
47 Particular paean penner
48 Ozone destroyers, for short
49 "What's Hecuba to him, ___ to Hecuba": Hamlet
50 Sinatra's "Meet ___ the Copa"
51 Biblical miracle setting
52 Police dept. personage
53 Touch
54 Law school newbie

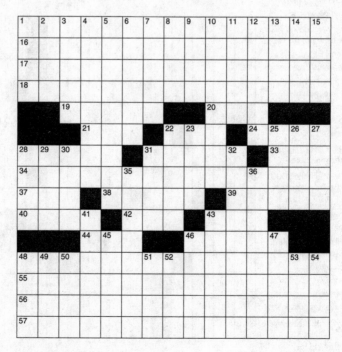

by Martin Ashwood-Smith

132

ACROSS

1 Domino's bottom?
11 Sing
15 Olympic Tower financier
16 Roman marketplaces
17 Lines to be cracked
18 Something to hold down
19 Asian silk center
20 Giving no performances
22 Aid in getting it together?
23 Off-limits
26 Al Bundy's garage, e.g.
28 Spot with a talking bear, maybe: Abbr.
31 XII, perhaps
33 Hailstorm, e.g.
34 Sarah Palin called herself an average one
37 How fresh paint glistens
38 "The Tourist" novelist Steinhauer
39 Best final result
41 Literary character who says "I'll chase him round Good Hope"
42 Kind of horoscope
44 Kids' party game
46 Bell heather and tree heath
48 Topic in a world religions course
49 Follower of Gore?
50 Like some laptop keyboards
52 Minable material
54 Part of un giorno
55 "I'll send for you ___": Othello
57 Record held for decades?

61 Swimmer featured in the 2013 film "Blackfish"
63 Important stud farm visitors
66 Ape's lack
67 Pre-Raphaelite ideal
68 Bad side of literature?
69 Sings

DOWN

1 Spotted South American mammal
2 The white surrounds it
3 99+ things in Alaska?
4 2008 title role for Adam Sandler
5 Buttercup family member
6 See 8-Down
7 Letter string
8 With 6-Down, old wheels
9 When hands are extended straight up and down
10 It may be over a foot
11 Closest bud, briefly
12 Head-turning cry
13 Make a fashionable entrance?
14 Its contents provide juice
21 Apprehended
24 Big name in Hispanic food
25 Juice
27 Sports stud
28 DC transformation location
29 Collection of green panels
30 CH₃COOH
32 Some pleas, briefly
35 Flair

36 Like some colors and cornets
40 Grp. concerned with feeding the kitty
43 Karaoke stand-in?
45 Raiser of dogs?
47 Penalty box, to sports fans
51 Trattoria dessert
53 "32 Flavors" singer Davis, 1998
56 "Barney Miller" Emmy winner Pitlik
58 Armenia's basic monetary unit
59 French suffix with jardin
60 Proposal figs.
62 Draught ___
64 Jubilant cry
65 Trash

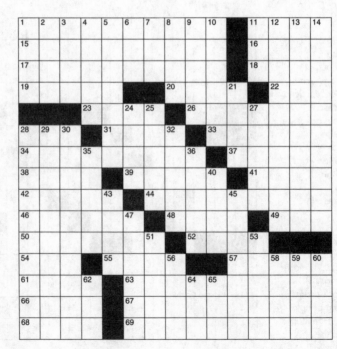

by Barry C. Silk

ACROSS

1 Common catch off the coast of Maryland
9 Light, in a way
15 Crude alternative
16 Jewelry box item
17 Like a bout on an undercard
18 Dickens's Miss Havisham, famously
19 ID clincher
20 Challenge to ambulance chasers
22 Arcade game prize grabber
24 Fiacre, to taxi drivers
27 "___ reminder . . ."
30 Nook occupier
31 Toshiba competitor
32 Some camcorders
33 Besmirch
36 Isaac Bashevis Singer settings
38 Culmination
39 Only proper noun in the Beatles' "Revolution"
41 "Something to Talk About" singer, 1991
42 Golf commentator's subject
43 Classic kitschy wall hanging
46 Slip for a skirt?
47 "Billy Bathgate" novelist
50 Ex-G.I.'s org.
53 Washington State mascot
54 Pre-W.W. I in automotive history
57 "If music be the food of love . . ." speaker in "Twelfth Night"
58 Cry of despair
59 Nothing: It.
60 Periods of warming . . . or cooling off

DOWN

1 M asset
2 Royal Arms of England symbol
3 Bone under a watchband
4 The Orange Bowl is played on it: Abbr.
5 Acupuncturist's concern
6 Croupier's stick material
7 Acknowledges
8 Tab carrier in a bar?
9 Tourist attraction on Texas' Pedernales River
10 Face in a particular direction
11 "Champagne for One" sleuth
12 Shot, informally
13 Serena Williams, often
14 Novel in Joyce Carol Oates's Wonderland Quartet
21 Exasperates
22 Cauldron stirrer
23 "The Avengers" villain, 2012
24 Bit of sachet stuffing
25 Classroom clickers of old
26 Singer who once sang a song to Kramer on "Seinfeld"
27 When "Ave Maria" is sung in "Otello"
28 1970s pact partly negotiated in Helsinki
29 Right hands: Abbr.
32 Arena
34 Orange garnish for a sushi roll
35 Fox hunt cry
37 Bay, for one
40 Prompt a buzzer on "The Price Is Right"
43 Unoccupied
44 Massive, in Metz
45 Block
46 Keep from taking off, as a plane with low visibility
47 Nobel category: Abbr.
48 Loughlin or Petty of Hollywood
49 Italian actress Eleonora
50 Let it all out
51 Unoccupied
52 Rolls of dough
55 One of the Ms. Pac-Man ghosts
56 "There is no ___ except stupidity": Wilde

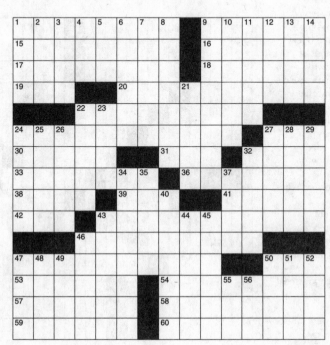

by Brad Wilber

134

ACROSS
1 Insignificant row
9 Traffic reporter's aid
15 Big rush, maybe
16 Twin's rival
17 Offerer of stock advice
18 Grown-up who's not quite grown up
19 No big shot?
20 Nasty intentions
22 Threatening word
23 Overseas rebellion cry
25 One may be played by a geisha
26 Wasn't given a choice
27 "You Be ___" (1986 hip-hop hit)
29 Super German?
31 Pressure
33 Launch site
34 Where many airways are cleared, briefly
35 Antithesis of 32-Down
37 Common sound in Amish country
39 Large amount
42 Classics with 389 engines
44 Scrammed
48 Like Fabergé eggs
51 Schoolyard retort
52 Carry ___
53 So great
55 Paving block
56 Golf lesson topic
57 Goes downhill
59 Troubling post-engagement status, briefly
60 Doctor
62 They were labeled "Breakfast," "Dinner" and "Supper"

64 2002 César winner for Best Film
65 Real rubbish
66 Least significant
67 It really gets under your skin

DOWN
1 Determine the value of freedom?
2 Carp
3 Scandinavia's oldest university
4 Sneeze lead-ins
5 Austrian conductor Karl
6 Recess
7 Be quiet, say
8 Savor the flattery
9 It's bad when nobody gets it
10 "The Guilt Trip" actress Graynor
11 Like some cartilage piercings
12 "Possibly"
13 Dream team member
14 Planet threateners
21 Like a top
24 Stain producers
26 Gallant
28 Result of knuckling down?
30 Hollow
32 Antithesis of 35-Across
36 Pageant judging criterion
38 Ed supporters
39 Park Avenue's ___ Building
40 Radical
41 Shaking
43 Sniffing a lot

45 What a slightly shy person may request
46 1967 Emmy winner for playing Socrates
47 "As you like it" phrase
49 What a bunch of footballers might do
50 Game in which the lowest card is 7
54 Marriott rival
57 Preventer of many bites
58 Bit of action
61 Household name?
63 Soreness

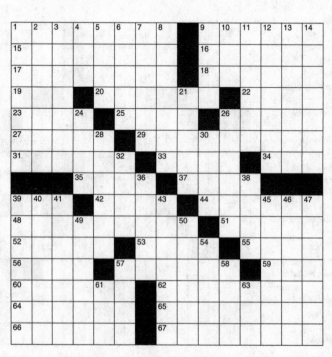

by Tom Heilman

ACROSS

1 African city of 4+ million whose name means, literally, "haven of peace"
12 Seeing things
14 "Why such a fuss?"
16 Start of a Jewish holiday?
17 Put one's two cents in?
18 Arizona's Agua ___ River
19 Not natural for
21 Like Beethoven's Piano Sonata No. 6 or 22
24 Tilting figure: Abbr.
25 ___ Ximénez (dessert sherry)
26 Manipulative health care worker
29 Smash letters
30 Destroy, informally
32 Range ridges
33 Classified
35 Eatery where the Tony Award was born
38 Pitch
39 Juan's "Hey!"
42 Perseveres
44 Some Deco pieces
46 Lead film festival characters?
47 Rhineland Campaign's arena: Abbr.
48 Frito-Lay snack
50 Silver of fivethirtyeight.com
52 California city near Fullerton
54 Author Janowitz
55 Opening line of a 1966 #1 Beatles hit
59 One-hit wonder
60 Events for some antiquers

DOWN

1 Demonstration exhortation
2 A bee might light on it
3 Some N.F.L.'ers
4 Irritate
5 Dopes
6 Restoration notation
7 Even though
8 Polynesian island chain?
9 Lee with an Oscar
10 Home row sequence
11 Kalahari Desert dweller
12 Irritability
13 Femme canonisée
14 Deli menu subheading
15 Foundation for some roofing
20 Silence
22 Verges on
23 Anticipate
27 Mind
28 Irritable state
31 Election surprise
33 What some bombs result in, in brief
34 Fanciful notions
35 Dead
36 Pair of boxers?
37 Give a makeover
39 Pontiac and others
40 "Star Trek" extra
41 It's definitely not the short answer
43 "That's that"
45 Fix a key problem?
49 Kind of yoga
51 Important info for people with connections
53 Clément with two Oscar-winning films
56 Düsseldorf direction
57 La la lead-in
58 Allen of play-by-play

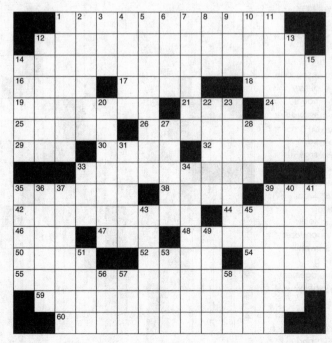

by Alan Arbesfeld

ACROSS

1 Made a seat-of-the-pants error?
11 "Your mama wears army boots," e.g.
15 Rioting
16 Popular pizza place, informally
17 Washington, D.C., has a famous one
18 Greets enthusiastically, in a way
19 One working in a corner in an office?
20 Eastern Woodlands native
22 Noted eavesdropper, for short
23 Covenants
25 Splendiferous
27 Bar supply
30 ___ Valley
31 Sulky
32 Tandoori-baked fare
34 "Yes" to an invitation
36 One way to stand
37 They may result when you run into people
40 Hognose snake
41 Of two minds
42 ___ work
43 Lender, legally speaking
45 Lo ___
47 50% nonunion?
48 "Gunsmoke" setting
49 Marina sight
51 Classic Northwest brewski
52 Charlie's land
54 Like a tennis match without a break?
58 Like many a gen.

60 Mother of Andromeda
62 "Iliad" locale
63 Settles in, say
64 Job application info, for short
65 Nootropics, more familiarly

DOWN

1 Internet prowlers
2 Hand or foot
3 Cry frequently made with jazz hands
4 Georg von ___
5 Vice president after whom a U.S. city is thought to have been named
6 Ninny
7 Best Picture of 1960, with "The"

8 ___ Palmas
9 Breastplate of Athena
10 "The High One"
11 Where a canine sits?
12 Whole
13 Winter Olympics sight
14 They use blue books
21 TV show headed by a former writer for "S.N.L."
24 "Mom" and "Mama's Family"
26 Poetic expanses
27 Grumpy
28 They use Blue Books
29 "The Wishing-Chair" series creator

33 Manage
35 Whiner, of a sort
38 Kind of compressor
39 Yankee, once
44 Passes
46 "Uh-uh!"
50 #2 pop
53 Title with an apostrophe
55 Appear stunned
56 Apothecary item
57 Din-din
59 Prefix with peptic
61 2 Tone influence

by Michael Ashley

ACROSS

1 Their drinks are not on the house
9 Rough limestone regions with sinkholes and caverns
15 Novel title character with a "brief, wondrous life"
16 Hawaii's Forbidden Isle
17 ". . . period!"
19 One buzzing off?
20 Three Stooges display
21 Some lab leaders, for short
22 Like most hall-of-fame inductees: Abbr.
23 Gave belts or socks
24 Swamp
25 Female friends, to Francisco
27 Early-millennium year
28 Jet black
29 Some are soft-shell
30 Spread out
32 He cast the Killing Curse on Dumbledore
33 What the Flying Wallendas refuse to use
34 Powerful Hindu deities
38 That same number of
40 Diner's words of thanks
41 Unlucky accidents, old-style
44 Co. led by Baryshnikov in the 1980s
45 It broke up in the age of dinosaurs
46 Not procrastinating
47 Midday assignation, in slang
49 Stink
50 Olive ___
51 More pointed

52 Give an underhanded hand?
53 Assertion more likely to be correct if 8-Down is given
56 Decision makers
57 Axis, e.g.
58 "Fingers crossed"
59 Whose eyes Puck squeezes magical juice on

DOWN

1 "Well done!"
2 With no dissenters
3 Common result of a slipped disk
4 Foil feature
5 Realty ad abbr.
6 Lies ahead
7 What a vacay provides
8 What an interrogator might administer
9 Bring home, as a run
10 Light as a feather
11 One in a cage
12 Confined
13 Vast historical region controlled by the Mongols
14 Kingdom next to Kent
18 See 24-Down
23 They aid responses, in brief
24 With 18-Down, life today
26 Transcend
30 Speaking of repeatedly, to a Brit
31 1984 award for Elmore Leonard
35 Drifting type

36 Good hand holding in Omaha Hi-Lo
37 It has the densest fur of any animal
39 Alpine skier Julia who won Olympic gold in 2006
41 Still-produced stuff
42 Slangy segue
43 Awful accident
45 Hazards
48 Afresh
51 Film and theater
52 Actor Rickman who played 32-Across
54 Low numero
55 ___ Fáil (Irish coronation stone)

by David Woolf

138

ACROSS

1 Air protection program?
10 Italian alternative
15 Tight squeeze for a couple?
16 Where Union Pacific is headquartered
17 1992 chart-topper that mentions "my little turn on the catwalk"
18 Tar
19 65-Across's title: Abbr.
20 Evian competitor
21 Gun shows?
22 A or O, but not B
24 First name in fashion
26 One going for the big bucks
27 ___ Fund Management (investment company)
29 Strike-monitoring org.
30 Contact on Facebook
31 Time reversal?
33 Tore to shreds
35 Diehard sort
38 Dangerous things to go on
39 Long, slender glass for drinking beer
41 River to the North Sea
42 Lowly one
43 Quarterly magazine published by Boeing
45 Norwegian Romanticist
49 Anti
50 Sch. in Madison, N.J.
52 ___ Gunn, "Breaking Bad" co-star
53 Killing it
56 Make a touchdown
58 Star opening?
59 Turning blue, maybe
60 Prevent a crash, say
62 Triumphant cry
63 "Buy high and sell low," e.g.
64 Baselines?
65 Case worker

DOWN

1 Springblade producer
2 Marmalade fruit
3 Green piece
4 Wall Street inits.
5 ___ Musk, co-founder of Tesla Motors and PayPal
6 Millan who's known as "the Dog Whisperer"
7 Temporarily inactive
8 ___ Place (Edmonton Oilers' arena)
9 Frozen food aisle eponym
10 See 11-Down
11 She loves, in 10-Down
12 "G-Funk Classics" rapper
13 Iroquoian tongue
14 Provincials
21 "Holy smokes!"
23 Long Island Rail Road station
25 Old phone trio
28 Spartan gathering place
30 Bakery/cafe chain
32 Schwab rival
34 Rhames of "Mission: Impossible"
35 Pioneering underground publication of the 1960s
36 Early tragedienne Duse
37 1990s sci-fi series
40 Alternative to die
41 In the direction of
44 Make further advances?
46 Sense
47 Former Italian P.M. Letta
48 Boot covering
51 Open, in a way
54 Kind of threat
55 Certain spirits
57 Frankie Avalon's "___ Dinah"
60 Org. with a top 10 list
61 Shopper's choice

by David Steinberg

ACROSS

1 Milk additive
6 TV actor who lived, appropriately, in Hawaii
14 Hoyt who wrote "Joy to the World"
15 Go-getter on the hunt?
16 Catch
17 Reverse order?
18 "Wrong" way to spell a world leader's name in a New York Times crossword, according to a 1999 episode of "The West Wing"
20 Gets ensconced
21 Altdorf's canton
22 19th-century abbot and scientist
24 Word that begins with an apostrophe
25 Cheese made from the milk of Friesian cows
27 Reposes
28 Relative of a leek
30 Otherworldly
32 Showing irritation
33 On-deck circle?
36 First name in pop
37 Arm bones
38 Charles who was born Angelo Siciliano
39 Reproductive cell
40 Bar in a shower stall
44 Moniker
45 Johns Hopkins program
47 Beat oneself up about
48 Authorized, as to read secrets
51 Paternity prover
53 Dicey issue
55 Light-reflecting shade
56 Deep-fried treat
57 Third-place finisher in 2004 and 2008
58 Unwelcome benchmark?
59 Cygnet's parents

DOWN

1 Language of Navarre
2 City that hosts the California Strawberry Festival
3 Places for races
4 Drapery attachment
5 Wee hour
6 One of the Bushes
7 Makes up (for)
8 Monstrous
9 Modelists' purchases
10 Took a powder
11 Milk additive
12 Stereo system component
13 Showing some wear?
15 Only so-called "Decade Volcano" in the continental U.S.
19 ___ González, longest-serving democratically elected Spanish P.M.
23 Star of Buñuel's "Belle de Jour"
26 Group that offers "protection"
28 Beloved, in Bologna
29 Possible skin test reaction
31 Cinematography choice
32 Scribes
33 Never mind
34 Phone line?
35 Title sort of person in 2008's Best Picture
36 Purina product
39 Officially make
41 Brand in the frozen food aisle
42 "Northanger Abbey" novelist
43 Dwindles to nothing, with "out"
45 ___ dish
46 Begins to develop
49 Each
50 Author Jaffe
52 Détente
54 Shell filler

by Patrick Berry

140

ACROSS

1 It includes pinning and throwing
8 "Chicago" setting
15 Rapture
16 Skyrocket
17 Prepare to pull the trigger
18 Couple seen at a baby shower
19 Hard knocks
20 It might hold up a holdup
22 Reason for a semiannual shift: Abbr.
23 Skunk and such
24 Star in Virgo
25 Aid in getting a grip
26 Check spec.
27 Abyss
28 Modern Persian
29 "That's clever!"
31 California's ___ Sea (rift lake)
32 Got a 41-Across on
33 Billy who played the Phantom in "The Phantom"
34 Person with small inventions
37 Slam dunk stat
41 Benchmark mark
42 They have seats
43 Crew's director
44 "Que ___-je?" ("What do I know?": Fr.)
45 "The Great Caruso" title role player
46 Perpetual 10-year-old of TV
47 Wile E. Coyote buy
48 Too, to Thérèse
49 Board game with black and white stones
50 Pupil of Pissarro
52 Like many laptop cameras
54 First name among Italian explorers
55 With ramifications
56 Galls
57 Does some farrier's work on

DOWN

1 One feeling 15-Across after Super Bowl III
2 Title name written "on the door of this legended tomb," in poetry
3 Home of Southeast Asia's largest mosque
4 News briefs
5 Colombian kinfolk
6 "___ see"
7 Like the human genome, before the 1990s
8 "St. John Passion" composer
9 Now, to Nicolás
10 Choice for a long shot
11 Sound in the comic "B.C."
12 Groveled
13 Tepid consent
14 Sitcom pal of Barbarino and Horshack
21 Grammy-nominated Ford
24 No-yeast feast
25 Parking meeter?
27 Cuts up
28 Adder's defense
30 They're off-limits: Var.
31 Pole star?
33 Its main island is Unguja
34 Asset in a drag contest
35 Whence a girl who's "like a samba," in song
36 Member of 31-Down's team
37 Geiger of Geiger counter fame
38 "You're not the only one!"
39 Recess for a joint
40 Reaches
42 Leisurely strolls
45 It's often parried
46 Impolite interruption
48 Indigo source
49 Spinal cord surrounders
51 Rescue vessel?
53 Relative of Aztec

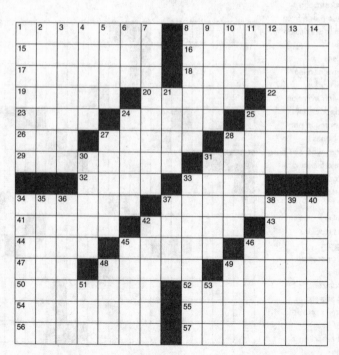

by Frederick J. Healy

ACROSS

1 Cartoon canary's bane
9 Lymph liquid
14 Launch
15 Many a predictable plot
16 Rests
17 One with a game collection, maybe
18 Gate announcement, briefly
19 Longtime model Parkinson of "The Price Is Right"
20 One with a game collection
21 Home to Bar-Ilan Univ.
22 Grp. supported by 17-Acrosses
23 Something groundbreaking
27 Post rival
32 "That is so obvious!"
33 What corned beef is often served on
34 Weights, to a weightlifter
35 Heart-felt thing?
36 Where to take stock?
37 Lamb accompaniment
39 Shade similar to bay
40 One getting into briefs?
41 Least brazen
42 "Eldorado" inits.
43 Forbid
44 Urban phenomenon
48 Coastal diver
49 Sun Devil Stadium's sch.
52 Chill
53 Labor leader?
55 Ray Charles's Georgia birthplace
56 A sprinkling
57 Inc. magazine topic
58 Voice of 1-Across

DOWN

1 Ton
2 Ton, e.g.
3 Quit running
4 Detoxing woe
5 Bagel source?
6 Many a Taiwanese
7 More than bickering
8 It has eight neighbors: Abbr.
9 Stars and stripes, say
10 Tod's sidekick on "Route 66"
11 Court records
12 Hammer and sickle holder, maybe
13 Trivial
15 Delta lead-in
22 Like many holiday letters
23 Jungian principle
24 In favor of the idea
25 Words before know and care
26 Total
27 See 29-Down
28 Sarcastic "I can't wait"
29 With 27-Down, her last film was "High Society"
30 Some food festival fare
31 French body of law?
33 Derby favorite
35 10 or 15 yards, say
38 One shot in a cliffhanger
39 Inner ear?
41 Stall near the stacks
43 Designer Geoffrey
44 Evidence of damage
45 John Paul II, e.g.
46 ___-call
47 Creator of bad apples?
48 Hartmann of talk radio
49 Mont. neighbor
50 Wrapped (up)
51 Grp. with national antidoping rules
54 It might end in "mil"

by Ned White

142

ACROSS

1. 1960s sitcom character with the catchphrase "I see nothing!"
11. Kvetch
15. Pitchblende, e.g.
16. Disney title character surnamed Pelekai
17. Singles collection?
18. Hostile
19. Malignant acts
20. "Not serious!"
21. Lose one's place?
22. Itches
23. Places gowns are worn, for short
24. Setting for many reprises
26. Elated outpouring
28. Hercules type
29. Result of some fermentation
33. Ingredient in Worcestershire sauce
35. Still in the 17-Across
37. Still
38. Second baseman in both of the Dodgers' 1980s World Series
40. Like South Carolina vis-à-vis North Carolina, politically
41. Storied abductee
42. Sports mascot who's a popular bobblehead figure
44. Ring
46. Comfort's partner
47. "The X-Files" project, for short
51. Verb in the world's first telegraph message
52. Watergate units: Abbr.
54. Embroidery loop

55. Brand once pitched by Garfield
56. Where filing work is done
58. Relative of aloha or shalom
59. Home of the W.N.B.A.'s Silver Stars
60. Transcendental aesthetic developer
61. Accent for plus fours, often

DOWN

1. Like many drafts
2. Lollipop selection
3. Tarte ____ (French apple dessert)
4. Uncooperative moods
5. What César awards honor
6. Stick close to
7. One paid to make calls
8. Considers
9. "Star Trek: T.N.G." role
10. Literary wife in "Midnight in Paris"
11. Nearly set?
12. Judicious state
13. Minor payment
14. Early riser?
23. Locales that may be well-supplied?
25. Digs on a slope
26. Recognition not sought by Benjamin Franklin
27. Rapper with the 2012 album "Life Is Good"
29. Clear one's way, in a way
30. Latin condenser
31. Cookware that's often hinged

32. Cared
34. Overcome by mud
36. Weir
39. Blue label
43. Lose
45. Medieval merchants' guild
47. Grain elevator components
48. Discount, in combination
49. Vodka ____
50. "There, there"
53. "Up to ____" (1952 game show)
54. Fancy spread
57. Show on Sen. Franken's résumé

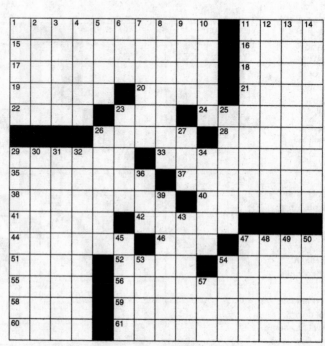

by Byron Walden and Brad Wilber

ACROSS

1 Innocent one
6 Short shift?
10 Judgmental clucks
14 Influential style of the 1960s
15 Au courant about
16 Home of Sunset and Paradise
17 Pitching staff work areas
19 Plea opener
20 Coffee order
22 Theology inst.
23 "Praise the Lord!"
26 "Stanley & Iris" director Martin
29 A bit of cheer?
32 "Aw, sorry about that . . ."
33 Here, to Henri
34 B, to scientists
36 Untwisted silk fibers
37 Ganache ingredient
40 Brisbane buddies
41 Country that split in two in 2011
42 22-Across subj.
43 Puts on a pedestal
45 Door sign
46 Combines
47 Cold war defense system
49 Semi part
51 Dancers known for their Japanese street-style wardrobe
57 Water bearer
59 Singer whose first top 10 hit was "Where Does My Heart Beat Now"
60 In Australia her name is Karen
61 1980s Chrysler offering
62 Harper Lee's given name
63 Castaway's spot
64 Amtrak stops: Abbr.
65 "Skyfall" singer

DOWN

1 "The aristocrat of pears"
2 On ___ with
3 Like one end of an electric cord
4 Nursing locale
5 "Hello, ___"
6 Subatomic particle more massive than an electron
7 Many a museum audio guide
8 Chinese menu words
9 Relative of a raspberry
10 Sushi order
11 Plot device?
12 Early "Doctor Who" villain
13 "Nurse Jackie" channel, for short
18 Musket loader
21 Make jokes about
24 Like many turkeys
25 Collectible cars
26 Encircled
27 Producer of cold cuts?
28 Carnival ride since 1927
30 Ones going in circles?
31 [Zzzzz]
34 Get moving
35 Anatomical knot
38 Prevaricate
39 Popular spring break locale
44 They may be offered by way of concessions
46 Withstood
48 Deplane in moments
50 NASA's Gemini rocket
52 ___ Bator
53 Wine-and-cassis drinks
54 Make angry
55 Idle
56 "The Mikado" weapon
57 Penultimate Greek letter
58 Grafton's "___ for Alibi"

by Elizabeth C. Gorski

144

ACROSS

1 Big name in 25-Across treatment
9 Air piece?
14 Shrugs, maybe
16 Take it as a sign
17 "The Help" co-star, 2011
18 Decorative moldings
19 First of a succession of 13
20 Coot
22 Johnny-jump-up, e.g.
24 Nude medium, often
25 See 1-Across
27 90° from ouest
28 Really
31 Area map
32 ___ d'âme (moods: Fr.)
33 Alternative to 53-Down
34 Secures
37 She's no puritan
40 Farm sounds
41 Station, e.g.
42 Repulsive
43 Get out of practice?
45 Sportscaster Nahan with a star on the Hollywood Walk of Fame
48 Keel extension
49 Unrefined type
50 Key setting
52 Like eggheads
56 Stockholder's group?
57 Universal work
58 Hack, say
60 Nonstop
61 Evidence of having worn thongs

62 Little ones are calves
63 Player of many a tough guy

DOWN

1 Olympian on 2004 and 2012 Wheaties boxes
2 Bach contemporary
3 Onetime pop star who hosted "Pyramid"
4 First name in erotica
5 Fortune subjects: Abbr.
6 Stalin defier
7 Stargazer's focus?
8 Street fair lineup
9 Lodge org.

10 Fryer seen at a cookout?
11 Harvard has an all-male one
12 Creation for many an account
13 Super Mario Bros. runner
15 Backing
21 ___ rating (chess skill-level measure)
23 So-far-undiscovered one
26 Name-dropper's abbr.?
29 Aid in making one's move?
30 So-far-undiscovered ones, briefly
32 Like a type B
34 Geishas often draw them
35 Wimp's lack

36 Wrest the reins
37 Crane arm
38 Ace's stat
39 Open love?
41 To the degree that
43 What mops may be made into
44 Feet with rhythm
45 Dealt with
46 Abercrombie design
47 Brought to ruin
51 Kick back
53 Alternative to 33-Across
54 Ripped
55 Drumroll follower
57 Group with family units
59 Actor Penn of "Van Wilder"

by James Mulhern

ACROSS

1 Kid in shorts with a cowlick
8 Soft soap relative
15 Twisting
16 Industrial production unit
17 What black licorice or blue cheese is, for many
19 What a parade may necessitate
20 Goulash
21 Give the ax
22 Organ showpiece
24 Things that are put on . . . or don't go off
25 Sound of a belt
28 Agitates
29 "Stand and fight" grp.
30 Like agateware and graniteware
32 One might be made for the shower
35 Goosed
36 Consolation prize recipient
37 Novel followed up by "The Boyhood of Christ"
38 Out to lunch
39 Need for muscle contraction, briefly
40 Person who may work a lot
41 One having a ball?
42 Like a Madrilenian millionairess
44 Apex
46 Geology topic
47 Plot element?
48 Singular publication
52 Line near the end of an infomercial
55 Get limited access?
56 Finish line?
57 Rural parents
58 Sexual desire, euphemistically

DOWN

1 Not much
2 Singular
3 Rushing home?
4 Bit of chichi wear
5 Smashed
6 Like a common printing process
7 The Skywalker boy, for short
8 Processes, as ore
9 Tennis star Petrova
10 Not suckered by
11 Inquiry made while half awake, maybe
12 Mojave Desert sight
13 Like some celebrities blogged about by Perez Hilton
14 Inn inventory
18 Chemistry Nobelist Hoffmann
23 Hernando's hundred
24 Go gaga (over)
25 English channel's nickname, with "the"
26 Being with une auréole
27 King John sealed it
29 Direct, as a confrontation
31 Israel Philharmonic maestro
32 Technology standard named for a Danish king
33 "Calm down now . . ."
34 Massachusetts motto opener
36 Hitch horses
38 All-Star 18 consecutive times from 1967 to 1984
40 "Where we lay our scene," in Shakespeare
42 Take up one more time, say
43 ___ Sendler, heroine of W.W. II's Polish Underground
44 Blocker working with a receiver
45 Out of sight
47 "Like ___ Song" (John Denver hit)
49 With 51-Down, unscented
50 Wind, in Chinese
51 See 49-Down
53 Midwest attachment?
54 Bearded ___ (reedling)

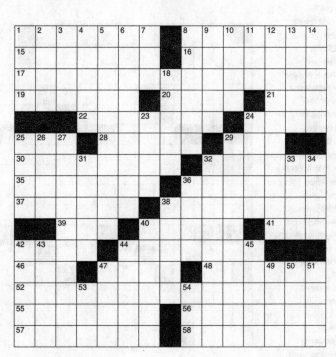

by Gary Cee

146

ACROSS

1 2015 Toronto event
11 Office staples
14 Slide
15 Protagonist in David Foster Wallace's "Infinite Jest"
16 "Corpus Christi" playwright
18 Ones united in France?
19 Manufacturer of boxy cars
20 Treasure
21 Loose end?
22 "Return to Never Land" role
23 Darkroom chemical solution
24 Pickle
25 Big gun
26 U.S. city that's almost as large in area as Delaware
35 Part of a French cabinet
36 Jumbo, e.g.
37 Shpilkes
38 Certain shell contents
39 Joan Sebastian's "___ y Más"
40 Pull out all the stops
43 Miracle site
45 Latin primer word
49 Hip to
50 Enterprise Klingon
51 Close call
52 Forrest Tucker's "F Troop" role
55 X-___ large
56 What solidifies things in the end?
57 Member of the E Street Band
58 Bit of forensic evidence

DOWN

1 Golfer Calvin
2 Quattro relatives
3 Quaint complaint
4 Husband of Otrera
5 TV ad unit: Abbr.
6 Not cover one's butt?
7 Formation from glaciation
8 Former first lady
9 List-ending abbrs.
10 When repeated, a breath freshener
11 Jacob's-ladder, for one
12 Make a little lower?
13 More artful
14 Tank gun first produced by the Soviets in W.W. II
17 Ottoman ruler nicknamed "The Lion"
22 19th-/20th-century U.S. portraitist
23 ___ Brunelleschi, Italian Renaissance architect who developed linear perspective
24 Coupling
25 1958 41-Down by Samuel Barber
26 Mennen line
27 Scandinavian goddess of fate
28 Suffix with pluto-
29 "Ocean's Eleven" activity
30 Cagney classic of 1935
31 Big name in modeling agencies
32 "South Park" boy
33 The Garden of England
34 Song and dance
40 Flag wavers?
41 25-Down, for one
42 Common cleanser
43 Neighbor of Gabon
44 Holder of Leia's secret
45 Legend maker
46 Cuban revolutionary José
47 "Little Miss Sunshine" co-star
48 Souvenir buys
50 Keen
51 Flue problem
53 Literary inits.
54 Real-estate listing abbr.

by Martin Ashwood-Smith

ACROSS

1 Locale that often includes a wet bar and large-screen TV
8 Picture with a number
15 Where it never gets above zero degrees?
16 One going around the bases?
17 Ends of some films
18 Warm-up?
19 Greasy spoon order
20 Where a bud hangs out
22 Successfully lure
23 Kind of figure
26 Highlighted, say
27 Toss
30 Mexican revolutionary of 1910
32 Moon of Mars
34 Draft pick?
38 Electric ___
39 Jacket option
41 "___ bad!"
42 Much of the Plains States
44 Palliate
46 Staple of the house in "The Real World"
48 Still
49 "___ con Dios"
52 Transport for Miss Gulch, in "The Wizard of Oz"
54 What a chair needs
56 Hawaiian for "white"
57 PC whiz
61 Controversial 1715 measure of Parliament
63 Touch-type?
65 Infomercial testimonial
66 Reply to a schoolmistress
67 It clears the air
68 "The Hangover" co-star

DOWN

1 Go well (with)
2 Soft shade
3 "The Sound of Music" chorus
4 TV game show on the Discovery Channel, 2005–12
5 Loved, with "up"
6 Person behind a curtain, maybe
7 Unreal
8 Joe
9 Handles online
10 Attend
11 Edward Murdstone, to David Copperfield
12 Sugar
13 Certain belly button
14 What polling may reveal
21 Chinese restaurant staple
24 ___ Belvedere (classic sculpture in the Vatican)
25 Great white shark prey
27 Particular, informally
28 "Clueless" protagonist
29 Hershey candy
31 Distilled pine product
33 Places to find in-flight magazines
35 Advance on a table
36 Actor Jay of "Jerry Maguire"
37 Leave in
40 Lock opener?
43 Unreal
45 Former
47 "So long"
49 South American carrier founded in 1927
50 Heartburn
51 Cries of pain
53 Nursed, with "for"
55 ___ Torres, four-time Olympic swimming gold medalist
58 Company that follows Shin Bet security procedures
59 Tight-lipped sort
60 Border lines?
62 "Bad!"
64 Popular wood for wood chips

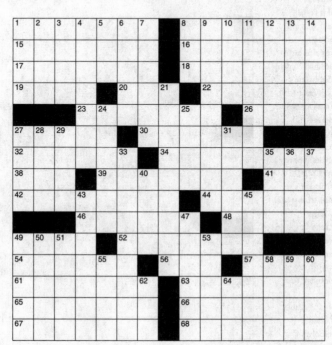

by Ian Livengood

148

ACROSS

1 Girl's name in #1 1973 and 1974 song titles
6 With 20-Across, where the first-ever crossword puzzle appeared
13 Reserved parking spaces and others
14 Less light
15 Form of many a birthday cake
16 Jojoba oil is a natural one
17 Lead-in to now
18 Home of MacDill Air Force Base
19 Had ___ (flipped)
20 See 6-Across
24 Legal attachment?
25 Light unit
26 Acclaim for picadors
28 Certain sultan's subjects
30 They're not team players
34 Lab dept.
35 La ___ (California resort and spa)
36 Extended trial
38 Not for the general public
39 Morlocks' enemy
41 Saxony, e.g.
42 Shot
45 Creator of the first crossword
49 Kingdom vanquished by Hammurabi
51 Actor Tom of "The Seven Year Itch"
52 Ranch sobriquet
53 1989 Peace Nobelist
55 Aviary sound
57 To a fault

58 Fruit whose name comes from Arawak
59 Year in which the first crossword appeared, on December 21
60 Firth, e.g.

DOWN

1 Where vaults can be seen
2 Jacket style
3 Noted geographical misnomer
4 "South Park" boy
5 Basic Latin verb
6 Hobbyist, e.g.
7 Jerry Orbach role in "The Fantasticks"
8 Early Chinese dynasty
9 Neighborhood org. since 1844
10 Chilling
11 Mulligans, e.g.
12 Mardi Gras group
14 Big sport overseas?
16 Babe in the woods
18 Sailors' chains
21 City on the Firth of Tay
22 "Star Wars" queen and senator
23 Canine vestigial structure
27 High-hatting
28 Cortés's quest
29 Graffiti, say
31 Like many nutrients
32 1, for one: Abbr.
33 Poor, as an excuse
37 Rock singer?

38 Key never used by itself
40 Formal confession
41 Toni Morrison novel
42 Obscure
43 Like some vin
44 R. J. Reynolds brand
46 Borders
47 Brass
48 Hemingway, notably
50 T. J. ___
54 "Vous êtes ___"
55 Staple of sci-fi filmmaking
56 Ostrogoth enemy

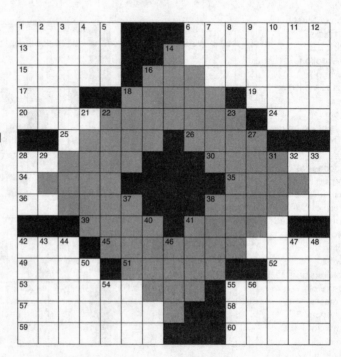

by David Steinberg and Todd Gross

ACROSS

1 Compliment after a dive
10 Word with cellar or door
15 2012 billion-dollar Facebook acquisition
16 Dermatologist's case
17 Things employed to show the passage of time à la "Citizen Kane"
18 Some saucers
19 Mixed ___
20 1950s–60s sitcom nickname
21 Cant
22 Identifies
24 Small jerk
26 Accord
27 Brown refreshers
30 Caustic soda, chemically
32 ___ kwon do
33 Gridiron datum: Abbr.
34 So-called "potted physician"
36 Oscar-nominated film featuring a dentist-turned-bounty hunter
40 Home of Sky Tower, the tallest free-standing structure in the Southern Hemisphere
41 "Uncle Tom's Cabin" girl
42 Morse bit
43 Contrarian's abbreviation
44 Island where Artemis was born
47 Phishing lures
49 Disperse
51 Double ___ Oreo
53 Lead-in to type
54 Two-master
57 Sushi fish

58 Leader of Uganda's independence movement
60 Subject of a landmark 2012 Supreme Court decision
62 Dice
63 Final say
64 Apply
65 Like Albert Einstein, ethnically

DOWN

1 Add zip to
2 "Hold on . . ."
3 Port on Lake Ontario
4 Result of drying out, maybe
5 Pasta, e.g., informally
6 "The African Queen" screenwriter
7 Attempt to cure
8 "Homicidal Psycho Jungle Cat" duo
9 Bounty letters
10 E, F and G in D.C.
11 Jennifer of "Bound"
12 Quite a long shot
13 Cause for some blacklisting
14 Who's who in publishing?
23 Move furtively
25 Class graded on a curve?
26 Gather at harvest
28 Whites, informally
29 Brown coat
31 Expressed some delight
35 Perfume holders
36 Some Lamaze assistants
37 Drink with a straw
38 Have no help

39 Some, in Salamanca
45 Parliamentary home
46 Newsman Ray
48 What stress may be good for
50 "Roasted in ___ and fire": Hamlet
52 Guy with a cooking show
55 Reassuring comment after a fall
56 Wide breach
59 What means the most at the end?
60 Beginnings of life
61 Bilk

by Ian Livengood and J.A.S.A. Crossword Class

ACROSS

1 Gut-busting side
11 Port. title
15 Alternative to 1-Across
16 Some GPS suggestions, informally
17 Shooting star?
18 College figs.
19 It means little in the Lowlands
20 Trimming gizmo
21 Like floppy disks, e.g.
22 Vino de ___ (Spanish wine designation)
23 Red shade
24 Santa Ana wind source
27 It may be up against the wall
29 Bring out
30 1975 hit song about "tramps like us"
33 Like Athena
34 Sharon's predecessor
35 Fig. for I, O or U, but not A or E
36 It may be said while wearing a toga
38 Manual series
39 Phoenix suburb larger than the Midwest city it's named for
40 Break through
41 Princess of ballet
43 Like red bell peppers
44 Orders
45 Key ring?
47 Scoutmaster, often
50 The moment that
51 It's not drawn due to gravity
53 Co-star in the U.S. premiere of "Waiting for Godot," 1956
54 Pride and joy
55 Abstainers
56 Question from a bully

DOWN

1 Slight pushes
2 One at the U.S. Mint?
3 Jonathan's wife in "Dracula"
4 A.L. East team, on sports tickers
5 Like many pregnant women
6 Where to get a cold comfort?
7 #1 spoken-word hit of 1964
8 "My Son Is a Splendid Driver" novelist, 1971
9 Castle of ___ (Hungarian tourist draw)
10 Old map abbr.
11 Like some pills and lies
12 Dilly
13 Bait
14 Listing on I.R.S. Form 8949
21 Summit success
22 Front runners
23 Engine buildup
24 Sound like a baby
25 Cartoon pooch
26 Hunky-dory
27 Rather informal?
28 Printer part
30 Port on the Adriatic
31 Like Bill Maher, notably
32 Supporter of shades
34 Unembellished
37 Stock to put stock in
38 Verbal alternative to a head slap
40 Go for a car-cramming record, say
41 Anciently
42 Tunisian money
43 ___ presto
45 Devotional period?
46 Insignificant
47 Twain's "celebrated jumping frog"
48 Talent show lineup
49 "___ Bones G'wine Rise Again" (spiritual)
51 Important card source: Abbr.
52 Deterrent to lateness or cancellation

by Frederick J. Healy

ACROSS

1 Company whose jobs are often changing?
10 Working group
15 Got to the bottom of
16 It takes a bow at a musical performance
17 1958 Buddy Holly hit
18 "Guaranteed relief every time" sloganeer
19 Historic leader?
20 "Dove ___" (Mozart aria)
21 Thing
22 Poetic contraction
23 Kind of strip
25 Workers' org. founded by Samuel Gompers
26 Farriers' tools
29 Letters signifying quality brandy
30 Grant-giving org.
31 Musical with the song "Written in the Stars"
33 Said "There, there" to, say
36 It makes the Statue of Liberty green
39 Guarantee
40 Very excited
42 The so-called Island of the Gods
43 Head for the hills
44 One can be tall
46 Jerry or Jerry Lee
50 Seine sight
51 Rappers' covers
53 Sign
54 Lane on Broadway
56 Attack
58 Telephone trio
59 Against a thing, at law
60 2010 Ke$ha chart-topper with a creatively spelled five-word title
62 Clichéd
63 Series of Nintendo games
64 Certain 49-Down
65 Watersheds

DOWN

1 18-footer, maybe
2 Measured two-dimensionally
3 Chickens for dinner
4 "Marvy!"
5 Surrealist Tanguy
6 Simon of Duran Duran
7 Russian ballerina Galina
8 Gets into Monk music
9 Eponym of a frozen food
10 It may be picked up in the woods
11 Do a driver's no-no
12 Axis, e.g.
13 Condition known medically as pes planus
14 1967 hit with the lyric "You know you're a cute little heartbreaker"
21 Wife, in Juárez
24 Sister of Helios
27 Sibling, at times?
28 Sound really good
32 007 player
34 Put to sleep
35 Auto racer Luyendyk
36 "Refudiate," e.g.
37 Mythical runner
38 1990s series initially set in the year 2193
41 Place for a plug
42 Mild Irish oath
45 Nike competitor
47 Move to and fro
48 Belong
49 Women's wear
51 Women
52 2005 horror sequel
55 Prefix with port
57 Fund-raising suffix
60 Iraq war subject, briefly
61 Volga tributary

by David Steinberg

152

ACROSS

1 Like many a fairy tale princess
8 Craft with one mast and one sail
15 Offering for continuing education
17 Totally gone
18 "___ I might . . ."
19 Pretend
20 Papua New Guinea port
21 One with a glazed-over expression?
22 Plant related to pepper
23 Places for shooting stars
24 Finished
25 They've been splintered
26 Boiling point at Roman baths?
27 Number tossed out
29 Glacial pinnacles
30 Longtime "Guiding Light" actress Beth
31 Hellenistic-era galley
32 Is offensive, in a way
33 Lost it
35 Left unsaid
36 Waterwheel parts
37 Learning the ropes
38 Depression specialist's subj.
39 Fix
40 Bullfighter's cloak
41 Vietnam's Dien Bien ___
42 Lacking
43 Like some uncared-for closets
44 Mudslinger, say

47 Lacked any supervision
48 Strawberry, for example
49 Voiced letters

DOWN

1 Potential beach closer
2 Aid in scaling down?
3 Hung in there
4 It prevents things from becoming 43-Across
5 Some, in Seville
6 Southern leader?
7 Southern and such
8 Hundreds
9 "___ Million" (Nathanael West novel)
10 Like some muscles and tendons
11 Frank's place
12 Taxing educational hurdle
13 One traveling around India with a trunk
14 Progress by intelligent design
16 Proust's Parisian courtesan
22 Campout dangers
23 One whose head is turned
25 Take the lead from?
26 Roll of candy
28 Wack, in hip-hop
29 Blockage-busting brand
31 Job-hunting consideration

32 Pop from a different line
33 Lacked in freshness
34 Hockey player Roloson and wrestler Johnson
36 Like pocketed bills
39 Barbizon School painter Jules
40 Brown shade
42 Court hearing
43 Brooklyn Park setting: Abbr.
45 Municipal div.
46 Before-long link

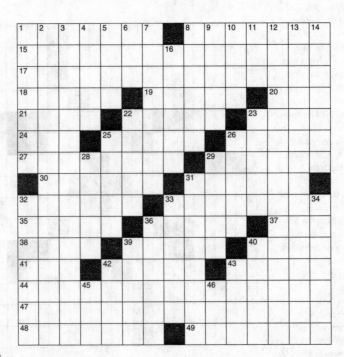

by Joe Krozel

ACROSS

1 Eaters of halal food
8 Like many mall fixtures?
15 Star of 2011's "Puss in Boots"
17 One shooting out on a golf course
18 Oil sources for oil paint
19 Mode
20 Mo. containing Constitution Day
21 Unhealthily light
25 From
29 It may be fat after a fight
32 Digs
33 Onetime Taliban stronghold
35 What twisty arrows warn drivers of
37 Bring into being
38 Hit film directed by James Cameron
39 Football linemen: Abbr.
40 Arctic or Antarctic fish-eater
41 It has left and right channels
42 Part of S.F.S.U.
43 How some hearts are broken
48 Car exhaust part
54 Potential pets
57 Worker whose charges may charge
58 Answer that avoids answering
59 Writer's field

DOWN

1 More, to a señor
2 Like surprises you'd rather not get
3 Youth
4 Chop source
5 They have keepers
6 Bit of D.J. equipment
7 Flat bottom
8 Hold hands?
9 Nav. position
10 Nestlé brand
11 Partridge family setting
12 Hanging out in galleries, say
13 Isle of Man man
14 "Nine Stories" title girl
16 Flat bottom
20 Web presence
22 "Natural Affection" playwright
23 Surgical aid
24 Big band
25 Done to ___
26 Foundering call
27 Black-and-white giants
28 Geologist's big break?
29 Couples' retreat
30 Rachel McAdams's "Sherlock Holmes" role
31 Choose to refuse
34 Big wheel at a party?
36 Beyond, to Browning
43 Put the finger on
44 Short plea
45 Some govt. raiders
46 Imitated Niobe
47 Dept. of Labor division
48 Stole option
49 Do one's part?
50 N.F.C. part: Abbr.
51 Concerning
52 Order
53 Except
55 Univ. helpers
56 Some 55-Down: Abbr.

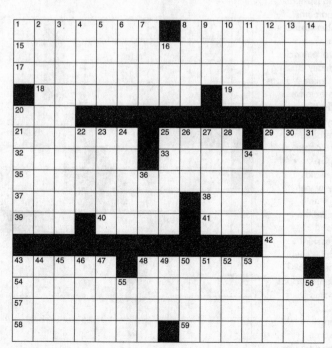

by Todd Gross and Doug Peterson

ACROSS

1 Aldrin, Armstrong and Collins
10 Large parts of some support systems?
15 Bit of the magic of Disney
16 Increased
17 Start practicing, as bad habits
18 University next to the Centers for Disease Control headquarters
19 A.B.A. team that signed Moses Malone out of high school
20 Yellow fever carrier
21 "Vexations" composer
22 Cause people to disbelieve, with "on"
24 Flintstones vitamins maker
25 Pull up stakes, informally
26 U.S. United Nations representative, 2005–06
30 Pfizer brand since 1997
32 Dunce cap-shaped
33 "The Great Santini" author
34 Nutty as can be
36 Kept slightly open artificially, maybe
37 Storms on the road
38 Spanish uncle?
40 Anne Brontë's first novel
42 The U.S.S. Constitution has three
47 Grounation Day celebrant

48 Snack item next to a dip bowl
50 With lid rattling, say
51 These days
52 Waterfall or rapid
53 Feature of many a pizzeria
54 Builds up
55 Sticks firmly

DOWN

1 A little above average
2 Loop taken on a drive?
3 Gertrude Stein or Alice B. Toklas
4 "___ could" (expression of regret)

5 Thornburgh's predecessor as attorney general
6 Mine entrance
7 Makeshift cat dish
8 Animal that has escaped from its owner
9 Fox Business Network show
10 Horrible
11 Provider of relief for a finger?
12 Roman count?
13 All in the family?
14 Le Carré specialty
23 Flashes
24 Ominous
26 Coastal setting of "The Birds"
27 Bistro offering

28 Bathroom item on a honey-do list
29 Bit of retribution
31 Locust tree feature
32 Cuban remnant
35 From Land's End, e.g.
36 Aces, nowadays
39 Will, if intentions bear out
41 De-ices, perhaps
42 Rules of conduct
43 Lead-in to God or Congress
44 Trinity member
45 Post-marathon posts
46 Wiped out
49 "Best friend" from Germany?

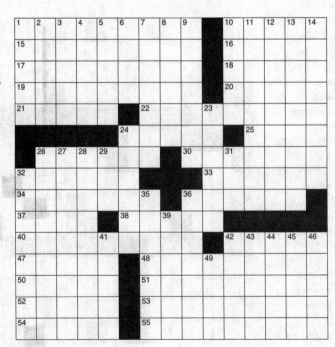

by Mark Diehl

ACROSS

1 Semimonthly tide
5 Mooring post on a ship
9 Head nurse on "Scrubs"
14 If you add up the pros and cons
16 Nautical direction
17 Pitcher of the only no-hitter in World Series history
18 Small truck manufacturer
19 Highly rated 1997 film with the song "Tupelo Honey"
20 Take in, possibly
21 Flogs
22 Like yoga instructors
23 Pink shade
24 Secures every share from
26 Early man?
28 Had some inventory problems
29 ___ lane
30 Berate profanely
33 Court
34 What mansions rarely are
36 "___ = Politics" (TV slogan)
37 Inventor given a gold medal by Titanic survivors
38 "Goodness me!"
41 U.K. Triple Crown racecourse site
42 Dance trio?
47 Suddenly took interest
48 Motivated
49 Go on
50 Communion place
51 Abject
52 Colorful Amazon swimmer
53 They're indispensable
54 Mrs. Charles Lindbergh
55 "The Lucy-___ Comedy Hour"

DOWN

1 "Well, of course"
2 Name on a famous B-29
3 Mammy's son
4 Adjective applied to ginger ale
5 Things towed along towpaths
6 Expanse beneath an arch?
7 Certain lymphocyte
8 Works behind a counter
9 Prompter
10 Get rid of
11 Like some store furniture
12 North American home of 30,000 islands
13 Tiramisu ingredient, often
15 Frequent photo prop for Will Rogers
25 "___ furtiva lagrima" (Donizetti aria)
26 Bourbon enemy
27 Blow out of proportion
28 Flat fish
29 Pleasantly rustic
30 The Village ___ (musical group with the 1963 hit "Washington Square")
31 Walked away with
32 Star of Ang Lee's "Hulk"
35 Looked for a phenomenon, maybe
36 Blackened
38 Leroux who created the Phantom
39 Premium number
40 What a dickey simulates
43 Lady of Paris
44 Junk car
45 Some funeral attendees
46 "We're Madly for ___" (old campaign song)

by Patrick Berry

ACROSS

1 Fiddlehead sources
6 Get chummy
11 Odeur detector
14 Phone query before a private conversation
16 Grp. with the top 10 album "Face the Music"
17 Emerge
19 Like many obscenities
20 Supporter of Yoda
21 Masters focus
22 Words before story or debate
24 Wrapped up
25 Dodgem feature
27 Euro forerunner
29 It first circulated in 2000
38 Great parking spot, slangily
39 Gate holder
40 Sultanas, say
41 Things often zapped
42 It shows many B&W pictures
43 South Georgia's Prince ___ Harbor
46 1960s TV actor whose name looks like a free offer?
50 Big revolver
53 "Mickey" singer Basil
54 Lighting problem?
57 Slice from beneath the ribs
60 Roquefort source
61 One of Washington's houses, e.g.
62 1976 Rodgers and Harnick musical about Henry VIII
63 Soft, meshed fabrics
64 Some are drug-induced

DOWN

1 Braves
2 Lose ground?
3 D.J.'s creation
4 Maxim's denial
5 Somme silk
6 "Cry, the Beloved Country" author
7 One way to pray
8 Match game?
9 America East sch.
10 Epi center?
11 Seti River setting
12 Opera's Obraztsova
13 Like a lot, maybe
15 Oppressed by the heat?
18 Kabbalah
23 Big leagues

25 Roosevelt established it as Shangri-La
26 Steeped in tradition
28 Vast
29 Pleasant treatment centers
30 Oberhausen opera highlight
31 Highly glazed fabric
32 Believers in raising spirits?
33 Sinks a sub?
34 Joltin' Joe, e.g.
35 "Lift Every Voice" author Guinier
36 ___ end
37 Genealogical line: Abbr.
43 Sleek fur
44 "The Little Prince" composer

45 Proposal for business expansion
47 "But not without ___": Pope
48 Golden Pavilion setting
49 Early New Yorkers
50 Early hour
51 Neck tie?
52 Is oppressed by the heat
55 Brief moment, briefly
56 He's 2, say
58 An expat may take it: Abbr.
59 One taken on a drive: Abbr.

by Martin Ashwood-Smith

ACROSS

1 Actress Stone and others
6 "Just playin' with ya"
10 Base characters?
14 Meccan, e.g.
15 Ones sitting on pads
16 Cut off one's ears?
17 One asking questions he already knows the answers to
19 Cousin of contra-
20 Highness
21 "Figures I'd have this problem!"
23 French expert in body language?
24 Draw back
25 Education dissemination locations
30 Solidifying agents
31 Vase lookalikes
35 Bouncing off the walls
36 Enclosure . . . and an alphabetical listing of letters not appearing elsewhere in this puzzle's answer
37 Sylvester's "Rocky" co-star
38 A Ford
39 "___ Girl" ("Bells Are Ringing" tune)
40 One swimming with flippers
46 Logical ending
49 Accessible for shooting
50 Like pool racks
52 Host of PBS's "Scientific American Frontiers"
56 Baseball All-Star Kinsler and others
57 "1984" shelfmate

59 Ordeal for jrs.
60 Part of some pools
61 Rose partially
62 Clinic shipments
63 Henry James biographer
64 Least desirable parts

DOWN

1 A.B.A. members' titles
2 Wailuku's county
3 California's ___ Woods
4 Wood shop shaper
5 "Scrooge" star, 1951
6 "Likely story"
7 Lawn flamingos and such
8 Pop alternative

9 With 12-Down, lidocaine delivery option
10 Risk board territory
11 Stack at IHOP, say
12 See 9-Down
13 Like some punk hairstyles
18 Cracked open
22 Stocking-up time?
23 Lay claim forcibly
25 Weak
26 Quaint euphemism
27 Film holders
28 True companion?
29 Pundit
32 Highness: Abbr.
33 Mass action
34 Mosel tributary
41 Begin a conversation with

42 Cut back
43 Contact liquid
44 Nail topper
45 Home to a much-visited tomb
46 Sticks in a makeup bag
47 Sweep the board?
48 Mosul money
51 The Charleses' pet
52 Not close
53 Like fashionable partygoers?
54 It may knock you out
55 Concert pieces
58 54-Down for a trip

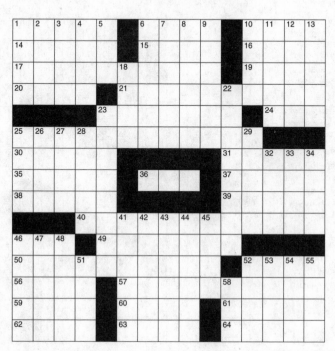

by Joe Krozel

158

ACROSS

1 Concern for a dermatologist
5 They often come with eggs
15 Catalan article
16 What cuts power in half?
17 Sheila's welcome
18 Opposite of "dissuaded from"
19 Coulee
21 Messed up
22 Roster curtailer: Abbr.
23 Product of some decay
25 Non-Hollywood, say
26 Bit of wet-weather wear
27 Packed things
29 Touchdown letters
30 Something stuck in a freezer?
33 Five in the ninth inning?
35 Step
36 Prefix with 11-Down
39 Signs near a teller's window, maybe
42 Some proctors, briefly
44 Of the essence
47 Silverwing flier
49 Prepare to send some mail
50 Route through a park, maybe
52 The toe of a boot?
53 Schnapps choice
55 Declamation stations
56 Many a crash cushion at a construction zone
59 Get 44-Down
60 Affection
61 Bananas
62 Civil engineering vehicle
63 School in the Piedmont region

DOWN

1 It's checked before taking off
2 Ripple
3 Dieter's design
4 Like many horror flick characters
5 One of the subjects of the best-selling '02 book "The Conquerors"
6 King Hussein Airport locale
7 Disgrace
8 Cod relative
9 Java, for one
10 Like the Phillies' caps
11 Word with career or goal
12 Falls short
13 Manx trait
14 Some ermines
20 Securing device
24 Her help was solicited in a hit song
25 P.R., e.g.
27 P.R. releases
28 Passing comment at a poker table
31 Shared funds
32 Symphonic score abbr.
34 Backed up
37 "Sold!"
38 Universidad de las Américas site
40 "Children of the Albatross" novelist
41 Osmose
43 Like much of Niger
44 Not so remote
45 Swiss alternative
46 Big coffee exporter
48 Quick and thorough learner
50 Like some canine teeth
51 Daughter of Zeus and Themis
53 "The Incredibles" family name
54 Aretha's Grammy-nominated sister
57 Bit of 1-Down
58 Photocopier abbr.

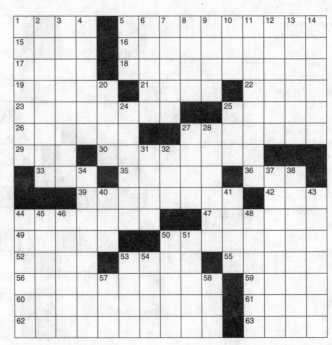

by Barry C. Silk

ACROSS

1 Title matchmaker of early 19th-century literature
5 Drifting type
9 Some help
14 With 21-Across, ship out?
15 Britain's Douglas-Home
16 Need for a 17-Across
17 Special delivery of a sort
20 Fluoride, e.g.
21 See 14-Across
22 Spots for rubs and scrubs
23 Is homesick, say
25 "Oedipe" opera composer, 1936
27 Response to being tickled
29 They often have quiet eyes
32 Moo ___
34 Santa's checking things
36 N.F.L. QB Kyle
37 Revolutionary Tribunal casualty
40 Verdugo of "Marcus Welby, M.D."
41 Oxford attachment?
42 Automne follows it
43 Fort's steep slope
45 Click beetle
47 Go at
49 98.6°, say
52 Korean War outbreak year
54 Starchy
56 African antelope
57 Discovery of Vitus Bering before his shipwreck
60 Paavo ___, track's Flying Finn

61 "Live at Red Rocks" pianist
62 Under tension
63 Some tides
64 City in Padua province
65 Shakespeare title contraction

DOWN

1 Steele work
2 Where "ayuh" is an affirmative
3 What 007 might shoot with
4 He declared "The planet has a fever"
5 Largest ethnic group in China
6 Pasternak mistress Ivinskaya
7 Implicatively
8 Large quantity
9 GPS screen abbr.
10 Curling rink line seven yards from the tee
11 Destination after a touchdown
12 Scholarship-offering org.
13 4-Down's grp.
18 Semicircular canals' locales
19 Burning solutions
24 2008 demolition target
26 Eolith or neolith
28 Fifth of fünf
30 Glam rock's ___ the Hoople
31 Old dagger
32 Hook helper
33 Dutch Golden Age painter

35 Dirty
38 Experiencing down time
39 Home of Sistan and Baluchestan
44 Spanish term of endearment
46 Printed slips
48 Really put out
50 "The X Factor" panelist, once
51 Things Santa checks
52 "Doctor Faustus" novelist
53 Footprint or fingerprint, say
55 Tears can create one
58 "Indeedy"
59 "___ Cried" (1962 hit song)

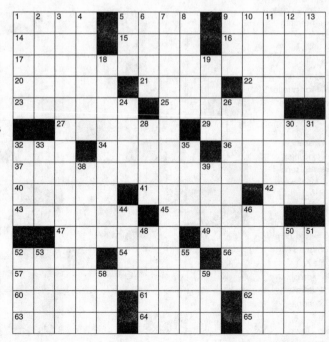

by Joel Kaplow

ACROSS

1 Navajo terrain
6 Chicken ___
10 Pack member, for short?
13 Top
14 What going 100 might result in
17 "You ___ one"
18 1980s–'90s hip-hop show co-hosted by Fab 5 Freddy
19 Ingurgitate
21 Delectable
22 Joins
24 Food item whose name means "pounded"
25 "Patton" setting
27 Relieve
28 They often accompany discoveries
29 Congregation, metaphorically
32 Org. studying viruses
35 Be daring
39 Sound after "Lower . . . lower . . . that's it!"
40 Noted entertainer with a whistle
41 Site of a religious retreat
42 Oaf
43 Sneeze cause
46 Salad bar offering
49 Writer about a bear
51 "Julie & Julia" co-star
53 Amass
56 "Bad for bacteria" brand
58 Setting for the 1996 documentary "When We Were Kings"
59 "Funny People" actor
60 "Pietà or Revolution by Night" artist
61 Jerk
62 Zip
63 "L'Amateur d'estampes" painter

DOWN

1 Subjunctive, e.g.
2 Dutch chess grandmaster Max
3 First N.B.A. player to light the Olympic cauldron
4 Caution
5 French nuns
6 Liberal arts dept.
7 Midway, e.g.
8 Fratricide victim of myth
9 "Meet the ___" (major-league fight song)
10 Bye lines?
11 Data
12 Artist's supply
15 Line at a water fountain, maybe
16 Burned out
20 Échecs piece
23 Modern-day pointer
25 Part of a bar order
26 "Dream on!"
27 King, e.g.: Abbr.
30 Like '40s boppers
31 Colossal, to Coleridge
32 Christmas order
33 Alter ___ amicus
34 Follow
36 It rolls across fields
37 Gorgon, e.g.
38 Business that's always cutting back?
42 Disinclined
44 Put on
45 Like some doughnuts and eyes
46 Makings of a model, maybe
47 Billet-doux recipients
48 Some bump producers
49 Computer that pioneered in CD-ROMs
50 Onetime Moore co-star
52 Longtime Yankee moniker
54 Nocturnal bear
55 No ___ (store sign)
57 Rhinology expert, for short

by Brendan Emmett Quigley and Caleb Madison

ACROSS

1 Like eaters of humble pie
7 Impossible dream
14 Clichéd company claim
15 Surveilled, say
16 Onetime pickling liquid
17 Pumpkin is rich in it
18 Party makeup?
20 Abbr. accompanying some dotted notes
21 Urban planting favorite
22 Half the time?: Abbr.
25 Makes less edgy
27 A weather strip may fit into it
29 Only Englishman named a Dr. of the Church
32 Tony's "Taras Bulba" co-star, 1962
34 Maneuver
35 Reckon
37 Producer of a blowout, maybe
39 Danny DeVito's "Throw Momma From the Train" role
40 Clock stopper, at times
42 Good dogs for pulling loads
43 Most negligible
45 Expect
47 Winged ___
48 Cobble, perhaps
50 More, in ads
54 Maker of fabrics with intricate designs
56 Tryst figure
59 Running quarterly, for short?
60 A 40-Across will watch for it
61 C_3H_8, e.g.
62 Like some words and swords
63 Reacted to a punch

DOWN

1 Alternatives to sales
2 Spartan toiler
3 ___ Express
4 What Jack got in exchange for a cow, in a children's story
5 Form of "sum"
6 Proper
7 Attributes (to)
8 Grand entrance?
9 Retort of contradiction
10 Longtime Dodgers coach Manny
11 Feta milk source
12 "Footloose" hero McCormack
13 Ending for AriZona flavors
15 Hardly abundant
19 N.L. Central city
22 Divvy up
23 Cabbage
24 Ocular irritants
26 "Bad" cholesterol, briefly
28 Inscrutable
29 Tiptoed, say
30 Spa handout
31 Subs
33 Body shop offering
36 Cheerleading outfit?
38 A 40-Across may call it
41 Like many bakers' hands
44 Walks heavily
46 Resembling
49 Collège, e.g.
51 Like the Navajo language
52 ABC's Arledge
53 Full of adrenaline
54 Shocks
55 World's largest fruit company
56 One-striper, briefly
57 Swiss stream
58 Spanish stream

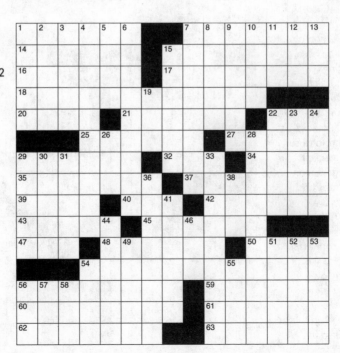

by Barry C. Silk and Brad Wilber

162

ACROSS

1 Fashion show disaster
4 Dated
7 Make a major decision?
9 Head honcho in baseball
11 Element in many semiconductors
13 Like galley slaves, typically
15 Late 1980s Cadillac
16 Literally, "the Stairway"
17 ___ Day
19 Makes a person less tense
20 Exceeds, as demand
21 Closet item, for short
24 Collection of Blaise Pascal writings
25 Middle of this century
28 Spanish queen and namesakes
30 Father-and-son Connecticut congressmen Thomas and Chris
31 Big ring
32 Buckle attachment
34 9-5 connector
35 Choice word?
36 With love
39 Long Island university
40 Like the relatives notified in emergencies, usually
41 Entices
42 Grass for some baskets
43 Economical
44 It might be tipped at a rodeo

DOWN

1 Fingers on a diamond
2 "That's my intention"
3 Quickly reproduces
4 Ship's boarding ladder
5 Keys and Markova
6 CeCe of gospel
7 Lavish events
8 Like John Kerry in 2004
9 Opposites of mansions
10 Food topping in France
11 Blast
12 Has no significance
13 They let traffic through after a crash
14 German article
18 Doesn't continue, as an argument
21 Maintainers of a sacred flame in ancient Rome
22 Made a commitment to play
23 Boxing Hall-of-Famer Primo
25 Sewers, often
26 Sends
27 ___ Hewitt, 2002 Wimbledon winner
29 Nascar driver Elliott
31 Eye
33 One side of a longstanding ad battle
35 Military encampment
37 Nose: Prefix
38 Sign for a musician not to play

by Joe Krozel

ACROSS

1 Stud, say
11 Court defendant: Abbr.
15 He played Don Altobello in "The Godfather Part III"
16 Fair
17 Side effect?
18 Hillbilly's plug
19 More, to a 37-Down
20 Eric of "Funny People," 2009
21 It's gradually shrinking in the Arctic
23 Lost traction
24 One punched in an office
25 Kitchen dusting aid
28 Admirable person
29 They might be left hanging
30 Not pussyfooting
31 1990s Indian P.M.
32 "Youth With a Skull" painter
33 Didn't use a high enough 45-Across, maybe
34 Carpenter's groove
35 Some E.M.T. cases
36 They stand for things
37 Kind of nut
38 Evenly matched
40 Employees at a ritzy hotel
41 Is routed by
42 Whiff
43 Hand holder?
44 Grain, e.g.
45 Ray blockage no.
48 Month whose zodiac sign is a fish
49 "Lady Baltimore" novelist, 1906
52 Prefix with 3-Down
53 "It'll be O.K." lead-in
54 Tummy filler
55 "Whoa, not so fast!"

DOWN

1 Appear thrilled
2 Two before Charlie
3 Computing 0s and 1s
4 Milk source
5 Sense, slangily
6 Aquila's brightest star
7 Secretive body part
8 Mariner's grp.
9 Outer: Prefix
10 Postapocalyptic best seller of 1978
11 Wraps up
12 Send
13 Flighty type
14 Drills, e.g.
22 League division
23 Criteria: Abbr.
24 Veers sharply
25 Friend one grows up with, often
26 "News to me!"
27 Reason for a track delay
28 "Faded Love" singer, 1963
30 Film with the tagline "Borat was SO 2006"
33 Where following a star might lead you
34 Shoulder press target, briefly
36 It's in front of the cockpit
37 South-of-the-border bad guy
39 Colorful additions to tanks
40 Beheld
42 Name in seven Shakespeare titles
44 Charges from counsel
45 They may be prayed to in Fr.
46 Graceful fairy
47 Part of a long neck
50 "Huh?"
51 "___ being Brand" (Cummings poem)

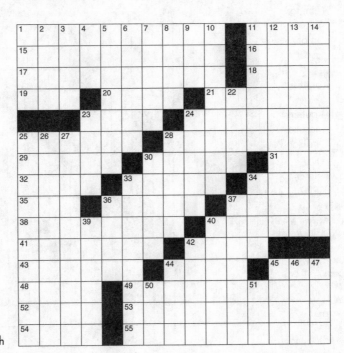

by Ian Livengood

ACROSS

1. Big chickens
9. Seat cushions?
15. Loose
16. Like Fiennes's Shakespeare
17. Supply in a camper's first-aid kit
18. Actress Matlin
19. W.W. II inits.
20. British meat pies
22. Soviet accords?
23. Maine's ___ Bay
25. Locks
26. Kind of cloud
27. Vertical: Prefix
28. Anderson who wrote "My Life in High Heels"
29. 1950s–'60s singer Jackson, the Queen of Rockabilly
30. Forum : Rome :: ___ : Athens
32. Go on
33. Exchange
36. Talking-tos
37. "Save the ___" (conservationists' catchphrase)
38. A park may have one
39. No challenge
40. See 51-Across
41. Stoked
45. Grand
46. Stern contemporary
47. Massey of "Frankenstein Meets the Wolf Man"
48. "This is a test. For the next 60 seconds . . ." org.
49. Beats
51. Notable stat for 40-Across
52. Nickname for Warren Weber in an old sitcom
54. Rowdy
56. "I'm a walking, talking ___": Larry David
57. Resting
58. Bee wine
59. Veteran

DOWN

1. Plain's opposite
2. Commensurate (with)
3. "It's about time!"
4. Doo-wop syllable
5. Grave, for one
6. "Confessions of a Drunkard" writer, 1822
7. Didn't have enough
8. "The Brandenburgers in Bohemia" composer
9. Scrabble accessory
10. Final pharaoh of the Fifth Dynasty, whose pyramid is near Cairo
11. Canon type, briefly
12. Retain
13. Classic actress who played the principal in "Grease"
14. Reel
21. Junior Jr.
24. Hat
26. Dish eaten with a spoon
28. "___ on First" (1981 comedian's biography)
29. Tune (up)
31. Hiking snack
32. Aid consideration
33. Big house
34. Offensive formation
35. Uncommitted
36. Sacagawea, for one
38. "In actuality . . ."
40. Minnesota senator Klobuchar
42. Homer's "dread monster"
43. Not home?
44. Picked up
46. Gossip opening
47. Key chain?
49. Italian lyrical verse
50. N.F.L. coach Jim
53. ___ Friday
55. Bit of news in the financial sect.

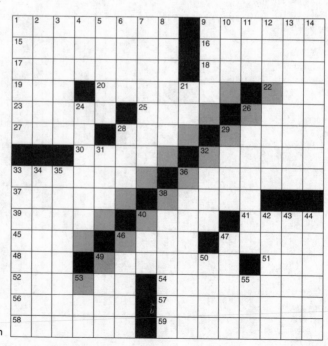

by Matt Ginsberg

ACROSS

1 Cuisine featuring nam prik
5 Identifies
9 Counterpart
13 Mezzo-soprano Marilyn
15 1968 Best Actor nominee for "The Fixer"
17 A blimp may hover over one
18 Induce squirming in, perhaps
19 Coat that's easy to take off
21 French loanword that literally means "rung on a ladder"
22 Colors
24 Perfect
25 It was MSNBC's highest-rated program when canceled in 2003
26 Antique shop purchase
29 Wizard's garment
30 Paper assets
36 Device with a hard disk
37 It has a denomination of $1,000
38 Homeric character who commits matricide
41 Weapons used to finish off the Greek army at Thermopylae
46 What a robot might resemble
47 To the left
48 Psychedelic 1968 song featuring a lengthy drum solo
51 What a whatnot has
52 Like molasses
53 Danger for a climber
54 President's daughter on "The West Wing"
55 Alternative to "your"
56 Company whose Nasdaq symbol is the company's name
57 Keep alive, as a fire

DOWN

1 Showed a bit more friendliness
2 Poet who gave us "carpe diem"
3 Singer at Barack's inauguration
4 Poor
5 Hymn sung to Apollo
6 Trees in Gray's country churchyard
7 Kaplan who co-hosted six seasons of "High Stakes Poker"
8 Acknowledge a commander's entrance, maybe
9 Pizza sauce
10 Not going with the flow?
11 Round-bottomed container
12 Letter on Kal-El's costume
14 One hanging at a temple
16 It's all in your head
20 Christmas green?
23 Gets the gist
25 Dimwit
27 "I hate it when that happens!"
28 Business often located near an interstate
30 Obstruct
31 Trunk item
32 Too accommodating for one's own good
33 Once-autonomous people of southern Russia
34 Sober
35 Nonwoody plant parts
39 Senate sheets
40 Make possible
42 Disobey the rule?
43 Baltimore's ___ Park
44 Begin with enthusiasm
45 Got a lot of laughs out of
47 1980s Tyne Daly role
49 Small quantity
50 Surrealism forerunner
51 Buddy

by Patrick Berry

166

ACROSS
1 Crowds around noisily
5 "In the Still of the Nite" doo-wop group, with "the"
15 Beginning of time?
16 Somewhat
17 Korean War weapon
18 Where to request a knish
19 "___ the brinded cat hath mewed": Shak.
21 Like sports cars, briefly
22 Reagan-era teen, e.g.
23 Modern-day stream
25 Burgeon
27 Like some shape shifters?
29 Cut bits from, maybe
33 What "–" means in a search query
34 Big ring rivals
36 Mark of a successful gunfighter
37 They cause blowups
39 Like many disabled vehicles
41 Positions
42 Helped supply a sushi restaurant, say
44 Promotions may require them, for short
46 Chile's main airline
47 Yarn identifier
49 Bar lines?
51 Washout
53 First bishop of Paris
54 "Looky here!"
57 ___ balls (chocolaty snacks)
59 1950 sci-fi classic
60 Medium relative
63 Mini successor

64 Spy's query at the start of a meeting
65 LeAnn Rimes's "Love ___ Army"
66 Like legal voters
67 Take out

DOWN
1 Like some top-10 people
2 Like bull's-eyes
3 One in a stag's litter
4 "Aah!"
5 Tricks
6 1969 Peace Prize agcy.
7 Certain stamp of approval
8 Fifth element, per Aristotle
9 Of atoms' spatial relationships

10 The Hebrew Hammer of the Cleveland Indians
11 J.F.K. speechwriter Sorensen
12 Horned mountain dweller
13 View from Memphis
14 Kerfuffle
20 Airport fleet
24 It's south of the Banda Sea
26 Hydroxyl compound
28 Tinkertoy bit
30 One of Henderson's record 1,406
31 Off-and-on
32 Bit of paste
35 2009 Tennis Hall of Fame inductee
38 Common portrait subject

40 Beat
43 Actress-turned-nun Hart
45 Abolhassan Bani-___ (first president of Iran)
48 Clawed
50 Russian playwright Andreyev
52 Guideposts magazine founder
54 "'Tis all a Chequer-board of Nights and Days" poet
55 Take on
56 Universal donor's type, briefly
58 Kitchen drawer?
61 Traffic violation, for short
62 Okla. City-to-Tulsa direction

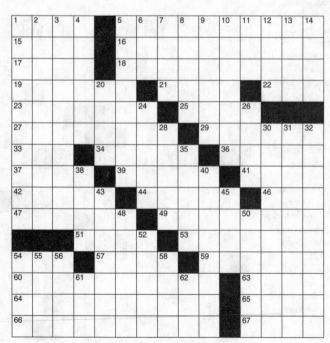

by Barry C. Silk

ACROSS

1 The miss in "Miss Saigon"
4 Burger go-withs
10 Big race sponsor
13 Dishes fit for astronomers?
16 Panglossian person
17 Asia-to-Africa link
18 Carmen ___ ("The Producers" role)
19 Interior decorator's suggestion
20 Southeast Asian holiday
21 Grp. concerned with bowls
23 Rout
26 Mean cur, typically
28 Ice cream mix-in
30 Place to go in Soho
31 See 32-Across
32 On the 31-Across side
34 ___ question
36 South Asian chant word
38 Had a lot to digest
40 Restless
41 Ear-related
43 Longtime Russian acronym
44 ___ Dogg Pound (rap duo)
45 Chihuahua scratch?
47 Adjust one's sights
49 Lays atop
51 Asset
53 King, in Cape Verde
55 Handy-andy's letters
56 Box-office take
58 SALT I and II, e.g.
60 Beloved "Immortal Beloved" piece
63 How this puzzle's black squares are arranged

64 They may have you in stitches, in brief
65 Gunsmith with Smith
66 One may say "I'm with stupid"

DOWN

1 "Take cover!"
2 Security requests
3 Star in Cetus
4 What an express often whizzes by: Abbr.
5 Hägar's wife
6 Polynesian farewell song
7 "Beau Geste" headgear
8 Responsibility for a groundskeeper
9 Grade sch. subject
10 Round-trip flight?
11 Tackles a tough task
12 W. Coast clock setting
13 Do some recharging
14 Center for cat-tails?
15 Highly decorated Bradley
22 Prefix with many fruit names
24 Georgetown athlete
25 Things worked under in a garage
27 "Sax All Night" New Ager
29 Mtge. broker's come-on
31 "SCTV" lineup
33 Hmong homeland
35 It is in Spain

37 It has a sticking point
39 Sandy shade
42 Pre-stunt provocation
46 Thing worked on in a garage
48 Second-largest city in Finland
50 Matched up, after "in"
52 Can
54 Exeter exclamation
57 Cut takers: Abbr.
59 Some kind of ___
60 6 letters
61 Fan setting
62 Apollo's chariot "passenger"

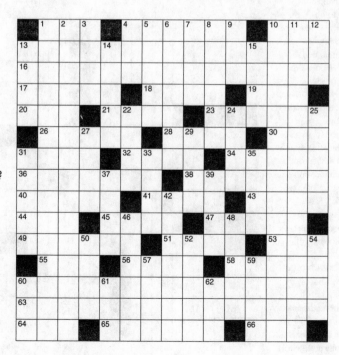

by Scott Atkinson

168

ACROSS

1 Gemini, Libra and Aquarius
9 Untrustworthy sort
15 Result of too much TV, it's said
16 Not bad, in Nantes
17 Common aquarium decoration
18 Promotional description for a coming show
19 Ancient key
20 Goat's call
21 "Green Book" org., familiarly
22 Home of the Dostoyevsky Literary Museum
23 Kitchen tool
24 Do stuff
29 Field marshals' commands
30 Thumbs-up
34 Monkey ladder vine
35 Holiday when sweeping and emptying the trash are considered bad luck
36 Vega of "Spy Kids"
37 Polyhedron part
38 Chaotic
40 Symbiotic partners of clownfish
41 "She is more precious than ___": Proverbs 3:15
45 Points
46 Garment originally made from caribou or sealskin
47 "___ Back" (2004 Kenny Chesney hit)
48 Tarzan trademark
52 Takes a powder
53 Steve Allen sidekick with the catchphrase "Hi-ho, Steverino!"
55 Cup alternative
56 Engaged, as a target
57 Keeping half the world down, say
58 Flock member

DOWN

1 "East of Eden" girl
2 Unrelenting
3 Pool accessory
4 Guru follower
5 "___ 500" (annual list)
6 Case study?
7 Cape Breton locale
8 Taco Bell offering
9 Dogs that ought to be great swimmers?
10 State of nervous tension
11 Test course challenges
12 Sphere of influence
13 Old country name or its currency, both dropped in 1997
14 "The Apostles" composer
22 Mrs. Václav Havel, the first first lady of the Czech Republic
24 Game part
25 "Celeste Aida," e.g.
26 Leopard's home?
27 Hall-of-Fame Cub Sandberg
28 Conniving
30 Imperial offering
31 "Smoke Gets in Your Eyes" composer
32 Wheelset piece
33 Exuberant cries
36 Byrd and others: Abbr.
38 Executive suite?
39 Fix up, in a way
40 Nobel-winning poet Heaney
41 Lacks a clear voice
42 "Say ___!"
43 Compound used to kill ants
44 Ramadi resident
48 River intentionally flooded in W.W. I
49 Michael who wrote "The Neverending Story"
50 Home of the international headquarters of Interpol
51 Time of forbearance
54 Reverend ___, onetime radio evangelist

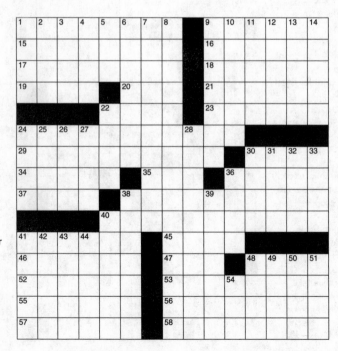

by Byron Walden

ACROSS

1 Many fans are running during this
9 Three-toed wading birds
15 Gets
16 Present-day cry?
17 A vegetarian isn't on it
18 Holds forth
19 Tycoon types
20 "Go ahead," to Shakespeare
21 Certain odor absorber
22 Tabulae ___
23 Storming-out sounds
24 Must-see
27 Spam protection items?
28 Like many bread knives
30 Grammy-winning Brian
31 Looks
32 ___ of Lagery (Pope Urban II's real name)
33 Brushing and such
35 Blood rival
36 Ivy supporters
37 It's developed in a sonata
38 Parts of kingdoms
39 Curtain fabrics
40 Needs for some games of tag
42 Noted 19th- and 20th-century portraitist
43 Flight from danger
44 Bump down

45 Immobilized during winter, say
46 "Not if my life depended on it!"
47 "Done"
48 Four-seaters, maybe?

DOWN

1 Clumsy
2 Queen Mary, for one
3 "Don't do it!"
4 TV Land staple
5 They often get depressed
6 Modern guest-list organizer
7 Onetime Virginia V.I.P.'s
8 Amphibious carrier, for short
9 Establishment where customers typically are seated
10 Singer with the 1994 #1 alternative rock hit "God"
11 Short, strong pan
12 They may be odd
13 Malcolm-Jamal's "Cosby Show" role
14 Plea for aid
20 Teases playfully
22 It hasn't yet been interpreted
24 Strikes out
25 What many crewmen carouse on

26 Deposited into a bank
28 Dancer who was a fan favorite?
29 Ones giving winner forecasts
31 Amass
34 Not belowdecks
35 Tiny biter causing intense itching
37 Sign of availability
39 "Swearin' to God" singer, 1975
40 Hardly a good looker
41 1966 A.L. Rookie of the Year
42 Ward on a set
43 Sock
44 Not quite make the putt, with "out"

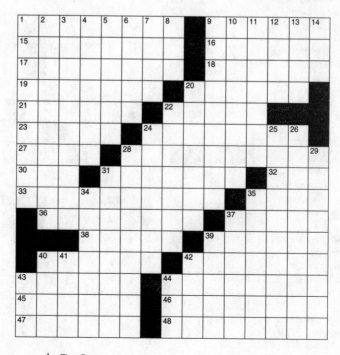

by Tim Croce

170

ACROSS

1 Regular fluctuation
11 Resourcefulness
15 Choose not to mess with
16 Stop shooting
17 Written between two rows of text
18 "But men are men; the best sometimes forget" speaker
19 Opposing
21 "Jelly Roll, Bix and ___" (1994 history of early jazz)
22 Lamb's "___ From Shakespeare"
23 Empty space
24 ___ of Denmark (James I's queen consort)
25 Fiber-rich fruits
26 Madrigal syllables
28 Crumbled ingredient in "dirt pudding"
29 Takes the big cheese down to size?
30 Surprising revelation
34 Superior facility
35 "You have been ___"
36 Salon selections
37 She bests Sherlock in "A Scandal in Bohemia"
38 Light
39 Snide remark
43 Items found in jackets
44 TV golf analyst who won three Masters
46 What tickets may get you
47 Some movies on TV are shown in it
50 Possible solution
51 Approximately
52 Film genre
53 Quick affair?
54 One attracted to vinegar
55 Terrible #2s

DOWN

1 "24" actress Cuthbert
2 Robert who won Oscars for both writing and directing "Kramer vs. Kramer"
3 1942 invasion site
4 Pay back
5 Square
6 "Burning Giraffes in Yellow" painter
7 More obdurate
8 Much earlier
9 Two stars of "Paper Moon"
10 One held in a trap
11 When the O.S.S. was formed
12 Reagan-era scandal
13 Subjects of many notices stapled to telephone poles
14 Part of a timing pattern on a football field
20 Winners of the longest postseason game in major-league history (18 innings, 2005)
25 Lead role in "Miracle on 34th Street"
27 Way to serve vegetables
28 1940s–'50s tough-guy portrayer Dennis
29 Gandalf the ___
30 Drinking to excess
31 Brought up incessantly
32 Aeschylus trilogy
33 "This Week at War" airer
34 Mineral found in igneous rocks
36 Took a mulligan on
38 Typical lab rat, e.g.
39 Circumferences
40 Yardbird
41 Cylindrical vessel with a flat bottom
42 Compounds found in wine
45 Ancient Mycenaean stronghold
46 Do without
48 Pointed, in a way
49 Stymie

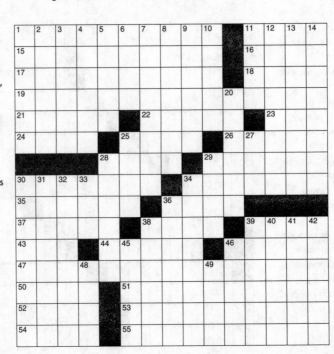

by Patrick Berry

ACROSS

1 It operates under a royal charter
7 1996 movie starring Michael Jordan
15 Swank in Hollywood
16 Popular mixer
17 Low 90s, say
18 "I get your point!"
19 Many a first-time voter in 1920
20 Hilarious
21 Bald person's envy, maybe
22 "Imperialism, the Highest Stage of Capitalism" writer
23 Born yesterday
25 Balrog slayer, in fiction
30 Errs
32 Case worker's org.?
34 Stand for something
35 Grind
36 Expert with computers
39 Kudzu, e.g.
40 Per ___
42 With 49-Across, figure skating practice
43 Well-being
44 Novelty shop purchase
47 Dish often served with soy sauce or miso
49 See 42-Across
51 Neighborhood vandalism ammo
53 Super item?
57 Hardly close-mouthed
59 It breaks the "I before E" rule
60 Lack of vitality
61 Many a role in the Jason Bourne films
62 Frank
63 Brandy brand
64 Pigpens

DOWN

1 Springtime period
2 Stadium shout-out
3 M.V.P. of Super Bowls XLII and XLVI
4 U.C. Santa Cruz athlete
5 It borders the South China Sea
6 Young and others
7 Movie component
8 Contacting via Facebook, in a way
9 Whistling thorn, e.g.
10 Ingredient in Buffalo wings
11 Bionomics: Abbr.
12 Part of a routine
13 Interjection that comes from the Latin for "weary"
14 Billy famous for infomercials
20 Rite of passage participant, often
24 Industrial container
26 "A Heartbreaking Work of Staggering Genius" author
27 Quadrennial sporting event
28 See-through object
29 Fugitate
30 Buck
31 Liberal arts college 20 minutes north of Manhattan
33 Charade
37 Merry-go-round fixture, to a tot
38 ___ high (about that tall)
41 Sales rep's reimbursement, maybe
45 Big list maker
46 "The Lion Sleeps Tonight" hitmakers, with "the"
48 Bowser in the Super Mario series, e.g.
50 Inconsequential
52 10-Down, e.g.
53 Physicist Ernst who studied shock waves
54 "___ told often enough . . ."
55 Range
56 Common conjunction
58 Chow
60 Nelson, e.g.: Abbr.

by Joel Fagliano

172

ACROSS

1 High clouds?
9 Ancient pentathlon event
15 Approximately .264 gallons
16 Div. created in 1969
17 It gets the word out
18 New Valentine's phrase added on Sweethearts candy in 2010
19 Prince Edward I. clock setting
20 Having an underwhelmed response
22 Essence
23 Thought after an after-afterthought: Abbr.
25 Freshen
27 Scramble
28 Hot
30 War cry of the '60s
32 Smooth
34 "The Da Vinci Code" albino
35 "Brokeback Mountain" director
36 Hot dog's relative
38 Cable inits.
39 ___ tree
42 "Alas!"
44 Flavor
46 Hands-in-the-air phrase
50 McCarthy cohort
51 Big name in educational funding
52 Spread
54 Birds of prey
55 Etiolates
57 Incipience
59 Grp. involved in the Abbottabad raid
60 Onomatopoeic game on "The Price Is Right"

62 Time near the end of a time range
64 It might have a crust
65 Sophocles tribute that begins "Numberless are the world's wonders . . ."
66 Language of the Afghan national anthem
67 Cry from an arriving group

DOWN

1 Medicate oneself, say
2 Rampaging
3 Check that's inked, perhaps
4 Sharp
5 Spray
6 Fur source
7 Fish of sufficient size

8 Fur sources
9 Slangy pronoun
10 They're near appendices
11 Stock in an adult store
12 Name-brand targets?
13 Words below an eagle
14 A biochemical solid
21 Dock, in a way
24 Itinerary abbr.
26 Spring locales
29 Character
31 Spikes
33 Spring locales
37 1997 Nielsen title role
39 Common admission requirement
40 Actor who might grin and bare it?
41 Director's cutoff

42 Chorus member?
43 Secrecy, with "the"
45 Game show purchase
46 Rare dynamic marking seen in Tchaikovsky's Sixth Symphony
47 Objects from everyday life
48 United group
49 "In order to know virtue, we must first acquaint ourselves with vice" speaker
53 Hold off
56 Sketch
58 Department head?
61 Conceptual art pioneer
63 Line from Homer

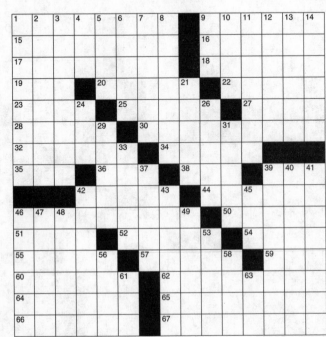

by David Quarfoot

ACROSS

1 Aunties' sisters
7 Gold medal
15 Fly
16 Prepare to take off, perhaps
17 Evers of civil rights
18 Quick seasonal greeting?
19 Ice cream gobbler's woe
21 A.L. East team, on scoreboards
22 Ear-relevant
23 Old Norse work
24 Orange exterior
25 United entities before 1991: Abbr.
26 "Get Smart" enemy agency
27 2008 Israeli political biography
28 Beater of a full boat in poker
30 Naturally bright
31 Develops
34 C₆H₆
35 Stilted-sounding "Consider it done"
36 "The Godfather" enforcer who "sleeps with the fishes"
37 "Cheers" alternative, in a letter
38 Providers of inside looks?
39 "Minnie the Moocher" feature
43 Archer of film
44 In a day, say
45 Solving aid
46 End of a line in England
47 Hit MTV series starting in 2009
50 Double grace period?
52 Start operating, datewise

53 Vronsky's love
54 Stoolies, often
55 Like clams during winter
56 1993 rap hit in which Snoop Doggy Dogg popularized the term "bootylicious"

DOWN

1 Relatives of merengues
2 Heads off
3 Where trapeze artists connect
4 Ancient talisman with mathematical properties
5 ___ advantage
6 One bound to do work

7 Ball wear
8 Popping Prozacs, perhaps
9 Common statue setting
10 Ask
11 Legendary raptor
12 Figure skater Brasseur
13 Directed attention (on)
14 Runs over
20 Goes over
24 Source of false returns
26 Film critic Pauline
27 Magazine articles
29 E-tailing specifications
30 They can get choppy
31 "Ponyo" writer/director Hayao ___

32 In unison
33 Booms
34 Pickle
36 Pierce with lines
38 "West Side Story" Oscar winner
40 Like the I.B.M. PC, often
41 Light show?
42 Minute
44 Four enter them, but only two survive
47 Tennis star Novotna
48 Over there, to bards
49 Practice with gloves on
51 Once known as

by Steven Riley

174

ACROSS

1 Stage Deli staple
12 Gas ending
15 Writer who held 14 honorary doctorates
16 Deliver hooks, e.g.
17 Stephen King's next novel after "Christine"
18 Many a cell product
19 Quito-to-Lima dir.
20 Bolted
21 Melodic passages
23 Bottom part
24 Oyster Bay hamlet
25 "Hammerklavier," for one
28 Is in the can
29 Singer of the 2011 #1 hit "Someone Like You"
30 Ranee's wear
31 Dreadlocks cover
32 NC-17, maybe
33 Grooved ring on many a ring
34 It may be open at a comedy club
35 Sound that a muzzle muffles
36 One active in the heat?
37 Black scavenger
38 They can answer the question "Who's your daddy?"
40 Jerboa's home
41 Origins
42 Volstead Act opponents
43 Throws together
44 Two-wheeled carriage
45 Away's partner
48 Accent reduction may be part of it: Abbr.
49 Great work
52 Computer add-on?

53 1951 Tony winner for "Call Me Madam"
54 The idiot brother in "Our Idiot Brother"
55 It borders the Land of Lincoln

DOWN

1 Disco swingers?
2 Plural suffix for conditions
3 Turner Prize institution
4 Part of une danse
5 Collectible record
6 Chutney-dipped appetizer
7 Pre-Soviet succession
8 One may provide passage
9 Health care grp.
10 Crevice-lurking predator
11 1957 hit for Perry Como
12 Like some blood
13 One passed out on New Year's Eve
14 What many fans generate
22 Ending for 23-Across
23 Having nothing to part with?
24 More likely to go off
25 Choice for a bed made in the kitchen
26 ___ Line (German/Polish border)
27 Novel
28 Staggers
30 Mennonites and others

33 Diamond lane
34 Gravitation consideration
36 They have job listings
37 Does over, as a document
39 French pronoun
40 Hand wringer's words
42 Overpower
44 Be unsettled
45 Damage control grp.
46 "Ev'rybody Wants to Be ___" (Disney film tune)
47 Novelist Bazin
50 "___ nuff!"
51 N.Y.C. commuting debut of 1904

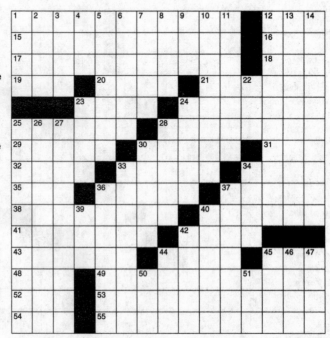

by Barry C. Silk

ACROSS

1 Pet subject
9 Presents itself
15 "My pleasure"
17 Dubious claim after crying wolf
18 They may be carted around
19 Defense option
20 Enough, to Étienne
22 Grammar subject
23 Guam-to-Tahiti dir.
25 Common canal locale: Abbr.
29 Great red spot?
37 Unlikely place to take one's business
38 Promise, e.g.
39 Weeps and wails
40 Old English letters
41 "The Black Cat" writer's inits.
42 "Yesterday," e.g.
47 Really tick off
52 Funny
55 Let go to pot?
56 1991 Jackie Chan film
60 Sign words often accompanied by an airplane symbol
61 Megillah book
62 One may get printed

DOWN

1 One of the Pointer Sisters
2 Some vaults
3 They're in the first draft
4 Kind of porridge
5 With 54-Down, kind of store
6 First name in 1970s tyranny
7 Giant among Giants
8 Words before problem or department
9 Drop ___ (be suggestive)
10 Dreaded believer?
11 Put under the table
12 Not peruse
13 Actress Watson
14 Admitted to a doctor's office
16 More or less follower
21 Mrs. F. Scott Fitzgerald and others
22 Like many monograms on clothing
24 Arrange for
26 Rather colloquial?
27 Much paper, originally
28 Compassion
29 33-Down, for one
30 Formed another congress
31 N.B.A. great Thomas
32 Pirates' hangout
33 Plains people
34 Like many bagged vegetables
35 Part of a Flintstone's yell
36 Consumes impolitely
43 Winged
44 Gas unit
45 Pirates' hangout
46 Starbucks has one
48 Gas units
49 Get a divorce
50 Make right
51 Sign of a narrowing path
52 John Paul II, e.g.
53 "Beowulf" or "Gilgamesh"
54 See 5-Down
57 "Tell Me More" broadcaster
58 Runner with a hood
59 Valuable stuff in a pocket

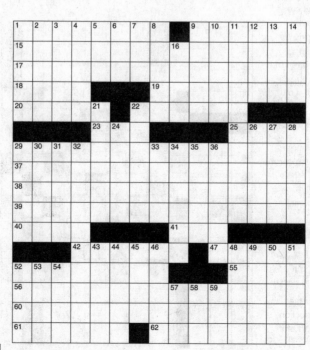

by Joe Krozel

176

ACROSS

1 Makeup of some insulating sheets
5 Vulcans and others
15 Sixth-day creation
16 Singer with a black V-shaped collar
17 Food product for the eco-conscious
19 "That man" in "I'm Gonna Wash That Man Right Outa My Hair"
20 It's often shown with hands
21 Word for a keeper?
22 Hands off
24 Approx. camera flash duration
26 Ending with plural, in Plymouth
27 Words before before
28 South Vietnam's ___ Dinh Diem
30 "Ooh-la-la!"
32 Across, in odes
33 Seize, old-style
35 Wine shop offering, informally
36 "The Girl I Knew Somewhere" group, with "the"
38 "My Best Friend's Girl" group
42 Harboring cold feelings?
43 It's often in the spotlight
45 Left-arrow abbr.
46 Language that gave us "catamaran"
48 Spotted à la Tweety Bird
49 Family
50 Gerrymander
51 Like many a teen idol
53 Ray with lines
55 National competitor
57 Selling point
59 Cloudless, in Saint-Cloud
60 Features of some Amerindian embroidery
63 Put in the spotlight
64 They have balls
65 Put through a chop shop, say
66 Brand name used by Jersey Standard

DOWN

1 Moved over, say
2 1781 Mozart premiere
3 Demographic lauded in a 1965 song
4 Not so scanty
5 Introspective query
6 Carnival follower
7 Hugo-winning 1994 memoir
8 Wheels from the Netherlands
9 Pleasing bank statement?
10 "Self-Reliance" essayist's inits.
11 Plane figs.
12 Fables, often
13 Knighted diamond magnate Oppenheimer
14 Spin out on the ice?
18 "___ Twelve Men" (Greer Garson film)
23 Old dagger
25 Trick
29 Beano alternative
31 Minute Maid brand
33 Holdover
34 "Vulcan's chimney"
37 Cityhopper carrier
39 Laugh hard
40 Geckos, e.g.
41 Guarantees
44 Not bound by 20-Across
46 Temple of Vesta locale
47 Group indiscriminately
49 Certain toast
50 ___-fire
52 Dirty
54 Defib setting
56 Dirty film
58 Where le nez is
61 She played Cécile in "Dangerous Liaisons"
62 Ending letters

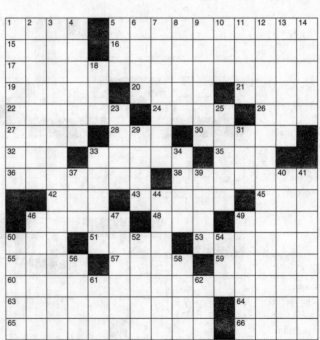

by Scott Atkinson

ACROSS

1 Letter carrier
8 Quaint place to live?
13 Extreme choice
16 Farmer's enemy
17 Much-favored person
18 Some subatomic particles
19 Retired
20 ___ Plus (razor brand)
22 Home to a school of pre-Socratic philosophers
23 Comedic duo?
24 Using an Rx, say
26 Ron who played Tarzan
27 Where your ship may come in
28 Loafs on the job
30 Filling point
34 "When I was a lad . . ."
36 Smooth
37 Six-time Tony winner of 1984
40 Stump the crowd?
41 Vet employer, maybe: Abbr.
42 16-Across, e.g.
43 Rambled
45 Bygone
46 86 or 99 on "Get Smart": Abbr.
47 Tangles
49 Chip in a dish, e.g.
53 Gush (over)
55 Round nos.
56 It's often backed up
57 Foreign assistance org. since 1961
59 Use advantageously, as an idea
61 Big name in watches
62 Place to find subs

63 Rob of "Melrose Place"
64 Discharged

DOWN

1 Word with square or number
2 Helpless?
3 "Can you beat that?!"
4 Bonanzas
5 Raised
6 Rule among true crime writers
7 Run wild
8 Physical "Psst!"
9 Grandnephew in 1960s TV
10 Not marked up
11 Cat's gift
12 Final words?
14 Passing remark?

15 "Gentle reader, may you never feel what I then felt!" speaker
21 Attach (to)
24 Instrument with a bell
25 Average
29 [This is scary!]
30 Lose it
31 Contents of the rightmost column of a table
32 Words of anticipation
33 Political writer ___ Bai
35 Scoop
38 Prizm and Spectrum, once
39 They're not hot for very long
44 Anchorage-to-Fairbanks dir.

48 Order: Abbr.
49 Contents of many outtakes
50 Wash against gently
51 Win by ___
52 Declined
54 Figure on the front of Olympic medals since 1928
56 Forward who wore #10
58 Elements of some lists
60 Quickly turn back

by Mike Nothnagel

ACROSS

1 Many a museum dinosaur display
8 Suited to the stage
15 What a telemarketer often hears before a click
17 Reward in the offing?
18 Three in a match, maybe
19 Covent Garden area
20 Taking some doing
23 Stains
27 Bleed (for)
31 Probably will
32 Back 40?
34 Nonstarter's lack
36 Threaten collapse
37 The Cherokee deemed it good training for war
38 Masters
39 Like Bacharach/David songs
40 Checked the meter?
42 Provider of up-to-the-minute info?
45 Follower of blood and guts
49 Might just
53 Scottie
54 Homemakers out on a limb?
55 Site of the first British colony in the Caribbean, 1624

DOWN

1 Leap-the-___ (world's oldest operating roller coaster)
2 Hungary's ___ Nagy
3 Doing the job
4 Huge-taloned menaces
5 Put down
6 Parmesan pronoun
7 Name meaning "grace"
8 Heroic son of Prince Anchises
9 Mustard family member
10 Easily snapping
11 He got a tennis scholarship from U.C.L.A.
12 Old bomber
13 Fat part
14 Reds great Roush
16 Traitors' Gate locale
20 Present
21 Senior
22 1930s film dog
23 Mandates
24 "___ signo vinces" (Constantine I's motto)
25 29-Down, for one
26 Two are often put in
27 "My Fair Lady" setting
28 Where to feel the beat?
29 Its capital is Wiesbaden
30 European city whose name sounds like two letters of the alphabet
32 Shameful gain
33 Nose-burning
35 Like much lumber
39 "The Last of the Mohicans" craft
40 Strawberry is one
41 One engaged in bucket-making
42 Toots
43 St. ___, Cornwall
44 Frobe who played Goldfinger
45 Sign letters on the cross
46 Execute a 47-Down, e.g.
47 See 46-Down
48 Rocky outcrops
49 China's ___ dynasty
50 Affliction a.k.a. "blue devils"
51 Strawberry was one
52 Chafe

by Robert H. Wolfe

ACROSS

1. "I'd like to hear any justification at all"
16. Young and inexperienced
17. "Yeah, and . . . ?"
18. Olympians brought them down
19. Flutter the eyelids, say
20. First name in horror
21. "I should ___ die with pity": King Lear
24. Surfing business?
27. Hole in the wall
30. "Roxana: The Fortunate Mistress" novelist
31. Antebellum Ohio, e.g.
34. Like much lumber
35. Intl. group whose biennial conferences are focuses of protest
36. Follower of grazing cattle
38. Put away
39. Word repeated before "lama sabachthani" in Mark 15
41. Frames wind up on them
43. Some crosses
45. "Love Actually" co-star, 2003
46. River that the dead drank from, in myth
47. You may leave them in stitches: Abbr.
48. "Das ___ gut!"
51. Bottom
53. Convertible
56. Bar cliché
61. It shows many flight numbers
62. Doesn't take the cake?

DOWN

1. You'll get it from CliffsNotes
2. Way to fry
3. Promise one will
4. Better
5. With 35-Down, have no malice
6. Quoted figs.
7. Sweet ending?
8. Big inits. in paperback publishing
9. Urban rumblers
10. Pulitzer-winning poet Armantrout and others
11. Ready for publication
12. What webpage sponsors may link to
13. Seat of Marin County, Calif.
14. "Listen up!" to Luis
15. State bordering the Pacific: Abbr.
21. Tangle up
22. One who shouldn't be helping
23. Winner of over 100 Pulitzer Prizes, briefly
25. Chiwere speakers
26. Time to abstain
28. Things done for fun, for short
29. From
31. Home of the U.S. Army Women's Museum
32. Upper house support
33. Misunderstands, say
35. See 5-Down
37. ___ volente
40. "Ow-w-w!"
42. They're hard to figure out
44. Always, in scores
49. "Rotten School" series author
50. Photographer's bath
52. Underscore neighbor
53. Mindless
54. Some MoMA works
55. Hide
56. Small bark
57. ___ good day
58. "Odi et ___": Catullus
59. 2000s, e.g.: Abbr.
60. One may be tight

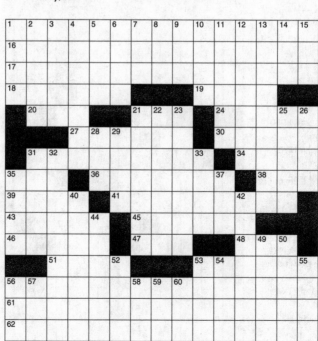

by Tim Croce

ACROSS

1 Skirt raisers?
9 Toward the tip
15 Equivalent of "ibidem"
16 __ 400 (Pennsylvania Nascar event)
17 They're often swiped at stores
18 Parnassian
19 Stereotypical bouncers
20 Do some post-harvesting work
21 Marion __, Emmy-winning actress on "Bewitched"
22 A hand
24 Singer in the "Odyssey"
25 "What __?"
26 Subject for Enrico Caruso
28 Kiss hit "Rock and Roll All __"
29 Western wear
31 Cousin of bridge
35 Discards
36 2001 presidential biography by Edmund Morris
40 Pull down
41 Michael who sang "I'm a lumberjack and I'm O.K."
42 Rudimentary run
46 Puts on a graph, say
48 Zero-deg. setting
49 Source of a feather in one's cap?
50 Symbol of power
52 TV hotline
54 Captured for posterity, maybe
55 Spanish port
56 Classic Lorre role
57 Jabbed back
58 Like classic stories
59 Macramé creators

DOWN

1 Helpful
2 Lorry supply
3 Shows reservations
4 Molière contemporary
5 Put to shame
6 "Heads up!"
7 Many an HBO show
8 Shrink time, say
9 8-Down, e.g.: Abbr.
10 Some toy bears, informally
11 They have two goals
12 Sets of friends
13 Liqueur sweetened with syrup
14 Locale in a much-studied 1934 photo
23 1970s–'80s N.B.A. nickname
26 Classical subject of a Velázquez painting in the Prado
27 Gone from a plate
29 "The Beverly Hillbillies" role
30 1920 Democratic presidential nominee
31 "Make a searching and fearless moral inventory of ourselves," in Alcoholics Anonymous
32 Digital bone
33 1980s–'90s Ford model
34 "Whatever"
37 Catchy tune
38 Medicinal tea source
39 Narcolepsy drug
42 Totally shaken
43 Family name in English literature
44 See 49-Down
45 Strong mounts
47 Walls of the heart
49 With 44-Down, it had its grand opening on 10/1/1982
51 Ranked player
53 __ the hat

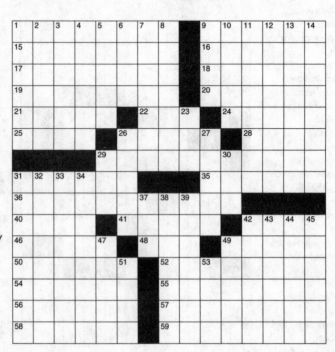

by Mark Diehl

ACROSS

1 One with a famous opening act?
8 Invite out for
13 They get the scoop at work
16 Run
17 Trying to win a radio contest, say
18 Figure in a doctor's office
19 Light breakfast
20 Liberal opening?
22 Notes come out of them
23 Old game co. that made D&D
24 Tree with catkins
26 Temporary retirements?
27 Intrepidity
29 "The Sorrows of Young Werther" author
31 Runs out of energy
33 Fix up
35 "Holy cow!"
36 Frustratingly difficult
39 Suffix with Caesar
40 Excrete
41 Swing wildly
42 11-Down, usually
44 Argument
46 Part of the intro to a piece of "Champagne Music"
47 Area in front of a basketball net, informally
49 ___-bear
52 Allocation of some pork spending?
53 A.L. East squad, on scoreboards
54 Quickly mount
57 Bit of funny business
59 Fools around
61 Advertiser with a computer-generated mascot

62 Game that gave rise to the expression "ace in the hole"
63 Thomas Cromwell's earldom
64 Positive or negative

DOWN

1 Fred has one in "Scooby-Doo" cartoons
2 Assistance for short people?
3 Thumb twiddler
4 Roll in a field
5 Do ___ (celebrate, sort of)
6 Player losing to the 49ers in Super Bowl XVI or XXIII
7 Intl. soccer powerhouse
8 Original airer of "The Jetsons"

9 ___ Crosley, author of the 2008 best seller "I Was Told There'd Be Cake"
10 Held back
11 Item in a trophy case
12 Cross-country trips, perhaps
14 Soul mate
15 N.F.L. All-Pro player Chris
21 What a fugue may be written for
25 "Passage to Marseille" actor, 1944
27 Valve opening?
28 Some flakes
30 Specialty doc
31 Connection indicators
32 "You're telling me!"
34 Discover, as a solution
36 21, often
37 2011 revolution locale

38 Item in a tent, maybe
43 "Ooh-la-la!"
45 "Better than nothing"
48 Informal approvals
49 Shoot up
50 "Breezing Up (A Fair Wind)" artist, 1876
51 When to celebrate el Día de los Reyes
55 "Outside the Lines" airer
56 Comprehensive
58 Boat navigator, informally
60 "___ Yu" (collection also known as "The Analects of Confucius")

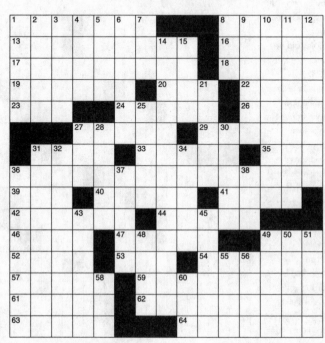

by Mike Nothnagel

182

ACROSS
1 Pettifog
9 Home of Texas A&M International University
15 Reprimander of Miss Gulch
16 Flew united?
17 Not covered anywhere
19 One in a powerful house
20 "Cats" Tony winner Trevor
21 Pop sharer
22 Legions
23 Heartless sort
25 Like many suites
26 Reason for a replay
27 "Join me?"
28 Prefix with -matic
29 Nautilus shell liners
30 "All Day Strong. All Day Long" sloganeer
31 Pole dance?
34 Their scales aid in location
36 "Do ___?"
37 Remove with leverage
39 Grp. on the floor
40 The health-conscious often take them
41 Bug about bills
44 Olden dagger
45 Uncommon delivery
46 Manager, briefly
47 Finishing touch on a diamond?
48 Dermatologist's concern
49 Affects radically
51 Events marked by large streamers
54 Was a real stinker
55 Pass
56 Meetings kept under wraps
57 Utterly unpredictable

DOWN
1 It's barely about a foot
2 Deliverer of the 1992 "Murphy Brown speech"
3 Relax during a massage, as a muscle
4 Bothered
5 Offers for lots
6 Drive away
7 Brown with the Band of Renown
8 Spring
9 Bit of rough housing
10 Kirk who played the first big-screen Superman
11 Mug, say
12 Program developments
13 Like raspberries
14 They're unmatched in footwear
18 "Hey, it's something to consider"
24 Transport
25 Bed for some kebabs
27 Tin finish?
29 Worker with vital information?
30 Film composer Clausen and others
31 Get off on the wrong foot
32 Erhard succeeded him in 1963
33 "The Vanishing American" novelist, 1925
35 Taking great pains
38 Shower surprise
40 Some quiet riots
41 "André" playwright William
42 1982 and 1991 Pulitzer winner for fiction
43 Ford's press secretary
46 Defense grp. formed in 1954
48 Four-time Gold Glove Award winner Boone
50 Man in la famille
52 Agreements
53 Duct lead-in

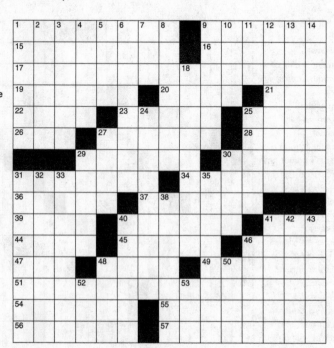

by Barry C. Silk

ACROSS

1 One called upon to decide
5 Back cover?
10 Keep the complaints coming
14 Pavlova of the ballet
15 Head stone?
16 Nondairy alternative
17 O.K.
20 First #1 hit for the Commodores
21 Counterfeit
22 Horse shows?
23 Hard to see through, say
24 Laid eyes on
25 Hardly seaworthy
26 Takes shape
27 Apple seed
30 About
31 One of Franklin's certainties
32 Little Tramp prop
33 Diagnosis deliverers: Abbr.
34 Expended some nervous energy
35 Commuting option in Georgia's capital
36 Jockey's uniform
37 First female chancellor of Germany
38 Attributes (to), with "up"
40 Former "CBS Morning News" co-anchor Bill
41 Spotlight
44 "Yeah, right!"
45 Play money?
46 The Donald's second ex
47 Small letter
48 Some ruminants
49 Bob ___, "To Kill a Mockingbird" villain
50 Santa ___ Valley (wine-growing region)

DOWN

1 Play group
2 Getting better
3 Not caught up
4 First son, sometimes
5 Warp drive repairman on the original "Star Trek"
6 Koran memorizer
7 Koran reciter
8 Like a town that used to be a ghost town
9 Schooner features
10 Sat on a sill, maybe
11 Finnish architect Aalto
12 Tries out for a part
13 Part of many a tech school's name
18 "The North Pole" author, 1910
19 Phone company offers
23 Hardly stocky
24 "The Battle of the ___" (D. W. Griffith film)
26 Pick-up sticks piece
27 English physician James who gave his name to a disease
28 Not ready to go, you might say
29 Ring
31 "I want the lowdown!"
32 Not drawn true to life
34 Starchy dish
35 Good reason for promotion
36 "Tom ___, Detective" (1896 novel)
37 Held in common
38 Part of a boomtown's skyline
39 Cause of careless mistakes
40 Rise
41 Utterly exhausted
42 Literary governess's surname
43 Courtroom cry

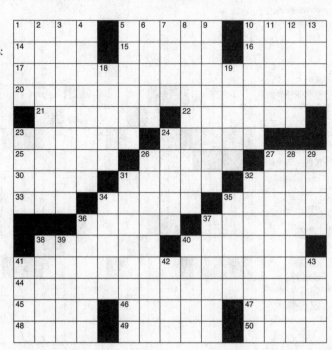

by Patrick Berry

184

ACROSS

1 Stuff between some cake layers
16 Brood terribly
17 They may perform minor surgeries
18 Menu general
19 Harbors
20 Jobs announcement?
21 Refreshment site
24 Thing that's picked
26 Old-time actresses Allgood and Haden
30 Ad ___
32 Tom Sawyer's half brother
34 Org. with lead concerns
35 Staff member checking the books
41 Self-correcting or self-cleaning, say
42 Put some matter in the gray matter?
43 "Nasty!"
44 Kill
45 Besides
46 Big pictures
49 Ball-bearing piece
51 Sycosis source, informally
55 Trucial States, today: Abbr.
57 Buzzsaw Brown, e.g.
59 Little Parisian?
60 Ruthless
66 Something baffling
67 Creates more incentive to win

DOWN

1 Poem comprised of quotations
2 Common language in Niger
3 Others, to Juan
4 Calculator button
5 In dire need of gas
6 First name in Polish politics
7 Literary lion
8 1955 sci-fi film that was one of the first to use Technicolor
9 Contracted time period?
10 More than mar
11 Killers that may go through hoops
12 City near Oneida Lake
13 ". . . ___ fool returneth to his folly": Proverbs 26:11
14 Thing to fry in
15 8-Down characters, briefly
22 She pounded the East Coast in 2011
23 Alternative to Tempur-Pedic
25 Luis in the Red Sox Hall of Fame
27 Like many things that come back
28 "Every man will be ___ if he can": Thoreau
29 South Asian wear: Var.
31 Moon of Jupiter
33 Ticket, informally
35 Color-streaked playing marble
36 Grp. involved with Brown v. Board of Education
37 McAloo ___ (burger at McDonald's in India)
38 About
39 Apollo's birthplace
40 Otherwise
47 Round dance officials
48 Hall-of-Fame jockey Earl
50 Olympic-level
52 Vertical, at sea
53 Nez ___
54 Ear protectors
56 Time to evolve?
58 Those, to Juan
60 Seagoing sort
61 Cry upon figuring out 66-Across
62 Trombonist Winding
63 Express
64 Time of year for much raking: Abbr.
65 Grp. with a piece plan?

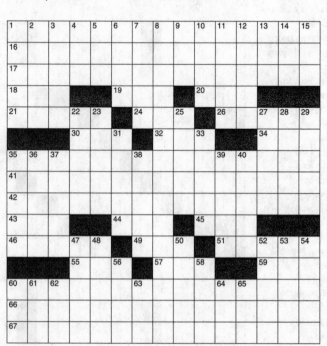

by Gary J. Whitehead

185

ACROSS

1 Goldeneye relative
5 Emergency extractor
15 "Must've been something ___"
16 No night owl
17 Jags of the 1960s and '70s
18 Eggbeater
19 Election extension?
20 Wrestling event
21 Only one of the 13 Colonies not touching the Atl. Ocean
22 Go crazy
24 Board provision
26 They're prepared to sell snake oil
27 Stock keeper
28 Third qtr. closer
31 See
32 Ferris wheel in Dallas that is the tallest in North America
34 Angle in botany
35 Support
36 El ___
37 Very turbulent situation
39 Slopes
40 Lifesaving squad: Abbr.
41 Wrong
42 Collector of dust bunnies
43 ESPN anchor Kolber
44 Word before and after "for"
45 Moolah
48 Ancient neighbor of Judah
49 Bladder
50 Follower of "Help!"
53 Feature of some lenses

54 ___ Line (international boundary)
55 Alfredo sauce brand
56 One concerned with bouquets
57 Buzz producers

DOWN

1 Wells Fargo Center event, informally
2 38-Down's second chance
3 They never end
4 Jazzman Montgomery
5 The Pink Panther and others
6 Showed delight, in a way
7 Certiorari, e.g.
8 Olympus OM-1, e.g.
9 Olive ___
10 Browning equipment
11 Smearing in ink?
12 "The fix ___"
13 Shedder of spores
14 Mother of the Valkyries
20 Three-time All-Star pitcher Pappas
23 "Mack the Knife" composer
24 Annual "Hot 100" publisher
25 They're historically significant
27 Generated
28 Cardinal for 22 years
29 Newark suburb
30 Security account?
32 Robe material
33 Fixes at an animal hospital

35 Complete
38 Person making a mark
39 Grouch
42 Crack investigator's target?
43 Buffalo pro
44 Quiet type
45 It's often knitted
46 Designer Gernreich
47 "___ Holden" (Irving Bacheller novel)
48 Very
51 "Still Crazy" star, 1998
52 Family nickname
53 Singsong syllable

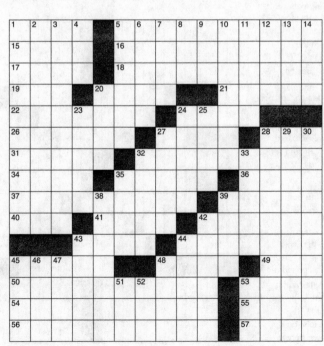

by Barry C. Silk

ACROSS

1. Fault line?
8. Rope holding down a bowsprit
15. Great part for Duvall?
16. 1945 Tommy Dorsey hit
17. Medium frequencies include them
18. Journalists James and James Jr.
19. Nigerian language
20. Ingredient in gourmet potato chips
22. ___ de guerre
23. Scary sucker, for short
25. Bastes
26. Look down
27. Shot stuff
29. LP insert?
30. Pungent fish topper
31. Longtime ace
33. Goes gray
35. Part of some fruit drink names
37. Film with the protagonist "Z"
38. Any of three title characters in a long-running Cartoon Network series
42. See 46-Across
46. With 42-Across, old ad mascot who sang "It's dandy for your teeth"
47. Worked (up)
49. Source of the word "robot"
50. Salad, often
51. ___ up (brawl)
53. Big name in jewelry retail
54. Mouths, to Marius
55. Spartan
57. Ad trailer?
58. Reaches the age of
60. It forms much of Lombardy's southern border

62. One
63. Central feature of St. Peter's Square
64. Taco alternative
65. "Coppelia" composer

DOWN

1. Parent's peremptory "reason"
2. Common barn roof
3. Passenger's status
4. Taxonomy suffix
5. Drum and bass parts
6. Through
7. Get heat from?
8. Part of French Polynesia
9. Some German models
10. Boom follower, maybe
11. Boom maker, once
12. Gnarly
13. Author of "The Stranger Beside Me," 1980
14. Beatles tune that begins "If you wear red tonight"
21. Like arias
24. Sugar
26. Dash
28. Oscar winner after "On the Waterfront"
30. Onetime Lake Texcoco dweller
32. Papuan port
34. Having five sharps
36. Drink that had a Wild Red variety
38. Drink that has a Ruby Red variety
39. Philippine province on Luzon
40. The Aggies of the Big West Conf.
41. "What ___?"
43. Steak or chop choice
44. Cover-up witnessed by millions?
45. Relatives of dik-diks
48. Car bar
51. So as not to be overheard, say
52. Alabama or Missouri
55. ___-Pacific
56. First name in long jumping
59. Small creature that undergoes metamorphosis
61. Clinton or Bush, once

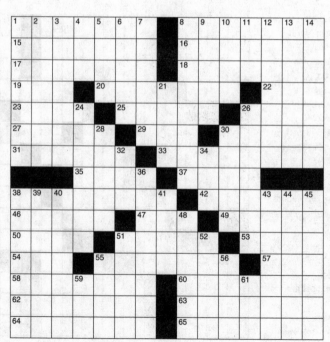

by Ned White

ACROSS

1 Drive-in theater, in old slang
11 Klutzes
15 Like some freely available software
16 Streaming video giant
17 What an up-and-coming band wants to snag
18 Keatsian or Horatian
19 Say "Ta-da!," say
20 "Hmm . . ."
22 "____ Maria"
24 PC file extension
25 The shakes, for short
26 Together
31 Cary of "The Princess Bride"
33 They might be cut at a salon
34 Kind of rock or candy
36 Not fancy at all
38 Bob Hope, for 18 Oscar ceremonies
39 When repeated, response to "Who wants ice cream?"
40 Traffic cone
41 Fidgeting during a poker game, e.g.
42 Grind
43 Dastard
44 Jai alai basket
46 Produces new music for, as a movie
48 Shake
49 Company name ender
51 Where Barry Bonds was an All-American, in brief
52 First female dean of Harvard Law School
56 Football Hall-of-Famer Marchetti
60 Michigan college
61 Craft in a "Star Wars" battle scene
63 Like some German nouns: Abbr.
64 Individually

65 Language from which "hubbub" comes
66 "The Case of the Demure Defendant" protagonist

DOWN

1 Offering from a Parisian butcher
2 Copycat
3 Like some Spanish wine
4 What people waving their arms might produce
5 It has more museums per capita than any other country: Abbr.
6 Lots
7 Fully exposed
8 Ready, in Rouen
9 Caesarean section?
10 Wired, in a way
11 Eager pupil's cry
12 Where to see some German models
13 Rubble neighbor
14 Is god-awful
21 ____ Avivian
23 Gripper
26 Scoffing comment
27 One hurling insults
28 Fictional narrator of "Legends of the Old Plantation"
29 Home to the Browns and the Reds
30 Bottom
32 Moe Howard catchphrase
35 Moe Howard, for Chris Diamantopoulos, in 2012
37 Tips
40 Ranks for jarheads: Abbr.

42 Sleeveless option
45 ____ Maria
47 Levelheadedness
48 ____ Dixon, self-styled seer who wrote an astrology book for dogs
50 "The Dark Knight" actor
53 "Great" detective of kiddie lit
54 Will of "The Waltons"
55 Way off
57 "Really?"
58 Literary captain who says "I am not what you call a civilized man!"
59 ____ Ishii ("Kill Bill" character)
62 Group of whales

by Natan Last

ACROSS

1 Drinking problem
9 If all goes swimmingly
15 Sugar
16 André and Mia adopted her
17 Change-producing agent
18 Water park recreation
19 Big dogs
20 1969 Tony winner for "Promises, Promises"
21 Colon's meaning, at times
22 When to see der Mond
23 Big name in gourmet chocolate
26 More likely to be bowdlerized
30 Chiwere speaker
31 Emmy-winning show of 2007, '08 and '09
35 Rom. tongue
36 Didn't demur
37 Face-topping figure
38 1955 Dior debut
40 Tiropita ingredient
41 Maximally mean
42 Nearly flawless bodies?
43 Place
46 1989 E.P.A. target
48 One in the closet
50 Starts to stagnate
54 Smallish printing format
55 Response to a surprising statement
56 One may be required to park
57 Start to squirm
58 2009–11 Republican National Committee chairman
59 Their voices really carry

DOWN

1 Fast shuffle
2 ___ Debevoise, Marilyn Monroe's "How to Marry a Millionaire" role
3 Some turnovers: Abbr.
4 It goes whichever way the wind blows
5 Apollo, for one
6 Sailor's behind
7 Piece offer?
8 Forest race of fantasy
9 Respecting
10 What seeds are often planted in
11 2008 Libertarian presidential candidate
12 Computing behemoth
13 Coordinate
14 Like best friends
23 Woman who "drank Champagne and danced all night," in song
24 Rom. tongue
25 Terse demurral
27 Posse, e.g.
28 Early radio receiver
29 Kin of -niks
31 Bits
32 Draft team
33 Reference
34 Rondos, e.g.
36 Big ray
39 Magic show?
40 Producer of the venom solenopsin
42 Annual George Jean ___ Award for Dramatic Criticism
43 Bazaar makeup
44 Indicator of silence
45 ___ Rios de Minas, Brazil
47 It might be a triple
49 Mechanical
50 Pen pals?
51 Quintillionth: Prefix
52 Locale in a Beatles title
53 Kikkoman options

by Caleb Madison

ACROSS

1 Ones pressed for cash, briefly
5 1997 #1 hit with a nonsense title
11 Many a bugger
14 See 63-Across
15 Code that's dangerous to break
16 Hermano de la madre
17 ___ en scène
18 More like a gymnast's body
19 Cartoon character who cries "You eediot!"
20 It may be acknowledged with a slap
23 Bad stroke
24 Back, in a way
25 Having the lead?
29 Real go-getter
30 Baker's dozen, maybe
33 Reading letters from the end?
34 TV's "hipster doofus"
37 Big name in footwear
39 Wish
40 Ticker with cachet
42 Watch it
47 Temporary
50 "9 to 5" director Higgins
51 Bad tool for a toddler to find
55 N.L. West team, on scoreboards
56 One seen in a shower
57 Ramirez of "Grey's Anatomy"
58 It's often illegal to hang one
59 Cry for more

60 2006–08 heavyweight champion Maskaev
61 Article in the Louvre?
62 High
63 With 14-Across, cruise bonus

DOWN

1 Tops
2 Wee bit
3 Fish out of water
4 Word chanted at a celebratory party
5 Routs, with "down"
6 When the Salt Lake City Olympics took place
7 Longtime first name in TV talk
8 Court paper showing one team's points
9 Comical Cheri
10 Adidas vis-à-vis Reebok
11 Alien
12 Like some navels
13 Jon Voight's New York birthplace
21 Air and water, e.g.
22 Yellow shade
26 Runaway
27 Organic compound
28 Scrappers put them up
31 Sprung thing
32 Response facilitator: Abbr.
34 What water lacks
35 When to get back to work, perhaps
36 Endpoint of pilgrims' progress?
37 Big name in frozen food
38 Circle
41 Snowboarders compete in them
43 Some Rodin pieces
44 Lye, for one
45 Like many grandstands
46 Tee off
48 Apropos of
49 Retail giant with the mascots Red Ruff and Blue Mews
52 Extra-bright
53 Bolted
54 He talked only to Wilbur

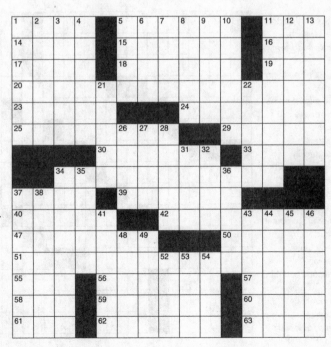

by Allan E. Parrish

ACROSS

1 One with a coat of many colors
10 Asian sea name
14 Girl group with a 1986 #1 hit
15 "Sì, mi chiamano ___" (Puccini aria)
16 Like telescopes
17 The Olympic Australis, e.g.
18 Unlocked?
19 1977 Paul Davis hit that spent 25 weeks in the Top 40
21 Negligible
22 Rubber
24 Old man
25 "___ Time," 1952 million-selling Eddie Fisher hit
26 Solitary places
27 ___ Humpalot, Austin Powers villain
29 Pro ___
30 City NNE of Toledo
31 Game in which players offer a few words
34 Swingers hit on them at parties
35 Manila airport name
36 Like hurricane weather
37 Punishment, metaphorically
38 Bill who composed "Gonna Fly Now"
39 Big trap
42 CBer's place
43 "Clamshell" computers of old
45 Kennedy Center happening
46 First, second and third
48 Historic D.C. theater
49 Beast fought by Heracles
50 Donning, as loafers
53 Gloom
54 Chilling
55 Short winter day?
56 They may be heard in a temple

DOWN

1 Redeem
2 Second Triumvirate member
3 David with a role for himself on TV
4 Muscle ___
5 Junk
6 California's Montaña de ___ State Park
7 Duchess of Cornwall
8 Mates
9 Dishes eaten with the hands
10 Topic for Catullus
11 Shred
12 Rain forest region
13 Resting spots by the water
14 "Stop!" overseas
20 Pasta go-with
22 Four-time Oscar nominee (never a winner) in the 1930s
23 Motivators
26 Doesn't merely observe
28 Heady time for soldiers
29 Rapid turnover
30 They're hard to see through
31 Organization of Afro-American Unity founder
32 School house?
33 Comic strip that Chic Young abandoned to create "Blondie"
34 No-goodnik
36 Touching bottom?
38 Pet peeve?
39 Herbert Henry Asquith's socialite wife
40 ___ Snow, Russell Brand's character in "Forgetting Sarah Marshall" and "Get Him to the Greek"
41 "___ That a Time?" (Weavers album)
44 Poet credited with popularizing haiku
45 They may be heard in a temple
47 Signs
48 Done, in Dunkirk
51 Wanamaker Trophy org.
52 Jewelry box item

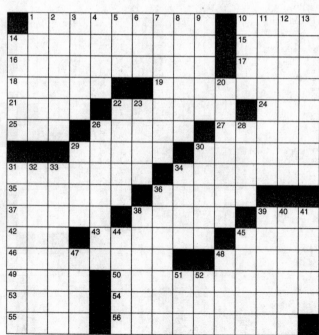

by Patrick Berry

ACROSS

1 Finery
8 Key for someone with 20/20 vision?
14 Audit targets
15 Concluding syllables
16 Take at an opportune time
17 Grooms
18 Modern chemistry experiment?
20 End of a dictionary
21 "The Scarperer" author
22 "Ciao"
24 "The cautious seldom ___": Confucius
25 Teary
27 ___ Fields
28 Winter ailment, informally
29 Get dressed for a party, say
31 52-Down unit
34 One who's blue, for short?
36 Poison ivy and others
37 Herb that causes euphoria
39 2022 World Cup host, maybe
41 Threshold
42 Raw
44 Lead character in Larry McMurtry's "Lonesome Dove"
47 Many a "Twilight" fan
49 Stick for a kite
50 Bankrupted
51 It might be covered by an umbrella
54 "Aladdin" princess
55 Remove spots from
56 Compass divisions
57 Most slapstick
58 Showcases of rock bands?
59 Ones who are hurting?

DOWN

1 Blow up, maybe
2 Fix for a wobbly table
3 Boot cover
4 Carving tools
5 A wolf may have one
6 Part of a jail cell
7 Prescription directive
8 Swept, say
9 Yards, e.g.
10 Command associated with numbers
11 "Couldn't agree with you more"
12 Seemed right
13 They go below signatures, briefly
15 Oct. 24
19 "Moby-Dick" setting
23 Lethal injection administerers
25 Hinged vessel, often
26 2001 British Open champion David
28 Britain's biggest-selling paper, with "The"
30 Certain board member: Abbr.
31 "Home Invasion" rapper
32 Avoid humiliation
33 Points in the direction of
35 First jazz musician to win a Pulitzer Prize
38 Raises
40 "Eugene Onegin" girl
43 Conditions, with "up"
44 Museum employees
45 Revolutionary state
46 Christmas tree base coverings
48 One who's really going places
50 Like the majority of Saudis
52 Informal pub
53 Brown green?
54 Prod

by Brendan Emmett Quigley

ACROSS

1 Accompanier of a thrown tomato
8 Reddish-orange gem
15 Settled
16 Like the sky
17 High-carb party snack
18 Midwest birthplace of Orson Welles and Don Ameche
19 Berry of "Mayberry R.F.D."
20 "Ha, see?!"
22 Heart, to Hadrian
23 Norway's Order of St. ___
25 Local protest acronym
26 Avoid work, in Britain
27 Try, informally
29 Jack-a-___ (hybrid dog)
30 Perfect Day maker
31 Green acres?
33 Basic bit of algebra
35 News newbie
36 Sartre's soul
37 Musée Rodin masterpiece
41 Home of the U.S. Army Airborne Forces
45 One of about a million on a jetliner
46 Fictional title sch. of a 1994 comedy film
48 Choice at some check-ins
49 "___ it!"
50 No-no for objectivity
52 Allowing no play
53 Adapted intro?
54 Make stylish
56 Bush much seen around Florida
57 Approach from out of nowhere
59 Stylish
61 Edible floppy disk?
62 Select from a menu
63 World's largest nocturnal primates
64 ___ Beer Night (1974 baseball promotion that ended in a riot)

DOWN

1 "I don't want to fight, man"
2 His opening line is "'Tis better as it is"
3 Like some markets and headphones
4 Bit of witchery
5 Brand with a paw print in its logo
6 Progeny
7 Advice from Dr. Ruth
8 Target of Fonzie's fist bumps
9 Impressionism?
10 One to walk with
11 Nigerian people
12 Pointless situation
13 Program guides
14 Talk of the town
21 Subj. in the 2007 documentary "Sicko"
24 Like some pullovers
26 Point out?
28 It might prevent a blackout
30 Friend of Pumbaa
32 "Are We There Yet?" airer
34 Skin pic?
37 Big name in weight-loss pills
38 Stowed
39 Prince of Darkness
40 Thin construction strips
41 Cool bit of trivia
42 For laughs
43 Like some fingernails and eyelashes
44 Bart Simpson catchphrase
47 Half-___
50 Rail nail
51 Tutu material
54 Make unbearable?
55 It may be unbearable
58 Andean tuber
60 Turn-of-the-century year

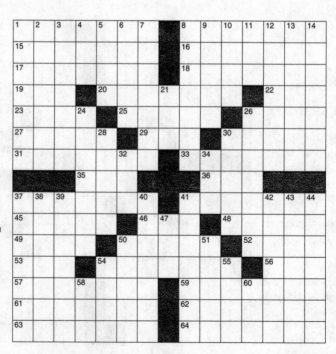

by Peter Wentz

ACROSS

1. Children's author Eleanor
6. Environment of many old PCs
11. Opposite of ample
13. Grapefruit taste-alike
14. Heated house for newborn chicks
16. Round number?
17. Restless, in scores
18. Go beyond seconds, say
19. Confirmation declaration
20. Some people in costume
21. "This doesn't exactly require a Ph.D."
23. What big banks underwent in 2009
24. ___ B (initial step)
25. They may be studied along with languages
33. What past performance may portend
35. Wild West symbol of authority
36. Practice at a track
38. Went for something else
39. SeaWorld attraction
40. Put people in their places?
41. Activity in "Ghostbusters"
42. Firewood measures
43. Attempt to recall the passed?

44. Stunned, in a way
45. German composer with a palindromic name

DOWN

1. Enclose in a recess
2. Eisenstein who directed "The Battleship Potemkin"
3. Some Asian believers
4. Hardly the self-effacing sort
5. Not so frantic
6. Really bothers
7. Give a smug look
8. Big name in diamonds
9. Last name in Chicago lore
10. It's unsettling to be out of them
12. Patch up, in a way, as a space shuttle
13. Quaint, dignified dance for couples
15. Valentine verse starter
16. Reach an agreement
22. Many a red dwarf
25. Things people "do" in the early afternoon
26. Mailbox checker's excited cry
27. Taught a lesson, maybe
28. Goes back on one's word?
29. Same old orders

30. Less congealed
31. Singer Morse with the 1952 hit "The Blacksmith Blues"
32. Giving expression to
33. Piñata-hitting occasion
34. Superlawyer Gerry who wrote "How to Argue and Win Every Time"
35. "___ no one"
37. "Old Time Rock & Roll" rocker

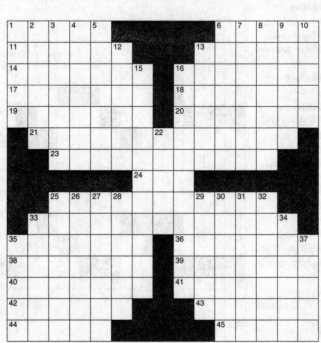

by Joe Krozel

194

ACROSS

1 Dessert for an infant
16 A straight shot it's not
17 "Bi-i-ig difference!"
18 Plea before going under
19 Him, in Hamburg
20 Certain chain unit: Abbr.
21 What's next to nothing in Nogales?
22 Paradise in literature
24 Produced some pitches
28 "Guten ___" (German greeting)
31 Beard growing out of an ear
32 San Francisco's ___ Valley
33 It may be pulled out while holding something up
38 Not so significantly
39 Cause for urgent action
40 Gothic leader?
41 Push around
42 Very conservative
43 [Don't touch my food!]
45 One chained to a desk, say
46 Certain chain units: Abbr.
47 Prefix with central
49 Going through
50 Fell
53 Tycoon who was the first person in New York City to own a car
59 Best seller that begins "Children are not rugged individualists"
60 Least accessible parts

DOWN

1 Eastern titles
2 Entirely, after "in"
3 Hodges who called baseball's "shot heard 'round the world"
4 Fay's "King Kong" role
5 "Absolutely!"
6 Taquería tidbit
7 Jet
8 Title in an order
9 Brand-new toy?
10 Net sales
11 Terminal list: Abbr.
12 Many stored hoses
13 Czech martyr Jan
14 Gen. Bradley's area: Abbr.
15 Person going into a house?: Abbr.
21 Man in a tree?
22 Liking a lot
23 Name shared by two U.S. presidents
25 Lets off the hook?
26 Unclaimed
27 Upper crust
28 Trouper's skill
29 New arrival of the 1950s?
30 More than fascinate
31 It shares a border with Switzerland
34 "___ said . . ."
35 Not single
36 Fixture in a doctor's office
37 Periodic law figs.
44 Change the borders of, say
45 Some pitch producers
46 Look a lot like
48 Dawdle
49 "___ l'amour"
50 2009 Wimbledon semifinalist Tommy
51 Best by a bit
52 Some branched pipes
53 Served the purpose
54 Urban trailer?
55 Went from soup to nuts, say
56 Syst. first implemented during W.W. I
57 Faze
58 Inits. of Ben Gunn's creator

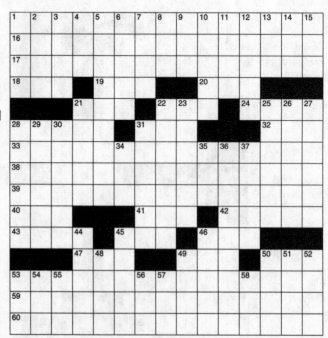

by Tim Croce

ACROSS

1 "I'm a Survivor" sitcom
5 "West Side Story" girlfriend
10 Cabinet maker?: Abbr.
14 Icelandic saga subject
16 Long way to walk?
17 "Chantez-Chantez" singer, 1957
18 It's 180° from X
19 Cell division?
20 Places to put up
21 It's taken by some coll. seniors
22 Business brass
24 Some encumbrances
25 Class Notes subject, informally
27 "___ Gott, vom Himmel sieh darein" (Bach cantata)
30 Memorial Day performance
31 Almost in vain
36 Road locomotives
37 Runners often seen in windows
38 Big names
39 Poetic period
40 Idaho motto opener
41 Big guns in the Mideast
43 Norman with a legendary swing
45 Flying ___
46 Put away
50 Kosher's Islamic equivalent
53 Digital protection
54 Water flow regulator
56 Dip ___ in
57 Trafalgar Square figure
58 Lacking
59 Took home courses?
60 Salinger girl

DOWN

1 Hester Prynne's stigma
2 Journalist Burnett of 55-Down
3 Aid in judging distances
4 School rings?
5 Some patient responses
6 Beverage once sold "in all popular flavors"
7 Press
8 Coastal plunger
9 Some pitcherfuls
10 Southeast Asian soarer
11 Toasts
12 First name in 2000 headlines
13 Venting aids
15 Director Angelopoulos who won the 1988 Palme d'Or
23 The Five ___, 1950s million-selling doo-wop group
24 Slow passage
25 "___ baby!"
26 Singer learning a script
28 Bonehead
29 "Iceland" star, 1942
30 Function of some forks
32 1970s Thunderbird options
33 Rose family member
34 Waldorf Astoria muralist
35 Tiger Express station brand
41 ___ Edibles (food shop on "The Facts of Life")
42 Spyder rival
44 South Korea's first president
46 Luzón, e.g.
47 Cardiological concern
48 River at Chartres
49 Conn of "Grease"
51 Its diameter is measured in picometers
52 Singer Lovich
55 Home of "Your Bottom Line"

by Martin Ashwood-Smith

ACROSS

1 Al Jazeera locale
10 Shot
15 2012 election issue
16 Set ___
17 Flip
18 Boss's directive
19 Mens ___
20 Soup flavorer
21 Source of some inside info?
22 Trouble in the night
24 Snarky reply after a lecture
26 W.W. II battle town
27 Bird named for its call
28 Foreign leader
29 Slip
31 Relishes
34 Leader given the posthumous title Rex Perpetuus Norvegiae
36 Trinity member
40 Jones's "Men in Black" role
44 Calculus, e.g.
45 Undercover wear?
48 Close up
49 Mates
50 Collegiate honor society of Bloomberg and Iacocca
53 Annie who voiced Bo Peep in "Toy Story"
54 Sticking points?
55 Cross reference?
57 Executed
58 Word with control or sight
59 Access provider
61 Some are bitter
62 Avalanche gear
63 Clipped
64 #1 on VH1's "40 Hottest Hotties of the '90s"

DOWN

1 Popular events for gamblers
2 The duck in "Peter and the Wolf"
3 It rates over 100,000 on the Scoville scale
4 Health advocacy abbr.
5 Grilling option
6 Berry variety
7 Nudist's lack
8 Shrinking body
9 Brief word
10 Noodles
11 '50s trial
12 Rock carrier
13 Dish containing masa
14 How one might speak
21 Where to pin a medal
23 First name in aviation
25 Major downer?
30 Taunt
32 Pause fillers
33 ___ Park, home of the San Diego Padres
35 Wedding wear
37 Spreadsheet command
38 Hockey shot involving two players
39 Story locale?
41 School grp.
42 Food whose name comes from the Tupi language of South America
43 "M*A*S*H" character from Toledo, Ohio
45 Military craft
46 "Pain Is Love" rapper
47 Beau
51 Big name in motels
52 Clean, in a way
53 What may represent "I" in American Sign Language
56 Game played across the world
59 Calculus abbr.
60 Setting in "Call of Duty: Black Ops," informally

by David Quarfoot

ACROSS

1 Field agents?
11 Amount to
15 Home of Owens Corning Corporation
16 First lady Harrison
17 Catchphrase of the '80s
18 Rock's Kings of ___
19 Big party
20 Big party
21 Coulrophobe's bugaboo
22 Extra turn in Monopoly
24 "Monster" actress, 2003
25 Explanatory lead-in
27 Composer/conductor Webern
28 What was yours at one time?
31 Puck, for one
33 Building with giant doors
35 Envy, anger or greed, maybe
36 Many a prom corsage
38 Napa Valley sight
39 Postal stamp on una carta
40 Patrick of "Barry Lyndon"
42 Dotted ones are half again as long
43 French cathedral city
48 Hard hits
49 Curly-haired toon
50 Possible result of an allergic reaction
51 Joe Hardy's girlfriend in the Hardy Boys books
52 What an ad blocker might block
54 Oater sound
55 Taking a load off
56 Big name in salad dressing
57 Current

DOWN

1 Shortchange
2 Duck and quail
3 "___ Walk" (Frost poem)
4 O'Connor of "Xena"
5 Setting for Yankees home games: Abbr.
6 Money-saving fast-food option
7 Nassau ___ liqueur
8 I = V/R
9 Accompanying
10 Like the K.G.B.: Abbr.
11 Excusing oneself from work, maybe
12 "Home on the Range" range
13 Treats to beat the heat
14 Kind of bed
21 Comparatively arch
23 Carnival booth with soda bottles
26 Jean, Jacques or Jean-Jacques
28 Like some paper punches
29 Do business?
30 They're usually found on the margins
32 Tomato
34 "Stand" band
36 "Walk On By" singer
37 Zesty casserole with a crust
41 Halloween personae
44 In the midst of
45 Overhauled
46 "The Vampire Diaries" girl
47 Rank smoke
49 Nobelist name of 1922 and 1975
52 D.E.A. target drug
53 Transportation for many a Little League team

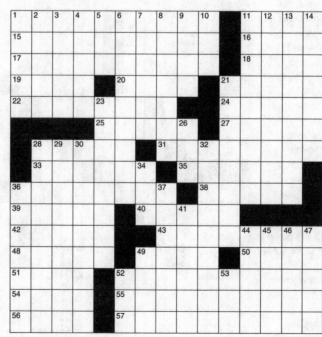

by Mark Diehl

198

ACROSS

1 Mass merchandise?
7 A nerd has a low one
15 Side effect or ride effect?
16 Where to select Select All
17 Won't shut up
18 Far Eastern marinade
19 "Les Misérables" feature
20 Avian abductors
21 One goes along the 38th parallel, briefly
22 Protective zoo feature
23 49-Across maker
25 Wind sound
26 Unthreatening sorts
28 Don Diego de la Vega, familiarly
29 Dir. from 30-Across to Norfolk
30 See 29-Across
31 Some change in Russia
32 Ab follower
33 Aid in getting around
34 Brown drawer
37 Father figure?
38 Alternative to mushrooms
41 Puts some black lines on
42 Youngest member of a 1990s girl group
44 Sign of spotlessness
45 Leave
46 Like anatomical anvils
47 ___ Tech
48 Lightsaber user
49 23-Across product
51 Slowly came through
53 Chao of George W. Bush's cabinet
54 Characteristic of salts
55 Try to get off the straight and narrow
56 Thriller killer?
57 Pulling together, say

DOWN

1 They'll get you going with the flow
2 Like many a juke joint
3 Good place to lay down arms
4 Subject of I.R.S. Form 8949
5 It's noble
6 Natural Bridges State Beach locale
7 Fee
8 Some classic theaters
9 Around
10 Reply to "Really?"
11 Tan in a bookstore
12 Material for a slag furnace
13 Hard-to-remove stain
14 Chain serving Torpedoes and Bullets
24 It's deposited in drops
25 Betray dejection
27 Roars
28 Drops off, with "out"
31 About whom Obama said "He is a jackass. But he's talented"
32 New circulator of 2002
33 All-Century Team member
34 Breaks
35 Nice country house
36 They bare arms
37 Preprandial performance
38 Big Chilean export
39 Focus of some fairs
40 Ordered
42 Obfuscates
43 Mexican motel
45 Ushered
48 Simple gymnastics move
50 One way to direct a helm
52 Casino spot

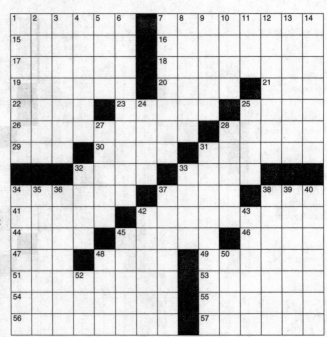

by Barry C. Silk

ACROSS

1 Party pooper
9 Tree related to the ylang-ylang
14 Local money?
16 Zombie's craving
17 Gridded display
18 Tourist buy in Mexico
19 Foible
20 Moolah
22 ___ Act
23 Ancient rival of Judah
25 "Growing Up ___" (2004–05 A&E reality show)
26 "___ Lisa"
27 Relatives of newtons
29 Algebraic unknowns
31 "Savvy?"
32 "Well, ___!"
34 Literally, "pick me up"
36 Beverage substitute
40 Too cute, say
41 Johnnie Walker blend
43 It's made every day
44 Parliament's end?
45 Dogma
47 German leader?
51 One crossing a line
53 Richard of NBC News
55 King who consulted the Witch of Endor
56 Chuck
57 "The Pianist" setting
59 Knoxville-based org.
60 Breakers ahead
62 Sweet spot
64 Serotonin, e.g.
65 Hierarchy
66 Classroom units
67 Captain of the Nebuchadnezzar, in "The Matrix"

DOWN

1 Cry when exposing something secret
2 Out of order
3 December birthstone
4 Actress Caldwell
5 "I ___ it!"
6 Accessory to a case
7 Foozler
8 Eagerly accepted
9 Forrest Gump's rank: Abbr.
10 Cell phone function
11 Intermittent
12 Stagger
13 "Gotta love him!"
15 Traveler in 1957 news
21 Main vein
24 There might be one on a hero
28 Tree whose leaves were once smoked by Indians
30 David who directed the final four Harry Potter films
33 55-Across, e.g.
35 Operations were once commonly performed in this
36 Resting place, informally
37 1991 Madonna hit
38 "Apollo 13" actor
39 Simulate, in a way
42 Subject of an air traveler's complaint
46 Old Chrysler make
48 "All or Nothing" rapper, 2005
49 Second-smallest member of the United Nations, by population
50 Bad looks
52 Flip one's lid?
54 Staples Center player
58 Wuss
61 Article in L'Express
63 Book before Phil.

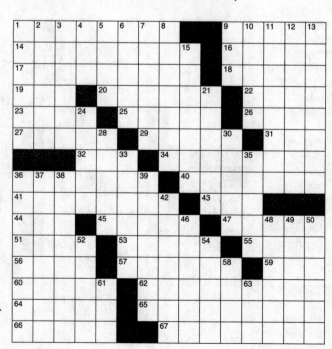

by Josh Knapp

ACROSS

1 Lower one's racket
10 Establish
15 1 + 1
16 Disperse again
17 Realized in the end
18 Emcee's delivery
19 Have mastery over
20 Part of a suite no.
21 Asian soup ingredients
23 Some antique buses
25 Wrangler's assent
27 Setting for many early online discussions
28 1999 Ron Howard bomb
29 Aunt or uncle's leader?
31 Honk off
32 They're found in orbits
35 Feature of many an Italian skyline
36 Evoker of 1950s nostalgia
39 What some vaccinations prevent
41 Knock
42 Person trying to move things?
44 Certify
46 "The __ Bride" (Rimsky-Korsakov opera)
47 Terminal division
51 What gums might do
53 Cause of a messy breakup?
54 Where the John Day R. flows
55 One might do a countdown
57 Engadget's co.
59 Coll. administration
60 Common desktop clutter
61 Fascinates

64 Like some kids' shoelaces
65 Most carefree
66 Journalist Ifill and others
67 Gumbo seasoning source

DOWN

1 Measure of popularity
2 Like someone who couldn't care less
3 Response to an accusation
4 Wring (out)
5 What les cheveux grows on
6 Like blood coursing through one's veins
7 On-site shucking sites
8 Dwarf
9 Compass letters

10 Sportscaster Andrews and others
11 Thrifty customer, e.g.
12 Like the developers of Skype
13 Big Red, in the N.C.A.A.
14 Dances country-western style
22 They were traditionally attached to factories
24 Ren's cousin of cartoondom
26 __-brained
30 Disappointed Olympic team members, maybe
33 Nigerian food staple
34 Fr. place name starter
36 Not all-out battle

37 Freak
38 Toast lead-in, at times
40 Vessel protected by Hera
43 "2 Broke Girls" co-star Dennings
45 Curb
48 Trial attorney, e.g.
49 Wright with an Oscar
50 Discharges
52 Hospital units
56 Yacht parts
58 "__ of Lambeth" (Maugham novel)
62 Its first pres. was Gen. Burnside
63 Picture file suffix

by Laura Sternberg

ANSWERS

1

```
MASS  ■ S T R I P M A L L S
ANTE  ■ H E A D T O T A I L
STAX  ■ M A K E S N O I S E
A I R Q U O T E S ■ A T A D
■ T U T O R ■ P P S ■
S P R I T ■ O M E L E T P A N
W E E Z E R ■ I M A C ■ R U E
A S K ■ R E P L I C A ■ I R A
M T V ■ R I E N ■ E N D S I T
P O I S O N P E N ■ P O O C H
■ E T S ■ E S I G N ■
A D H D ■ E D S H E E R A N
B R E A K A D A T E ■ A I L S
C O R K A G E F E E ■ R O O F
S P R A Y O N T A N ■ S T E W
```

2

```
H I V E ■ P R O P E R ■ T R A
A H E M ■ R O X A N E ■ W E T
N E R O ■ E V E R Y S O O F T
D A M ■ U S E S ■ A T M F E E
B R E A K S ■ ■ L E A R N
R Y E B E E R S ■ F E N C E D
A A R E ■ V O T E R S ■ E E S
■ T H E A R T I S T ■
C P R ■ E N D U R E ■ A M C S
L O O K A T ■ G E N E P O O L
I D L E D ■ ■ D E A D W E
F R O T H S ■ B O Z O ■ E P I
B A D T O T H E B O ■ B L O G
A C E ■ M Y E L I N ■ B U S H
R E X ■ E X M A T E ■ C N E T
```

3

```
G U F F ■ O P E R A S ■ O H O
A P I A ■ L A M E S T ■ B E N
S P L I T S V I L L E ■ R E M
B E E R B E L L Y ■ A S I D E
A R M ■ S N O ■ E M C E E D
G L E N ■ V A G A B O N D S
S I N U S ■ E R R O R ■
■ P U T P E N T O P A P E R
■ P A Y I N ■ T I M E S
P O L I C E C A R ■ O P T O
I T U N E S ■ E S T ■ O R A
G O M E R ■ H A N K A A R O N
L O M ■ A R E Y O U B L I N D
E L O ■ C A R L I N ■ B U Y S
T E X ■ E M B A R K ■ A M M O
```

4

```
B A B Y S L I N G S ■ P O L S
A D I E U A D I E U ■ L I E U
L O C A L C O L O R ■ A L G A
S N O R K E L E D ■ S I T A R
A I R S ■ S E M I N O L E
M S N ■ L E O ■ S A G ■ W I Z
■ F A U X D I A M O N D
■ D A D D Y I S S U E S
■ H O T D O G S T A N D
G E T ■ E R E ■ S I D ■ T A D
A L T E R A N T ■ G E R I
G L E N S ■ B I D P R I C E S
M U D D ■ C A M E R A S H O P
A V I A ■ P R O J E C T I L E
N A S T ■ U S N A V Y S E A L
```

5

```
G R E G ■ S C A B ■ T W I T S
A U N A T U R E L ■ S A G A N
S P A R E T I R E ■ K N U R L
S E C R E T S A U C E ■ A A H
Y E T ■ S E C T ■ I D U N N O
■ S H R O O M S ■ S O T S
■ M I L O ■ R O C K E D I T
S A G I T T A ■ P O I S O N S
T R U E S E L F ■ B O N O
A M E S ■ R E A C H I N
T A S T E R ■ T H A T ■ A P E
E L S ■ Z I S F O R Z E B R A
C A N T I ■ O R A L E X A M S
A D O R N ■ B E T A D E C A Y
R E T I E ■ S E E N ■ D I N A
```

6

```
■ S K I P J A C K S ■ H A M M
S T E T S O N H A T ■ A Q U I
L A Y S I E G E T O ■ D U D S
A L U M S ■ S H O E ■ A F T
P E P E ■ C I T Y P L A Z A
■ T A S E ■ S E D U C E
M A R C H H A R E ■ A D M I N
O C A R I N A ■ G O N E B A D
A T T I C ■ C O R P O R A L S
T O P E K A ■ H E I R
■ F O R E T A S T E ■ A B L E
E L I ■ N O T A ■ B R O I L
L O S T ■ D E N T A L E X A M
A V O W ■ D A T A M I N E R S
L E N O ■ S T A M P P A D S
```

7

```
R E F R I G E R A T O R C A R
A C E U P O N E S S L E E V E
C H A R L O T T E A M A L I E
K O R ■ A G R E E R S ■ L A D
■ ■ O N L Y ■ D I T S ■ ■
S H A N T Y ■ ■ S E E K E R
A E R E O ■ B E S T D R A M A
P A C A ■ B I T E S ■ B L O G
O V E R S I Z E D ■ P I E T A
R E D T A G ■ ■ E R A S E S
■ H O L M ■ E L O N ■
S H E ■ T O E C L I P ■ E M S
C A R L O S T H E J A C K A L
A L L A M E R I C A N H E R O
T E E T E R O N T H E E D G E
```

8

```
P I N T O B E A N ■ I L I K E
A C E O F B A S E ■ N O S I R
G O O N S Q U A D ■ F I N D S
E N D N O W ■ P L A I N T S ■
■ A E R I E ■ O P E C ■
S O D ■ T N T ■ W A L L M A P
P L A Y S G O D ■ D O Y L E
E L I A ■ S N I P S ■ T F A L
R I S K Y ■ S E A C H A R T
M E T E O U T ■ R N A ■ I M S
■ T U S H ■ F D R J R ■
L A Y A B E T ■ P R E L I M
W O M Y N ■ R A D I O W A V E
I L I A D ■ I C A L L E D I T
N A N K I ■ O H H E L L Y E S
```

9

```
■ S H O C K S ■ A M I G O
■ S T A Y A T H O M E D A D
■ S P A R E N O E X P E N S E
C H I N T Z E S ■ F E T U S ■
H A R D C ■ L O A D ■ M T V
E W E ■ R A D I U M ■ O B O E
■ L A T E N T ■ S T E V E
D E F I N E S ■ R E W I R E S
A R I S E ■ A L A N I S ■
L I R A ■ B L I N D S ■ F B I
I C E ■ G A T E ■ S M I R K
■ B A B E S ■ W A R M O V I E
T A N E H I S I C O A T E S
I N T E R N E T R A D I O ■
P A S T Y ■ T H E R E F
```

10

```
S A M B A S ■ ■ G A M B I A
T R I E D O N ■ C U I S I N E
I T S A Z O O ■ O L D S T E R
M I D S E N T E N C E ■ P R O
S C O T S ■ H A T H ■ F A T S
O L E S ■ M I S O ■ S E R I O
N E S ■ C E N T R I P E T A L
■ ■ B U D G E T C U T ■
C O N A N O B R I E N ■ H A N
A P E R Y ■ U N O S ■ P E L E
N E E R ■ W R E N ■ P R A D A
I N D ■ T I G R I S R I V E R
T E N M I L E ■ S L O V E N E
B R O I L E R ■ T A L E N T S
E S T A T E ■ G E T S E T
```

11

```
D I S C ■ S A G A S ■ A P P S
O N T H E C L O C K ■ D R I P
P A P A Y A T R E E ■ V O L E
P H A S E R ■ O T T ■ I P S E
L O U T S ■ Q U I C K S A N D
E L L E ■ L U N C H M O N E Y
R E S ■ S A I D ■ B A R E R ■
■ B O U T ■ D O R Y ■
■ S H A U N ■ R O O T ■ T O W
S P E L L C H E C K ■ W E R E
H E A D S H O P S ■ J A N E T
E A R P ■ P B R ■ R U S T I C
A R I A ■ A B O M I N A B L E
V E N T ■ D I V I N G B E L L
E D G E ■ S T E A K ■ I D Y L
```

12

```
M A J O R ■ C S P O T ■ C R O
A R U B A ■ U N I T Y ■ O E D
R E S I N ■ T A X I S Q U A D
K A T E ■ T I P ■ S O U R C E
E R A ■ B A T C H ■ N E S T S
T U S C A N ■ H A S ■ B E S T
■ G E O R G I A D O M E ■
■ C A R R O T J U I C E ■
■ S E A T F I L L E R S ■
D A F T ■ M A R ■ F E R R I S
U N L I T ■ S I N U S ■ O N E
B I O N I C ■ E E L ■ B R A N
O M A G A Z I N E ■ L I L T S
S A T ■ R A N D D ■ A D O R E
E L S ■ A R T S Y ■ V E G A S
```

13

```
W A V E L E N G T H S ▦ A R P
I M A G I N E T H A T ▦ B O A
D A N G E R M O U S E ▦ O T S
E S S ▦ W O E S ▦ B E A V I S
▦ ▦ ▦ F I L A ▦ T E R S E S T
S H T E T L ▦ S H E E P I S H
W O R T H ▦ F O U N D ▦ T E E
I N I T ▦ B E A D S ▦ B A R B
S E P ▦ L A M P S ▦ D E L I A
S Y L L A B U S ▦ K E L L E R
C H E A T E R ▦ B O I L ▦ ▦
H O T T E R ▦ S E E R ▦ D A X
A N I ▦ H U N T A N D P E C K
R E M ▦ I T S A M I R A C L E
D Y E ▦ T H A T S G E N I U S
```

14

```
C A M P U S M A P ▦ P A S T A
O H I O S T A T E ▦ A X I O M
S A M E S E X M A R R I A G E
A B E ▦ T A E ▦ R A I N M A N
▦ ▦ O R E L S E ▦ G A G ▦ ▦
R O G U E S ▦ Y E O H ▦ C E O
A P R I L ▦ J E R U S A L E M
S T A N ▦ S P L I T ▦ G E R E
P I P S Q U E A K ▦ A G A I N
S C H ▦ R I G S ▦ O V I N E S
▦ ▦ O C T ▦ H I R E E S ▦ ▦
I M A F O O L ▦ N A N ▦ L G A
S E L F D R I V I N G C A R S
M O V I E ▦ F I N G E R T I P
S W A T S ▦ T A K E S T E P S
```

15

```
C H I D E ▦ C R I M E B O S S
O A S E S ▦ D U D E R A N C H
S T U B S ▦ S T A L I N E R A
S E P I A ▦ ▦ T E A S E R ▦
E M P T Y W O R D S ▦ I E D
T A O S ▦ A C N E ▦ N E E D S
S I S ▦ A V O C A D O S ▦ ▦
▦ L E A V E N ▦ D R E A M S
▦ ▦ C O R N M E A L ▦ R I D
P I S A N ▦ O I N K ▦ N O L E
A N O ▦ T R A D E M A R K S
S T U C C O ▦ ▦ A T A R I
T A T A M I M A T ▦ M A N O R
I C E P A L A C E ▦ A L G A E
S T R E S S A T E ▦ S E E D S
```

16

```
A P P E T I Z E R ▦ ▦ R I S K
P E A S H O O T E R ▦ A C T I
H E R C U L E A N E F F O R T
I D S ▦ S A Y S I D O ▦ N A E
D E E D ▦ ▦ ▦ O C C U R
S E R U M ▦ S A C K D R E S S
▦ ▦ ▦ C E D A R R A P I D S ▦
▦ ▦ C H A R L I E R O S E ▦
▦ T H E T I M E W A R P ▦ ▦
P R E S S P A S S ▦ N U M B S
R O A S T ▦ ▦ ▦ P E R U
E C T ▦ E M B R A C E ▦ K I R
T H E T W I L I G H T Z O N E
T E R I ▦ A A M E E T I N G S
Y E S M ▦ T E E N A N G S T
```

17

```
C H R I S S Y ▦ A R A P A H O
H O E C A K E ▦ L U N U L A R
E N D E D I T ▦ M E T G A L A
M E D I A N ▦ R A D I S S O N
L Y I N ▦ C E Y ▦ ▦ K E G
A P T ▦ D U O S ▦ C C L A S S
B O O T Y L I C I O U S ▦ ▦
▦ T R U S T F U N D B A B Y
▦ ▦ N O R S E D E I T I E S
M T D A N A ▦ D I S C ▦ K A T
E V E ▦ ▦ P O E ▦ B E H R
T E C H B L O G ▦ A G A S S I
E X I T R O W ▦ S M A S H U P
R E D T I D E ▦ G O T S O R E
S C E P T E R ▦ T R O O P E D
```

18

```
K N I T C A P ▦ T S P ▦ S P Y
N O S H A D E ▦ I P A D P R O
E N T E R I N ▦ R I T E A I D
E C H E L O N ▦ E N H A N C E
S E A M O S S ▦ S N O R K E L
▦ ▦ ▦ T E T ▦ ▦ ▦ A S S
S T A R S T R U C K ▦ I H O P
H O L A ▦ R O G U E ▦ R O V E
Y E L L ▦ O T H E R W O M A N
▦ ▦ D A Y ▦ ▦ ▦ E R E ▦
C A S I N O S ▦ B I O M A S S
O P T S O U T ▦ O D W A L L A
P R A L I N E ▦ T A N D O O R
S I L E N C E ▦ C H I A N T I
E L K ▦ T E D ▦ H O T M E S S
```

19

```
A N D W E R E O F F ■ S I T E
P E R I W I N K L E ■ E T A L
S T A L E B R E A D ■ T O N Y
E S M E ■ C A D S ■ M A L E S
■ ■ ■ L A G ■ H A I R D Y E
S T O W A G E ■ M O N E Y ■
C A P O N E ■ G O L D C O I N
A L E R T ■ D A B ■ M O U S E
T I N K E R E D ■ P E R S O N
■ S E R T A ■ C O L D O N E
S C O R N E D ■ L A D ■
C L U B S ■ L A I C ■ A L B A
H E R E ■ W I T C H T R I A L
M A C E ■ I N T H E W I N G S
O R E S ■ G E N E R A L T S O
```

20

```
O F F E D ■ S A H L ■ S Z A
D R I V E S ■ O R E O T H I N
S E R I A L ■ S C A T H I N G
■ S E L F I M P O R T A N C E
O H H I ■ C I A ■ T A T T E R
I M O N ■ E R D O S ■ S O D S
N E S T E D ■ S H A L T ■
K N E E C A P ■ O N T H E G O
■ N O N O S ■ D R E X E L
A T I T ■ D R E A M ■ S C A D
D E N I E D ■ T R I ■ P A R S
L A B O R I N T E N S I V E ■
I R O N I C A L ■ D O R A D O
B A R S C E N E ■ S P I T U P
S T N ■ A D O S ■ S T E P S
```

21

```
N E S S ■ A D A G E ■ P R A T
O C T A ■ T U P A C ■ F I S H
W H A T S T H E B I G I D E A
L O T I O N ■ G A Z E A T
E B E R T ■ M C S ■ M E S S I
T O M E ■ P E O N S ■ R H Y S
M O O ■ B A G N O L D ■ O A T
E M T ■ I R A Q W A R ■ T S O
S E T ■ D E D U C T S ■ G A S
E R O S ■ D E E R E ■ J U B A
E S S E X ■ T S A ■ F A N C Y
■ L I G H T B U L B ■
L A T I N O ■ R O B U S T
A V E N G E ■ N A E N A E
B A D A S S ■ S T R O D E
```

22

```
S H O N D A ■ C H E A T D A Y
T O P O U T ■ R O G U E O N E
A M E N D S ■ A L A N A L D A
R E D O S E ■ W E N T T O I T
G A P S ■ A C L U ■ A R E S
A L I ■ P I P E T S ■
Z O E K A Z A N ■ N O T B A D
E N C A S E S ■ C O R E L L I
S E E T H E ■ K E S T R E L S
■ Y E S A N D ■ W A H
C R O P ■ D E E P ■ F A T E
L I M E A D E S ■ I S O P O D
O V E R L A P S ■ M U R A N O
M A G R I T T E ■ A P E R C U
P L A Y T E S T ■ S E X T E T
```

23

```
S I X P A C K ■ B O O H I S S
C O R O L L A ■ O N V A C A Y
A D A P T O R ■ D E A D E N D
N E Y O ■ S E E Y A ■ I M I N
T V S ■ B E N D S ■ S T A T E
R I P P E D ■ G U A M ■ N Y Y
O C E A N ■ S E R I E S ■
N E X T G E N ■ F R A T B R O
■ S A M O A S ■ G A B O R
C A R ■ L O W S ■ T O R Q U E
O P E N S ■ Y O D E L ■ J L O
B A N A ■ S O F A R ■ P O E T
A T E C R O W ■ N E O L I T H
L O G R O L L ■ A S H A N T I
T W E E Z E S ■ E A S Y T E N
```

24

```
C R I P ■ M A N T A ■ P S I S
L E N T ■ A R E E L ■ O H N O
A N T O I N E T T E ■ L I M A
S T I L L L I F E ■ B A R A K
S A F E L Y ■ L A C E R A T E
I C A M E ■ B I T E S I Z E D
C O D Y ■ T U X E D O S ■
S P A ■ R A T A T A T ■ L A C
■ P A R T N E R ■ W I L L
G R E A T O D D S ■ H A S T O
N E U R O T I C ■ T O R T E S
A P L A N ■ A H O Y T H E R E
W O O S ■ F L I P P H O N E S
A R G O ■ B E L I E ■ L U G E
T T Y L ■ I D L E S ■ S P O T
```

25

```
T A B L E S C R A P ▦ A S I S
A L P I N E L A K E ▦ R I C A
K A L E C A E S A R ▦ E D E N
E M U ▦ A S A P ▦ P H T E S T
I O S ▦ S O N ▦ B W A H A H A
▦ P E N ▦ G R A Y A R E A ▦ ▦
▦ B I A S ▦ S A I L S ▦ M E N
L I N T ▦ S K U N K ▦ B E T A
U G H ▦ S U I N G ▦ A I D S ▦
S P A R E S E T ▦ C F O ▦ ▦ ▦
T H R O A T S ▦ S A C ▦ M T A
S A M O S A ▦ P U C E ▦ O W N
F R O M ▦ I V E C H A N G E D
O M N I ▦ N O P R E S S U R E
R A Y E ▦ S W E E T T A L K S
```

26

```
S C H L U B B Y ▦ P O T A S H
P L E A S U R E ▦ O P O R T O
Y O U D A M A N ▦ L E M M O N
B U R L ▦ M I S S E D W O R K
O D I E ▦ E N I A C ▦ A R K S
A L S ▦ P R E G N A N T ▦ ▦ ▦
T I T L E ▦ D N A T E S T S ▦
S K I E R S ▦ ▦ S C O R E D ▦
▦ E C O C I D A L ▦ K N A V E
▦ ▦ P E T O D O R S ▦ G E M
A R C O ▦ C R O W E ▦ M I R E
B I L L B O A R D S ▦ I C A N
A P E D O M ▦ N O T A L E N T
R E F I L M ▦ E S U R A N C E
E N T I T Y ▦ D E P E N D E D
```

27

```
M S G ▦ G A S C A P ▦ H B O
O L I V E G A R D E N ▦ E R R
C O M E A T M E B R O ▦ A A S
H O M E R ▦ B E L ▦ M A T Z O
A P E D ▦ C A P O ▦ E L H I ▦
▦ ▦ U S O ▦ S C R A B B L E
L O W B L O W ▦ K A N S A N S
I R E ▦ E L I ▦ E T S ▦ R U T
L E T M E I N ▦ R E N T S T O
T O N E P O E T ▦ D O I ▦ ▦
▦ T O L D ▦ S H I M ▦ S A S S
C H O S E ▦ T E D ▦ A S K U P
A I D ▦ B O O Z E C R U I S E
S N L ▦ T H R A S H M E T A L
E S E ▦ S E X T O Y ▦ A N T
```

28

```
▦ M A L A L A ▦ P A C T S
▦ C A P E M A N ▦ E M C E E
▦ C A R P A I N T ▦ C O R E R
W A N T A D ▦ D I G ▦ R I T E
I M T I R E D ▦ V I C O D I N
N E O N A T E ▦ A M U S E M E
D O R A T H E E X P L O R E R
▦ ▦ ▦ ▦ ▦ D M X ▦ ▦ ▦ ▦ ▦ ▦
S A I N T P E T E R S B U R G
I G N O B L E ▦ R A P I N O E
T R A N S A M ▦ S T Y G I A N
S E T H ▦ N Y C ▦ T W O P L Y
P E R E S ▦ E M U L A T E D
A T A R I ▦ R O S E R E D ▦
T O P O L ▦ S N O R E D ▦
```

29

```
▦ C L O W N C A R S ▦ T I A S
T R E E H O U S E S ▦ O N M E
R E T R O G R A D E ▦ U D O N
Y D S ▦ G O A P E ▦ G R I N S
▦ ▦ F O O D ▦ F O L I A G E
A R G U E D ▦ M I D A S ▦ ▦
S E A N S ▦ C O N E S T O G A
T A U N T ▦ A L E ▦ S T R A W
I D L E H A N D S ▦ C R E P E
▦ ▦ L E N D S ▦ T E A S E S
A M S C R A Y ▦ S H I P ▦ ▦
P U P A E ▦ C R E E L ▦ S P A
P R E K ▦ W A I T L I S T E D
L A C E ▦ I N S O M N I A C S
E L K S ▦ T E E N A G E R S
```

30

```
S T R I P P E R S ▦ W A R E S
T H E M O L D A U ▦ A B O V E
Y O G A P A N T S ▦ T I M I D
▦ ▦ ▦ L U N A ▦ H O T D A T E
O C T I L E ▦ A I R L I N E R
F L U V I R U S ▦ N E N E ▦
F I R E S ▦ R I C O ▦ G M C S
A N N ▦ M A G N E T O ▦ P I P
L E E S ▦ R E I D ▦ B S I D E
▦ ▦ R I D E ▦ N E W S C R E W
A G E R A N G E ▦ W O O E R S
C O S P L A Y ▦ W E L T ▦ ▦
T O Q U E ▦ O P E R E T T A S
U S U R Y ▦ Z A P A T I S T A
P E E R S ▦ A L T W E E K L Y
```

31

```
S H O U T I N G ■ M A I D S ■
N E W M E D I A ■ E X T O L S ■
O I L P A I N T ■ R E I N I N ■
O D E ■ G E O R G ■ S U M O
P I T A S ■ B R I E F ■ T E C
■ B E T A ■ D R A C H M A
■ T R A L A L A ■ T R O O P
W H I T E B L O O D C E L L S
A R D E N ■ K N E A D E D
S E E D I E R ■ T A T I
S E S ■ C O U C H ■ S T A R T
A S H E ■ C E L E B ■ L A W
I T A L I E ■ A D E L A I D E
L A R S O N ■ N O B I G G I E
■ R E E S E ■ S T E P O N I T
```

32

```
A T F I R S T ■ C H E A P I E
T R A C E E E L L I S R O S S
T E L E V I S I O N P I L O T
A X L E S ■ T A S T Y ■ A L A
C E O S ■ E R I E S ■ E R A T
H S N ■ C R U S T ■ W R O T E
■ K A I N E ■ D O R I E S
■ C R A N K S ■ H O W O D D
B A A B A A ■ M O V E R ■
A B D U L ■ W I N E D ■ L A T
S O I L ■ L E A D S ■ T E C H
E C O ■ L L A M A ■ P E S T O
T H E B O O K O F M O R M O N
W O R L D S E R I E S R I N G
O N A T E A R ■ T W E E Z E S
```

33

```
B B C A M E R I C A ■ U F O S
A B O M I N A T E S ■ H A L T
S Q U I L L I O N S ■ A L M A
E S P ■ K I T ■ T A B U L A R
■ C B S T V ■ S O L I N G
P T B O A T ■ I T S Y ■ N R A
O I L E R ■ A P B I O ■ L I Z
C M O N ■ C S P A N ■ J O V E
K E W ■ B R I A R ■ L A V E R
E T S ■ A A A S ■ S A B E R S
T R A S H Y ■ S P U R S ■
C A P I T O L ■ A B C ■ A W E
O V A L ■ L E A D P E N C I L
M E R L ■ A N I M A N I A C S
B L T S ■ S A L A R Y H I K E
```

34

```
S W I P E R N O S W I P I N G
H I G H M A I N T E N A N C E
I D L E S P E C U L A T I O N
M E O W ■ S T E N C H ■ T S E
S R O ■ M H Z ■ S H O J I ■
■ T R E S S ■ S L E A Z Y
■ S T A T E C A R ■ E S T E E
B R A T ■ T H R E E ■ S O S A
A T P A R ■ E A T S D I R T
M A D M E N ■ N I C H E ■
■ A I D A N ■ C A L ■ C A T
K A N ■ B E E P E R ■ B O F A
A C C O U N T I N G E R R O R
T H E C L A W S C O M E O U T
Y E R T L E T H E T U R T L E
```

35

```
C R O C E ■ A L T A ■ A N T ■
H O L D M Y B E E R ■ S A W S
E P I C P O E T R Y ■ C N E T
Z E N ■ T U T O R ■ C O N E Y
■ S Y N S ■ A C O L Y T E
D E F A N G ■ A P H I D S ■
A L I V E ■ A L I E N A T E D
F I R E S ■ B O N ■ O S A G E
T E S T T U B E S ■ P I T O N
■ T H E R E S ■ R E C E S S
O R D E R L Y ■ T O R E
H E A D S ■ R A I S A ■ G T O
M Y N A ■ T O N E I T D O W N
S E C T ■ C A N I N E U N I T
■ S E E ■ U D O N ■ D I E G O
```

36

```
T A L L I E S U P ■ G A T O S
O C E A N L I N E R ■ A L A M O
S T I C K Y R I C E ■ B A K E D
C E L E B ■ T S A R ■ S E G A
A D A ■ L I T ■ L E S ■ P A C
■ H O R A C E ■ P O S A D A
■ B O T O X I N J E C T I O N
■ P A R T N E R D A N C I N G
F I T N E S S C E N T E R S
E N M E S H ■ E D G E R S
L O O ■ T O T ■ O D S ■ S I T
T C B Y ■ T U M S ■ T E A M O
S H I E D ■ B R O G R A M M E R
A L L A Y ■ A I R P O R T B A R
D E E R E ■ S T A Y S S A N E
```

37

```
D O Y O U H E A R M E ■ D R S
O V E R Z E A L O U S ■ E E K
P A T R O N S A I N T ■ C G I
E L I ■ A R E S ■ C E R E A L
■ ■ I D Y L ■ S H E E P L E
C E N S U S ■ W I I M O T E S
A B O M B ■ B A T E ■ S I M S
M O T ■ A I R K I S S ■ C E O
E L A S ■ L I E N ■ U C O N N
R A C E B I B S ■ G R U N T S ■
A S H C A K E ■ D Y E D ■ ■
S C A T H E ■ L I M B ■ H A J
H A N ■ A I D E S D E C A M P
O R C ■ I K E A C A T A L O G
P E E ■ S E E D O Y S T E R S
```

38

```
C O M I C S A N S ■ C R A G
O P E N L Y G A Y ■ L U L L
P E A C E S I G N ■ S A B L E
E R N ■ O O N A C H A P L I N
S A G A ■ P G T H I R T E E N
■ ■ I L L S ■ N G O
A T R I A ■ T A P D A N C E S
H A L ■ S K I P A S S ■ H O E
H U S H P U P P Y ■ S A I N T
■ I A N ■ D O L L ■
S U R P R I S E M E ■ A L T O
T H A N K S O B A M A ■ P H U
R U N E S ■ D E T O X D I E T
I R I S ■ A R T D E A L E R
P A N S ■ S T E E L B L U E
```

39

```
S L O G A N ■ B A R N U M
H A I R B O W ■ A V I A T E
A T L A N T A N ■ M A S S E S
■ Y E S Y E S ■ T E A R S
C I A ■ G O N D O L A ■ L O Y
A N I T A ■ E F F O R T S
S P R I T ■ S L A B ■ E T A S
T U P P E R W A R E P A R T Y
S T O P ■ E O N S ■ A S I A N
■ R I C A R D O ■ R E P R O
S O T ■ A L L E G R O ■ S I D
E X C O N ■ D R O I D S ■
C L O W N S ■ S O C I A L I Q
T I D I E D ■ D E S S E R T
S P E E D S ■ S T E A K S
```

40

```
H A M M ■ C H U P A C A B R A
E C R U ■ H E S I T A T I O N
R U M S ■ U N D E R S T O O D
T R O T ■ T R A D E T A L K S
Z A M B E Z I ■ P S I
■ E S P ■ S I T N S P I N
■ R E N T A C O P ■ G O O S E
D E M I ■ H I N E S ■ C L A W
O N I C E ■ G A R L I C K Y
H O T E L B A R ■ E N E ■
■ G R R ■ C D D R I V E
S U P P R E S S E D ■ T R I X
I L L B E T H E R E ■ E A R P
B E E R C O O L E R ■ A Q U A
S E A S O N P A S S ■ M I S T
```

41

```
T I G E R S H A R K S ■ T U B
I N O C U L A T I O N ■ O N E
B O O K S O N T A P E ■ M I A
E N D ■ S O D A S ■ E N S O R
R E S H I P S ■ G R E E N S
■ M A Y ■ B A R E B A C K
L I E O N ■ B O R E D ■ V A I
I M A S ■ L A I T Y ■ B E R N
O Y S ■ W A R N S ■ W O R D S
N O T C H I N G ■ P I X ■
S U C C O R ■ B O D Y B A G
G R O S S ■ H U L L O ■ E R E
A M A ■ W H E R E S W A L D O
T A S ■ H E L E N K E L L E R
E N T ■ O H M Y D A R L I N G
```

42

```
O N T A P E ■ S A S S E D
M A R T I N I ■ E V O N N E
A D U L T I N G ■ R E B A T E
N I A ■ T A C O N I C ■ P A P
I N N S ■ C H I E F ■ S O I L
S E T U P ■ A N G ■ A P P L Y
■ B E E R G O G G L E S ■
■ Z O R O A S T R I A N ■
■ C O R R E C T I O N S ■
I R O N Y ■ T E A ■ G H A N A
N U T S ■ M E A T Y ■ Y S E R
C I O ■ B I R D I E S ■ S A N
E S P I A L ■ Y O S E M I T E
P E I R C E ■ N E M E S E S
T R A S H Y ■ S I T I N S
```

43

```
L E A D E R O F T H E P A C K
A L F A R O M E O S P I D E R
G O I N G B A C K T O C A L I
■ C L E O ■ R U Y ■ C A P E S
L U I S ■ ■ ■ N O T H ■ T S P
I T S ■ P L E D G E ■ C O T Y
B E T A R A Y ■ A N G O R A ■
■ ■ L I R E ■ M A U L ■ ■
■ G O D E E P ■ E C S T A S Y
N O L O ■ D O R S E T ■ I M O
O R D ■ C O P A ■ ■ G R E W
M I S D O ■ P U P ■ D U M A ■
A L A I N R E N E L E S A G E
A L L O V E R C R E A T I O N
M A T R Y O S H K A D O L L S
```

44

```
T H U M B ■ L A S E ■ T S P
G A R B A G E B A G ■ I T E M
I T S A L I V I N G ■ M E N U
F H A ■ C R I E D ■ R E A C T
■ ■ G O D S ■ P L U M M E T
A M A I N ■ B A O B A B ■
C U R V Y ■ P O P P Y C O C K
C I T E S ■ E X E ■ S H A L E
T R I M E S T E R ■ L I T U P
■ F E A R E D ■ I N S E T
A V I A T O R ■ C A P E ■
L O C H S ■ S L U R P ■ M O M
E L I A ■ D O U B L E W I D E
E V A N ■ J U N I O R P R O M
■ O L D ■ S T A T ■ S M O R E
```

45

```
F R I G G A ■ C R U S A D E S
L O G O U T ■ H A R P S E A L
I N L A S T ■ U N G U L A T E
N C O ■ H U G G E D ■ D E E
G O O D S E N S E ■ E A R P
■ R O A R ■ G R E G ■
M A J O R L E A G U E G A M E
P R I V A T E P R A C T I C E
G E N E R A L A U D I E N C E
■ G O E R ■ B E T S ■
A T O N ■ T A B L E T O P S
T R I ■ E M B R Y O ■ H E T
W A S H R O O M ■ U N E A S Y
A N T I G O N E ■ P A T R O L
R E S T O R E D ■ E N C A S E
```

46

```
A F C ■ A G E N T ■ M A T
C L A M ■ D R I E R ■ C O L E
C A S A B L A N C A ■ U C L A
E S T R E E T ■ K I S S C A M
S H O R T R I B ■ N E P A L I
S Y R I A ■ N O U S E ■ S O N
■ A T V ■ E N T I C I N G
■ T I G E R P R O O F I N G
H E R E S H O W ■ P I T ■
A L I ■ T E X A N ■ C A P O S
N E S T E A ■ R E L A T E T O
G C H O R D S ■ M A R I N E R
M O S S ■ S O M E P E O P L E
A M E S ■ E L I A S ■ N A L A
N S A ■ T O N N E ■ L O T
```

47

```
■ S L A P D A S H ■ H O A R D
S T A R E I N T O ■ E D G E R
L E N D A N E A R ■ L I N D Y
A L D O ■ T W I N ■ D E U C E
S M A R M ■ N E W T ■ S H Y
H O U S E M D ■ R O A D I E
■ M A I T A I ■ P E N D
■ Q U E E N V I C T O R I A
O U S T ■ T E X T E D ■
P A S C A L ■ E R E A D E R
E T E ■ G E A R ■ S L O M O
N O N C E ■ B E T S ■ P R A Y
B R A U N ■ R U R I T A N I A
A Z T E C ■ A S I R E C A L L
R E E D Y ■ M E X I C A N S
```

48

```
L A P E L M I C ■ D A S H I T
O N A L E A S H ■ A R M A N I
A N I M A T O R ■ D R I V E L
T I N ■ D E L I S ■ T E X T
H E E D ■ ■ A S P ■ R E A P S
■ ■ E S C ■ T R O U ■ B E A
■ H A W A I I A N S H I R T
■ C A T E B L A N C H E T T
M I C H E L I N G U I D E
I N K ■ T E A M ■ E N E ■
D E A L S ■ D I M ■ R I M E
R A T A ■ S N A P E ■ C A N
A S H M A N ■ G L A D H A N D
S T O P G O ■ L I N G E R I E
H E N S O N ■ E A S Y R E A D
```

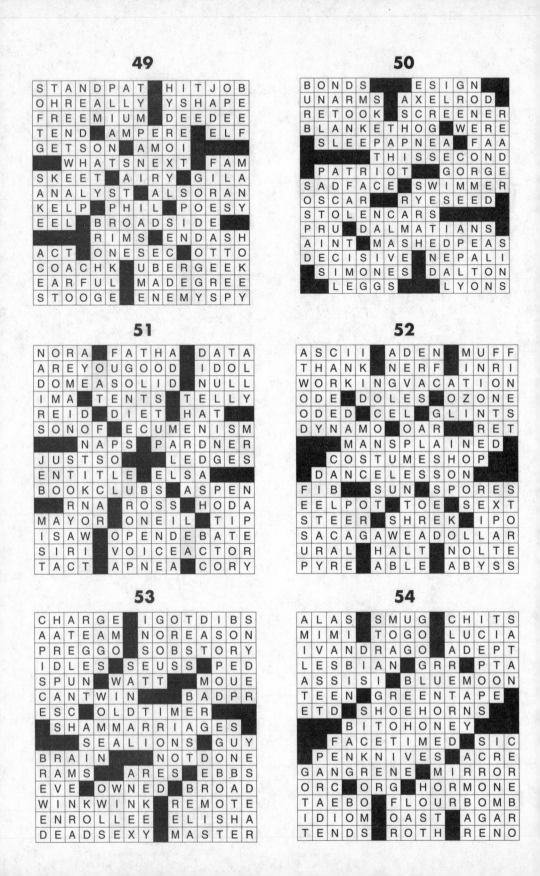

49

50

51

52

53

54

55

```
O A S I S ■ T B S P ■ ■ U V E A
G R O U P P H O T O ■ R O E S
R E A D Y O R N O T ■ B I L K
E S P ■ C R E E P ■ M A C Y S
■ ■ T A T E ■ A L O N E ■ ■
C L A I M S ■ S H E R L O C K
R O V E S ■ S E E N O E V I L
E G A D ■ P I T A S ■ G E N E
D O N T B E M A D ■ M E R C I
O N T H E D O T ■ D A N S O N
■ G E T I N ■ F O R D ■ ■
C H A K A ■ S T A I R ■ B L T
H O R N ■ F A M I L Y T R E E
U P D O ■ B Y A N Y M E A N S
M E E T ■ I S N T ■ E A T A T
```

56

```
C R A S H P A D S ■ ■ P E C
D O C T O R D O O M ■ M O M A
S O M E T I M E S Y ■ A L E S
■ S E T T L E S O N ■ M O R T
■ ■ I O N ■ A R A M I S
■ W R A P S ■ H A S A B A L L
S H E S ■ E V I L ■ J E L L O
K I C K ■ C O R F U ■ A L I T
I L I A D ■ T E A R ■ R E V S
P E T N A M E S ■ B A S T E
I S A Y N O ■ S A G ■ ■
N A T O ■ T I P O N E I L L
T W I N ■ O V E R A N D O U T
R A V E ■ R E S T R A I N T S
O Y E ■ S T A T S G E E K
```

57

```
L E F T J A B ■ A L L O W M E
I S U R E D O ■ P E E P E R S
S P R E A D O N E S W I N G S
S A R A N ■ K I X ■ E T R E
O N I T ■ D I N A R ■ P E N
M O E ■ A R E A M A P ■ R E C
E L R O N D ■ S N O C O N E
■ P E R M ■ L E O ■ ■
M E N S W E A R ■ A T T I C A
A M A ■ W R I S T S ■ S A N
R A M P ■ I C E E ■ L I M O
S N E A D ■ E O N ■ M I N E D
B A T S I N T H E B E L F R Y
A T A T R O T ■ C A R L O A N
R E G A T T A ■ A D V E R S E
```

58

```
S U G A R M A M A ■ C O S T
A M A T E U R I S H ■ L U K E
B A L A N C E D U E ■ E R I N
E M O T I O N ■ B L O O M S
R I P ■ U T T E R S ■ B O P
■ O W S ■ U S E D T O B E
K A Z A A M ■ M A W ■ A R I E
A M A S S E S ■ I C E C O L D
L O P E ■ M E L ■ A N I S E S
E R A S A B L E ■ L O T ■
S A T ■ F R A I S E ■ M A A
A L I C I A ■ U N O C A R D
L I S A ■ N E X T D O O R T O
A T T A ■ E X T R A F R I E S
D Y A N ■ S C A R S D A L E
```

59

```
G U A R ■ R I N D ■ F R A T
O N S A L E N O W ■ G R E C O
A S I F I C A R E ■ R E T R Y
T H A T S A L I E ■ A E R O S
S Y N ■ P S A ■ B A D C O P
■ ■ L E T T S ■ P S Y C H O
A S F A R ■ H I D E ■ C O O P
S C A M ■ R E L A X ■ L O B E
E R T E ■ A R T Y ■ D E L E D
S A F E S T ■ S T A R S ■
■ P I X I E S ■ R E Y ■ B R A
T I N C T ■ P H A R M A R E P
A R G U E ■ A U D I O T A P E
L O E S S ■ S L E E P O V E R
I N R E ■ M A R S ■ P O L Y
```

60

```
I P A S S ■ T A P E ■ P D A
M O N A E ■ I M A X ■ B R U N
D I D J A ■ M O T O R B I K E
O S H A ■ T B S ■ I B E A M
W O O K I E E ■ L P S ■ S K I
N N W ■ N A R C O L E P T I C
■ ■ P A B L O C A S A L S ■
■ D E C L A R A T O R Y ■
■ D A R L E N E L O V E ■
D O N E A N D D O N E ■ L A S
R T E ■ I D S ■ F I R E A X E
O C C U R ■ A F C ■ S T I X
P O O P E M O J I ■ A T I L T
I M O N ■ G U A C ■ M E N L O
T S K ■ M I R E ■ T E X A N
```

61

S	T	A	R	S	H	I	P	S		S	O	N	I	A
C	H	I	C	K	A	S	A	W		A	X	O	N	S
R	E	L	A	Y	R	A	C	E		M	E	S	S	I
U	T	E			D	W	E	E	B		N	E	T	S
B	A	D	P	R				T	A	M		S	E	A
			R	I	M		F	E	T	A		T	R	I
		T	O	B	E	C	O	N	T	I	N	U	E	D
	W	H	A	T	S	H	O	U	L	D	I	D	O	
C	H	E	M	I	C	A	L	P	E	E	L	S		
R	E	M		P	A	N	S			S	N	L		
E	R	A		S	L	C				S	A	L	E	M
S	E	T	H		S	E	V	E	N			O	V	A
T	A	R	O	T		D	A	T	A	M	I	N	E	R
E	M	I	L	E		I	N	A	M	O	M	E	N	T
D	I	X	I	E		T	E	L	E	P	O	R	T	S

62

N	E	S	T	C	E	P	A	S		A	M	P	A	S
A	L	P	H	A	M	A	L	E		L	A	R	C	H
M	A	U	I	W	O	W	I	E		A	G	I	T	A
A	I	R	S		J	A	G		A	N	I	M	A	L
T	N	T		H	I	T	H	E	R		C	E	L	L
H	E	S	S	E			T	A	C	O		R	O	W
			C	A	L	I		T	A	N	L	I	N	E
	C	L	O	R	O	X		E	N	R	O	B	E	
C	H	I	T	O	W	N		N	E	A	R			
H	U	M		F	R	A	T		M	E	R	C	H	
I	G	O	R		E	Y	E	C	U	P		A	H	A
C	A	R	A	T	S		J	O	N		E	T	A	L
A	L	I	V	E		C	A	N	D	Y	G	I	R	L
N	U	D	E	S		I	N	D	I	E	G	O	G	O
A	G	E	N	T		G	O	O	D	A	S	N	E	W

63

D	R	Y		L	O	O	F	A		A	S	A	N	A
J	U	M	B	O	T	R	O	N		C	A	B	O	T
E	S	C	A	P	E	K	E	Y		E	R	N	I	E
D	E	A	N	S	L	I	S	T		T	O	E	S	
			K	I	L	N		A	V	E	N	G	E	D
M	A	D	E	D	O		S	K	I	N	G	A	M	E
E	V	A	D	E		B	L	E	D		S	T	A	T
N	E	T		D	E	L	I	R	I	A		I	K	E
A	R	I	A		G	U	M	S		L	A	V	E	R
C	A	N	T	L	O	S	E		W	A	D	E	R	S
E	G	G	H	A	S	H		P	E	N	S			
	E	P	I	C		P	O	R	T	H	O	L	E	S
B	J	O	R	K		I	M	O	N	A	R	O	L	L
M	O	O	S	E		N	A	V	A	L	B	A	S	E
W	E	L	T	Y		K	N	O	P	E		F	E	W

64

S	P	A	M	B	O	T	S		P	A	C	M	A	N
H	O	M	E	C	U	R	E		U	S	H	A	P	E
O	H	I	G	E	T	I	T		R	A	I	D	E	D
P	L	E	A		S	G	T	P	E	P	P	E	R	
			D	R	E		L	A	M		S	A	I	L
	F	E	E	T		E	R	A	S		S	T	U	
P	I	T	T		T	R	I	T	E		T	I	X	
A	H	T	H	I	S	I	S	T	H	E	L	I	F	E
J	O	S		E	L	R	O	Y		S	O	N	S	
A	N	T		D	E	A	F		J	A	N	K		
R	E	O	S		D	N	C		A	W	E			
	C	A	T	T	R	E	A	T	S		W	E	A	N
H	A	T	A	R	I		T	O	P	F	O	R	T	Y
U	S	E	R	I	D		A	T	E	A	L	I	V	E
B	E	E	R	M	E		N	E	R	D	F	E	S	T

65

F	O	O	L		Z	E	B	R	A	F	I	N	C	H
E	D	N	A		A	Q	U	A	M	A	R	I	N	E
L	O	I	S		F	U	Z	Z	Y	N	A	V	E	L
T	R	O	T		T	A	Z	O			E	T	D	
	E	N	T	A	I	L		R	O	M	A	N		
S	A	R	O	N	G		T	B	I	L	L			
A	T	I	L	T		C	H	A	L	K	L	I	N	E
G	E	N	E		R	I	C			T	W	I	X	
O	R	G	A	N	B	A	N	K		T	H	A	N	E
			V	E	R	B	S		P	I	A	N	O	S
		M	E	A	R	A		M	U	S	T	N	T	
E	L	I			P	H	I	L		J	A	C	K	
C	A	S	T	A	S	P	E	L	L		A	S	H	E
O	N	E	I	D	A	L	A	K	E		Z	E	K	E
N	A	R	C	O	L	E	P	S	Y		Z	E	A	L

66

B	O	I	N	G			H	E	A	D	E	R		
E	N	C	O	R	E		C	U	R	S	I	V	E	
T	E	E	B	O	X		R	E	L	I	E	V	E	S
T	I	D	E	W	A	T	E	R	A	C	C	E	N	T
A	D	U	L	T	M	A	L	E	S			R	O	O
S	A	P	P	H	I	R	E	S		B	B	G	U	N
			R	A	N	A	T		F	I	L	E	T	
		H	I	R	E	S		J	A	N	U	S		
		R	A	Z	E	D		B	A	R	G	E		
M	E	D	E	A		C	R	I	M	E	B	O	S	S
A	M	F			T	E	E	N	P	E	O	P	L	E
L	O	A	N	T	R	A	N	S	L	A	T	I	O	N
A	V	I	A	R	I	S	T			O	T	T	A	W	A
L	E	T	T	U	C	E			W	E	L	T	E	R
A	S	H	L	E	E					R	E	E	D	Y

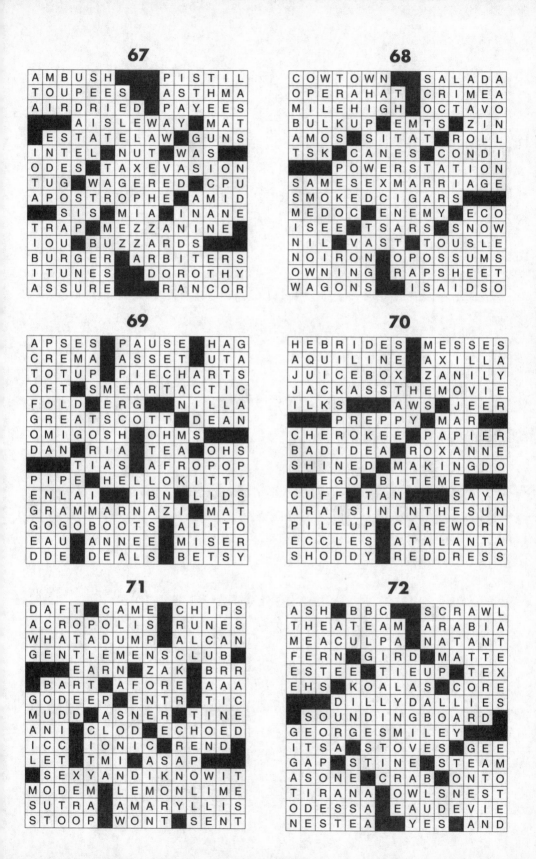

67

A	M	B	U	S	H			P	I	S	T	I	L
T	O	U	P	E	E	S			A	S	T	H	M	A
A	I	R	D	R	I	E	D		P	A	Y	E	E	S
		A	I	S	L	E	W	A	Y		M	A	T
	E	S	T	A	T	E	L	A	W		G	U	N	S
I	N	T	E	L		N	U	T		W	A	S
O	D	E	S		T	A	X	E	V	A	S	I	O	N
T	U	G		W	A	G	E	R	E	D		C	P	U
A	P	O	S	T	R	O	P	H	E		A	M	I	D
	S	I	S		M	I	A		I	N	A	N	E
T	R	A	P		M	E	Z	Z	A	N	I	N	E
I	O	U		B	U	Z	Z	A	R	D	S
B	U	R	G	E	R		A	R	B	I	T	E	R	S
I	T	U	N	E	S		D	O	R	O	T	H	Y
A	S	S	U	R	E		R	A	N	C	O	R

68

C	O	W	T	O	W	N		S	A	L	A	D	A
O	P	E	R	A	H	A	T		C	R	I	M	E	A
M	I	L	E	H	I	G	H		O	C	T	A	V	O
B	U	L	K	U	P		E	M	T	S		Z	I	N
A	M	O	S		S	I	T	A	T		R	O	L	L
T	S	K		C	A	N	E	S		C	O	N	D	I
		P	O	W	E	R	S	T	A	T	I	O	N
S	A	M	E	S	E	X	M	A	R	R	I	A	G	E
S	M	O	K	E	D	C	I	G	A	R	S
M	E	D	O	C		E	N	E	M	Y		E	C	O
I	S	E	E		T	S	A	R	S		S	N	O	W
N	I	L		V	A	S	T		T	O	U	S	L	E
N	O	I	R	O	N		O	P	O	S	S	U	M	S
O	W	N	I	N	G		R	A	P	S	H	E	E	T
W	A	G	O	N	S		I	S	A	I	D	S	O

69

A	P	S	E	S		P	A	U	S	E		H	A	G
C	R	E	M	A		A	S	S	E	T		U	T	A
T	O	T	U	P		P	I	E	C	H	A	R	T	S
O	F	T		S	M	E	A	R	T	A	C	T	I	C
F	O	L	D		E	R	G		N	I	L	L	A
G	R	E	A	T	S	C	O	T	T		D	E	A	N
O	M	I	G	O	S	H		O	H	M	S
D	A	N		R	I	A		T	E	A		O	H	S
	T	I	A	S		A	F	R	O	P	O	P
P	I	P	E		H	E	L	L	O	K	I	T	T	Y
E	N	L	A	I		I	B	N		L	I	D	S
G	R	A	M	M	A	R	N	A	Z	I		M	A	T
G	O	G	O	B	O	O	T	S		A	L	I	T	O
E	A	U		A	N	N	E	E		M	I	S	E	R
D	D	E		D	E	A	L	S		B	E	T	S	Y

70

H	E	B	R	I	D	E	S		M	E	S	S	E	S
A	Q	U	I	L	I	N	E		A	X	I	L	L	A
J	U	I	C	E	B	O	X		Z	A	N	I	L	Y
J	A	C	K	A	S	S	T	H	E	M	O	V	I	E
I	L	K	S		A	W	S		J	E	E	R
	P	R	E	P	P	Y		M	A	R
C	H	E	R	O	K	E	E		P	A	P	I	E	R
B	A	D	I	D	E	A		R	O	X	A	N	N	E
S	H	I	N	E	D		M	A	K	I	N	G	D	O
	E	G	O		B	I	T	E	M	E
C	U	F	F		T	A	N		S	A	Y	A
A	R	A	I	S	I	N	I	N	T	H	E	S	U	N
P	I	L	E	U	P		C	A	R	E	W	O	R	N
E	C	C	L	E	S		A	T	A	L	A	N	T	A
S	H	O	D	D	Y		R	E	D	D	R	E	S	S

71

D	A	F	T		C	A	M	E		C	H	I	P	S
A	C	R	O	P	O	L	I	S		R	U	N	E	S
W	H	A	T	A	D	U	M	P		A	L	C	A	N
G	E	N	T	L	E	M	E	N	S	C	L	U	B
		E	A	R	N		Z	A	K		B	R	R
	B	A	R	T		A	F	O	R	E		A	A	A
G	O	D	E	E	P		E	N	T	R		T	I	C
M	U	D	D		A	S	N	E	R		T	I	N	E
A	N	I		C	L	O	D		E	C	H	O	E	D
I	C	C		I	O	N	I	C		R	E	N	D
L	E	T		T	M	I		A	S	A	P
	S	E	X	Y	A	N	D	I	K	N	O	W	I	T
M	O	D	E	M		L	E	M	O	N	L	I	M	E
S	U	T	R	A		A	M	A	R	Y	L	L	I	S
S	T	O	O	P		W	O	N	T		S	E	N	T

72

A	S	H		B	B	C		S	C	R	A	W	L
T	H	E	A	T	E	A	M		A	R	A	B	I	A
M	E	A	C	U	L	P	A		N	A	T	A	N	T
F	E	R	N		G	I	R	D		M	A	T	T	E
E	S	T	E	E		T	I	E	U	P		T	E	X
E	H	S		K	O	A	L	A	S		C	O	R	E
		D	I	L	L	Y	D	A	L	L	I	E	S
	S	O	U	N	D	I	N	G	B	O	A	R	D
G	E	O	R	G	E	S	M	I	L	E	Y
I	T	S	A		S	T	O	V	E	S		G	E	E
G	A	P		S	T	I	N	E		S	T	E	A	M
A	S	O	N	E		C	R	A	B		O	N	T	O
T	I	R	A	N	A		O	W	L	S	N	E	S	T
O	D	E	S	S	A		E	A	U	D	E	V	I	E
N	E	S	T	E	A		Y	E	S		A	N	D

73

```
. R A M A D A . . T R U M B O
D E L O V E L Y . A E G E A N
O S O L E M I O . P A G A N S
D I N E R O . U R A L . S G T
O N E S . T I R E S . C U B A
. . M A G E S . D O R A G . .
. S H I P O F T H E L I N E .
. H O U S E T R A I N I N G .
P O U N D S T E R L I N G . .
R U N T O . H E E L S . . . .
O L D S . P I T A S . D E V O
L I B . M I S O . I C E C A P
O H I O A N . G A D A B O U T
N A T U R E . O V E R A L L S
G N E I S S . . E S P R I T .
```

74

```
W A S H D I S H E S . G R A D
A C T I O N H E R O . A C N E
F R O S T N I X O N . Z A G S
F E M S . M A O . H A D I T .
L A P . L O O P . B U S O N I
E G O . I N N O C E N T M A N
S E N T R A . D O E . R E L Y
. . H A K E . T R O I . . . .
S O L I . I R A . K A P P A S
C R A N K C A L L E R . E D T
R E S O A K . B I G S . T H E
A G O N Y . B E L . S T E W .
P A R T . M A R K O M E A R A
E N D O . A N T I V A X X E R
S O A P . S C A M A R T I S T
```

75

```
M I S H M A S H . A N E M I A
A L O U E T T E . D O R A G S
D O N T S T O P . U S M I N T
M I N . H U R . E L E A N O R
A L E G . K E N T S . M R I .
N O T I C E . C O S . D E E D
. . B A L L O U . A R N I E .
. T H I N K I N G A B O U T .
C H I L E . N O H E L P . . .
A R A L . G E M . R E I N E D
N E W . T O N Y S . T E R R .
T E A S E T S . E A R . A R A
A T T H A T . T O M O R R O W
B O H E M E . S U I T A B L E
S N A P O N . O L D S T Y L E
```

76

```
R I T Z B I T S . . S C R E W
A M A Z O N A N T . W A I V E
P I C T O G R A M . A N T E D
. N O O B . O P I U M D E N S
. . P O I . . S P Y . . . . .
T R I . I N E S S E . C A S T
R A R E S T A M P D E A L E R
I B E L I E V E I C A N F L Y
C I N D E R E L L A T E A M S
K N E E . A S T E R S . S A T
. . R E C . . S R I . . . . .
S L O W S T A R T . I S T O .
L A M A S . L E A D G L A S S
A R E N A . A N N E H E C H E
B A N D Y . I G E T T H A T .
```

77

```
A B U S E . M E N D . O L D S
L A S T C H A N C E . M E E T
C R U S H I N G I T . E A V E
A R R . O N B A S E . G R I P
Z A P S . T U G . N B A J A M
A G E N T . N E W T O . E T O
R E D E E M . M A I N I T E M
. . A N Y S E C O N D . . . .
K I C K E D I N . N E L L I E
I M O . T E X T S . T E E N Y
S A M O S A . P P P . D O T E
S L E W . R E A R E D . N O L
C I N E . S T R E A M L I N E
A V O N . I N T E R V E N E S
M E W S . R A Y S . S E E D S
```

78

```
S I L I C O N C H I P . V J S
A V O C A D O R O L L . E O N
Z O N E D E F E N S E . R Y E
E R G . T A S K . A F I R E .
R I I S . S I T E S . A Z I Z
A E S O P . R E D O . C O D E
C S H A R P . D A R K E N E D
. . P O O F . T E N S . . . .
D I R E W O L F . L O W T A R
U S E D . C O O P . B A H I A
S U L U . H O R U S . P E R T
T R A P S . R E N T . D A B .
M E T . T O M A T O S A U C E
O D E . A L I C E W A L K E R
P O D . B E C H D E L T E S T
```

79

```
CATSPAJAMAS ■ MFA
ATOMICCLOCK ■ OIL
FORINSTANCE ■ ONT
FLUTE ■ RITE ■ DEO
ELSE ■ TIMESTAMP ■
■ LACES ■ CURE
CONVENED ■ COUSIN
AVOIDED ■ SOARING
BETRAY ■ FUNFACTS
SRTA ■ ROMAS ■
■ SOLDIERON ■ LESS
ELO ■ ALEC ■ BALOO
WEB ■ RIDESHOTGUN
EPA ■ KEEPTALKING
STD ■ ODDSANDENDS
```

80

```
FETE ■ ALDA ■ ATHOS
AGOG ■ LEON ■ CHARY
COPA ■ GENT ■ ERNES
ASSN ■ AZTEC ■ ONIT
DUH ■ ATNO ■ WADE
ERECTS ■ HAVISHAM
■ FLORIDATECH ■
■ FLEXITARIAN ■
■ PALEBLUEDOT ■
ANNOTATE ■ PREFAB
BOER ■ NEAP ■ RKO
BOAT ■ ETTAS ■ VIES
OGRES ■ IATE ■ ALSO
TIEUP ■ CLIP ■ PLUM
TERRY ■ SLOT ■ ESPY
```

81

```
MECCA ■ LSD ■ VIVID
ONYOU ■ ETA ■ PRONE
BACONATOR ■ SALSA
ICANTWAIT ■ QUAD
LTD ■ MATCHPOINTS
■ CAY ■ MOW ■ TIE
IMPLY ■ SCAPEGOAT
MAIA ■ EQUUS ■ ALTO
ALEPHNULL ■ WIDEN
TLC ■ AVE ■ JOT ■
ASEASYASPIE ■ BBS
LAMB ■ MIAMIHEAT
ONEAL ■ IDRISELBA
STATE ■ SEC ■ MILER
SALES ■ HAH ■ ERASE
```

82

```
FASCIAS ■ PIRATES
ARCADIA ■ ARACHNE
REAPERS ■ CONCISE
PARIAHS ■ ANTESUP
OWESTO ■ MANTRA
SAUCERS ■ BATTLES
TYPE ■ NOWIN ■ SERT
■ BIZ ■
RUST ■ BEZEL ■ PRIE
ANTIWAR ■ TAPIOCA
MAIMED ■ SENDER
ALFREDO ■ LATERON
DEFINES ■ ELUSIVE
ARECIBO ■ ALLAGES
STREETS ■ SEAPORT
```

83

```
DASHCAM ■ ETRADE
ENTERKEY ■ DREVIL
PERFECTO ■ GENEVA
EMOTE ■ AURAS ■ MIN
NIPS ■ ERROR ■ CANT
DAS ■ LUZON ■ CORER
■ CARAT ■ SHEILA
AWAYONHOLIDAY ■
SNARLS ■ EXITS ■
HASTA ■ BRIMS ■ MAR
ACHE ■ DOLCE ■ SAGA
GOD ■ YODEL ■ MIXER
UNODOS ■ FEMININE
ADWARE ■ TAILENDS
RANTED ■ NOSWEAT
```

84

```
MENACHEM ■ ABLAZE
APOLLOVI ■ LOOSED
HOTTOWEL ■ TAXING
ACHENE ■ IBIS ■ AMI
THERE ■ ITEM ■ ETON
MARS ■ DNATESTING
ALE ■ BEARATTACK ■
■ HAPPYMEAL ■
■ TEASEAPART ■ JAW
DOGKENNELS ■ MUSH
INGE ■ DINE ■ SANKA
END ■ SECS ■ BARKAT
TARZAN ■ ICEGIANT
EGOIST ■ OGEEARCH
DEPTHS ■ NINTHTEE
```

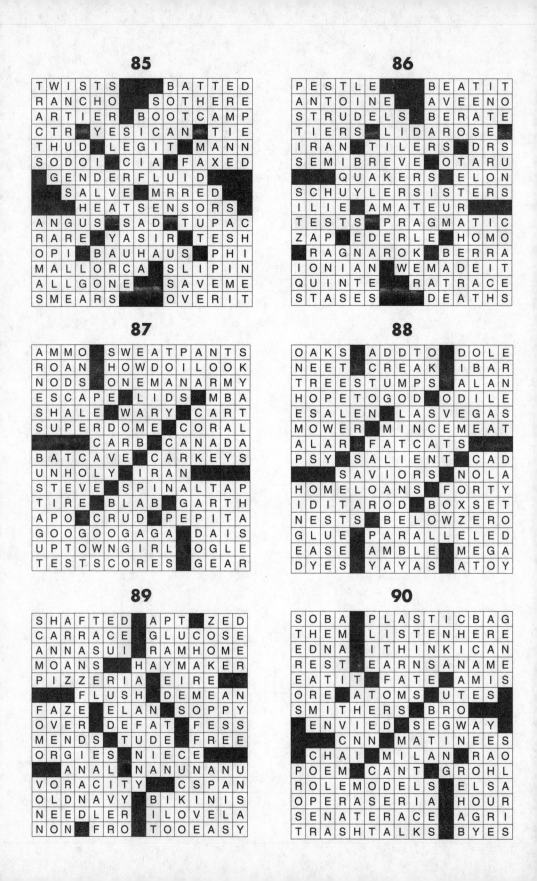

85 86 87 88 89 90

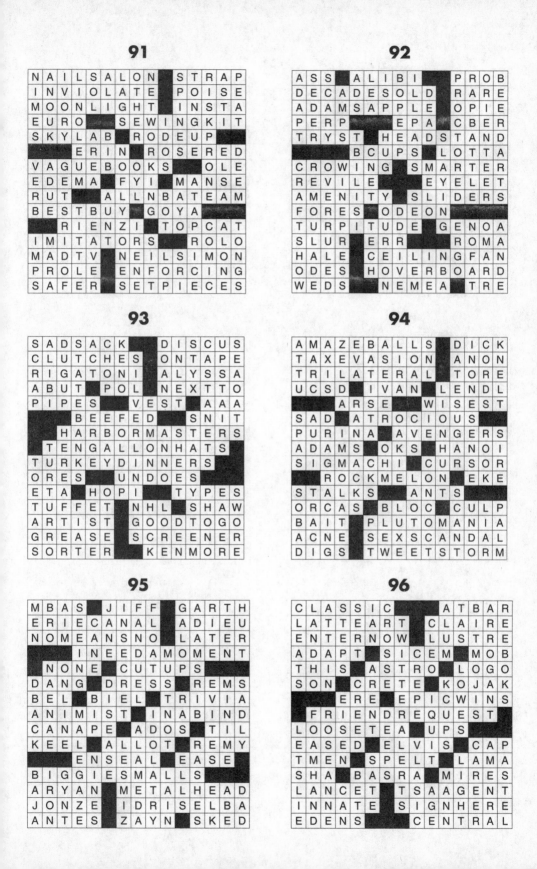

91

```
N A I L S A L O N ■ S T R A P
I N V I O L A T E ■ P O I S E
M O O N L I G H T ■ ■ I N S T A
E U R O ■ ■ S E W I N G K I T
S K Y L A B ■ R O D E U P ■ ■
■ ■ ■ E R I N ■ R O S E R E D
V A G U E B O O K S ■ ■ O L E
E D E M A ■ F Y I ■ M A N S E
R U T ■ ■ A L L N B A T E A M
B E S T B U Y ■ G O Y A ■ ■ ■
■ ■ R I E N Z I ■ T O P C A T
I M I T A T O R S ■ R O L O
M A D T V ■ N E I L S I M O N
P R O L E ■ E N F O R C I N G
S A F E R ■ S E T P I E C E S
```

92

```
A S S ■ A L I B I ■ ■ P R O B
D E C A D E S O L D ■ R A R E
A D A M S A P P L E ■ O P I E
P E R P ■ ■ E P A ■ C B E R
T R Y S T ■ H E A D S T A N D
■ ■ ■ B C U P S ■ L O T T A
C R O W I N G ■ S M A R T E R
R E V I L E ■ E Y E L E T
A M E N I T Y ■ S L I D E R S
F O R E S ■ O D E O N ■ ■ ■
T U R P I T U D E ■ G E N O A
S L U R ■ E R R ■ ■ R O M A
H A L E ■ C E I L I N G F A N
O D E S ■ H O V E R B O A R D
W E D S ■ N E M E A ■ T R E
```

93

```
S A D S A C K ■ D I S C U S
C L U T C H E S ■ O N T A P E
R I G A T O N I ■ A L Y S S A
A B U T ■ P O L ■ N E X T T O
P I P E S ■ V E S T ■ A A A
■ ■ B E E F E D ■ S N I T
■ H A R B O R M A S T E R S
■ T E N G A L L O N H A T S
T U R K E Y D I N N E R S
O R E S ■ ■ U N D O E S
E T A ■ H O P I ■ T Y P E S
T U F F E T ■ N H L ■ S H A W
A R T I S T ■ G O O D T O G O
G R E A S E ■ S C R E E N E R
S O R T E R ■ K E N M O R E
```

94

```
A M A Z E B A L L S ■ D I C K
T A X E V A S I O N ■ A N O N
T R I L A T E R A L ■ T O R E
U C S D ■ I V A N ■ L E N D L
■ A R S E ■ W I S E S T
S A D ■ A T R O C I O U S
P U R I N A ■ A V E N G E R S
A D A M S ■ O K S ■ H A N O I
S I G M A C H I ■ C U R S O R
■ R O C K M E L O N ■ E K E
S T A L K S ■ A N T S
O R C A S ■ B L O C ■ C U L P
B A I T ■ P L U T O M A N I A
A C N E ■ S E X S C A N D A L
D I G S ■ T W E E T S T O R M
```

95

```
M B A S ■ J I F F ■ G A R T H
E R I E C A N A L ■ A D I E U
N O M E A N S N O ■ L A T E R
■ I N E E D A M O M E N T
■ N O N E ■ C U T U P S
D A N G ■ D R E S S ■ R E M S
B E L ■ B I E L ■ T R I V I A
A N I M I S T ■ I N A B I N D
C A N A P E ■ A D O S ■ T I L
K E E L ■ A L L O T ■ R E M Y
■ ■ E N S E A L ■ E A S E
B I G G I E S M A L L S
A R Y A N ■ M E T A L H E A D
J O N Z E ■ I D R I S E L B A
A N T E S ■ Z A Y N ■ S K E D
```

96

```
C L A S S I C ■ ■ A T B A R
L A T T E A R T ■ C L A I R E
E N T E R N O W ■ L U S T R E
A D A P T ■ S I C E M ■ M O B
T H I S ■ A S T R O ■ L O G O
S O N ■ C R E T E ■ K O J A K
■ ■ E R E ■ E P I C W I N S
■ F R I E N D R E Q U E S T
L O O S E T E A ■ U P S
E A S E D ■ E L V I S ■ C A P
T M E N ■ S P E L T ■ L A M A
S H A ■ B A S R A ■ M I R E S
L A N C E T ■ T S A A G E N T
I N N A T E ■ S I G N H E R E
E D E N S ■ C E N T R A L
```

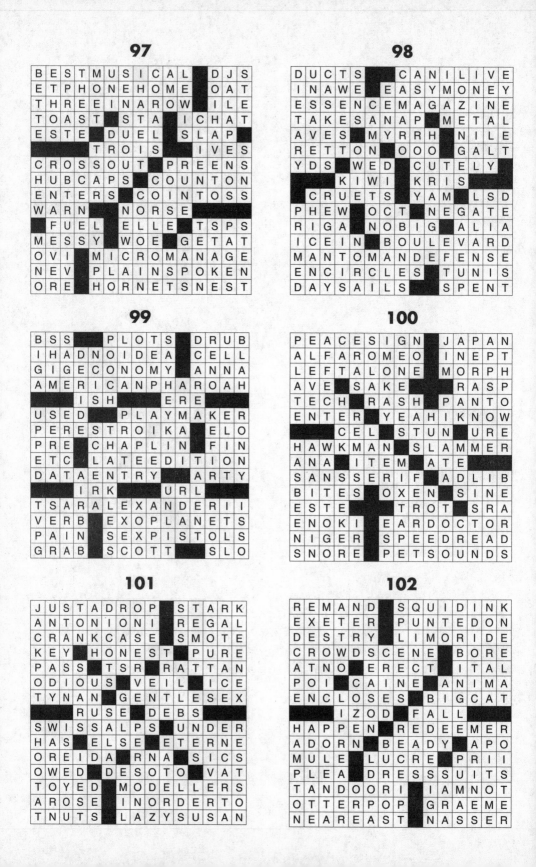

97

```
B E S T M U S I C A L  ■ D J S
E T P H O N E H O M E  ■ O A T
T H R E E I N A R O W  ■ I L E
T O A S T ■ S T A ■ I C H A T
E S T E ■ D U E L ■ S L A P
■ ■ T R O I S ■ ■ I V E S
C R O S S O U T ■ P R E E N S
H U B C A P S ■ C O U N T O N
E N T E R S ■ C O I N T O S S
W A R N ■ N O R S E ■ ■
■ F U E L ■ E L L E ■ T S P S
M E S S Y ■ W O E ■ G E T A T
O V I ■ M I C R O M A N A G E
N E V ■ P L A I N S P O K E N
O R E ■ H O R N E T S N E S T
```

98

```
D U C T S ■ C A N I L I V E
I N A W E ■ E A S Y M O N E Y
E S S E N C E M A G A Z I N E
T A K E S A N A P ■ M E T A L
A V E S ■ M Y R R H ■ N I L E
R E T T O N ■ O O O ■ G A L T
Y D S ■ W E D ■ C U T E L Y
■ K I W I ■ K R I S ■
■ C R U E T S ■ Y A M ■ L S D
P H E W ■ O C T ■ N E G A T E
R I G A ■ N O B I G ■ A L I A
I C E I N ■ B O U L E V A R D
M A N T O M A N D E F E N S E
E N C I R C L E S ■ T U N I S
D A Y S A I L S ■ S P E N T
```

99

```
B S S ■ P L O T S ■ D R U B
I H A D N O I D E A ■ C E L L
G I G E C O N O M Y ■ A N N A
A M E R I C A N P H A R O A H
■ I S H ■ E R E ■
U S E D ■ P L A Y M A K E R
P E R E S T R O I K A ■ E L O
P R E ■ C H A P L I N ■ F I N
E T C ■ L A T E E D I T I O N
D A T A E N T R Y ■ A R T Y
■ I R K ■ U R L ■
T S A R A L E X A N D E R I I
V E R B ■ E X O P L A N E T S
P A I N ■ S E X P I S T O L S
G R A B ■ S C O T T ■ S L O
```

100

```
P E A C E S I G N ■ J A P A N
A L F A R O M E O ■ I N E P T
L E F T A L O N E ■ M O R P H
A V E ■ S A K E ■ R A S P
T E C H ■ R A S H ■ P A N T O
E N T E R ■ Y E A H I K N O W
■ C E L ■ S T U N ■ U R E
H A W K M A N ■ S L A M M E R
A N A ■ I T E M ■ A T E ■
S A N S S E R I F ■ A D L I B
B I T E S ■ O X E N ■ S I N E
E S T E ■ T R O T ■ S R A
E N O K I ■ E A R D O C T O R
N I G E R ■ S P E E D R E A D
S N O R E ■ P E T S O U N D S
```

101

```
J U S T A D R O P ■ S T A R K
A N T O N I O N I ■ R E G A L
C R A N K C A S E ■ S M O T E
K E Y ■ H O N E S T ■ P U R E
P A S S ■ T S R ■ R A T T A N
O D I O U S ■ V E I L ■ I C E
T Y N A N ■ G E N T L E S E X
■ R U S E ■ D E B S ■
S W I S S A L P S ■ U N D E R
H A S ■ E L S E ■ E T E R N E
O R E I D A ■ R N A ■ S I C S
O W E D ■ D E S O T O ■ V A T
T O Y E D ■ M O D E L L E R S
A R O S E ■ I N O R D E R T O
T N U T S ■ L A Z Y S U S A N
```

102

```
R E M A N D ■ S Q U I D I N K
E X E T E R ■ P U N T E D O N
D E S T R Y ■ L I M O R I D E
C R O W D S C E N E ■ B O R E
A T N O ■ E R E C T ■ I T A L
P O I ■ C A I N E ■ A N I M A
E N C L O S E S ■ B I G C A T
■ I Z O D ■ F A L L ■
H A P P E N ■ R E D E E M E R
A D O R N ■ B E A D Y ■ A P O
M U L E ■ L U C R E ■ P R I I
P L E A ■ D R E S S S U I T S
T A N D O O R I ■ I A M N O T
O T T E R P O P ■ G R A E M E
N E A R E A S T ■ N A S S E R
```

103

A S S E T	T E S T M A T C H
S T A L E	A P P I A N W A Y
Q A N D A	R A I N S T O R M
U N D E R	H U T C H I S O N
I D B R A C E L E T	L O L A
T E A	T R E E S	C A M E L
H E R B	A L T	S O B E R S
E A T S	S H O O
A C H E B E	S E E	R O S E
B R A T S	B I T E S	W P A
R U S H	L A N A T U R N E R
E M B O W E R E D	R E G A L
A B E V I G O D A	E V O K E
S L E E P O N I T	L U A U S
T E N N E S S E E	Y E L P S

104

H E Y M R D J	A S C R I B E
I C K Y P O O	M A R I N E S
T O N S I L S	A D E P T A T
C L O T	L E G	A T T E N D
H E W E D	P E T H A I R
R I G H T H A N D M A N
S A W Y E R	A I R	E S T E
P E A	T E A R S U P	O W E
E R R S	C S A	O U T F O R
C O M E G O W I T H M E
H E I R E S S	A A R G H
G H E T T O	E G O	B O S E
M I A H A M M	A N N A S U I
A D R E N A L	R E E L S I N
J E T S O N S	P R B L I T Z

105

T H E W H O	S N A P	J E T
R E N A I L	T O B E S U R E
A N G L E D	A M B R O S I A
Y I E L D S	S E A O T T E R
S E L A	A S H	E T H I C
C O W H E R B	A F A R
A L T E R	O S H A	T I N O
L O E S S E R	I N A H E A P
A S S T	V T E N	L A D L E
S A T E	E U R O P O P
L A V I N	O S H	P O G S
P A T E N T E D	O N E S E T
I M O N F I R E	B A N K S Y
N O R S E M A N	I D E A T E
E S S	R E S T	C A D R E S

106

M A T T D A M O N	P A S S E
S P E E D D A T E	I N A L L
R E L A T E S T O	E N I A C
P R E K	N C O S	C E N T I
R O O M	S E X T E D
G E S S O	T A B O O
I T H A C A	N U F F S A I D
S T A R K L Y	B T W E L V E
H U G I T O U T	C O R D O N
H E M E N	R E A R S
G N O M E S	D U C K
S A W I V	I T C H	D U P E
P I N T O	M A L E N U R S E
O V E T T	P L E A S E S I R
T E R S E	S K I P C L A S S

107

K I D N E Y B E A N	L A T E
A N Y O N E E L S E	E R I S
T R E N C H C O A T	G E N T
Z E D	A I R F R A N C E
L U L U	U L U L A T E
S H I I T E S	L I S T
W A R G A M E	E X T E N D S
U H O H	N C A A
M A N T R A S	B R A D A W L
S U V A	R E V E R S E
S E V E N A M	U B E R
P L E C T R U M S	G W B
L E G O	I R A Q I D I N A R
I V A N	C A Y U G A L A K E
T E N D	E I S E N H O W E R

108

S O T	H A B E R D A S H E R
W H O	O N C L O U D N I N E
E P A	R I C K Y N E L S O N
E L F M A N	H A N S	M R T
T E A R S	B A L E	K A M A
S A R I	W O R F	A N S E L
O S E	W A X T A B L E T
P E T M I C E	M A E W E S T
H I T O R M I S S	R P I
G O E T H	B A L K	M S R P
A R E A	O R L Y	T I V O S
S S W	G A I L	W O N O U T
L I E D E T E C T O R	I T E
O N L I N E F O R U M	C U R
G O L D E N S P I K E	E P S

109

```
O M A H A █ E L M S █ S E R F
H E L E N █ K I C K B O X E R
C A P R I █ G E R A L D I N E
A T H O M E █ S I T U A T E D
L E A N E R S █ B E E P █ █
C A B S █ R E F █ B O O S T
U T E █ N A I L C L I P P E R
T E T █ A N N U L A R █ E L I
T R I B U T E B A N D █ N F C
A S C O T █ S I C █ P E S O
█ █ A I R S █ R E O R D E R
S C O T L A N D █ T H E F E D
A R T M U S E U M █ A L I K E
K A T E S P A D E █ R A R E R
E B O N █ S K E W █ E W E R S
```

110

```
G O D E L E S C H E R B A C H
P R I V A T E A U D I E N C E
S U M A N D S U B S T A N C E
█ █ D E S █ G R E A T █ █
P A N E S █ P H I L █ I N D S
O R O S █ B E T S █ A F O O T
T A K █ Z O R A █ C R I N G E
S P O K E O F F T H E C U F F
D A M A S K █ E R O S █ S O A
A H I N T █ Z W E I █ L E O N
M O S S █ D E W Y █ P A R D O
█ A T A R I █ A I M █ █
O N E S E C O N D P L E A S E
P U T S T H E K I B O S H O N
S T A T E A S S I S T A N C E
```

111

```
A T W A R █ F L E E █ S A P S
B U R M A █ R A I L █ C L A W
O N I O N R I N G S █ R E N E
D E S K █ O N T H E L E V E L
E S T █ P U G E T █ E W E L L
█ B A L L E R I N A S █
P R A G U E █ N E E D █ P B S
D Y N A S T S █ S A F A R I S
Q E D █ S T E P █ R O D E O S
█ P I E A L A M O D E █
G E O R G █ T A C I T █ M A P
E R G O N O M I C S █ L P G A
I R I S █ B A T E S M O T E L
C O V E █ I T E S █ I R E N E
O R E S █ T E D S █ L E D T O
```

112

```
A B L E █ M S N B C █ A B R A
N A A N █ I L I E D █ M E A N
T Y P E W R I T E R S T A N D
F A D █ H O T S P O T █ R D A
A R E N A S █ █ M E C C A N
R E S E T █ A N N █ P O U L T
M A K E M I N E A D O U B L E
█ D E L I C I O U S █
S I D E W A L K A R T I S T S
O T E R O █ L S D █ S N A R E
M E S S R S █ █ M I S L E D
E M E █ R A D I O A D █ T V A
S O R R Y F O R T H E W A I T
A N T I █ E L A T E █ E I N E
Y E S M █ S E N O R █ T R O D
```

113

```
P E D I C A B █ B R A P A D S
A R I G A T O █ E A T E N U P
P A N A R A B █ R I H A N N A
A S K █ L L B █ T S A R I S M
█ T O O L S █ I N L E T S
J U S T A S E C O N D █
U N I O N S H O P S █ M O E T
B U R P S █ E N E █ W E L S H
A M I S █ M A C N C H E E S E
█ R I D E S H O T G U N
S T R A W S █ S E A L S █
W E E L A S S █ C L E █ I R E
A P L E N T Y █ R U B S O U T
B E A R D E N █ E P I C W I N
S E X T A P E █ T A T I A N A
```

114

```
X E N O █ A L I S T █ G R A F
A T O N █ L E N T O █ H A L O
C H O C O L A T E S H A K E S
T A K E N O P R I S O N E R S
O N S █ C U T A N D P A S T E
█ G U T █ M O T █
Z A I R E █ S E A W O R T H Y
A R N O █ S P U R N █ A S I A
K I C K S T A R T █ O N K E Y
█ P E R █ M F G █
I M A G I N E T H A T █ S A M
C O M E T O T H E R E S C U E
A P P L E P I E A L A M O D E
R U L E █ A R U D E █ U N I T
E P E E █ D E N S E █ G E T S
```

115

```
M I C H E L E B A C H M A N N
S T R A T E G I C R O U T E S
T H E L A T E L A T E S H O W
■ A T T S ■ R I P ■ S E E N ■
N C I S ■ S I O U X ■ D I A Z
C A N ■ E P A U L E T ■ S T E
O N S T A R ■ S C R A M M E D
■ A S I F ■ O O P S ■ ■ ■ ■ ■
A F L U T T E R ■ X E S O U T
D O E ■ S E R A P E S ■ V S O
O R A L ■ S R T A S ■ B E B E
■ S V E N ■ A R I ■ T E R P ■
H U E V O S R A N C H E R O S
U R B A N D I C T I O N A R Y
P E E R A S S E S S M E N T S
```

116

```
J I M M Y F A L L O N ■ P B J
A R E Y O U R E A D Y ■ A L A
K I N G S R A N S O M ■ R O C
E S S O ■ L B S ■ R E R A C K
S H A D S ■ I C K ■ T I C K S
■ ■ ■ ■ O S C A R S ■ S H A Q
T I S S U E ■ P I E ■ K U D U
O T H E L L O ■ S A G E T E A
G A O L ■ M A C ■ M O D E S T
A L O E ■ A T O A S T ■ ■ ■ ■
P I T C H ■ S N L ■ O M E G A
A C E T I C ■ S A W ■ A L U M
R I M ■ M A G I N O T L I N E
T Z U ■ O R I G I N A L S I N
Y E P ■ M E A N S T R E E T S
```

117

```
P O V E R T Y R O W ■ G A R R
U R A N I U M O R E ■ E P E E
C A R R O T C A K E ■ L P G A
E N Y A ■ U A R ■ D I A L U P
■ ■ ■ G A S ■ ■ P E N T E L ■
E S T E R ■ S T E A D I C A M
W A R S A W P A C T ■ N I T E
O N E ■ B O L S T E R ■ D I A
K T E L ■ R E T I R E M E N T
S A G E G R E E N ■ B E R G S
■ C U T S I N ■ ■ F A N ■ ■ ■
B L A S T S ■ O N O ■ D I S K
C A R O ■ O T H E R W O M A N
U R D U ■ M S M A G A Z I N E
P A S T ■ E A S T O R A N G E
```

118

```
B U R J K H A L I F A ■ P I C
O N A U T O P I L O T ■ G M A
W I S D O M T E E T H ■ T M S
E X P O S I T S ■ O L D H A T
■ ■ ■ L E O ■ A M E R I C A
C I A L I S ■ S T A T E R U N
A S I A N ■ S U I T E ■ T L C
N O R M ■ S E N D S ■ Y E A H
T M C ■ M A I N E ■ S E E T O
H E L S I N K I ■ C O R N E R
A T E I N T O ■ E O N ■ ■ ■ ■
C R A N I A ■ C R O N Y I S M
K I N ■ M A J O R L E A G U E
I C E ■ A N D S O I T G O E S
T S R ■ L A S T R E S O R T S
```

119

```
C L A S P I N G ■ A N G L E
L A S E R B E A M ■ B O R A X
I N A N I M A T E ■ C R A V E
N O R A D ■ L E T T ■ Y O U
G L U T E I ■ E A S T E R N
T I L E ■ R U M O R H A S I T
O N E ■ C O N A R T I S T S ■
■ ■ L A N D L I N E S ■ ■
■ F O U R L E T T E R ■ O F T
C O I N P U R S E S ■ B R I E
H U L K I N G ■ S C L E R A
A L P ■ G O B S ■ R A G E S
I T A L Y ■ N O T R E D A M E
S I N A I ■ E Y E O P E N E R
E P S O N ■ S T E T S O N S
```

120

```
P I Z Z A J O I N T ■ W I F E
A N T I M A T T E R ■ A L A S
W H I T E N O I S E ■ L L C S
N I L ■ S E E S T O ■ K A T O
■ S E T ■ S N L ■ G O T ■
■ ■ H T S ■ T I E O N E O N
I N H E R I T ■ N E W W A V E
B I O D A T A ■ G R E A S E S
A T T A C K S ■ S I S T E R S
R E T R E A T S ■ E T E ■
■ O K S ■ E P S ■ R A W ■
L O T S ■ S T E P O N ■ S A Y
Y U R I ■ R E N O N E V A D A
I Z O D ■ I S C R E W E D U P
N O T E ■ S T E E L T R A P S
```

121

```
A S K O V E R ■ P T B O A T S
R A I S E D A N E Y E B R O W
A L L K I D D I N G A S I D E
R O M A N ■ I N N E R ■ S I E
A M E R ■ M A J O R ■ S T E T
T E R ■ T I T A N ■ K N I F E
■ B A K E S ■ D E A D O N
■ I B I S E S ■ P E E P E R ■
A M A Z E D ■ M A L L S ■
R I L E D ■ B U S T S ■ S H E
A T I T ■ P E S T S ■ V T E N
P A N ■ S E I K O ■ K A R A T
A T E E N A G E R I N L O V E
H O S T I L E T A K E O V E R
O R E S T E S ■ L E E R E R S
```

122

```
L I A R S ■ B L A S T I T
U N D O C K ■ C O M E O N S
S A S S O N S ■ S A N T A N A
T W O S T E P S ■ F E T T E R
F O R E T E L L S ■ S L U R S
U R B S ■ P I A M A T E R S ■
L D S ■ B A T T A L I O N
■ L E T T E R M E N
■ C O N C E R T O S ■ S E A
■ T O U G H R O A D ■ M A G I
C O N G A ■ S O L O H O M E R
L O C A L S ■ F E V E R I S H
A L E N C O N ■ C A R E S T O
M E D I A T E ■ R E S E E S
P R E S T O S ■ S O N D E
```

123

```
G E R M I N A T E ■ L U C I A
O V E R T A K E S ■ A N O D E
D O M E S T I C P A R T N E R
I K I D ■ A R S ■ S K I D O O
V E T ■ A L A ■ G A S L O G S
A S S I S I ■ A R P ■ F R O
■ C H A N G E ■ O N E A L
M C G E E ■ O N E ■ P O E M S
A L O E S ■ L E T T E R ■
M E T ■ S A W ■ A R M P I T
M A T D O W N ■ A G A ■ A M Y
A R E O L A ■ E S T ■ A G A R
M I N D I N G T H E S T O R E
I N I G O ■ A R E A C O D E S
A G N E S ■ T E R M I N A T E
```

124

```
P A W P R I N T ■ M E A N T O
R E E L E D I N ■ I N F E R S
O R N A M E N T A L T R E E S
P O T T I E S ■ L E I ■ D E I
O B S E S S ■ B I S C A Y N E
S A O N E ■ P I E T I N
A T U S ■ M I G N O N E T T E
L I T ■ B I G B A N G ■ H U A
S C H O O L M A T E ■ C E R T
■ D A L E N E ■ B E R N E
T I M E S I N K ■ G E R M A N
I W O ■ T O T ■ B A R T O L I
L I S T E N S T O R E A S O N
T S H I R T ■ R U N T I E S T
S H E E S H ■ I T I S N T S O
```

125

```
S A N T A N A ■ N E T F L I X
C H U N N E L ■ O X I D A T E
A I R T A X I ■ S P R A Y E R
L T S ■ G U M S H O E ■ A M O
D U E T ■ S O L O S ■ T W I X
E N R O N ■ N O W ■ G R A Z E
D A Y L I L Y ■ S P L A Y E D
■ K E Y ■ D I P ■
E T A I L E D ■ I Q T E S T S
N O T E S ■ I N C ■ Z Z T O P
C O E N ■ I V I E S ■ E U R E
A S I ■ A M O E B A S ■ N N E
M O N S T E R ■ A M I S T A D
P O T O M A C ■ T O R P E D O
S N O C O N E ■ H A I R D O S
```

126

```
A C T F I V E ■ O F F C A S T
F A I R B A N K S A L A S K A
F R E E A S S O C I A T I O N
A L G O R E ■ M A N X ■ M P G
B E A N S ■ P O R T ■ M O J O
L A M S ■ B U D S ■ L O V E S
E S E ■ B R N O ■ R O O
■ E S P R I T D E C O R P S ■
■ A I M ■ R A M P ■ L I D
S K O R T ■ H A S P ■ N O L O
A A H S ■ S A G E ■ J A W E D
I B M ■ Z E R O ■ D U P I N G
D O Y O U W A N N A D A N C E
H O M E L E S S S H E L T E R
I M Y O U R S ■ C L A M O R S
```

127

```
F A W N ■ A B B A ■ ■ T A S K S
E C H O ■ H E A R ■ ■ I R E N E
M E A T T H E R M O M E T E R
A S T A R ■ T R Y M E ■ T W A
■ ■ H R A P ■ ■ S A G A L
P L A Y M E O R T R A D E M E
S A P ■ S O X E R ■ P I S A N
E S P O ■ N Y T O L ■ A T N O
U S E A S ■ G I N O S ■ H O T
D O N T E V E N G O T H E R E
■ ■ S H E E N ■ ■ P I E S
C T N ■ K E A T S ■ L Y C E E
W H E R E S T H E R E M O T E
T A X E R ■ E U R O ■ A R A L
S I T E S ■ D R E W ■ N E T S
```

128

```
N A S T Y G R A M ■ N A P E S
I N T H E R E A R ■ O R R I N
P A R A S A I L S ■ B O O N E
S L O W ■ S D I ■ G O A T E E
■ ■ S T P ■ Y S I D R O ■
S R O ■ U S U A L L Y ■ T E D
C A M E R A S H Y ■ S T Y L I
A D A P T T O ■ F S H A P E D
R A H A L ■ P R O P O N E N T
F R A ■ E Y E E X A M ■ S A O
■ ■ B A D E N D ■ M E T ■ ■
S T E P I N ■ Z I A ■ E S A U
M I A T A ■ P O O L H A L L S
U L C E R ■ E N T O U R A G E
G E H R Y ■ D E A T H S T A R
```

129

```
S T I L L D R E ■ A L B A
C O N E H E A D S ■ M E A N
A R C T A N G E N T ■ O A T S
R E L I S T S ■ O R I E N T E
F A U N A S ■ T W I N B I L L
A D D O N ■ J E T P L A N E
C O E N ■ G A L I L E E
E R S ■ D E S E R E T ■ L O B
■ ■ D E T O X E D ■ J O N I
■ S T E A R N E S ■ T A M E S
T H E O R E M S ■ L I M B I C
Y E S D E A R ■ S A N T A N A
P A S A ■ L A B O R P A R T Y
E T A T ■ Z E N G A R D E N
A H S O ■ L E O N T Y N E
```

130

```
W H I P I T ■ S P A C E J A M
H A M E L S ■ C O C A C O L A
A M P S U P ■ H I T S O N G S
T R U T V ■ O M N I S ■ K O S
S A D O ■ N A U T ■ P Y R E
U D E ■ K I T T Y K E L L E Y
P I N C E N E Z ■ R D A ■ ■
G O T O V E R ■ M A G N U M S
■ ■ R I T ■ T A K E O N M E
J O H N N Y C A K E S ■ D M X
A N A S ■ O X E N ■ G E M S
R E V ■ H E L P S ■ G O R G E
J O E B O X E R ■ M O N G O L
A N N E R I C E ■ F A Z O O L
R E S T S T O P ■ A T O D D S
```

131

```
M A D E M I N C E M E A T O F
E C O N O M I C W A R F A R E
L O S A N G E L E S T I M E S
S P E C I A L I N T E R E S T
■ ■ S T E M S ■ ■ I S S ■
■ ■ O D E ■ F F F ■ T R E E
S T U R M ■ B E E F S ■ A X L
M O R S E C O D E S I G N A L
O J S ■ N I L E S ■ L A K M E
G O A L ■ M A X ■ T V S ■
■ ■ U G A ■ ■ P I E R O ■
C O M M E R C I A L R A D I O
F R E E T R A N S L A T I O N
C H A N S O N S D E G E S T E
S E T S O N A P E D E S T A L
```

132

```
P I Z Z A C R U S T ■ B L A B
A R I O N A S S I S ■ F O R A
C I P H E R T E X T ■ F O R T
A S S A M ■ D A R K ■ K I T
■ ■ N O G O ■ M A N C A V E
P S A ■ N O O N ■ P E L T E R
H O C K E Y M O M ■ W E T L Y
O L E N ■ A P L U S ■ A H A B
N A T A L ■ H O T P O T A T O
E R I C A S ■ S E C T ■ T E X
B A C K L I T ■ D A T A ■ ■
O R A ■ A N O N ■ O L D I E
O R C A ■ B R O O D M A R E S
T A I L ■ I T A L I A N A R T
H Y D E ■ N A M E S N A M E S
```

133

```
B L U E C R A B ■ L O W F A T
O I L S H A L E ■ B R O O C H
N O N T I T L E ■ J I L T E E
D N A ■ ■ T O R T R E F O R M
■ ■ C L A W C R A N E ■ ■ ■ ■
P A T R O N S A I N T ■ A S A
E B O O K ■ N E C ■ R C A S ■
T A R N I S H ■ S H T E T L S
A C M E ■ M A O ■ ■ R A I T T
L I E ■ V E L V E T E L V I S
■ ■ ■ F A L L E N H E M ■ ■ ■
E L D O C T O R O W ■ ■ V F W
C O U G A R ■ B R A S S E R A
O R S I N O ■ I M R U I N E D
N I E N T E ■ D E T E N T E S
```

134

```
S Q U A B B L E ■ J A M C A M
E U P H O R I A ■ O R I O L E
T I P S H E E T ■ K I D U L T
B B S ■ M A L I C E ■ E L S E
A B A S ■ K O T O ■ H A D T O
I L L I N ■ W U N D E R B A R
L E A N O N ■ P I E R ■ E R S
■ ■ ■ S O U P ■ C L O P ■ ■ ■
S E A ■ G T O S ■ L I T O U T
E X Q U I S I T E ■ C A N S O
A T U N E ■ S U C H ■ S E T T
G R I P ■ D E C A Y S ■ M I A
R E V I S E ■ K R A T I O N S
A M E L I E ■ U T T E R R O T
M E R E S T ■ P E T P E E V E
```

135

```
■ D A R E S S A L A A M ■ ■ ■
■ C O N T A C T L E N S E S ■
W H A T S T H E B I G D E A L
R O S H ■ A N T E ■ F R I A ■
A L I E N T O ■ I N F ■ K N T
P E D R O ■ O S T E O P A T H
S R O ■ N U K E ■ A R E T E S
■ ■ ■ T O P S E C R E T ■ ■ ■
S A R D I S ■ T O S S ■ O Y E
P R E S S E S O N ■ E R T E S
E F S ■ E T O ■ C H E E T O S
N A T E ■ ■ B R E A ■ T A M A
T R Y T O S E E I T M Y W A Y
■ F L A S H I N T H E P A N ■
■ ■ E S T A T E S A L E S ■ ■
```

136

```
B U T T D I A L E D ■ G I B E
O N A R A M P A G E ■ U N O S
T I D A L B A S I N ■ M O B S
S T A P L E R ■ S A C ■ N S A
■ ■ ■ P A C T S ■ L O V E L Y
I C E ■ S I M I ■ I N A P E T
N A N S ■ L E T S ■ A S I D E
B R I E F E N C O U N T E R S
A D D E R ■ T O R N ■ S C U T
D E B T E E ■ M E I N ■ E N S
S A L O O N ■ S L O O P ■ ■ ■
O L Y ■ N A M ■ O N S E R V E
R E T D ■ C A S S I O P E I A
T R O Y ■ T A K E S A S E A T
S S N S ■ S M A R T P I L L S
```

137

```
C A S H B A R S ■ K A R S T S
O S C A R W A O ■ N I I H A U
N O I F S A N D S O R B U T S
G N A T ■ I D I O C Y ■ T A S
R E T ■ S T R U C K ■ M I R E
A M I G A S ■ M I I ■ O N Y X
T A C O S ■ O P E N E D ■ ■ ■
S N A P E ■ N E T ■ D E V A S
■ ■ ■ A S M A N Y ■ G R A C E
H A P S ■ A B T ■ P A N G E A
O N I T ■ N O O N E R ■ A D O
O Y L ■ A C U T E R ■ A B E T
T H E T R U T H W I L L O U T
C O U R T S ■ A L L I A N C E
H O P E S O ■ L Y S A N D E R
```

138

```
A P P L E C A R E ■ R A N C H
D O U B L E B E D ■ O M A H A
I M T O O S E X Y ■ M A T E Y
D E T ■ N A Y A ■ O A T E R S
A L E R ■ R A L P H ■ ■ D O E
S O R O S ■ N L R B ■ P O K E
■ ■ ■ S T E T ■ S A V A G E D
Z E A L O T ■ ■ B I N G E S
A L E Y A R D ■ T Y N E ■ ■ ■
P E O N ■ A E R O ■ G R I E G
C O N ■ D R E W U ■ A N N A
O N F I R E ■ L A N D ■ T R I
M O L D Y ■ F O R C E Q U I T
I R U L E ■ B A D A D V I C E
X A X E S ■ I N S P E C T O R
```

139

```
B O S C O   ■   J A C K L O R D
A X T O N   ■   R E T R I E V E R
S N A R E   ■   A B O U T F A C E
Q A D D A F I   ■   N E S T L E S
U R I   ■   M E N D E L   ■   T I S
E D A M   ■   L I E S   ■   C H I V E
■   A L I E N   ■   P A I N E D
■   L I F E P R E S E R V E R   ■
C E L I N E   ■   U L N A E
A T L A S   ■   O V U M   ■   S O A P
T A G   ■   P R E M E D   ■   R U E
C L E A R E D   ■   D N A T E S T
H O T P O T A T O   ■   W H I T E
O N I O N R I N G   ■   N A D E R
W E T P A I N T   ■   S W A N S
```

140

```
J U J I T S U   ■   J A Z Z A G E
E L A T I O N   ■   S H O O T U P
T A K E A I M   ■   B O O T E E S
S L A M S   ■   A L A R M   ■   D S T
F U R S   ■   S P I C A   ■   V I S E
A M T   ■   D E P T H   ■   F A R S I
N E A T I D E A   ■   S A L T O N
■   A C E D   ■   Z A N E   ■
F I B B E R   ■   H A N G T I M E
A P L U S   ■   P A N T S   ■   C O X
S A I S   ■   L A N Z A   ■   B A R T
T N T   ■   A U S S I   ■   P E N T E
C E Z A N N E   ■   B U I L T I N
A M E R I G O   ■   A T A C O S T
R A N K L E S   ■   R E S H O E S
```

141

```
P U D D Y T A T   ■   P L A S M
I N I T I A T E   ■   C L I C H E
L I E S D O W N   ■   H U N T E R
E T D   ■   D I A N   ■   A R C A D E
■   I S R   ■   N R A   ■
A F I R S T   ■   K E L L O G G S
N O D U H   ■   J E W I S H R Y E
I R O N   ■   P U L S E   ■   B A R N
M I N T J E L L Y   ■   C O C O A
A T T O R N E Y   ■   C O Y E S T
■   E A P   ■   B A R   ■
S P R A W L   ■   T E R N   ■   A S U
C O O L I T   ■   H E R C U L E S
A L B A N Y   ■   O N E O R T W O
R E O R G   ■   M E L B L A N C
```

142

```
S G T S C H U L T Z   ■   C R A B
U R A N I U M O R E   ■   L I L O
D A T I N G P O O L   ■   U G L Y
S P I T E   ■   I K I D   ■   S H O W
Y E N S   ■   O R S   ■   A C T T W O
■   P A E A N   ■   H E M A N
B I O G A S   ■   T A M A R I N D
U N M A T E D   ■   S I L E N C E
S T E V E S A X   ■   R E D D E R
H E L E N   ■   M R M E T   ■
W R E A T H   ■   A I D   ■   S E T I
H A T H   ■   A P T S   ■   P I C O T
A L P O   ■   N A I L S A L O N S
C I A O   ■   S A N A N T O N I O
K A N T   ■   A R G Y L E S O C K
```

143

```
B A M B I   ■   M I N I   ■   T S K S
O P A R T   ■   U P O N   ■   U T A H
S A L E S R O O M S   ■   N O L O
C R E A M A N D S U G A R   ■
■   S E M   ■   G L O R Y B E
R I T T   ■   R A H   ■   T O O B A D
I C I   ■   B O R O N   ■   F L O S S
M E L T E D C H O C O L A T E
M A T E S   ■   S U D A N   ■   R E L
E X A L T S   ■   M E N   ■   A D D S
D E W L I N E   ■   C A B   ■
■   H A R A J U K U G I R L S
P A I L   ■   C E L I N E D I O N
S I R I   ■   K C A R   ■   N E L L E
I S L E   ■   S T N S   ■   A D E L E
```

144

```
P R O A C T I V   ■   B B G U N
H A S N O I D E A   ■   P U L S E
E M M A S T O N E   ■   O G E E S
L E O I   ■   O L D G E E Z E R   ■
P A N S Y   ■   O I L   ■   A C N E
S U D   ■   E V E R S O   ■   P L A T
■   E T A T S   ■   P U M A
O B T A I N S   ■   J E Z E B E L
B A A S   ■   A I R E R   ■
I C K Y   ■   D I S B A R   ■   S T U
S K E G   ■   O A F   ■   O C E A N
■   B O O K S M A R T   ■   H E R D
M O V I E   ■   B R E A K I N T O
O N E N D   ■   S A N D A L T A N
B E R G S   ■   S T A L L O N E
```

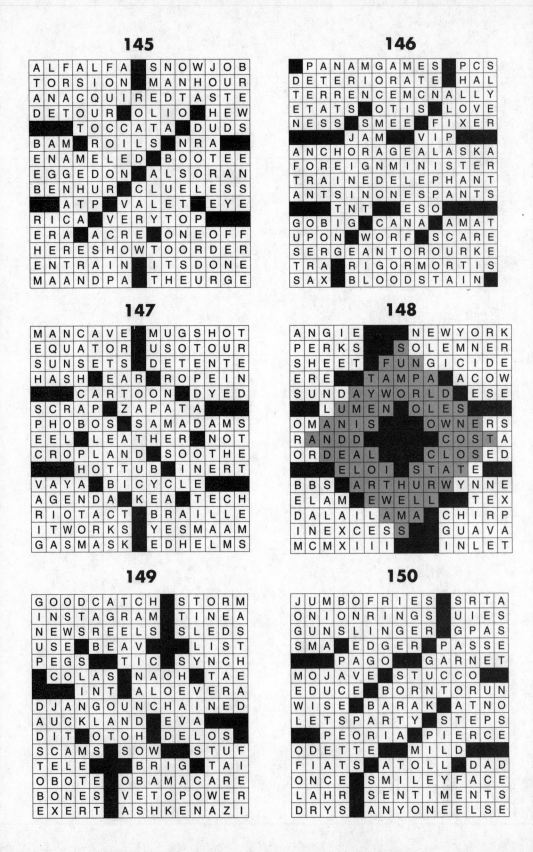

145

A	L	F	A	L	F	A	■	S	N	O	W	J	O	B
T	O	R	S	I	O	N	■	M	A	N	H	O	U	R
A	N	A	C	Q	U	I	R	E	D	T	A	S	T	E
D	E	T	O	U	R	■	O	L	I	O	■	H	E	W
■	■	T	O	C	C	A	T	A	■	D	U	D	S	■
B	A	M	■	R	O	I	L	S	■	N	R	A	■	■
E	N	A	M	E	L	E	D	■	B	O	O	T	E	E
E	G	G	E	D	O	N	■	A	L	S	O	R	A	N
B	E	N	H	U	R	■	C	L	U	E	L	E	S	S
■	A	T	P	■	V	A	L	E	T	■	E	Y	E	■
R	I	C	A	■	V	E	R	Y	T	O	P	■	■	■
E	R	A	■	A	C	R	E	■	O	N	E	O	F	F
H	E	R	E	S	H	O	W	T	O	O	R	D	E	R
E	N	T	R	A	I	N	■	I	T	S	D	O	N	E
M	A	A	N	D	P	A	■	T	H	E	U	R	G	E

146

■	P	A	N	A	M	G	A	M	E	S	■	P	C	S
D	E	T	E	R	I	O	R	A	T	E	■	H	A	L
T	E	R	R	E	N	C	E	M	C	N	A	L	L	Y
E	T	A	T	S	■	O	T	I	S	■	L	O	V	E
N	E	S	S	■	S	M	E	E	■	F	I	X	E	R
■	■	■	J	A	M	■	■	V	I	P	■	■	■	■
A	N	C	H	O	R	A	G	E	A	L	A	S	K	A
F	O	R	E	I	G	N	M	I	N	I	S	T	E	R
T	R	A	I	N	E	D	E	L	E	P	H	A	N	T
A	N	T	S	I	N	O	N	E	S	P	A	N	T	S
■	■	T	N	T	■	■	E	S	O	■	■	■	■	■
G	O	B	I	G	■	C	A	N	A	■	A	M	A	T
U	P	O	N	■	W	O	R	F	■	S	C	A	R	E
S	E	R	G	E	A	N	T	O	R	O	U	R	K	E
T	R	A	■	R	I	G	O	R	M	O	R	T	I	S
S	A	X	■	B	L	O	O	D	S	T	A	I	N	■

147

M	A	N	C	A	V	E	■	M	U	G	S	H	O	T
E	Q	U	A	T	O	R	■	U	S	O	T	O	U	R
S	U	N	S	E	T	S	■	D	E	T	E	N	T	E
H	A	S	H	■	E	A	R	■	R	O	P	E	I	N
■	■	C	A	R	T	O	O	N	■	D	Y	E	D	■
S	C	R	A	P	■	Z	A	P	A	T	A	■	■	■
P	H	O	B	O	S	■	S	A	M	A	D	A	M	S
E	E	L	■	L	E	A	T	H	E	R	■	N	O	T
C	R	O	P	L	A	N	D	■	S	O	O	T	H	E
■	■	H	O	T	T	U	B	■	I	N	E	R	T	■
V	A	Y	A	■	B	I	C	Y	C	L	E	■	■	■
A	G	E	N	D	A	■	K	E	A	■	T	E	C	H
R	I	O	T	A	C	T	■	B	R	A	I	L	L	E
I	T	W	O	R	K	S	■	Y	E	S	M	A	A	M
G	A	S	M	A	S	K	■	E	D	H	E	L	M	S

148

A	N	G	I	E	■	■	N	E	W	Y	O	R	K
P	E	R	K	S	■	S	O	L	E	M	N	E	R
S	H	E	E	T	■	F	U	N	G	I	C	I	D	E
E	R	E	■	T	A	M	P	A	■	A	C	O	W
S	U	N	D	A	Y	W	O	R	L	D	■	E	S	E
■	L	U	M	E	N	■	O	L	E	S	■	■
O	M	A	N	I	S	■	■	O	W	N	E	R	S
R	A	N	D	D	■	■	C	O	S	T	A
O	R	D	E	A	L	■	C	L	O	S	E	D
■	E	L	O	I	■	S	T	A	T	E	■
B	B	S	■	A	R	T	H	U	R	W	Y	N	N	E
E	L	A	M	■	E	W	E	L	L	■	T	E	X
D	A	L	A	I	L	A	M	A	■	C	H	I	R	P
I	N	E	X	C	E	S	S	■	G	U	A	V	A
M	C	M	X	I	I	I	■	I	N	L	E	T

149

G	O	O	D	C	A	T	C	H	■	S	T	O	R	M
I	N	S	T	A	G	R	A	M	■	T	I	N	E	A
N	E	W	S	R	E	E	L	S	■	S	L	E	D	S
U	S	E	■	B	E	A	V	■	L	I	S	T
P	E	G	S	■	T	I	C	■	S	Y	N	C	H
■	C	O	L	A	S	■	N	A	O	H	■	T	A	E
■	I	N	T	■	A	L	O	E	V	E	R	A
D	J	A	N	G	O	U	N	C	H	A	I	N	E	D
A	U	C	K	L	A	N	D	■	E	V	A
D	I	T	■	O	T	O	H	■	D	E	L	O	S
S	C	A	M	S	■	S	O	W	■	S	T	U	F
T	E	L	E	■	B	R	I	G	■	T	A	I
O	B	O	T	E	■	O	B	A	M	A	C	A	R	E
B	O	N	E	S	■	V	E	T	O	P	O	W	E	R
E	X	E	R	T	■	A	S	H	K	E	N	A	Z	I

150

J	U	M	B	O	F	R	I	E	S	■	S	R	T	A
O	N	I	O	N	R	I	N	G	S	■	U	I	E	S
G	U	N	S	L	I	N	G	E	R	■	G	P	A	S
S	M	A	■	E	D	G	E	R	■	P	A	S	S	E
■	P	A	G	O	■	G	A	R	N	E	T
M	O	J	A	V	E	■	S	T	U	C	C	O
E	D	U	C	E	■	B	O	R	N	T	O	R	U	N
W	I	S	E	■	B	A	R	A	K	■	A	T	N	O
L	E	T	S	P	A	R	T	Y	■	S	T	E	P	S
■	P	E	O	R	I	A	■	P	I	E	R	C	E
O	D	E	T	T	E	■	M	I	L	D
F	I	A	T	S	■	A	T	O	L	L	■	D	A	D
O	N	C	E	■	S	M	I	L	E	Y	F	A	C	E
L	A	H	R	■	S	E	N	T	I	M	E	N	T	S
D	R	Y	S	■	A	N	Y	O	N	E	E	L	S	E

151

```
J I F F Y L U B E ■ S T A F F
U N R A V E L E D ■ C E L L O
M A Y B E B A B Y ■ E X L A X
P R E ■ S O N O ■ E N T I T Y
E E R ■ N O P E S T ■ A F L
R A S P S ■ V S O P ■ N E A
■ A I D A ■ S O L A C E D
P A T I N A ■ S U R E T Y
A T I N G L E ■ B A L I ■
L A M ■ T A L E ■ L E W I S
I L E ■ D O R A G S ■ I N K
N A T H A N ■ G O A T ■ G H I
I N R E M ■ W E R W H O W E R
S T A L E ■ M A R I O K A R T
M A X I S ■ D R A I N A G E S
```

152

```
R E S C U E D ■ C A T B O A T
E X T E N S I O N C O U R S E
D E A D A S A D O O R N A I L
T R Y A S ■ L E T O N ■ L A E
I C E R ■ B E T E L ■ S E T S
D I D ■ S E C T S ■ C C X I I I
E S T I M A T E ■ S E R A C S
■ E H L E R S ■ B I R E M E ■
S M E L L S ■ W E N T W I L D
T A C I T ■ V A N E S ■ N E W
E C O N ■ D E S E X ■ C A P A
P H U ■ O U T O F ■ M O T H Y
D I R T Y P O L I T I C I A N
A N S W E R E D T O N O O N E
D E E P R E D ■ S O N A N T S
```

153

```
M U S L I M S ■ T E E N A G E
A N T O N I O B A N D E R A S
S P R I N K L E R S Y S T E M
■ L I N S E E D S ■ S T Y L E
S E P ■
P A L I S H ■ A S O F ■ L I P
I S I N T O ■ T O R A B O R A
D A N G E R O U S C U R V E S
E N G E N D E R ■ A L I E N S
R T S ■ T E R N ■ S T E R E O
■ S A N
I N T W O ■ M A N I F O L D ■
D O M E S T I C A N I M A L S
E L E P H A N T T R A I N E R
D O N T A S K ■ L E T T E R S
```

154

```
C R E W M A T E S ■ D C U P S
P I X I E D U S T ■ R A N U P
L A P S E I N T O ■ E M O R Y
U T A H S T A R S ■ A E D E S
S A T I E ■ C A S T D O U B T
■ B A Y E R ■ R E L O
■ B O L T O N ■ L I P I T O R
C O N O I D ■ C O N R O Y
I D I O T I C ■ W E D G E D
G E O S ■ N O M A S ■
A G N E S G R E Y ■ M A S T S
R A S T A ■ N A C H O C H I P
A B O I L ■ I N O U R T I M E
S A U L T ■ S T O N E O V E N
H Y P E S ■ H O L D S F A S T
```

155

```
N E A P ■ B I T T ■ C A R L A
O N B A L A N C E ■ A B E A M
D O N L A R S E N ■ T O N K A
U L E E S G O L D ■ A L T E R
H A R D S E L L S ■ L I T H E
■ R O S E ■ B U Y S O U T
■ B O Y ■ R A N S H O R T
H O V ■ S W E A R A T ■ W O O
O N E S T O R Y ■ C N N
M A R C O N I ■ G O S H
E P S O M ■ C H A C H A C H A
S A T U P ■ B E S T I R R E D
P R A T E ■ A L T A R R A I L
U T T E R ■ N E O N T E T R A
N E E D S ■ A N N E ■ D E S I
```

156

```
F E R N S ■ P A L U P ■ N E Z
A R E Y O U A L O N E ■ E L O
C O M E I N T O T H E O P E N
E D I T E D O U T ■ C A N E
S E X ■ E N D O F ■ C L A D
■ C A R ■ E C U
S A C A G A W E A D O L L A R
P R I M E R E A L E S T A T E
A I R P O R T T E R M I N A L
S E E D L E S S R A I S I N S
■ A D S ■ T C M
O L A V ■ T A K E I ■ O R B
T O N I ■ P Y R O M A N I A
T E N D E R L O I N S T E A K
E W E ■ S T A T E S E N A T E
R E X ■ L E N O S ■ C O M A S
```

157

E	M	M	A	S		I	K	I	D		U	M	P	S
S	A	U	D	I		M	I	C	E		R	E	A	P
Q	U	I	Z	M	A	S	T	E	R		A	N	T	I
S	I	R	E		J	U	S	T	M	Y	L	U	C	K
			M	A	R	C	E	A	U		S	H	Y	
L	E	C	T	U	R	E	H	A	L	L	S			
A	G	A	R	S						E	W	E	R	S
M	A	N	I	C		B	O	X		T	A	L	I	A
E	D	S	E	L					I	M	E	T	A	
		D	E	E	P	S	E	A	D	I	V	E	R	
Q	E	D		I	N	R	A	N	G	E			
T	R	I	A	N	G	U	L	A	R		A	L	D	A
I	A	N	S		A	N	I	M	A	L	F	A	R	M
P	S	A	T		G	E	N	E		S	A	T	U	P
S	E	R	A		E	D	E	L		D	R	E	G	S

158

LUMP · HASHBROWNS
UNES · SQUAREROOT
GDAY · TALKEDINTO
GULCH · BLEW · ETAL
ALPHARAY · INDIE
GALOSH · PISTOLS
ETA · POPSICLE
ENS · NOTCH · DIS
ENDORSES · TAS
CRUCIAL · CESSNA
LOGON · BIKEPATH
OMAN · PEAR · PODIA
SANDBARREL · NEAR
ENDEARMENT · GAGA
ROADGRADER · ELON

159

EMMA · HOBO · AHAND
SAIL · ALEC · VOICE
SINGINGTELEGRAM
ANION · AWAY · SPAS
YEARNS · ENESCO
TEEHEE · STORMS
SHU · REINS · ORTON
MARIEANTOINETTE
ELENA · SHIRE · ETE
ESCARP · ELATER
ASSAIL · NORMAL
MCML · PRIM · ORIBI
ALEUTIANISLANDS
NURMI · TESH · TAUT
NEAPS · ESTE · ALLS

160

MESAS · PARM · CIG
OUTDO · STEEPFINE
OWEME · YOMTVRAPS
DEVOUR · LUSCIOUS
ENROLLS · PESTO
TUNISIA · RID
AHAS · SHEEP · NIH
PUSHTHEENVELOPE
AHH · HARPO · APSE
LUG · RAGWEED
BACON · AAMILNE
AMYADAMS · RACKUP
LISTERINE · ZAIRE
SETHROGEN · ERNST
ASS · DART · DEGAS

161

SHAMED · CHIMERA
WECARE · SHADOWED
ALEGAR · CAROTENE
POLITICALDNA
STAC · GINKGO · AMS
BLUNTS · TSLOT
STBEDE · YUL · PLOY
TOTALUP · POTHOLE
OWEN · REF · AKITAS
LEAST · PLANON
ELM · RESOLE · XTRA
JACQUARDLOOM
PARAMOUR · COINOP
FAIRPLAY · ALKANE
CROSSED · REELED

162

RIP · SAW
GOPRO · SELIG
GALLIUM · CHAINED
ALLANTE · LASCALA
SAINTVALENTINES
SETSONEATEASE
OUTSTRIPS
VAC · PENSEES · MML
ENAS · DODDS · PEAL
STRAP · TIL · EENIE
TENDERHEARTEDLY
ADELPHI · NEAREST
LURESIN · ESPARTO
SPARING · STETSON

163

```
B A B E M A G N E T   R E S P
E L I W A L L A C H   E X P O
A F T E R T A S T E   C H A W
M A S   B A N A   S E A I C E
    S L I D   S T A P L E R
S I F T E R   C L A S S A C T
C H A D S   B L U N T   R A O
H A L S   F R I E D   D A D O
O D S   N O U N S   B E T E L
O N E T O O N E   V A L E T S
L O S E S T O   H I N T
M I T T E N   F E E D   S P F
A D A R   O W E N W I S T E R
T E R A   T H E R E T H E R E
E A T S   E A S Y D O E S I T
```

164

```
R O A S T E R S   T U S H E S
O N T H E L A M   I N L O V E
C A L A M I N E   M A R L E E
O P A   P A S T I E S   D A S
C A S C O   H A I R   O O R T
O R T H   L O N I   W A N D A
    A G O R A   N A T T E R
S W A P O U T   S E R M O N S
T I G E R S   T H E M E
A S N A P   A R O D   A G O G
T H O U   I M U S   I L O N A
E B S   R H Y T H M S   R B I
P O T S I E   H O O L I G A N
E N I G M A   I N R E P O S E
N E C T A R   S E A S O N E D
```

165

```
T H A I   P E G S   M A T E
H O R N E   A L A N B A T E S
A R E N A   E M B A R R A S S
W A T E R B A S E P A I N T
E C H E L O N   T I N C T S
D E A D O N   D O N A H U E
    C U R I O   R O B E
S T O C K S A N D S H A R E S
T I V O   T N O T E
O R E S T E S   A R R O W S
P E R S O N   L I B E R A L
  I N A G A D D A D A V I D A
B R I C A B R A C   G O O E Y
R O C K S L I D E   E L L I E
O N E S   E B A Y   T E N D
```

166

```
M O B S   F I V E S A T I N S
O N E O   A L I T T L E B I T
S T E N   K O S H E R D E L I
T H R I C E   A E R O   X E R
W E B C A S T   R I S E
A M O E B O I D   C E N S O R
N O T   S U M O S   N O T C H
T N T S   T O W E D   L O C I
E E L E D   R E L O S   L A N
D Y E L O T   L E G A L E S E
    F L O P   S T D E N I S
O H O   O R E O   I R O B O T
M I N D R E A D E R   N A N O
A R E W E A L O N E   I S A N
R E G I S T E R E D   D E L E
```

167

```
  K I M   S H A K E S   S T P
R A D I O T E L E S C O P E S
E T E R N A L O P T I M I S T
S I N A I   G H I A   A R T
T E T   N C A A   T H R A S H
  B I T E R   O R E O   L O O
S A F E   A L E E   Y E S N O
K R I S H N A   F E A S T E D
I T C H Y   O T I C   T A S S
T H A   P E S O   R E A I M
S E T S O N   P L U S   R E I
  D I Y   G A T E   P A C T S
M O O N L I G H T S O N A T A
N O N C O N T I G U O U S L Y
O R S   W E S S O N   T E E
```

168

```
A I R S I G N S   S L E A Z E
B R A I N R O T   P A S M A L
R O C K C A V E   I T S B I G
A N K H   M A A   T H E I R A
    O M S K   Z E S T E R
H A I R L A C Q U E R
A R M Y G R O U P S   O K A Y
L I A N A   T E T   A L E X A
F A C E   D I S O R D E R L Y
    S E A A N E M O N E S
R U B I E S   D O T S
A N O R A K   I G O   Y E L L
S C R A M S   L O U I S N Y E
P L A Q U E   L O C K E D O N
S E X I S T   A D H E R E N T
```

169

H	O	T	S	P	E	L	L	■	S	T	I	L	T	S
A	C	H	I	E	V	E	S	■	H	O	H	O	H	O
M	E	A	T	D	I	E	T	■	O	R	A	T	E	S
F	A	T	C	A	T	S	■	B	E	I	T	S	O	■
I	N	S	O	L	E	■	R	A	S	A	E	■	■	■
S	L	A	M	S	■	C	A	N	T	M	I	S	S	■
T	I	N	S	■	S	A	W	T	O	O	T	H	E	D
E	N	O	■	G	A	N	D	E	R	S	■	O	D	O
D	E	N	T	A	L	C	A	R	E	■	C	R	I	P
■	R	O	O	T	L	E	T	S	■	T	H	E	M	E
■	■	P	H	Y	L	A	■	V	O	I	L	E	S	■
■	L	A	S	E	R	S	■	S	A	R	G	E	N	T
H	E	G	I	R	A	■	R	E	L	E	G	A	T	E
I	C	E	D	I	N	■	I	L	L	N	E	V	E	R
T	H	E	E	N	D	■	M	A	I	T	R	E	D	S

170

E	B	B	A	N	D	F	L	O	W	■	W	I	T	S
L	E	A	V	E	A	L	O	N	E	■	W	R	A	P
I	N	T	E	R	L	I	N	E	D	■	I	A	G	O
S	T	A	N	D	I	N	G	A	G	A	I	N	S	T
H	O	A	G	Y	■	T	A	L	E	S	■	G	A	P
A	N	N	E	■	F	I	G	S	■	T	R	A	L	A
■	■	■	O	R	E	O	■	■	G	R	A	T	E	S
S	H	O	C	K	E	R	■	P	R	O	W	E	S	S
W	A	R	N	E	D	■	D	Y	E	S	■	■	■	■
I	R	E	N	E	■	A	I	R	Y	■	G	I	B	E
L	P	S	■	F	A	L	D	O	■	F	I	N	E	S
L	E	T	T	E	R	B	O	X	F	O	R	M	A	T
I	D	E	A	■	G	I	V	E	O	R	T	A	K	E
N	O	I	R	■	O	N	E	N	I	G	H	T	E	R
G	N	A	T	■	S	O	R	E	L	O	S	E	R	S

171

T	H	E	B	B	C	■	S	P	A	C	E	J	A	M
H	I	L	A	R	Y	■	C	O	C	A	C	O	L	A
A	M	I	N	U	S	■	O	K	A	Y	O	K	A	Y
W	O	M	A	N	■	P	R	I	C	E	L	E	S	S
■	M	A	N	E	■	L	E	N	I	N	■	■	■	■
■	■	N	A	I	V	E	■	G	A	N	D	A	L	F
S	I	N	S	■	A	B	A	■	E	A	S	E	L	■
T	O	I	L	■	T	E	C	H	Y	■	V	I	N	E
A	N	N	U	M	■	T	O	E	■	E	A	S	E	■
G	A	G	G	I	F	T	■	R	A	M	E	N	■	■
■	■	■	L	O	O	P	S	■	E	G	G	S	■	■
M	A	S	T	E	R	K	E	Y	■	A	G	A	P	E
A	L	P	H	A	B	E	T	■	A	N	E	M	I	A
C	I	A	A	G	E	N	T	■	D	I	R	E	C	T
H	E	N	N	E	S	S	Y	■	M	E	S	S	E	S

172

P	O	T	S	M	O	K	E	■	D	I	S	C	U	S
O	N	E	L	I	T	E	R	■	A	L	E	A	S	T
P	A	S	Y	S	T	E	M	■	T	E	X	T	M	E
A	S	T	■	T	E	P	I	D	■	A	T	T	A	R
P	P	P	S	■	R	E	N	E	W	■	O	L	I	O
I	R	A	T	E	■	R	E	B	E	L	Y	E	L	L
L	E	G	A	T	O	■	S	I	L	A	S	■	■	■
L	E	E	■	H	A	M	■	T	L	C	■	U	P	A
■	■	■	S	O	S	A	D	■	S	E	A	S	O	N
P	R	A	I	S	E	G	O	D	■	S	N	E	R	D
P	E	L	L	■	S	O	W	E	D	■	E	R	N	S
P	A	L	E	S	■	O	N	S	E	T	■	N	S	C
P	L	I	N	K	O	■	L	A	T	E	D	A	T	E
P	I	E	T	I	N	■	O	D	E	T	O	M	A	N
P	A	S	H	T	O	■	W	E	R	E	H	E	R	E

173

M	A	M	M	A	S	■	T	O	P	P	R	I	Z	E
A	V	I	A	T	E	■	U	N	L	O	O	S	E	N
M	E	D	G	A	R	■	X	M	A	S	C	A	R	D
B	R	A	I	N	F	R	E	E	Z	E	■	B	O	S
O	T	I	C	■	E	D	D	A	■	P	E	E	L	■
S	S	R	S	■	K	A	O	S	■	G	O	L	D	A
■	■	■	Q	U	A	D	S	■	S	U	N	L	I	T
M	A	T	U	R	E	S	■	B	E	N	Z	E	N	E
I	S	H	A	L	L	■	B	R	A	S	I	■	■	■
Y	O	U	R	S	■	M	R	I	S	■	S	C	A	T
A	N	N	E	■	S	O	O	N	■	C	L	U	E	■
Z	E	D	■	J	E	R	S	E	Y	S	H	O	R	E
A	M	E	N	A	M	E	N	■	O	P	E	N	O	N
K	A	R	E	N	I	N	A	■	N	A	M	E	R	S
I	N	S	E	A	S	O	N	■	D	R	E	D	A	Y

174

H	O	T	P	A	S	T	R	A	M	I	■	A	N	E
I	S	A	A	C	A	S	I	M	O	V	■	B	O	X
P	E	T	S	E	M	A	T	A	R	Y	■	P	I	C
S	S	E	■	T	O	R	E	■	A	R	I	O	S	I
■	■	■	B	A	S	S	■	S	Y	O	S	S	E	T
S	O	N	A	T	A	■	D	O	E	S	T	I	M	E
A	D	E	L	E	■	S	A	R	E	E	■	T	A	M
L	E	W	D	■	B	E	Z	E	L	■	M	I	K	E
A	R	F	■	R	A	C	E	R	■	R	A	V	E	N
D	N	A	T	E	S	T	S	■	D	E	S	E	R	T
G	E	N	E	S	E	S	■	W	E	T	S	■	■	■
R	I	G	S	U	P	■	S	H	A	Y	■	F	A	R
E	S	L	■	M	A	S	T	E	R	P	I	E	C	E
E	S	E	■	E	T	H	E	L	M	E	R	M	A	N
N	E	D	■	S	H	O	W	M	E	S	T	A	T	E

175

```
A D O P T I O N   A R I S E S
N O N E E D T O T H A N K M E
I M E A N I T T H I S T I M E
T E A S     M A N T O M A N
A S S E Z   S Y N T A X
      E S E       I S T H
T R I P L E W O R D S C O R E
R E S I D E N T I A L A R E A
I M I T A T I O N B U T T E R
B E A T S O N E S B R E A S T
E T H S       E A P
    B A L L A D   S T E A M
P E C U L I A R     A N T E
O P E R A T I O N C O N D O R
L O N G T E R M P A R K I N G
E S T H E R   A R R E S T E E
```

176

```
M I C A   A L I E N R A C E S
A D A M   M E A D O W L A R K
D O L P H I N S A F E T U N A
E M I L E   T I M E   S T E T
R E F E R S   M S E C   I S E
O N O R   N G O   S O H O T
O E R   R E A V E   Z I N
M O N K E E S   T H E C A R S
    I L L   X E N O N   R E W
  T A M I L   T A W   T Y P E
R I G   C U T E   L I O T T A
A V I S   M A R T   C L A I R
P O R C U P I N E Q U I L L S
I L L U M I N A T E   F E E T
D I S M A N T L E D   E S S O
```

177

```
M A I L B A G   T O W N E
A L L O R N O N E   A P H I S
G O L D E N B O Y   P I O N S
I N B E D   A T R A   E L E A
C E E S   O N M E D S   E L Y
    B A Y   D O G S I T
B R I M   O N C E   S U A V E
L A C A G E A U X F O L L E S
O R A T E   S P C A   P E S T
W E N T O N   O L D
A G T   S N A F U S   F L A W
F A W N   E S T S   P L A N A
U S A I D   S E I Z E U P O N
S E I K O   N A V A L B A S E
E S T E S   E G E S T E D
```

178

```
D I O R A M A   A C T A B L E
I M N O T I N T E R E S T E D
P R I C E O N O N E S H E A D
S E T S     W E S T E N D
    N O T E A S Y
D I S C O L O R S   A C H E
I N T E N D T O   L A S H E S
C H A N C E O F S U C C E S S
T O T T E R   L A C R O S S E
A C E S   C O W R I T T E N
    S C A N N E D
  B I G H A N D   I E S T
H A V E A G O O D M I N D T O
A B E R D E E N T E R R I E R
N E S T E R S   S T K I T T S
```

179

```
G I V E M E O N E R E A S O N
I N O N E S S A L A D D A Y S
S O W H A T E L S E I S N E W
T I T A N S   S T I R
  L O N   E E N   E T A I L
  C R A N N Y   D E F O E
  F R E E S T A T E   S A W N
W T O   C O W B I R D   E A T
E L O I   F I L M R E E L S
L E F T S   N E E S O N
L E T H E   E R S   I S T
  R U M P   R A G T O P
Y O U R P L A C E O R M I N E
I N S T R U M E N T P A N E L
P A S S E S O N D E S S E R T
```

180

```
U P D R A F T S   A P I C A L
S E E A B O V E   P O C O N O
A T M C A R D S   P O E T I C
B R U I S E R S   T H R E S H
L O R N E   A I D   S I R E N
E L S E   A M O R E   N I T E
      J E A N J A C K E T S
S P A D E S     T O S S E S
T H E O D O R E R E X
E A R N   P A L I N   A B C S
P L O T S   G M T   E G R E T
F A S C E S   B A T P H O N E
O N T A P E   A L I C A N T E
U G A R T E   R I P O S T E D
R E R E A D   K N O T T E R S
```

181

```
A L I B A B A . . . A S K T O
S O D A J E R K S . B L E E D
C A L L I N G I N . C O P A Y
O N E E G G . N E O . A T M S
T S R . A L D E R . N A P S .
. V A L O R . G O E T H E . .
. D I E S . R E H A B . B O Y
L I K E H E R D I N G C A T S
E A N . E G E S T . Y O Y O .
G L O S S Y . P O I N T . . .
A T W O . P A I N T . . S H E
L O I N . T O R . L E A P O N
A N T I C . K I L L S T I M E
G E I C O . S T U D P O K E R
E S S E X . N O N Z E R O . .
```

182

```
S Q U A B B L E . L A R E D O
A U N T I E E M . E L O P E D
N A K E D A S A J A Y B I R D
D Y N A S T . N U N N . S I S
A L O T . B E A S T . P O S H
L E T . W A N T T O . I D I O
. . N A C R E S . A L E V E
M A Z U R K A . A T L A S E S
I D A R E . P R Y O F F . . .
S E N S . S T A I R S . D U N
S N E E . Q U I N T . S U P E
T A G . B U R N . U P E N D S
A U R O R A E B O R E A L I S
R E E K E D . O V E R T A K E
T R Y S T S . W I D E O P E N
```

183

```
C O I N . S H I R T . C A R P
A N N A . C A M E O . O L E O
S T A M P O F A P P R O V A L
T H R E E T I M E S A L A D Y
. E R S A T Z . O A T E R S .
S M E A R Y . S P I E D . . .
L E A K Y . J E L L S . P I P
I N R E . T A X E S . C A N E
M D S . P A C E D . M A R T A
. . S I L K S . M E R K E L .
. C H A L K S . K U R T I S .
D R A W A T T E N T I O N T O
E A S Y F O R Y O U T O S A Y
A N T E . M A R L A . N O T E
D E E R . E W E L L . Y N E Z
```

184

```
C H O C O L A T E M O U S S E
E A T O N E S H E A R T O U T
N U R S E C L I N I C I A N S
T S O . H A S . M A C . . . .
O A S I S . N I T . S A R A S
. . . R E M . S I D . E P A
I N T E R N A L A U D I T O R
M A I N T E N A N C E F R E E
M A K E A M E N T A L N O T E
I C K . E N D . T O O . . . .
E P I C S . T E E . S T A P H
. . U A E . A L E . P E U
T A K E N O P R I S O N E R S
A H A R D N U T T O C R A C K
R A I S E S T H E S T A K E S
```

185

```
S M E W . J A W S O F L I F E
I A T E . E A R L Y R I S E R
X K E S . W H I R L Y B I R D
E E R . M E E T . P E N N A .
R U N W I L D . M E A L . . .
S P I E L S . B A R N . S E P
G E T I T . T E X A S S T A R
A X I L . A E G I S . P A S O
M A E L S T R O M . C A N T S
E M S . T O R T . D R Y M O P
. . S U Z Y . M E A S U R E .
B R E A D . M O A B . S A C .
R U B B E R S O U L . T I N T
O D E R N E I S S E . R A G U
W I N E T A S T E R . A L E S
```

186

```
I G O O F E D . B O B S T A Y
S A N T I N I . O P U S O N E
A M B A N D S . R E S T O N S
I B O . S E A S A L T . C R I
D R A C . D R U B S . P O U T
S E R U M . M N O . A I O L I
O L D P A L . G R I Z Z L E S
. . C R A N . A N T Z . . .
A Q U A T E E N . B E A V E R
B U C K Y . H E T . C Z E C H
S I D E . M I X I T . Z A L E
O R A . A U S T E R E . L I B
L I V E S T O . R I V E R P O
U N I F I E D . O B E L I S K
T O S T A D A . D E L I B E S
```

187

```
P A S S I O N P I T ■ O A F S
O P E N S O U R C E ■ H U L U
R E C O R D D E A L ■ O D I C
C R O W ■ L E T M E T H I N K
■ A V E ■ E X E ■ D T S ■
I N U N I S O N ■ E L W E S ■
B A N G S ■ H A R D ■ H A T E
E M C E E ■ I D O ■ P Y L O N
T E L L ■ T O I L ■ F I E N D
■ C E S T A ■ R E S C O R E S
J A R ■ I N C ■ A S U ■
E L E N A K A G A N ■ G I N O
A L M A ■ T I E F I G H T E R
N E U T ■ O N E A T A T I M E
E R S E ■ P E R R Y M A S O N
```

188

```
S P I L L A G E ■ A T B E S T
H O N E Y B U N ■ S O O N Y I
A L T E R A N T ■ T U B I N G
M A S T I F F S ■ O R B A C H
■ ■ I S T O ■ ■ N A C H T
L I N D T ■ R A C I E R ■
O T O E ■ T H I R T Y R O C K
L A T ■ S A I D Y E S ■ X I I
A L I N E D R E S S ■ F E T A
■ B A S E S T ■ N I N E S ■
S T E A D ■ A L A R ■
H A N G E R ■ P L A T E A U S
O C T A V O ■ I S T H A T S O
P E R M I T ■ G E T A N T S Y
S T E E L E ■ S T E N T O R S
```

189

```
A T M S ■ M M M B O P ■ S P Y
T R I P ■ O M E R T A ■ T I O
M I S E ■ W I R I E R ■ R E N
O F F E N S I V E R E M A R K
S L I C E ■ ■ F I N A N C E
T E T H E R E D ■ T I G E R
■ ■ D O N U T S ■ Z E D S
■ C O S M O K R A M E R ■
M C A N ■ P L E A S E ■
R O L E X ■ S P E C T A T E
S T O P G A P ■ C O L I N
P E R M A N E N T M A R K E R
A R I ■ M E T E O R ■ S A R A
U I E ■ E N C O R E ■ O L E G
L E S ■ S T O N E D ■ S I D E
```

190

```
■ C A L I C O C A T ■ A R A L
B A N A N A R A M A ■ M I M I
A S T R O N O M I C ■ O P A L
S H O R N ■ I G O C R A Z Y
T I N Y ■ G A L O S H ■ P O P
A N Y ■ J A I L S ■ I V A N A
■ ■ F O R M A ■ M A D R I D
M A D L I B S ■ P I N A T A S
A Q U I N O ■ G U S T Y ■
L U M P S ■ C O N T I ■ M A W
C A B ■ I B O O K S ■ G A L A
O R D I N A L S ■ F O R D S
L I O N ■ S L I P P I N G O N
M U R K ■ H A N G I N G O U T
X M A S ■ O R G A N I S T S ■
```

191

```
R E G A L I A ■ C S H A R P
E V A D E R S ■ U L T I M A S
S E I Z E O N ■ N E A T E N S
I N T E R N E T D A T I N G ■
Z E E S ■ B E H A N ■ T A T A
E R R ■ S A D E Y E D ■ M R S
■ ■ S T R E P ■ D U D E U P
I S S U E ■ D E M ■ V I N E S
C A T N I P ■ Q A T A R ■
E V E ■ N A T U R A L ■ G U S
T E E N ■ R O O S T ■ S U N K
■ F R O Z E N D A I Q U I R I
J A S M I N E ■ L A U N D E R
O C T A N T S ■ I N A N E S T
G E O D E S ■ S A D I S T S
```

192

```
B O O H I S S ■ J A C I N T H
A T P E A C E ■ U P A B O V E
C H E X M I X ■ K E N O S H A
K E N ■ S O T H E R E ■ C O R
O L A V ■ N I M B Y ■ D O S S
F L I N G ■ P O O ■ S E R T A
F O R E S T S ■ X T I M E S Y
■ ■ C U B ■ ■ A M E ■
T H E K I S S ■ F T B R A G G
R I V E T ■ P C U ■ A I S L E
I D I D ■ S L A N T ■ T A U T
M A L ■ S P I F F U P ■ J E B
S W O O P I N ■ A L A M O D E
P A N C A K E ■ C L I C K O N
A Y E A Y E S ■ T E N C E N T
```

193

E	S	T	E	S	■	■	■	M	S	D	O	S
M	E	A	G	E	R	■	■	P	O	M	E	L	O
B	R	O	O	D	E	R	■	C	A	L	I	B	E	R
A	G	I	T	A	T	O	■	O	V	E	R	E	A	T
Y	E	S	I	T	I	S	■	M	A	S	K	E	R	S

■ I T S E L E M E N T A R Y
■ ■ S T R E S S T E S T S
■ ■ ■ ■ A T O
■ ■ L I T E R A T U R E S
■ F U T U R E R E S U L T S

T I N S T A R ■ R U N L A P S
R E C H O S E ■ M A N A T E E
U S H E R E D ■ S L I M I N G
S T E R E S ■ ■ S E A N C E
T A S E D ■ ■ ■ R E G E R

194

S T R A I N E D P E A C H E S
R O U N D A B O U T R O U T E
I T S N O C O M P A R I S O N
S O S ■ I H N ■ I S L
■ U N O ■ S A L ■ S U N G
A B E N D ■ A W N ■ N O E
C O N C E A L E D W E A P O N
T O A L E S S E R E X T E N T
I M M E D I A T E D A N G E R
N E O ■ C O W ■ M O S S Y
G R R R ■ P E N ■ M T S
■ E P I ■ V I A ■ H E W
D I A M O N D J I M B R A D Y
I T T A K E S A V I L L A G E
D E E P E S T R E C E S S E S

195

R E B A ■ A N I T A ■ P R E S
E R I C T H E R E D ■ H A L L
D I N A H S H O R E ■ I I I I
A N O D E ■ I N N S ■ L S A T
■ C E O S ■ ■ ■ L I E N S
A L U M ■ A C H ■ T A P S
T O L I T T L E P U R P O S E
T R A C T I O N E N G I N E S
A I R C O N D I T I O N E R S
■ V I P S ■ E E N ■ E S T O
E M I R S ■ ■ G R E G
D I S C ■ I C E D ■ H A L A L
N A I L ■ S L U I C E G A T E
A T O E ■ L O R D N E L S O N
S A N S ■ A T E I N ■ E S M E

196

D O H A Q A T A R ■ P H O T O
O B A M A C A R E ■ A T R A P
G O B A N A N A S ■ S E E M E
R E A ■ D I L L ■ C T S C A N
A P N E A ■ I S T H A T A L L
C A E N ■ N E N E ■ R E Y
E R R O R ■ E A T S U P
S T O L A V ■ ■ T H E S O N
■ ■ A G E N T K ■ S T O N E
P J S ■ S E A L ■ C R E W
T A U B E T A P I ■ P O T T S
B R I A R S ■ I N R I ■ D I D
O U T T A ■ L O G I N N A M E
A L O E S ■ I C E S K A T E S
T E R S E ■ M A R K Y M A R K

197

S C A R E C R O W S ■ C O S T
T O L E D O O H I O ■ A N N A
I W A N T M Y M T V ■ L E O N
F E T E ■ B A S H ■ C L O W N
F R E E R O L L ■ R I C C I
■ ■ I M E A N ■ A N T O N
■ T H I N E ■ W O L F G A N G
■ H A N G A R ■ M O T I V E
W R I S T L E T ■ V I N E S
A E R E O ■ M A G E E
R E S T S ■ C H A R T R E S
W H A M S ■ B O O P ■ W E L T
I O L A ■ P O P U P V I D E O
C L O P ■ C H I L L A X I N G
K E N S ■ P R E S E N T D A Y

198

O R G A N S ■ S O C I A L I Q
N A U S E A ■ E D I T M E N U
R U N S O N ■ T E R I Y A K I
A C C E N T ■ R O C S ■ D M Z
M O A T ■ A M A N A ■ M O A N
P U S S Y C A T S ■ Z O R R O
S S E ■ E R I E ■ K O P E K S
■ ■ E L U L ■ C A N E
S C H U L Z ■ M O N K ■ L S D
C H A R S ■ B A B Y S P I C E
H A L O ■ L E T B E ■ O T I C
I T T ■ J E D I ■ W A S H E R
S E E P E D I N ■ E L A I N E
M A R I T I M E ■ S E D U C E
S U S P E N S E ■ T E A M E D

199

B	U	Z	Z	K	I	L	L	■	■	P	A	P	A	W
U	N	I	O	N	D	U	E	S	■	F	L	E	S	H
S	T	R	E	E	T	M	A	P	■	C	A	R	T	A
T	I	C	■	W	A	M	P	U	M	■	R	I	O	T
E	D	O	M	■	G	O	T	T	I	■	M	O	N	A
D	Y	N	E	S	■	X	A	N	D	Y	■	D	I	G
■	■	D	U	H	■	T	I	R	A	M	I	S	U	■
C	R	E	A	M	E	R	■	K	I	T	S	C	H	Y
R	E	D	L	A	B	E	L	■	B	E	D	■	■	■
A	S	H	■	C	R	E	E	D	■	S	O	F	T	G
S	C	A	B	■	E	N	G	E	L	■	S	A	U	L
H	U	R	L	■	W	A	R	S	A	W	■	T	V	A
P	E	R	I	L	■	C	O	O	K	I	E	J	A	R
A	M	I	N	E	■	T	O	T	E	M	P	O	L	E
D	E	S	K	S	■	M	O	R	P	H	E	U	S	■

200

Q	U	I	E	T	D	O	W	N	■	E	R	E	C	T
S	N	A	K	E	E	Y	E	S	■	R	E	S	O	W
C	A	M	E	T	O	S	E	E	■	I	N	T	R	O
O	W	N	■	E	X	T	■	W	O	N	T	O	N	S
R	E	O	S	■	Y	E	P	■	U	S	E	N	E	T
E	D	T	V	■	G	R	E	A	T	■	R	I	L	E
■	■	E	Y	E	B	A	L	L	S	■	A	L	P	■
S	H	A	N	A	N	A	■	T	E	T	A	N	U	S
P	A	N	■	M	A	R	K	E	T	E	R	■	■	■
A	V	E	R	■	T	S	A	R	S	■	G	A	T	E
R	E	C	E	D	E	■	T	N	T	■	O	R	E	G
R	A	D	I	O	D	J	■	A	O	L	■	G	R	E
I	C	O	N	S	■	I	N	T	R	I	G	U	E	S
N	O	T	I	E	■	B	R	E	E	Z	I	E	S	T
G	W	E	N	S	■	S	A	S	S	A	F	R	A	S

The New York Times

SMART PUZZLES

Presented with Style

Available at your local bookstore or online at www.nytimes.com/nytstore

✦ St. Martin's Griffin

f facebook.com/NewYorkTimesCrosswordPuzzle